CONTROLLING INTEREST

The Canadian Gas and Oil Stakes

CONTROLLING INTEREST

The Canadian Gas and Oil Stakes

David Crane

McClelland and Stewart

McClelland and Stewart Limited
The Canadian Publishers
25 Hollinger Road
Toronto, Ontario
M4B 3G2

Canadian Cataloguing in Publication Data
Crane, David.
  Controlling interest

ISBN 0-7710-2328-6

1. Petroleum industry and trade – Canada.
2. Petroleum industry and trade – Government
ownership – Canada. 3. Gas industry – Canada.
4. Energy policy – Canada. I. Title.

HD9574.C32C72   333.8 '2315 '0971   C82-094446-7

Printed and bound in Canada

Contents

It has been my good fortune to work with two of Canada's greatest journalists, Martin Goodman and Mark Gayn. Both of them encouraged me to write this book but, tragically, neither lived to see it published. This book is for them.

Foreword

Canadians are a lucky people. Nature's lottery has left us with abundant natural resources, oil and gas among them. But we are also a careless people. Rich in resources, we have been poor in policy. And nowhere, perhaps, have we been quite so poor as in our stewardship of the irreplaceable gas and oil reserves that are vital to the well-being of all people in Canada.

They are the property of every Canadian. Yet their control and ownership, and with these, the key decisions affecting their development and supply, have been allowed to fall largely into the hands of multinational corporate interests whose priorities and goals will not always be compatible with the public goals and priorities of Canada.

Not only did we, through our federal and provincial governments, yield access to our oil and gas on easy terms to foreign-controlled corporations, but we have actually financed these companies' expansion through government tax and other policies. The oil multinationals brought in little money of their own, and yet there has been virtually no need for them to sell shares to raise money. They soon became exporters of capital – paying head office, and funding resource development elsewhere.

In the 1970s, the importance of oil and gas was underlined by OPEC's 1973-74 quadrupling of oil prices and its 1979 action in doubling them again. The oil supply embargo by OPEC's Arab members in 1973 also drove home the strategic importance of energy self-sufficiency. If Canadians ever felt that they could be complacent about who dominated their oil and gas industry, they could afford that luxury no longer. They saw the worth of foreign-controlled oil and gas companies in Canada multiply several times as non-resident shareholders cashed in on the rapid rise in value of the country's reserves. Clearly, this industry was going to become much more powerful in the Canadian economy. Should Canadians be expected to pay much higher prices and provide such generous tax incentives for the benefit of foreign parent companies and their shareholders, and still at the same time leave the decision-making power in this giant industry to non-residents?

The answer could only be no. As we entered the 1980s, faced with the need for a decade or more of massive oil and gas development to achieve self-sufficiency, the case for Canadianization seemed clear-cut. Gas and oil were now recognized as strategic commodities essential to the political and economic security of Canadians. Moreover Canadians would, as before, be paying much of the cost of developing these energy resources anyway. The oil majors were openly hostile to the idea of higher levels of Canadian participation in the wealth and direction of their industry. Many subsidiaries allowed no Canadian participation at all. And none could claim that head-office ambitions did not take automatic precedence over Canadian aspirations – as well as Canadian talents to develop the new technology for getting at the Alberta tar sands, Arctic, and offshore reservoirs. Since the multinationals were that kind of beast, and since too they were sitting on most of these reserves, Canadianization would have to include land policy reform and buy-ups of some of the companies. Canadians could look outside and judge whether any other country would accept such massive foreign ownership and control in one of its most important and dynamic industries. Even the National Energy Policy goal of 50-per-cent Canadian control by 1990 still allowed for 50-per-cent foreign control, a high level of foreign participation by any standard.

That is what this book is all about – to show how careless policies in Canada over-rewarded the multinationals and why it is so important that Canadians, at a minimum, manage to reach the target of 50-per-cent control of production revenues by 1990.

The book would not have been possible without help from many different people. Certainly it would have been impossible without the co-operation and understanding of the Toronto *Star*, notably its publisher, Beland Honderich, and its former editor-in-chief, Denis Harvey. The Canadian Institute for Economic Policy provided generous research assistance while its chairman, Walter Gordon, also gave much encouragement. Others whose help has been invaluable include Bill Hopper, Joel Bell, and Bob Foulkes at Petro-Canada, David Scrim, an independent consultant, Norman Miller of EPI Resources, Evelyn Gigantes on research, and a number of people in the public service, including various officials at Statistics Canada. Some corporations in the oil industry were also helpful, even though this book is not one they would have wished for. Imperial Oil, Shell Canada, and Gulf Canada were particularly forthcoming, and never declined to answer a question. The same cannot be said, unfortunately, of others in the industry.

A special acknowledgement must go to my editor, Richard Howard, who has done so much to make the book readable, although a great deal briefer, and to Linda McKnight and Jack McClelland at McClelland and Stewart for their patience with my struggle to get the work done. Thanks are also due to Beverly Nathan who persevered with the typing of my seemingly endless manuscript and, last but obviously not least, to Françoise Hébert, whose constant presence and support made this book happen.

D. C.
Toronto
February 1982

Chapter 1

The Bombshell

Some events become turning points in a country's history. For Canadians, the 28 October 1980 introduction of the new National Energy Program was almost certainly such an event. The budget read to a packed House of Commons that evening by finance minister Allan MacEachen, and the accompanying program document[1] unveiled by energy minister Marc Lalonde, amounted to a set of blueprints with which Canadians were to gain control of at least half of their country's oil and gas production by the year 1990. The scene was set for a historic reversal of a process that was as old as the twentieth century and a little older. The people of Canada, through their national government, were moving to enforce their sovereign right to the use of, and the rich economic fallout from, a crucial resource that had always really, of course, been theirs.

A mere 50 per cent has all the ring of a modest ambition, a typically Canadian half measure; yet in the circumstances it was ambitious enough. For while oil and gas formed one of the most important industrial sectors in the country's life, they had long been and in 1980 still remained overwhelmingly foreign-owned and -controlled. In 1979, five foreign-controlled oil companies accounted for 52 per cent and 14 foreign-controlled companies accounted for 82 per cent of Canada's oil production.[2] Similarly, six foreign-controlled companies accounted for 51 per cent while 12 foreign-controlled companies accounted for 68 per cent of Canada's natural gas production. Of the top 25 oil and gas firms in Canada, 17, including the six largest, were foreign-controlled; of the top ten, only one, Petro-Canada, was controlled by Canadians.

The current state of domination in the oil and gas industry was not, however, the only item of concern. The oil majors held most of the tar sands and over 60 per cent of the frontier lands,[3] includ-

11

ing the potentially rich Hibernia field off Newfoundland and the reserves near Sable Island by the Nova Scotia coast, as well as much of the potential in the Beaufort Sea and Mackenzie Delta region. As these sources of supply came into production, foreign domination might well become even more pronounced. Through the 1980s, for example, it was expected that foreign-controlled companies would account for up to 70 per cent of tar sands production, even though Petro-Canada was likely to emerge as an important partner, along with the Alberta government, in all sands projects. Their ownership of the land, moreover, gave the oil majors a considerable say in the timing of reserves development. And as the experience of the 1960s and 1970s had shown, their parent companies had the last word on how Canadian resource development was to be paced.

At the same time, the high level of foreign ownership meant that the escalating value of Canada's oil and gas resources was accruing to the non-resident owners of the oil and gas majors. In the years 1970-79, the asset value of foreign-controlled oil and gas companies had tripled, from $10.5 billion to $31.9 billion, while the shareholders' equity had grown from $6.7 billion to $17.2 billion, and it was the accumulation of reinvested profits that funded this growth.[4] During the 1970s, the oil and gas industry rode high on sharply rising profits – profits for foreign-controlled companies rose more than eightfold, from $666 million in 1970 to $5.4 billion, 71 per cent of total industry profits, in 1979 – and massive increases in the value of the companies. This steep curve was reflected on the Toronto Stock Exchange. From 1970-79, the average annual return on oil and gas stocks was 35.5 per cent, while the average for all listed companies was just 7 per cent. In the five years after the energy crisis, 1974-79, the industry recorded an annual yield of 44 per cent as against 7.6 per cent for all TSE-listed companies. The average oil stock rose 350 per cent in value in 1973-79 as compared with 150 per cent in other industries. In 1976, the TSE composite index had risen to 2400 but the oil and gas index had risen to more than 5000.[5] (Even a year after the NEP, the composite index was 1800, the oil and gas index 3500.) As Petro-Canada's chairman put it: "Over the past few years, it has been easier to make a buck in the oil business than in any other sector of the Canadian economy. Anyone who doesn't believe me ought to try the fishing business for a while, or the manufacturing of shoes, auto parts, or clothing."[6]

Much of this quick wealth was hemorrhaging out of the country. The industry talked about Canada's need for foreign capital, but the flow of funds was in the opposite direction as dividends were raised, capital repatriated, and Canadian-generated treasure used to support exploration and development in the United States and elsewhere. In 1979, 14 of the largest foreign-controlled companies paid out $438 million to non-resident shareholders in dividends and equity reduction; in 1979, dividends and equity reduction amounted to 26 per cent of these firms' paid-up capital. During the 1980 federal election campaign, Pierre Trudeau claimed that "several multinationals operating in Canada have profits so large that they're shifting hefty sums out of the country."[7] An aide named two of them as Mobil and Standard of California. The money outflow is made up of more than dividends and interest: there is a wide range of intercorporate transfers, for research and development, patents, engineering consulting from head office, and management fees, as well as the transfer pricing mechanism under which an oil company buys oil owned by its parent company at a price higher than it would pay to an independent supplier. Even the companies' retained earnings statements can be misleading, as Canadian retained earnings may be used to provide funds or finance equipment purchases for the foreign parent. Texaco, for example, used its Canadian subsidiary to finance drilling equipment costs for Texaco operations in the United States. Many of these transactions show up as expenses for the Canadian subsidiary and income for the parent. The figures are extremely difficult to obtain.

By the fall of 1980, it was clear that industry profits and cash flow were going to soar over the next four to five years. One Bay Street analysis showed cash flow for the oil- and gas-producing sector rising from about $6 billion in 1979 to at least $12 billion by 1984, and possibly more than $16 billion if Alberta's 1980 proposals for higher oil prices were adopted.[8] Operating profits would climb from just over $7 billion in 1979 to at least $14 and possibly close to $21 billion in 1984. Cash flow would explode at an annual rate of 16 to 23 per cent from 1979 to 1984, while operating profits grew at an annual rate of 16 to 24 per cent in the same period.

The oil and gas share had gone from 12 per cent of the country's total industrial assets in 1974 to 19 per cent in 1978. Even these figures were understated, as industry financial statements did not indicate the value of reserves held in the ground. Similarly, net income after taxes had grown from 17 per cent of the non-financial corporate economy in 1974 to 27 per cent in 1978.[9] By 1980, the oil and gas industry was clearly outpacing the rest of the economy. In 1974 it had accounted for 7 per cent of the Gross National Product: by 1980, this had risen to more than 10 per cent. The oil industry's 1980 after-tax profits were 29.7 per cent of all non-financial industries' profits, as compared with the 15.3 per cent of 1972; at the same time, the return on shareholders' equity had risen to 21.4 per cent in 1980 as compared with 14.9 per cent for other non-financial industries, while the return on capital employed was 14 per cent in the oil and gas industry as against 10.7 per cent in other non-financial industries.[10] A 1979 study by the federal energy department confirmed the apprehension that rapidly growing oil industry cash flow would transform these companies into huge, multi-resource conglomerates. Diversification into non-resource industries could be accelerated, the study said, "thereby increasing foreign ownership and control of Canadian industry generally."[11] In effect, Canadians, through their tax concessions and the prices they were paying for oil and gas, would be providing the cash flow for foreign-controlled oil and gas companies to buy up Canada.

A continuing diversion of financial resources towards the oil and gas industry, then, could have critical effects on Canada's industrial structure just as the global rise in oil prices is changing the world's industrial structure. According to a Stanford University study, exaggerated returns from oil and gas are drawing off capital that is urgently needed for innovation in other industries, and thus for economic growth and increased productivity in the economy generally. These returns are likely to be reinvested inefficiently while other industries are starved for capital to put into new products and new technology: "The overwhelming bulk of capital for new enterprises is now controlled by the oil producers."[12] The consequence of this is that "the surplus available for productive investment in industrial countries is rapidly diminishing, and what innovations we can afford will be needed simply to provide substitutes for mineral imports and are unlikely to spur additional productivity growth." Moreover, "increased resource rents to petroleum and related industries have offset the profits of other major industries in the industrial countries and these sectors will find it increasingly hard to develop the new technology that is necessary for balanced economic growth."[13] Even the broadly conservative U.S. *Business Week*, in an article on the implications of oil profits, warned that "the oil giants appear to have more money than they can invest efficiently."[14] Higher oil prices, it said, were bringing "a large-scale redistribution of wealth and income from consumers and corporations to the oil industry," with long-term implications for the U.S. economy – and when this was written, the United States already had a windfall profits tax. Oil profits by 1980 accounted for 40 per cent of U.S. manufacturing profits as compared to 15 per cent in 1972. Such a massive shift, *Business Week* predicted darkly, could slow economic growth, with tougher conditions for other industries stemming from poor investments by cash-flush oil companies unloading ''more money than they know what to do with,'' and aggravate inflation, as non-oil companies raised their prices in an attempt to offset declining profit margins weighed down by high costs. The same article quoted U.S. business economists who worried that oil profits were burgeoning at the expense of some industries – for example, airlines and trucking – and causing hardship for such others as automobile manufacturing and parts. A 1981 House of Representatives Committee on Energy and Commerce report warned that soaring oil prices meant the redirection of economic strength and investment capital into the oil industry at the expense of the rest of the industrial base.[15] The 56 oil and gas companies within *Fortune*'s 500 saw their profits rise from 24.4 per cent in 1978 to 42.2 per cent of the 1980 total, accounting for 98 per cent of the total profit growth for the 500. Because Canadian price increases were more restrained, the numbers were less dramatic; 18 oil and gas companies, however, two of them Canadian-controlled in 1977 and four in 1980, accounted for 28 per cent in 1977, and, in 1980, 32 per cent of the profits of Canada's top 200 corporations, and of the $6.3-billion increase in profits in the top 200 between 1977 and 1980, $2 billion, or 32 per cent, had accrued to the same 18 companies. Arguing that the industry was reaching the point where it could not continue to raise spending on exploration and development, U.S. economists said that the soaring cash flow could lead either to a wave of conglomerate takeovers by oil companies or – and they saw this as preferable – to bigger dividend payouts for investors. While bigger dividend payments would recycle oil industry cash back to U.S. shareholders, including pension funds and other institutional investors, this was not an option for Canada, where the bulk of dividend payments go to non-residents. Higher dividends would mean an enormous outflow of funds from Canadian consumers to foreign parent oil corporations.

Whereas Canadian energy policies up to the early 1970s had stressed development as the key problem, ownership now became more critical. The Trudeau government had blocked two important takeovers in the resources sector and established the Canada Development Corporation and Petro-Canada to upgrade Canadian ownership. Canada had been a country rich in resources but poor in policy, and the 1970s saw a determined effort to find a better balance. The new thrust found echoes in Alberta, where previous policies had encouraged foreign-controlled companies to dominate much of the industry. In 1972, a group of Alberta officials spelled out for the government of Peter Lougheed why it was important that future tar sands development be Canadian-owned: "The most direct reason . . . is that the dividends and capital gains . . . will accrue to Canadians. This will tend to increase the availability of capital for future investments."[16] The oil majors' corporate strategies, they contended, did not include the promotion of such Canadian interests as the processing of resources into petrochemicals, the development of new technology in Canada by Canadians, or the fullest possible use of Canadian engineers, scientists, and technologists in Canadian projects. By requiring Canadian participation in tar sands operations, Alberta would make it possible for Canadians to earn new wealth from their resources as well as benefit from high Canadian content: "Thus, the intimate involvement of Albertans and Canadians in the development of the tar sands is seen as a means by which to develop Canadian technology, the Canadian economy, and ultimately the Canadian society."[17] These civil servants had seen at first hand how the absence of a pro-Canada policy left it open for the majors to exploit Alberta's resources without regard for the interests of Albertans and Canadians generally. Alberta's wide-open policies were also attended by long-term costs "arising from exported energy, technology, job opportunities, and environmental damages, in addition to the depletion of non-renewable resources."

Though there was a growing consensus that the foreign-dominated oil and gas sector was already over-powerful in the economy, there was also recognition that oil and gas prices would have to be raised, while the mammoth costs of new tar sands and frontier projects would require massive public risk sharing in the form of tax incentives. If prices were increased, however, Canadians would pay while non-residents reaped the gains. University of British Columbia economist John Helliwell calculated in 1979 that if prices were to reach world levels by 1985, the pre-tax profits from western Canada's conventional oil and gas would approach one third of total pre-tax corporate profits in the entire Canadian economy. "Put another way, profits in oil and gas production, after royalties but before income taxes, are likely to rise more than tenfold between 1974 and 1985, while similarly defined profits for the rest of the economy are projected to rise less than threefold, along with aggregate wages and salaries and nominal GNP as a whole . . . profit changes of this magnitude would represent an unparalleled shift in economic power in Canada."[18] The potential outflows were reckoned as very large indeed: "The 1985 net cash flow to non-frontier oil and gas producers, and the private shareholders in Syncrude, after all royalties, taxes, and capital expenditures required to develop the new conventional oil and gas discoveries forecast by the National Energy Board, is likely to exceed $8 billion per year under existing tax and royalty systems." Of the $8 billion in money to spend, 90 per cent, or $7.2 billion, would be in the hands of foreign corporations. Nor was there much prospect that the oil and gas industry would pay heavily in taxes: while revenues in the industry rose from $1.6 billion in 1970 to $14 billion in 1979, taxes paid went up from a mere $200 million in 1970 to just $1.5 billion in 1979. In the light of such analyses as these, the tired approach that relied on foreign-controlled companies reinvesting their earnings from old oil and gas would become less and less defensible as these giants grew more and more powerful, and the opportunity for Canadians to own a greater share of one of their country's most promising economic sectors became dramatically more remote. There had already been a high price for waiting. The oil and gas industry had risen in value from $10 billion in 1970 to more than $40 billion by 1980, and might be worth more than $100 billion in another ten years' time.

In preparing the National Energy Program, then, the federal authorities faced some chilling realities about fast-growing foreign control, aided and abetted by high domestic prices and hefty tax subsidies, over resources that were in law, under the Crown, the patrimony of every Canadian. And there were other factors urging change. With the OPEC crisis of 1973-74, oil had emerged clearly as a strategic commodity, vital to the national security and fundamental economic well-being of Canadians. In 1980, oil and gas supplied 57 per cent of Canada's energy needs; it was expected that in the year 2000, oil and gas would still be supplying about half the country's total needs.[19] Moreover, foreign hegemony in this industry had even complicated Canada's relations with other countries on occasion. When, just after World War II, Mexico had offered cheap oil or petroleum products to balance its trade, Imperial reminded the federal government of that nation's "unsatisfactory expropriation of oil properties,"[20] and argued that the deal would endanger jobs in Canada; at the beginning of the 1970s, a similar proposal for direct trading by Venezuela was also turned down for fear of offending the oil majors.

With this as background, the mood was changing. Federal

energy minister Marc Lalonde told U.S. investors shortly before the National Energy Program was announced that "foreign ownership and control of the petroleum sector increases the prospects that control of other sectors may slip from Canadian hands. No nation which seeks to independently control its own destiny can afford to permit the commanding heights of its economy to be controlled by foreigners." He went on to state: "We are simply not prepared to see the indefinite extension of foreign control. Canadians must be partners, not just employees, in our future oil and gas industry."[21] On the fateful 28 October, three goals were spelled out: "At least 50-per-cent Canadian ownership of oil and gas production by 1990; Canadian control of a significant number of the larger oil and gas firms; an early increase in the share of the oil and gas sector owned by the government of Canada."[22] The policy aimed, then, at both ownership and control. Ownership by itself was not enough, since the oil majors could sell more of their shares to Canadians without giving up control, the power to make the key decisions on investments, major profits, sourcing, research, and corporate strategy. Only with majority controlling ownership of some of the largest companies would Canadians really be in a position to direct the industry's future, from Canada-based head offices.

Under the NEP, a wide array of policies would encourage Canadian majority ownership. Some tax write-offs such as depletion allowances were to be replaced by direct grants – the Petroleum Incentives Program weighted in favour of Canadian-controlled companies. This measure would scale down the role of tax incentives in financing the growth of foreign-controlled concerns. Excess profits were to be reduced by a new petroleum and gas revenue tax, so that the oil majors and their non-resident shareholders would not wax rich on hiked-up prices for old oil and gas. Land rules were to be changed in the frontier regions, making Petro-Canada or another Crown agency a 25-per-cent partner in all oil and gas developments, while a minimum 50 per cent of Canadian participation would be required in any Canada Lands production. At the same time, Petro-Canada was instructed to begin discussions with industry to negotiate the takeover of several foreign-controlled firms. And to ensure greater industrial benefits from oil and gas developments in the future, the government announced plans to ensure more Canadian content in resource projects and push for a much higher level of research and development in Canada.

What was being proposed in fact, was a decade-long restructuring of one of Canada's most important industries. Not surprisingly, the ownership and excess profits provisions were quickly and harshly attacked. "We are left in a state of utter disbelief," the Canadian Petroleum Association announced.[23] The association, its membership dominated by the multinationals, accused the federal government of virtually ignoring the need to increase supplies: the NEP "focuses on Canadianization of the oil industry and increasing the government's revenues from the oil industry, which we judge to be lower priorities than supply security in terms of national interest." When its own public-opinion surveys found that 84 per cent of Canadians supported the government's ownership goals, and that 61 per cent favoured even stronger measures for reaching these goals, with 70 per cent feeling that more Canadian ownership would translate into jobs and economic stimulus for Canada,[24] the CPA raised $4 million from its members for a national advertising campaign, mainly on television, to sway public opinion.[25]

Canadians could achieve self-sufficiency, the campaign ran, only by allowing the oil majors a preponderant role: "Simply stated, Canada needs the financial muscle, the project management skills, and access to technology of the major multinationals, now more than ever. Conventional oil exploration can be handled by a diversity of small and large firms. The multi-billion-dollar oil sands and offshore developments, however, are highly dependent on the access to world technological and financial pools available only through the majors. If they are discouraged, these projects may not proceed on time. If these megaprojects do not go, there will be no opportunity for Canadians to own even a portion of them. If you want to win the Olympic high jump, you look for an athlete that can jump seven feet, not seven who can jump a foot. Canada needs the big jumpers as well as the little hoppers to make the leap to energy self-sufficiency. . . . Once we are self-sufficient, we can then afford to consider accelerated Canadianization if we still think it necessary."[26]

The petroleum association also took the line, adopted by many of the oil companies and other critics in the business community, that "acquisition of existing companies, whether by the public or private sector, is a misallocation of scarce capital. There is no virtue in borrowing foreign or Canadian capital to buy out foreign investors."[27] This was an unusual argument, as the association's members had never, in a half century and more of buying out Canadian-owned companies, seen their own takeovers as "misallocations of scarce capital." Even in the late 1970s, the majors were continuing to absorb companies while ruing the constraints of the Foreign Investment Review Agency screening process; and in the United States, takeovers were proceeding at an even faster and more massive rate, as the oil majors scooped up mining companies, meat packers, department stores, packaging companies, and electric-motor manufacturers, as well as other oil companies. Moreover, the petroleum association's shifting position on its financial needs could only heighten public suspicion. In 1979 and again in 1980, the CPA had argued that oil self-sufficiency could be achieved by 1990 only through much higher prices and even more generous tax incentives, a sweeter deal from government.[28] Yet after the National Energy Program was announced, an association spokesman said that under the previous tax system the industry had been confident of attaining oil self-sufficiency by 1990.[29]

In reaction to the NEP, the oil majors went on strike. Mobil Canada slashed its 1981 investment budget from $359 million to $195 million. Chevron Standard claimed that it had to have an after-tax rate of return in excess of 20 per cent, and that Hibernia oil would not be developed unless there were changes in federal pricing and tax policies. Texaco Canada announced that it would not be able to mount its oil sands and Atlantic offshore projects without major revisions in the program. Imperial Oil reduced exploration in western Canada by about one third, announced the postponement of its Judy Creek enhanced recovery project, and put the Cold Lake tar sands project on hold. Amoco Canada reduced 1981 spending by about 56 per cent. Shell Canada suspended the Alsands tar sands project.

Imperial portrayed the NEP as a wholesale assault on "proven industry performers," and, following the CPA line, went on to question whether Canadian-controlled companies could do the job: "Unfortunately, some – though certainly not all – of the companies who allegedly stand to benefit from the budget have not yet developed the expertise and resources necessary to tackle the really mammoth projects – in the oil sands, and in the Arctic and the Atlantic offshore – on which future self-sufficiency will depend to a major extent."[30] Gulf Canada argued that the government was trying to do too much too soon, and choosing to ignore an existing trend towards increased participation: in terms of asset values, "by the end of 1979, Canadian ownership was about 34 per cent and growing. If this accelerating trend continued, it is apparent that the government's original objective of 50 per cent of industry assets by 1990 would be achieved early in the 1980s. This trend would be even further accelerated if the government provided incentives for Canadian investors to purchase and hold shares in Canadian oil companies."[31] This way of looking at Canadianization is misleading. In the first place, asset values shown on company balance sheets represent, not current market value, but the depreciated, original cost of investment; asset values are only priced at market when a firm is being sold. The assets on an oil company's books do not reflect the value of its oil and gas reserves or its land position. A sharp increase in Canadian asset ownership did certainly occur through takeovers by Petro-Canada, Nova, and other Canadian companies, but the value of their assets acquired in the late 1970s was being compared with the much older and non-market-value assets of companies like Imperial and Gulf. Moreover, asset values alone do not tell us what proportion of industry assets are Canadian-controlled.

Like most of the oil majors, Shell made it clear that it was in no rush to increase Canadian ownership through the sale of shares. "Changes in Shell Canada's ownership structure, as a short-term response to the NEP, are not warranted," the company insisted.[32] For one thing, it had "not been prepared to embark on such a fundamental change in corporate structure because of the need to protect its internal reputation and name which has significant marketing value, and of the desire not to eliminate the ongoing, free, two-way flow of technical information covering all aspects of the business." Shell had anticipated government policies to favour companies under Canadian control, and about five weeks before the NEP budget it issued a statement declaring that "the federal government target of 50-per-cent Canadian ownership of the petroleum industry assets seems likely to be achieved well before that date – even if no additional preference is given to Canadian-owned companies."[33] And commenting on that budget – even though, like many of the oil majors in Canada, Shell had never offered common shares to Canadians except in takeovers, options for executives or employee benefit plans – the company maintained that "Canadians have always had, and continue to have, opportunity to invest in the oil business through purchase of the shares of operating companies, drilling funds, or by starting grassroots new ventures as they have chosen to do in large numbers."[34] Yet the following year brought these words from a Shell executive who was also chairman of the CPA: "In the case of the Canadianization objectives the target of 50-per-cent Canadian control as well as at least 50-per-cent Canadian ownership by 1990 virtually assumes that the objective can only be achieved through government purchase of several private companies."[35]

21

Shell based much of its attack on the assumption that the new Canadian owners would not be as effective as managers. Take-overs such as Petro-Canada's acquisition of Petrofina, Shell's president argued, "will create no new industrial activity, and will find no additional oil."[36] He ignored the Canadian needs for access to corporate cash flow and land for exploration, and the probability that Canadian-controlled companies, qualifying for higher exploration and development incentives, would in fact accelerate investment. At the same time, he claimed that among Canadians "there is also clear sentiment against moving towards nationalization of the industry – which I suspect may exist because of the strong negative impressions many people have on the success and effectiveness of nationalized industries and businesses in Britain and other countries." The industry's attempt to portray Canadianization as a dangerous exercise in nationalization and socialism was a scare tactic that backfired. Canadians had always lived with a mixed economy, and had no ideological fear of public ownership. Ontario Hydro and Quebec Hydro, Alberta Government Telephones, Air Canada, Canadian National, the Wheat Board, and De Havilland Aircraft are simply a few examples of our successful, effective, publicly owned enterprises.

Like Shell, Texaco took a harsh line. The company called for world prices within two years, elimination of incentives and other measures favouring Canadianization, withdrawal of special treatment for Petro-Canada in Canada Lands, and a pledge by government not to use oil and gas revenues to buy into or take over existing companies.[37] Like other NEP opponents, the chairman of Texaco argued that the industry would have been 50-per-cent Canadian-owned, in terms of assets, by the end of the decade, "but the National Energy Program may have slowed or halted that very desirable trend by diminishing the market value of the shares of the international affiliates – thereby reducing the likelihood of transfers of shares to Canadians."[38] Unless Canadian policies helped boost the price of oil majors shares substantially, the company would sell no more shares to Canadians. In truth, few new shares had been made available to Canadians through the 1970s, in spite of repeated government pleas: Texaco itself had offered no new shares on the Canadian market since 1948.

Some of the most antagonistic reaction against the idea of Canadianization came, paradoxically, from the subsidiary of British Petroleum, which had itself been controlled for many years by the British government to protect that nation's strategic interests. Referring to the March 1980 throne speech that had heralded the

NEP, BP Canada chairman Derek Mitchell commented: "Pity it had to talk about a Petroleum Price Auditing Agency – yet another government agency to monitor and report on oil company costs, profits, expenditures, and levels of Canadian ownership. Pity it had to go on to talk about providing 'new preferential rights on federal lands for Petro-Canada and other Canadian companies.' Pity it had to specify a target of 50-per-cent Canadian ownership of the petroleum industry by 1990. Do these measures help find one barrel of oil or one cubic foot of gas? I don't think so . . . all of this is remarkably irrelevant to the job that has to be done."[39]

There were reactions even more extreme than this. John Masters, president of Canadian Hunter Exploration, accused Ottawa of trying to slash the value of the oil majors so that they could be picked up at distress prices: "I think it's the same kind of tactics the Nazis used to drive the Jews out of Germany. They ran through the streets and smashed store windows and then told the German businessmen to buy them out. Now, Trudeau and his people are smashing in the U.S. oil companies and actually advising the Canadian companies to go buy them out. It's so disreputable, I can't believe it."[40] Tough censure came too from the *Financial Times of Canada*: "Slowly, the federal government is taking control of Canada's oil and gas resources – from exploration through to distribution – just as the socialist or fascist governments of Mexico, Iran, Saudi Arabia, and the Soviet Union control their energy resources. And in those countries, millions of people go freezing in the dark, under government control, and without freedom."[41] The Canadian Manufacturers' Association, whose members include Imperial, Gulf, Shell, Texaco, Suncor, and BP, labelled the NEP "a major fiasco," and the plan to provide for 25-per-cent public ownership of all Canada Lands oil and gas fields as "particularly odious." Association chairman Ted Newall saw it as "quite unnecessary that there be, as the minister of finance said in his recent budget address, 'an early increase in the share of the oil and gas sector owned by the government of Canada.' . . . We believe Canadianization can and should be achieved by putting incentives in place for individual Canadian investors, Canadian-owned companies, and various institutional pools of funds, and not through nationalization."[42] (Newall did not go on to specify what kinds of incentives would be needed.) With an even more comprehensive representation from the oil multinationals, the Canadian Chamber of Commerce issued the call for a massive anti-NEP lobby[43] and was soon passing an emergency anti-NEP resolution in response to an appeal from the

Calgary Chamber.[44] The Calgary spokesman was also the president of Chevron Standard, which not only has no Canadian shareholders, even though it is one of the biggest oil companies in Canada, but is not even incorporated in Canada, operating instead purely as a branch of its U.S. parent.

Various shades of outrage were voiced by other Canadians as well. Royal Bank chairman Rowland Frazee said the program should be scrapped.[45] And Darcy McKeough, the former Ontario treasurer turned president of Union Gas, gave a series of speeches arguing that "we have options: Canadianization versus the ending of our reliance on insecure and foreign sources of supply."[46] In other words, Canadians could not have both. McKeough left no doubt where his sympathies lay: "Having enough energy is more important than how much it costs or who finds, produces, or owns it." Canadians had to reduce their dependence on OPEC, and they could do this only by providing strong incentives for the multinationals. According to McKeough, who chose to pass over the fast-growing capability of public and private Canadian enterprises, we could not afford to antagonize the oil majors because they were the ones with the expertise, dynamism, and financial resources to meet the country's future energy needs. With others in the industry, he saw self-sufficiency as the overriding concern. In the words of the CPA's 1981-82 chairman, like his predecessor a senior executive of a foreign-controlled oil company: "Instead of arguing over ownership and control, the country should be directing all its efforts to finding and developing more oil."[47]

This negativism came as no surprise from an industry that had refused compliance over the previous fifteen years with the requests of successive governments for greater Canadian participation, and demonstrated its clear hostility towards the establishment of Petro-Canada. One multinational executive, Ross Hennigar of Suncor, did ask after the NEP was announced: "Can we, as Canadians, really object to the goal of increased Canadian ownership of our resources? Is this not, in fact, a completely understandable and legitimate aim for any country? We are talking about a non-renewable resource, a birthright which, once expended, is gone forever. Can we not, as an industry, accept the need for increased Canadian ownership of the oil industry and offer to help achieve this aim in a manner and within a time frame equitable to all concerned?"[48] His was a lone voice, however, in an industry that had been trying to dissolve the slow bonding of government policy for a decade past with its dark warnings of discouragement, jeopardized momentum, and skittish foreign investors, and had characterized the thrust behind the 1973 establishment of the Foreign Investment Review Agency (FIRA) as "negative nationalism," a foolish denial of bread and butter. "I hardly think that the fellow out working in a plant today who is getting very high wages is worrying very much about foreign ownership," Imperial's chairman had told a parliamentary committee in 1973.[49]

Equally unsurprising was the hostile and at times inflammatory reaction that came from the United States. Official Washington reacted with one of the most extraordinary communications ever sent by the State Department to a Canadian government.[50] While the confidential note was withdrawn at President Reagan's order, "it was mostly an atmospheric or tonal problem," Secretary of State Alexander Haig explained at an Ottawa press conference.[51] But the issues it raised continued to be stressed by American officials, as well as by Reagan himself, in a July 1981 Washington meeting and another in Grand Rapids, Michigan, with Prime Minister Trudeau. Certainly, the tone of the note was remarkable. Challenging almost every aspect of the National Energy Program, it read as though it had been dictated by the oil moguls themselves. Canada should reconsider its pricing policy, tax changes, Canadian content requirements, Canadianization goals, and measures to raise Canadian participation in the Canada Lands of the far North and Atlantic offshore.

In effect, the U.S. government wanted the NEP buried. The move to world prices should be made "as soon as practicable," under "a realistic pricing policy" that would mean world levels for the Suncor and Syncrude tar sands plants as well as for all future sands developments. Canada, moreover, "should carefully consider the impact of PGRT [the 8-per-cent petroleum and gas windfall profits tax] on its investment climate and production potential." Canada's move to give incentive preferences to Canadian-controlled oil and gas companies was attacked as being in violation of the Organization for Economic Co-operation and Development international investment code; even though Canada had reserved the right in 1976 to have special policies on foreign ownership, this "did not alter Canada's fundamental adherence to the consensus and basic commitment to the principle." The U.S. note opposed the creation of a natural gas bank unless its facilities were made available to foreign-controlled along with Canadian-controlled companies, and it was critical of the government's instruction to the National Energy Board to ensure that smaller Canadian-controlled gas companies had a chance to share in export business. The message from Washington also assailed the

50-per-cent Canadian ownership rule for oil and gas ventures on Canada Lands in the far North and offshore, on the grounds that it "could force the sale of substantial foreign investments at an artificially reduced level which would be less than fair market value." The existence of "an insufficient number of interested and financially capable Canadian buyers available to purchase foreign firms' equity . . . could depress foreign asset values, particularly of those investments located in the higher cost areas such as the Beaufort Sea. The United States government believes the program should not be applied retroactively where substantial foreign investments have already been made."

When it came to the plan for stiff Canadian content requirements in Canada Lands, tar sands, and heavy oil projects, the U.S. actually threatened economic retaliation. Not only were Canada's plans contrary to GATT, but they "would risk impairing the value of the many significant tariff concessions negotiated and bound by the government of Canada in the Tokyo Round and previous multilateral trade negotiations, in return for which the United States made many concessions of advantage to Canada. The Canadian policy, if strictly enforced, could have serious adverse effects on the U.S., especially on exports of energy-related goods to Canada, which in 1979 totalled $452 million. Many other U.S. exports of products used by energy producers would undoubtedly also be affected. Should the balance of concessions be disturbed, the United States would be obliged to consider how a new balance might be achieved." Canada should state publicly the private assurances given the United States, in a 17 December 1980 note, that the Canadian content program would "not be implemented in ways that require the non-competitive use of Canadian goods and services for projects on Canada Lands." The American note was backed by intense lobbying, complete with hints from the Reagan administration that it would unleash the dogs of Congress. Clearly, Canada's oil and gas program clashed with the new administration's aim to reduce barriers against foreign investment and encourage the growth of multinational corporations. FIRA was one target. "I am frankly surprised that a major developed country, provider and host for so much international investment, would adopt such nationalistic and short-sighted policies," Robert Hormats, assistant secretary for business, commented to a Washington audience: "Furthermore, such policies, if unchallenged, are likely to encourage other countries to adopt, or increasingly resort to, similar measures."[52] And another State Department official, Lawrence Eagleburger, announced that while the U.S. did not oppose the Canadianization goal, this must be achieved "in ways that are consistent with accepted international principles and are equitable to those who have made a major contribution in developing Canada's energy resources."[53] He said that Canada should impose its 25-per-cent back-in only on future oil and gas discoveries, a change that would exempt the oil and gas fields likely to start producing in the 1980s and 1990s, and that it should also drop its discrimination in favour of Canadian-controlled companies under the exploration grants program. But the strongest opposition to the NEP came from William Brock, the president's special trade representative, who continued his attack even after Canada and the United States had agreed, at an October 1981 Ottawa meeting attended by U.S. treasury secretary Donald Regan, finance minister Allan MacEachen, and external affairs minister Mark McGuigan, to turn to quiet diplomacy. After a particularly threatening note from Brock late in 1981, McGuigan arranged a special meeting with U.S. Secretary of State Haig during a Brussels NATO conference to lodge his complaint. For all this, however, U.S. pressure did not seriously abate: the office of the U.S. trade representative announced in August that it was beginning a formal inquiry to determine whether the republic was being adversely affected by FIRA; the Commerce Department sent a questionnaire to the *Fortune* 500 corporations that summer seeking evidence of allegedly unfair Canadian practices that would allow a formal investigation under the U.S. 1974 Trade Act; and later in the year, the Department of the Interior invited public views on whether Canadian companies should be excluded from exploration and development on federal lands under the Mineral Leasing Act.

U.S. business antagonism was even feistier. Typically of many business spokesmen, American Petroleum Institute and Union Oil of California chairman Fred Hartley misrepresented the National Energy Program: "The nationalistic move by that government in its desire to achieve total or majority ownership and control of all oil companies realistically can set back Canada's desire to reach petroleum self-sufficiency by many, many years."[54] The NEP was "a tragedy for Canada and also will cause severe losses in cash flow and earnings for both the U.S. and Canadian oil companies." And Mobil executive vice-president Alex Massad contended that "Canada now ranks among the bottom quarter of countries as a favourable place to look for oil."[55] There was no sign, however, that Mobil was ready to sell its Canadian interest or encourage Canadians to participate as shareholders in its subsidiary's activities. At the same time, George Ball, a senior U.S. investment banker and former high-ranking State Department functionary who often acts as an unofficial diplomat for U.S. multinationals, was attacking the NEP as a symptom of nuisance nationalism: "Perceptive Canadians have long understood the benefits derived from sharing the United States' capital, technology, and managerial skills. Just as our country financed its explosion of railroad building during the nineteenth century largely with money from abroad, principally the United Kingdom, the Canadian economy has benefited enormously from the influx of American capital."[56] What he conveniently ignored was that nineteenth-century British financing took the form of bonds, which, when repaid, left Americans the owners of their economy, whereas U.S. investment in Canada, and most particularly in the oil and gas industry, took the form of equity, with which the foreign investor retained permanent ownership. The cancellation of the fat tax benefits for U.S.-controlled firms and the new 50-per-cent-Canadian far North and offshore rule would, according to Ball, require "foreign-owned properties to be sacrificed" to Canadian buyers. And his outburst went beyond the NEP to include FIRA as well: "It is worth noting that, with the exception of France, the Western democracies abjure the type of foreign investment screening procedures adopted by Canada." In fact many countries, including Japan, Britain, Sweden, Australia, West Germany, and even the United States, have restrictions on foreign ownership. Nonetheless, came Ball's parting shot, "I hope that the Canadian government and the Canadian people will recognize realistically that discrimination begets retaliation. So long as such manifest unfairness continues, it generates pressures for restrictionist and protectionist measures."

In a special study on Canada's energy program, the New York investment banking firm of Brown Brothers Harriman and Co. went as far as to claim that Canada was actually obliged to maintain tax and pricing policies satisfactory to the oil and gas industry – including, of course, the oil majors – in order to live up to its "commitment to help assure energy security for its NATO allies and industrial countries generally."[57] The bankers held that without a favourable tax and pricing regime and a welcome mat for "the technical, managerial, and financial assets of the large multinational oil companies – especially valuable in difficult areas such as the Canadian frontier – the goal of self-sufficiency is not likely to be achieved." Even with Canadian-controlled companies increasing exploration, the foreign-controlled companies ac-

28

counted for 67 per cent of exploration spending in 1979, and these firms would see their exploration costs rise by 40 per cent: "The strengths of the multinationals . . . are still much needed to achieve production potentials. For example, the multinationals have greater flexibility in procuring and mobilizing rigs."

American business publications pounced on the new Ottawa policies too, though, like the political and business communities, they made little effort to understand the Canadian situation, let alone give their readers that side of the story. "As if the U.S. did not have enough trouble overseas, the Canadians have picked this time to throw the kind of nationalist fit usually associated with emerging nations," fumed a *Business Week* editorial.[58] The magazine accused the Canadian government of "catering to nationalist feelings and to the deep-rooted jealousy of the U.S." In a later editorial, *Business Week* upbraided Canada for "breaking all the rules of civilized commerce and investment. Reciprocity can be, as the dictionary defines it, an exchange of favours. It can also be a necessary act of self-defence."[59] A similar tone surfaced in the *Wall Street Journal*'s repeated attacks. Just before Prime Minister Trudeau's 1981 visit to Washington, the *Journal* announced: "It's time for Mr. Reagan to give his northern counterpart a stern talking to about the way the world works in the economic relations among nations. The prime lesson ought to be that you can't promulgate the kind of xenophobic national energy program that Canada is currently pressing without driving away foreign capital and reaping a backlash from the nations you're turning against."[60] In fact, the U.S. had already implied that resolution of other issues would depend on Canada's backing down on both the NEP and a proposed expanded role for FIRA. Brock, for example, linked the successful negotiation of differences over the Canada-U.S. auto pact to the resolution of these issues,[61] and Beryl Sprinkel, treasury undersecretary for Monetary Affairs, warned on a visit to Ottawa that "if there is no give" on the Canadian side, "I would not be surprised to see, unfortunately, retaliatory action in the trade and investment area."[62]

To be sure, not all U.S. oil companies pressed the panic button. Jerry McAfee, the retiring chairman of Gulf Oil, said that "Canada is still a good place to do business. . . . We'll be there for a long time."[63] All the same, American threats were graphic enough to alarm some Canadian businessmen. "I doubt Reagan will send in the Marines to protect oil assets against confiscation," a leading stockbroker warned, "but don't rule out retaliation from the U.S. in some form."[64] For its part, Canada's Business Council on National Issues fired off a memorandum to industry minister Herb Gray expressing alarm at the possibility of foreign retaliation and advocating a rapid retreat from the Canadian ownership policies.[65]

What was remarkable about this American criticism was its sheer intensity. The United States had quickly come to accept radical upheaval in the OPEC states, including their nationalization of U.S.-owned oil industries, and the strict policies of Britain and Norway for the development of their oil and gas. Yet when Canadians came up with policies that were more moderate than these, reaction in the U.S. was swift and angry. It was bad enough that tribes once hostile should kick out again; the Canadian thing, however, coming in the wake of all that, was seen as a callous defection of blood brothers, a literal last straw. Some of this may also have been due to the long-standing American view of Canada as a secure, back-up resource base. Certainly, during the 1960s and into the 1970s, Canada had taken on increasing importance in the eyes of the oil majors as a well to quench the growing U.S. thirst. The National Petroleum Council, for example, in a comprehensive, government-backed 1972 review of the U.S. energy outlook, noted the role Canadian resources, in particular tar sands oil and natural gas, could play in alleviating American shortages in the 1980s and 1990s. Canadian liquid hydrocarbon shipments to the U.S., the oil industry body predicted, would rise from 1.6 million barrels a day in 1970 to 4.7 million by 1985, while by the year 2000 the tar sands alone would be supplying 5 million barrels a day to the U.S. Gas would also be in the picture: "It is anticipated that increased volumes of Canadian gas will become available as exploration and development programs intensify and transmission systems are constructed."[66] But probably an even more important factor behind their anger was the tendency of many in the U.S. to see Canada as simply an extension of their own country. Some prominent Americans went as far as to accuse Prime Minister Trudeau of deliberately antagonizing the United States to bring Canadians together. "Indeed Americans – or some American interests – may find themselves paying part of the price for a United Canada," speculated the Atlantic Council.[67] This blue-ribbon group of U.S. business, government, and academic figures led by former Nixon official Willis Armstrong urged the Reagan administration to seek relaxed rules on foreign ownership from Canada. A similar and equally irresponsible charge was made by Harald Malmgren, a former U.S. trade official, and Marie-Josée Drouin, executive director of the Hudson Institute of Canada, an affiliate of the U.S. think-tank headed by futurist Herman Kahn, in an article in the prestigious U.S. journal *Foreign Affairs*: "As Quebec expressed its separatist views more clearly and the other provinces sharpened their differences over the economic and political dimensions of provincial relations, the federal government saw that the weak sense of Canadian identity provided an opportunity to exploit anti-Americanism."[68]

While the European reaction to Canada's new policy was not as strident as the American, it too was largely hostile. The Commission of the European Community commented in a diplomatic note that "Canada's decision to follow an isolated course in the field of energy policy will seriously affect international and bilateral relations."[69] The Europeans were especially critical of the Canadianization proposals: "It should be pointed out that the practice in the Community is not to take into account the nationality of individuals, companies, or shareholders of the companies applying for subsidies." Moreover, the NEP "'buy Canadian' rules, quite apart from conflicting with specific GATT obligations like the government procurement code, are contrary to the spirit of the international trading system." To be sure, the ECC note blithely ignored Europe's own long-standing, highly protectionist policies in agriculture, telecommunications, and electric power, as well as Britain's and Norway's North Sea policies.

In replying, Ottawa indicated that Canada would stand its ground. Its note to the ECC confirmed that "increased Canadian control and ownership in the energy sector is a central and nonreversible element of the NEP. Foreign companies currently control 70 per cent of the petroleum industry and 80 per cent of its cash flow. Canada's objective is to increase domestic ownership to a level of 50 per cent by 1990, a modest goal by any standard. These plans should come as no surprise to other countries. The Energy Strategy for Canada (1976) states clearly that 'the federal government is committed to greater Canadian content and participation in resource development.' "[70] Ottawa also reminded the Europeans that Canada had reserved the right to adopt foreign-ownership policies when signing the 1976 OECD declaration on international investment, and that the International Energy Agency long-term co-operation program of 1976 contained "an explicit exemption for Canada for the provision of Chapter V, which deals with national treatment of foreign investment." As for European complaints regarding procurement, Canada answered that the program "will be carried out in ways consistent with Canada's obligations under the GATT. The onus will be on Canadian firms to remain competitive if they wish to win contracts."

For all the attacks from without, there was clearly support

within Canada for this important policy shift. Public-opinion surveys such as the one conducted by the Canadian Petroleum Association drew an overwhelming positive reaction from the man on the street. Reinforcement came as well from a number of prominent Canadians. With McKeough and the Ontario Progressive Conservative right wing decrying the dramatic changes of the NEP, Premier William Davis stood before an audience of U.S. and Canadian business executives and insisted: "As a moderate Canadian nationalist throughout all my years in public life, I strongly disagree with the suggestion that Canada's long-standing comradeship with America and, indeed, its alliance with free and responsible nations around the world, are under review or, in any way, in doubt."[71] Davis also rejected the view of *Business Week* and other U.S. critics that the Canadian energy policy debate was plunging Canada into recession: "The most significant and immediate threat to our economy is the monetary policy of the United States Federal Reserve and its enthusiastic adherents in our national capital." Nationalism in Canada, Davis said, was "a positive force. It is not an erratic impulse and has never been dangerously excessive . . . I think it can be fairly said that Canadian nationalism has always been positive, growth-oriented, and outward looking. The distinguished Canadian historian and economist, Harold Innis, advised that 'nationalism provides the only sure base for internationalism.' I think that has been true for Canada and will remain so."

Even the chairman of a major multinational, Paul Paré of Imasco, argued that Canadians had a right to be concerned about the behaviour of subsidiaries which operated strictly as branch plants: "Such foreign-controlled companies give a bad name to other foreign-owned companies. . . . They are headed in Canada by 'paper' boards of directors and 'red-telephone' chief executives, in the sense that they cannot make a move without permission of the foreign parent company. . . . I think Canadians have every right to be dissatisfied with that kind of economic colonialism. . ."[72] (While Paré mentioned no company by name, he could have been talking of Mobil, Amoco, Chevron Standard, Canada-Cities Service, or Texaco.) Another maverick sympathizer, this time from the banking community, was Nova Scotia chairman C. E. Ritchie, who told his 1981 annual meeting in Halifax: "I believe that even the NEP's harshest critics would agree that the government had some pretty contentious issues to face up to. One of those issues revolved around the very large windfall-type increases in revenue flows and asset values that had already occurred and were going to keep accruing to established internationally controlled producers. When combined with the various tax concessions that were also most helpful to established concerns, this represented a massive new obstacle to even the most constructive of Canadian ambitions to develop strong new domestic industrial capability."[73]

The Major Projects Task Force, a group of some 80 business and labour leaders co-chaired by Robert Blair of Nova and Shirley Carr of the Canadian Labour Congress, endorsed the NEP with the recommendation that preference be given to foreign debt capital rather than foreign equity or ownership capital "in view of the higher long-run cost of the latter, particularly in relation to resource industries."[74] This counsel was especially remarkable in that Canada's financial community had usually favoured foreign equity investment on the grounds that debt repayment had to be made regardless of economic conditions, whereas equity returns in the form of dividends could be reduced or delayed if profits were weak or non-existent.

One of the first companies to support the government's 1990 Canadian ownership goal was Nova. Indeed, this attitude had been spelled out years earlier by Nova's president Robert Blair, who told the Toronto Society of Financial Analysts in 1974 that his company was for greater Canadian ownership "because we believe that there are real and large quantitative and qualitative advantages to the community from a degree of local ownership and control – whether the big community be Canada or Alberta or Edmonton or Calgary. These advantages arise from the existence and growth of strong companies whose ultimate headquarters and whose decisions are located in the said community. These advantages could be contrasted with what prevails when whole industries, or large parts of an industry, operate in the same given community through the branch offices or subsidiaries of foreign-owned or -controlled companies."[75] A similar message was sounded by Nova shortly before the NEP was unveiled, as company president Robert Pierce announced: "One easily recognized benefit of economic nationalism and Canadian ownership is that more money generated by Canadian industry stays in Canada than under any other scenario. Another less visible but at least equally and maybe even more permanent benefit is that Canadian ownership allows Canadian management to be management in the full sense of the word. . . . These people no longer have to answer to someone outside Canada concerning these decisions. At the same

33

time, these Canadian managers are fulfilling their potential without leaving their families or birthplace."[76] Pierce saw other benefits as well. Canadian ownership that meant Canadian executives like those at Nova were involved in the entire decision-making process for important petrochemical, pipeline, exploration, and manufacturing projects. Moreover, Canadian-owned companies were making an important contribution to the economy by upgrading resources, for example to petrochemicals: "Instead of simply exporting raw materials, many Canadian-owned firms are deciding to manufacture products in Canada which are internationally competitive. Such decisions have several effects. They create additional Canadian employment. They increase our areas of specialization and further expand and strengthen our domestic industrial base." Pierce went on to argue that "in addition to raising new equity for Canadians, Canadian-owned companies are more likely to look at Canada first when reinvesting their corporate earnings. To the extent that such earnings remain within the country, funds are available as required to revitalize the domestic industrial base." And Canadian-owned companies were more likely to turn to other Canadian companies as supplies of new technology, thus providing important industrial spin-offs. Finally, "in terms of good corporate citizenship, the cultural and social aspirations of a country are considered more by companies headquartered in that country. This is not only because they can profess greater altruism, but, more importantly, they can claim greater understanding and self-interest."

But would Canadians actually reap these benefits? The goal of the National Energy Program was to create an oil and gas industry that by 1990 would be much different from what it had been in 1980. Lalonde had promised that "Canadians will be major stockholders in every large firm and some of today's largest companies will be predominantly Canadian-owned. The role of Petro-Canada will also have expanded, so that all Canadians will participate through a larger public role."[77] And immediately after the program was unveiled, the minister had flown to New York to tell U.S. investors: "We know what we are doing. We really do mean it. . . . We are prepared to face the short-term consequences of a long-term policy for which there is no alternative."[78] It remained to be seen whether Canada would succeed. Powerful forces were arrayed against Canada's energy goals, and corporate interests could, as always, find solace in the fact that corporations outlive governments. It would take a determined national commitment to sustain the thrust of the National Energy Program.

Notes

1. Department of Energy, Mines and Resources. *The National Energy Program*. Ottawa 1980.
2. *Oilweek*, 15 June 1981.
3. *The National Energy Program*.
4. Statistics Canada.
5. Paul Halpern, University of Toronto. Quoted by T. A. Wilson, University of Toronto, Institute for Policy Analysis, to the Ontario Economic Council, September 1979.
6. W. H. Hopper, Petro-Canada, to the Financial Post Conference "Year One: What's Ahead after 12 Months of NEP," Calgary, 27 October 1981.
7. Toronto *Star*, 27 January 1980.
8. Robert H. Robinson, "Profitability of Canadian Producing Sector." Toronto, Gardiner, Watson, 30 September 1980.
9. Department of Energy, Mines and Resources. *Taxation and Revenue Sharing*. Ottawa 1979.
10. Petroleum Monitoring Agency. *Canadian Petroleum Industry: 1980 Monitoring Survey*. Ottawa 1981.
11. *Taxation and Revenue Sharing*.
12. Clark W. Reynolds, "The New Terms of the Trade Problem." Stanford University 1980.
13. Reynolds, "The New Terms of the Trade Problem."
14. *Business Week*, 18 August 1980.
15. "The Changing Distribution of Industrial Profits: The Oil and Gas Industry within the Fortune 500, 1978-1980." Staff Report for the Subcommittee on Oversight and Investigations of the Committee on Energy and Commerce, U.S. House of Representatives. Washington 1981.
16. "Report of the Conservation and Utilization Committee of the Alberta Government to the Executive Council on Fort McMurray and an Athabasca Tar Sands Development Strategy." Edmonton 1972.
17. "Report of the Conservation and Utilization Committee."
18. John F. Helliwell, Department of Economics, University of British Columbia, to the Canadian Tax Foundation, Toronto, 26 November 1979.
19. National Energy Board. *Canadian Energy Supply and Demand 1980-2000*. Ottawa 1981.
20. J. S. Ewing, unpublished history of Imperial Oil. See n. 3, p. 71.
21. Hon. Marc Lalonde, Minister of Energy, Mines and Resources, to the American Stock Exchange Seminar, Calgary, 16 September 1981.
22. *The National Energy Program*.
23. Canadian Petroleum Association press release, 29 October 1980.
24. Decima Research Ltd., cited in CPA press release.
25. *Globe and Mail*, 16 September 1981.
26. Hans Maciej, Technical Director, Canadian Petroleum Association, to the Economic Seminar, Calgary, 23 April 1981.
27. Maciej speech.
28. *Globe and Mail*, 31 July 1980.
29. *Globe and Mail*, 21 January 1981.
30. J. G. Livingstone, Imperial Oil Ltd., to the Canadian Club of Vancouver, 2 December 1980.
31. Jerry McAfee, Gulf Oil Canada, to the Fifth National Northern Development Conference, Edmonton, 3 November 1980.

32. C. William Daniel, president, Shell Canada, in the Annual Report for 1980. Toronto 1981.
33. Shell Canada. "Comments by Shell Canada Ltd. on the Petroleum Industry Monitoring Survey (1979)."
34. D. J. Taylor, senior vice-president, Shell Canada, to the Institute of Canadian Bankers, 2 December 1980.
35. Jack McLeod, Shell Canada Resources, to the annual *Port* day, Sydney, N.S., 4 June 1981.
36. C. William Daniel, president, Shell Canada Limited, to the Faculty of Management Studies, University of Toronto, 19 February 1981.
37. R. W. Sparks, chairman, Texaco Canada, to the Toronto Society of Financial Analysts, 5 March 1981.
38. R. W. Sparks, chairman, Texaco Canada, to the Annual General Meeting of Shareholders, Toronto, 24 April 1981.
39. Derek Mitchell, chairman, BP Canada, to the Annual Meeting of Shareholders, 25 April 1980.
40. Toronto *Sun*, 7 November 1980.
41. *Financial Times of Canada*, 9 February 1981.
42. J. E. Newall, Canadian Manufacturers' Association, to the Western Food Processors' Association, Vancouver, 5 February 1981.
43. *Globe and Mail*, 23 January 1981.
44. *Oilweek*, 28 September 1981.
45. Rowland Frazee, chairman, Royal Bank, to the annual meeting, Montreal 1981.
46. Hon. Darcy McKeough, president, Union Gas, to the Toronto Kiwanis Club, 20 May 1981.
47. Clem Dumet, chairman, Canadian Petroleum Association, Calgary, 9 July 1981.
48. Ross Hennigar to the Canadian Institute of Mining and Metallurgy, 11 December 1980.
49. W. O. Twaits, chairman, Imperial Oil Limited, to the House of Commons Committee on Finance, Trade and Economic Affairs, Ottawa, 13 June 1973.
50. U.S. Department of State. "Note on the National Energy Program to the Government of Canada." Washington, 5 March 1981.
51. Alexander Haig, Ottawa, 11 March 1981.
52. Robert D. Hormats, U.S. Department of State, to the Plenary Session of the Economic Policy Council of the United Nations Association, Washington, 18 September 1981.
53. Lawrence Eagleburger, U.S. Department of State, Center for Inter-American Relations. New York, 1 October 1981.
54. Fred Hartley, chairman, American Petroleum Institute, to the American Petroleum Institute Annual Meeting, San Francisco, 11 November 1980.
55. *Business Week*, 8 December 1980.
56. George Ball to the subcommittee on Oversight and Investigations of the Energy and Commerce Committee, U.S. House of Representatives, Washington, 19 June 1981.
57. Brown Brothers Harriman and Co. "Canada's Proposed National Energy Program." New York, 6 February 1981.
58. *Business Week*, 17 November 1980.
59. *Business Week*, 8 June 1981.
60. *Wall Street Journal*, 9 July 1981.

61. *Globe and Mail*, 18 February 1981.
62. *New York Times*, 9 July 1981.
63. *New York Times*, 5 July 1981.
64. Michael Graham, vice-president, A. E. Ames and Co., in *Alberta Report*, 3 April 1981.
65. Business Council for National Issues to the Hon. Herb Gray, Minister of Industry, Trade and Commerce, 6 July 1981.
66. National Petroleum Council. "U.S. Energy Outlook." Washington 1972.
67. Toronto *Star*, 25 July 1981.
68. Marie-Josée Drouin and Harald B. Malmgren. "Canada, the United States, and the World Economy." *Foreign Affairs*, New York, Winter 1981-82.
69. Commission of the European Communities. "Note to the Government of Canada." Brussels, 20 February 1981.
70. Government of Canada. "Note to the Commission of the European Communities." 27 March 1981.
71. William Davis, Premier of Ontario, to the International Conference of the Young Presidents' Organization, Toronto, 5 June 1981.
72. Paul Paré, chairman of Imasco, Ltd., to the Canadian Lumbermen's Association, Montreal, 12 February 1981.
73. C. E. Ritchie, chairman, Bank of Nova Scotia, to the Annual Meeting of Shareholders, Halifax, 14 January 1981.
74. "Major Canadian Projects, Major Canadian Opportunities. A Report by the Consultative Task Force on Industrial and Regional Benefits from Major Canadian Projects." Ottawa 1971.
75. Robert Blair, president, Alberta Gas Trunk Line Ltd., to the Toronto Society of Financial Analysts, 26 February 1974.
76. Robert Pierce, president of Nova – an Alberta Corporation, to the Ecole des Hautes Etudes Commerciales, University of Montreal, 3 June 1980.
77. Marc Lalonde, Minister of Energy, Mines and Resources, to an American Stock Exchange conference, Calgary, 16 September 1980.
78. Marc Lalonde to the Financial Post Conference "Sharing Canada's Energy Wealth," New York, 18 November 1981.

Chapter 2

The Growth of Concern

The issue of control in the oil and gas sector took on a whole new dimension in the year 1947, when a big strike at Leduc, near Edmonton, came as long-awaited confirmation that Canadians were sitting on an impressive bank of reserves. And it was soon clear that the foreign-controlled oil majors would be dominating that sector over a generation of dynamic growth which would transform the country from a substantial importer into a substantial producer of oil and gas.

The dawning awareness of the far-reaching implications of all this surfaced in, of all places, a confidential 1952 study by the federal Department of Defence Production.[1] It estimated that 85 per cent of western Canada's proven reserves were already owned by U.S.-controlled companies, with Imperial alone accounting for about half the grand total. By contrast, Canadian-controlled firms held only 10 per cent of proven oil reserves. The fully integrated oil giants – companies such as Imperial, British American/Gulf, Shell Canada, McColl-Frontenac/Texaco, and Standard Oil of California – were probably even more dominant in Canada than they were in the United States, active in every phase from exploration to marketing, and thus "able to avoid many of those risks which from time to time threaten smaller firms in only one branch of the industry." The federal researchers also pointed out how the nature of the majors' growth patterns discouraged domestic participation. More than half of this growth had been underwritten from retained earnings and tax incentives, another 20 to 25 per cent of the funds were raised by floating bond issues with long-term investors – U.S. insurance companies, for example, or Canadian investment houses – and an additional 10 per cent of their new debt had been financed through short-term bank loans. "The balance, which has rarely exceeded 15 per cent, has been raised by offering preferred and common stock issues to the general public. . . . Control, therefore, tends to remain firmly in the hands of existing shareholders. This is the case even though a large proportion of the new moneys being made available to the Canadian oil industry continues to be provided by a fairly wide-spread appeal to the public for funds. These are generally raised by selling 'safer' securities like bonds.''

Moreover even when equity shares were made available, only a small proportion were offered in Canada, with the general result that "most Canadian money finding its way into the domestic oil industry has gone towards the purchase of bonds with a limited life and a guaranteed rate of interest, rather than into the riskier and frequently more lucrative field of outright ownership. In the future there will probably be even less opportunity for Canadian nationals to participate in the ownership of the major oil companies. The main reason for this is that the most difficult phase as far as raising new funds is concerned in Canada, is largely over.'' This was in 1952! And "it looks as if internal company financing out of retained profits will play a more rather than a less important role in providing fresh capital for the industry's expansion program here.'' Over the following quarter century, in fact, there would be few new issues from the majors to make it possible for Canadians to gain admittance to the management of their own oil and gas resources. "On the other hand, dividend and interest payments to foreign investors are, in a few years' time, likely to be much larger than they are at present.'' The net effect of this process would be a $25-million annual drain by the mid-'50s from an industry in which average rates of return were running "considerably higher than those on foreign investments in other industries.'' American oil companies were earning 15 per cent and British firms 14 per cent on their investments at the time of the study, as compared with an average of 7 per cent for U.S. and British investments in other Canadian industries.

All this information collected in the early 1950s was kept from the Canadian public. Defence production minister C. D. Howe was not the sort of man to help heighten citizen concern about foreign ownership. Ironically, these were the years in which much of the country's known western oil reserves were being found. Of the 30.8 billion barrels discovered in Alberta between 1946 and 1979, 74 per cent were found before 1960, and of the oil found in this early period, 35 per cent was discovered by Mobil, 16 per cent by Imperial, 9 by Texaco, and 6 by Gulf, with other, minor finds by such foreign-controlled concerns as Chevron (Standard Oil of California), Shell, Hudson's Bay Oil and Gas, Amoco Canada,

Canadian Superior, Atlantic Richfield, Ashland, and Husky. The principal Canadian-controlled oil company active in this period was Home Oil, which accounted for 8 per cent of the 1946-60 finds.[2] While the story of natural gas in Alberta is somewhat different, the role of the foreign-controlled majors was significant there as well. The years before 1960 saw the discovery of 56 per cent of the gas found in Alberta from 1946 to 1979, and seven foreign-controlled firms – Mobil with 14 per cent, Shell with 14, Gulf with 9, Chevron with 7, and Hudson's Bay Oil and Gas with 5 per cent – accounted for 59 per cent of this total.

In fact, though the tidal wave of foreign-controlled oil companies seeking land and Canadian firms to take over came in the 1950s and 1960s, outside interest in the country's oil prospects dates back to the late nineteenth century and the dawn of the petroleum age. By 1880, John D. Rockefeller and his giant Standard Oil octopus were embarked on a process that culminated in the takeover of what was then and remains today Canada's biggest oil company, Imperial, for the then perceptible price of $350,000. The year 1911 saw the arrival in Canada of the Royal Dutch/Shell group, Standard's great global rival. Thereafter Canada's oil and gas business was largely under foreign control. Some indigenous competitors did emerge. The British American Oil Company, founded in 1906, became a takeover target: one-third held by Imperial at one point, B-A was eventually absorbed by the Gulf empire in the 1940s. Another Canadian-controlled firm, McColl-Frontenac, was taken over by Texaco in the late 1930s. And Canadian Oil, the sole remaining big, integrated, domestically controlled company, with its own wells, refinery, and chain of service stations trading under the White Rose name, was picked up by Shell in the early '60s.

In the pioneer years, there had also been some British interest in the strategic value of Canada's still largely undiscovered oil. Especially after Winston Churchill's elevation as First Sea Lord, the Admiralty, converting from coal to oil as part of its program to increase potential effectiveness against the German fleet, was anxious to secure the imperial supply. Even after the acquisition of Anglo-Persian, which later became British Petroleum, Whitehall kept close watch on Canadian developments, and its attitude inspired a 1914 order in council from the Borden government stipulating that any company applying for oil and gas leases in western Canada must be British- or Canadian-controlled.

This new regulation came into effect shortly before the discovery of oil in Alberta's Turner Valley by Calgary Petroleum

Products, later acquired by Imperial. The find precipitated a wild and speculative boom; companies mushroomed overnight, and it was hard to tell whether their main purpose was to raise money to find oil or simply to fleece the innocent and greedy of their savings. The Turner Valley development also unleashed an intense rivalry between Standard Oil's Imperial and Royal Dutch/Shell, which was considered as a British company, both of them anxious to be part of western Canada's highly promising oil play. As Walter Teagle, then Imperial's president, wrote to C. O. Stillman, a vice-president of Imperial: "You realize fully the importance of the discovery of a productive oil field in Canada and how such a discovery would affect our own business. For this reason it seems to me that we should be very much alive to the situation and if there is any likelihood of paying production being developed in Canada we should, if possible, try and arrange to be in on the ground floor with leases of our own, so that from the very outset we might occupy as important a position as producers of oil in Canada as we now occupy as refiners and distributors."[3] At the time this was written, Imperial had over 80 per cent of Canada's refining capacity. Avid for the western stakes, the company set out to thwart the federal regulation, reinforced in 1915 by another order in council under the War Measures Act, by stockpiling mineral rights on freehold land owned by the railways, the Hudson's Bay Company, and private farmers – Imperial's great 1947 Leduc discovery would be made on freehold land. In 1917, an exploration company, Northwest, was set up to acquire leases in Alberta and the Territories; holding at the outset only 28 per cent of Northwest's shares so that it could qualify as a Canadian company, Imperial assumed full ownership two years later when Ottawa relaxed its rules. Thus did Standard Oil contrive, despite its citizenship, to emerge as the leading oil firm in western Canada; its 1919 Norman Wells strike was the first of any significance since Turner Valley in 1914.

Throughout this early period, evidence of concern by Canadians over growing foreign control was never wanting. At the time, prior to its takeover of Imperial, when Standard was positioning itself to become the dominant player in the country's oil industry, it lobbied for a number of changes in Canadian legislation, notably a cut in the tariff on imported oil, the right to import oil products by tanker, and approval for the sale of oil and oil products by tank wagon. John Fraser, MP for Petrolia in Ontario, warned Prime Minister Sir Wilfrid Laurier that these changes would mean disaster for the Canadian industry: "Canadians would be placed at the mercy of a large and powerful foreign corporation. Competition would be impossible, for Standard also had access to American crude oil, alone had the money to buy and operate lake tankers, alone had the funds to build large fleets of horse-drawn tank wagons."[4] Nonetheless, in June 1897 Parliament went ahead to approve a reduced tariff on imported oil and permit imports by tanker. In the following year, Standard acquired control of Imperial, and in 1899 a federal mines report acknowledged that "the petroleum industry of Canada is now practically controlled by one corporation, which is understood to be a branch of the American industry."[5] Evidence of concern along these lines moved Imperial's own historian to record that "in these years was laid the foundation for an attitude on the part of the Canadian company which, for a long time, caused its officials to shrink from any public mention of their Standard affiliation as something only slightly more acceptable than leprosy."[6]

One reason for public concern – aside from a general dislike of Mr. Rockefeller, whose buccaneering exploits were often spread across the front pages of Canadian and U.S. newspapers – was the belief that the Standard group was misusing its monopoly to force up oil prices in Canada. According to one report, a February 1899 Toronto gathering of top executives from 17 large Canadian companies, including Massey-Harris, Dominion Bridge, and Dominion Glass, drafted an angry letter to Laurier complaining that "since the Standard Oil Company secured the control of the product there has been a tendency to curtail the supply and reduce the quality, and in some cases to cut it off altogether, as well as to advance the price materially."[7] The companies had cause to complain. In earlier, more competitive days, they had been persuaded to switch from coal to oil: now they were stuck with the higher prices.

Later, Canadians were roused by Shell's repeated though ultimately unsuccessful efforts between 1917 and 1919 to obtain a Middle-East-type oil concession covering much of western Canada. W. A. MacRae, Alberta MLA for the Peace River area, wrote a two-part series for *Saturday Night*'s financial section in 1919, outlining the Shell proposals under the headlines: "Open Your Mouth and Shut Your Eyes," "And We'll Take Your Oil Land, Wherever it Lies."[8] What the company wanted was exclusive exploration rights for 250,000 square miles of Alberta, the Yukon, and the Northwest Territories, with long-term concessions including the free grant of land for pipelines, storage and refining sites, duty-free imports of plant and equipment, the continuation of existing incentives for oil production until 1930, and after that, a ceiling on royalties of three cents a barrel, no land rental charge, complete exemption from taxation for 15 years, and the right to dispose of any of its land to whomever it chose and for whatever price it wished. In return for all this, once Shell had earned itself a 6-per-cent cumulative return on capital, it would split further profits with the federal government. MacRae damned the application as barefaced begging, and issued the dramatic warning that the granting of a monopoly on Canada's oil patch could, when "our neighbours to the south . . . have none for export," ruin the immense potential benefits for this country and leave its people as "the wage slaves of a concessionnaire."

Similar sentiments were expressed in a series of articles entitled "Canada's Oil For Canadians" that was sent back to the Toronto *Evening Telegram* from Edmonton and other places in Alberta the same year.[9] The author, G. C. Potter, described the intense rivalry over the western concessions, and added: "But there are some disinterested persons in this part of the west who do believe that the federal government should take warning by the way in which others of the Canadian great natural resources have been exploited by a few capital combinations and save this treasure. It is here for the people. This view increases with the growth of rival interests. The idea is crystallizing that the investigation should be made by the government and the product, if discovered, handled as a public asset. There are economic students in the west who point to the incalculable advantage Ontario has gained from the Hydro organization and the great oil industry is in many respects parallel."

One westerner, Col. James K. Cornwall, president of Northern Trading and the Athabasca Fur Company, told the *Telegram* reporter in the expansive style of the day that "if the Dominion government had a million dollars to cover this field thoroughly it would ultimately mean before the sum was expended that the reservoir would be tapped. After that taxes in this Dominion would be a thing of the past." "At no other time in the history of the Dominion," Potter perorated, "has a big man with big vision and with public ownership sympathies been so important to Canada as today." One such spokesman was Sir Adam Beck, the founder of Ontario Hydro, who gave a speech in Stratford calling on Ottawa to take over the oil business in western Canada and develop it for the public benefit. And officials in the Interior department – the minister then was Senator James Lougheed, grandfather of the present premier of Alberta – were among others pushing for state ownership. Citing the profiteering record of the "Oil Trust," government petroleum engineer S. E. Slipper insisted that even "admitting the objections to government operation of industrials . . . Canada could successfully handle the northern oil fields as she now operates her northern railways. . . . If a huge railway system can be operated by a company of this kind there is no reason why an oil enterprise could not be successfully operated on the same basis."[10]

These proposals remained just that, however, and in the years between the wars the foreign-controlled companies kept tightening their hold. With the ending of Canadian ownership regulations in 1920, Imperial moved to take over the largest oil- and gas-producing firm in Alberta, Calgary Petroleum Products. One of the key figures in this young Canadian operation was R. B. Bennett, a Calgary lawyer who went on to be prime minister of Canada in the years 1930-35. Bennett helped negotiate the deal with Imperial after a 1920 fire had wiped out the company refinery, which it lacked the capital to rebuild. Imperial created Royalite Oil and Calgary Petroleum shareholders received 20 per cent of the shares. With Royalite, Imperial became the major producer in Turner Valley, Canada's only oil field of any note until the Leduc discovery of 1947. And this was not all: among the many other independent Canadian firms Imperial absorbed in this period, either directly or through subsidiaries, were Southern Alberta Oil (another Turner Valley pioneer), Southwest Petroleum, Southern Lowery Oils, and Mayland Oil. At the same time, Imperial set up Foothills Oil and Gas in 1927 as a wholly-owned subsidiary for land acquisition, and it succeeded in gaining control of about 75 per cent of the Turner Valley field. Northwest too was still active, acquiring land for Imperial and operating as a drilling contractor. Many of the firms Imperial bought still had minority shareholders. Bennett, who acted for the giant on company acquisitions and leases, advised Imperial not to buy these shareholders out, arguing that their existence provided some protection against radical federal or provincial legislation on oil industry ownership and control.[11]

Meanwhile, sensitive as always about public awareness of its U.S. ownership, Imperial tried hard to sell the idea that it was really a Canadian company with Standard of New Jersey a passive shareholder. In 1915, Walter Teagle, the American president of Imperial, wrote to Standard that he had checked the proofs of a series of articles sent him prior to publication, and "the corrections eliminated any reference to Imperial as a subsidiary of the Standard Oil Co. (New Jersey)." A year later, he was writing Standard about an entry for the Moody Manual Co.: "I would be glad if the article when it finally appeared made no mention of the stock which the Standard Oil Co. (New Jersey) has in the company."[12] Another tactic was concealment of company interests. In 1924, Imperial built a small refinery in Coutts, Alberta, but kept its ownership of the company, Maple Leaf Petroleum, secret. It set up Consumers Gasoline Supply in the early 1920s to operate filling stations in Ontario and Quebec, again concealing its ownership. During the 1930s, Imperial resisted pressure to bring the Esso brand name into Canada, because Canadians did not like Standard Oil of New Jersey. Over this objection, however, the name was finally introduced into Canada in 1935.

After an important Alberta discovery by a Canadian-controlled firm, Turner Valley Royalties, in 1936, more U.S. companies began moving into the Canadian West. The trend was further encouraged by Mexico's 1938 nationalization of foreign oil companies and the approach of world conflict. By the time the Leduc field was tapped, these firms were solidly established. But it took Leduc and Imperial's 1948 Redwater strike to prove beyond doubt that Alberta was a highly promising oil region. The result was that "the American companies rushed for exploration reservations in such numbers that the province was soon plastered with their filings from border to border. Imperial Oil, being first on the ground, took out millions of acres of reservations and was the first to make mincemeat of the province's naive notion that it could limit the acreage any company could inventory."[13] Canadian-owned firms found that there was little land left for them to drill.

U.S. domination of the Canadian industry was also strongly abetted at this time by American tax laws offering generous incentives for U.S. companies to engage in foreign activities. It was also the period of the Cold War, a time of close resource planning between the two countries that made radical new Canadian policies on foreign ownership improbable. And in addition to its Cold War concern about continental security, Washington was seriously preoccupied about future resource supplies. In 1952, the so-called Paley Report from the President's Materials Policy Commission forecast that U.S. oil consumption would more than double, from 2.4 billion barrels in 1950 to 5 billion barrels in 1975, and that the United States would become heavily dependent on imported oil supplies.[14] Other American studies by the Chase Manhattan Bank and Resources for the Future also predicted rising U.S. oil-imports dependence. A growing number of U.S. policy-makers and oil industry planners began to see Canada as a future source of supply, reversing its half-century role as a net importer of American oil. In 1955, Canada became a net exporter of oil to the United States.

Not only was there an absence of Canadian measures to strengthen Canadian ownership, in spite of the findings of such studies as Defence Production's 1952 analysis, but foreign-controlled companies even had better access to Canadian savings. The oil majors could borrow against their refining and marketing assets, something that Canadian oil independents, who lacked such assets, could not do. Moreover foreign subsidiaries in Canada could borrow from Canadian banks on the basis of parent-company guarantees. As the Royal Bank spelled it out in 1956: "Large United States oil corporations often find it expedient to use this method of financing the operations of Canadian affiliates and by doing so, eliminate the necessity of tying up their own funds in the subsidiary's development programs."[15] The savings of Canadians were available through the Canadian banking system to reinforce the tax and other advantages foreign-owned oil companies had over Canadian-owned ones.

Another problem for Canadian firms as the 1950s passed into the 1960s was that production capacity far exceeded actual production. At the beginning of the '60s, for example, oil companies in Alberta were producing at about 40 per cent of capacity. Large firms were much better able to sit on reserves than small ones were. This was a factor that increased the vulnerability, as it restricted the options, of the remaining Canadian companies. And in the early '60s, in fact, the Canadian-controlled oil industry was engulfed by the biggest takeover frenzy in its history, giving the eight major internationals by 1962 some 60 per cent of oil production, and about 95 per cent of refining capacity; in Alberta, the 14 top companies held 63 per cent of the oil and gas lands.

But while the late 1950s and early 1960s saw the consolidation of ownership and control by the oil majors, they also saw a resurgence of public concern. A 1957 study for the Royal Commission on Canada's Economic Prospects – the Gordon Commission – was optimistic about oil and gas growth prospects but pessimistic about increasing Canadian participation or reducing the roughly 80-per-cent foreign ownership of the industry. For one thing, the oil majors had the money: "In recent years high bidding in provincial government land sales has prohibited the smaller companies with limited capital resources from acquiring land in the more favourable oil and gas areas."[16] Access to land for exploration and development was essential; if Canadian companies could not afford to outbid the majors when Crown reserves were auctioned by provincial governments, they were doomed to an inferior role from the start. And because of the economic imperative favouring the big integrated companies that could spread risk around and finance the large-scale capital investments which were needed, "the internationally owned and controlled firms will probably continue to dominate all phases of the oil industry in this country. Meanwhile, most Canadian independents, lacking these strengths, have little chance of becoming majors in the Canadian oil and gas industry during the next 20 to 30 years."

Moreover, like the Defence Production writers of 1952, the Gordon Commission researchers saw few opportunities for Canadians to become important shareholders in existing foreign-controlled companies. Given retained earnings and easy access to credit, the oil majors' growth was assured. And a further problem was that when oil subsidiaries in Canada did issue new shares for sale, they reserved huge blocks for their parent companies so that their control would not be reduced. "Unless the policy of a number of the major companies changes in this respect," the commission's paper explained, "there may be even less opportunity for Canadian nationals to buy into the oil industry in the future. The most difficult phase, in so far as the raising of investment capital is concerned, is largely over. Revenues from the sale of crude oil production are now on the increase. Within the next few years they may be sufficient to cover the industry's total expenditures on exploration, development, and production. No longer will parent companies be required to pour millions of dollars into Canada with little chance of earning a return for a decade or more. Also, there is less likelihood of companies like Imperial Oil selling, outright, their interests in subsidiary companies in order to obtain sufficient funds to carry on an accelerated program of exploration and development. From now on, therefore, it looks as if the plowing back of retained profits from crude sales and Canadian refinery operations will play a much more rather than a less important role in the providing of future capital for growth in this country."

In its 1957 final report, the Gordon Commission acknowledged that Canadians needed foreign capital and technology to help achieve high rates of economic growth, but expressed strong concern that so much of the foreign investment was in the form of equity or shares, especially in subsidiaries of major foreign companies, instead of bonds: "There is a snowballing effect about investments in equities. If a substantial part of earnings are retained and reinvested, the original investment tends to increase at a relatively fast rate."[17] Much of the postwar growth in the foreign share of the Canadian economy had come about as a result of the reinvestment of retained earnings. This was especially true in the resource industries. The commission went on to point out some special factors underlying the growth of foreign ownership in the oil and gas and other resource sectors. American corporations were generating large profit flows and their executives were looking beyond the U.S. borders for lucrative opportunities; there was U.S. government support for the development of raw-materials sources outside the United States to meet future security and industrial needs; U.S. tax incentives encouraged Americans to go abroad to explore for oil and gas. The commission also found that "many Canadians are worried about such a large degree of economic decision making being in the hands of Canadian companies controlled by nonresidents. This concern has arisen because of the concentration of foreign ownership in certain industries, because most of it is centred in one country, the United States, and because most of it is in the form of equities which, in the ordinary course of events, are never likely to be repatriated."

Aside from the general fear that such a high level of U.S. control might lead to considerable integration of the Canadian economy into the U.S. economy, economic domination of Canada by the United States, and Canada's eventual loss of political independence, there was the more immediate fear that the goals of foreign parent companies might be in conflict with Canada's best interests. "For example, in the oil industry the same large international companies, or their affiliates and subsidiaries, which broadly speaking dominate the producing, refining, and marketing sections of the Canadian industry, are the principal suppliers of crude oil to the large market centred in Montreal, and are important suppliers in most areas of the United States. The immediate and continuing interest of the Canadian subsidiaries of these companies, and indeed of Canada, is to find increasing markets for Canada's oil in the United States, or failing that, perhaps in the Montreal area. Without growing markets a large part of the oil being discovered in western Canada would have to be 'shut in,' perhaps for some considerable period. The importance and the immediacy of this problem of markets for the oil industry in Canada is clear enough to Canadians. Quite understandably, it may appear somewhat less important and less immediate to those in other countries who control the situation and who have worldwide interests to consider." And indeed, this very issue soon became a cause of direct conflict between the interests of the oil majors and the Canadian independents, with the oil majors coming out the winners. The Gordon inquiry worried too that foreign-controlled companies would tend to charge their parent companies too little for raw materials and overpay for what they acquired from them – for example, research and development fees or imported oil. Canadian tax authorities could try to detect such attempts to avoid Canadian taxes, but, the commission said: "It is not always easy to establish fair prices in such inter-company arrangements, which are difficult to investigate and police." Finally, the report warned that foreign subsidiaries tended more often than not to buy U.S. or other foreign-manufactured equipment instead of seeking out Canadian suppliers.

Analysing the Canadian predicament, the commission made a number of important recommendations. It called for greater reliance on foreign capital in the form of bonds and mortgages, a minimum of 20- to 25-per-cent Canadian ownership of foreign-owned companies operating in Canada, and various measures – more Canadians in senior management positions and the appointment of independent Canadians to the subsidiaries' boards of directors – to make these companies more Canadian in outlook. In addition, it proposed that foreign-owned companies retain Canadian engineering and other professional and service personnel, obtain their supplies, material and equipment in Canada, and issue public financial statements on their Canadian operations. Proposed as voluntary measures, these were largely ignored by the industry in Canada, as were subsequent appeals by the Canadian government to foreign-controlled corporations in the oil and gas and other foreign-dominated industries. The commission's appeal to federal and provincial governments that Canadian participants be required in future oil and gas exploration permits and leases also fell largely on deaf ears, especially in British Columbia, Alberta, and Saskatchewan.

Viewed a quarter century later, the commission's thinking seems remarkably prescient. Almost all the issues featured in the National Energy Program of 1980 had been canvassed by the Gordon Commission in 1957. Yet at the time, the Gordon Report had little impact on Canadians, and especially not on the policy-makers and politicians in Ottawa and the western provinces. To be sure, there were some votes for greater Canadian participation, but in the late 1950s these were few and far between. One was that of James H. Gray, a westerner appalled by the natural-resources takeover, who campaigned from the editorial pages of the *Farm and Ranch Review* and later the *Western Oil Examiner*. On one occasion, using the example of the Interprovincial Pipeline from Edmonton to

Superior, Wisconsin, he pointed out that much of the money came from Canadians who bought pipeline bonds, while the oil majors had invested the equity capital. Canadians, Gray wrote, "will get a fixed interest on their money, if the pipeline is a financial success. Twenty years from now they will get all their money back, if the pipeline is a financial success. And at that stage, if it is a success, it will be owned by the Standard Oil Co. of New Jersey, which owns the majority of the common shares. . . . It is too bad that the people who paid for the steel and the cost of the installation will never own it."[18]

The problem, in Gray's view, was a Canadian obsession with financial security and hence a preference for bonds over shares, along with a notable lack of interest on the part of Ottawa. In his autobiography, Gray wrote of a trip to Ottawa in the early 1950s to discuss the rapidly tightening grip of the foreign-owned oil companies with the assistant deputy finance minister. His expostulations were all for naught, and as Gray rose to leave, the official told him: "I don't give a damn who owns this country, as you put it, as long as we have the power to tax, because whoever has the power to tax calls the tune!"[19] Yet this indifference was not universal. Gray was quick to point to the fivefold oversubscription by Albertans for shares in the newly created Alberta Gas Trunk Line (now Nova) in 1957: "The first and most obvious implication is that Canadians are now more eager than they have been to invest their money in the equity side of oil and gas development. Secondly, the notion that Canadians could not have financed Trans-Canada [Pipeline] is preposterous on its face." As his March *Western Examiner* editorial argued, there was a lesson for the Alberta government: "Albertans want to participate in the building of their province and their country. Should the government not now take steps to re-examine its reservations and leasing laws to give Canadians the sort of advantage they deserve in obtaining access to develop? With over 84 million acres in Crown land under reservation and lease in Alberta, the scope for Canadian money is obviously limited."

The decision of the newly elected Progressive Conservative government of John Diefenbaker in 1957 to downplay the Gordon recommendations and ignore such western voices as Gray's was particularly surprising in that the party had, in opposition, vehemently opposed the St. Laurent Liberal government's plan to give financial assistance to a company controlled by U.S. interests for the building of the trans-Canada natural gas pipeline. Ottawa's stipulation that the line follow an all-Canadian route through

50

northern Ontario, instead of a more southerly route crossing the United States, meant higher construction and steel costs, and the promoters of the Trans-Canada Pipe Line Company applied for a subsidy. The best that commerce minister C. D. Howe could wring from his Cabinet colleagues was an agreement that the Industrial Development Bank, a subsidiary of the Bank of Canada, should become a financial partner. Under the deal worked out over ten weeks, the IDB would require common shares and convertible debentures in the project which, if fully converted, would give the Canadian government control of the company.

But here was the rub. U.S.-controlled firms in Alberta had been reluctant to sell gas to the pipeline company, even though the Alberta government was pressing them to do so. One company, though, Gulf Canadian Ltd., had agreed to supply about 40 per cent of Trans-Canada's gas needs, but with a big "if." The "if" was its U.S. parent. According to an unpublished history of the Trans-Canada Pipe Line Company negotiations by one of its key financial advisers, Deane Nesbitt of Nesbitt, Thomson: "Gulf Oil had established a policy . . . that it would not sell to a company either controlled by government, or one which could be controlled by a government through the exercise of rights."[20] When the deal was made with Governor James Coyne of the Bank of Canada, the president of Gulf in Pittsburgh, J. K. Whiteford, "categorically refused to sign a contract with Trans-Canada," and would not be budged. What this meant was that a project negotiated with the government of Canada and approved by the governments of Alberta and Ontario for shipping Alberta's natural gas to Ontario consumers was being vetoed by a U.S. oil company. Without the Gulf gas contract, Trans-Canada could not arrange the necessary private-sector financing and delivery contracts to place its orders for steel pipe.

When Trans-Canada "reported Gulf's decision to Mr. Coyne, the latter flew into a rage. He considered it a flagrant defiance of the government of Canada by a foreign company." According to Nesbitt, "the Trans-Canada representatives listened to a lengthy tirade against Whiteford and his company, which ended up with the statement by the governor that he would have the company named on the floor of the House of Commons." The Trans-Canada people went after Gulf again, but "Whiteford's position remained adamant. He categorically refused to sell gas from Gulf Oil to a company that could be controlled either by the government or a government agency." This episode amply demonstrates the power of foreign-controlled oil companies in Canada at this time, and it reveals as well that on real issues of policy, the management of the Canadian subsidiary was irrelevant. Canada had to negotiate directly with the parent. Nor was Gulf alone in its refusal to deal with a Canadian pipeline company that might have government participation. Nesbitt tells us that "other oil companies had expressed the same view."

The other revelation, in the face of Gulf's ability to veto the financing arrangements for the pipeline – one of the most important megaprojects of the period and one vital to the development of Canada's natural gas industry – was the unwillingness of Canadians to challenge the oil multinationals. Alberta Premier Ernest Manning, according to a letter written by Coyne, "had been surprised and disturbed by the Gulf Oil Co.'s attitude,"[21] and C. D. Howe, with the other members of the St. Laurent government who were anxious to see this national project proceed, must have been similarly upset. Yet nothing was done. The CCF's House of Commons leader, M. J. Coldwell, argued that "it would be intolerable if American corporations prevented Canadians from using their own natural resources;"[22] Ottawa should cancel Trans-Canada's charter and build the pipeline itself. Instead, the Ottawa and Alberta governments bowed to the power of Gulf, accepted a lengthy delay in the project, and told the Trans-Canada promoters to find a deal that the U.S. oil companies would accept.

What the U.S. companies wanted was the southern route instead of the all-Canadian one. Gulf announced that it would become a major investor in Trans-Canada if this route was followed. Fortunately, the St. Laurent government stood firm at least in its refusal to see the line go through the U.S. As Trans-Canada negotiated a new approach, under which Ottawa and Ontario would build the northern Ontario section through a separate Crown corporation, Gulf raised new difficulties: "Canadian Gulf was demanding an increased price, and as a result considerable difficulty was being experienced in concluding a contract with that company. In addition, the renegotiation clauses which Gulf was insisting upon at the time virtually set the company up as the rate regulating body for Trans-Canada."[23] Moreover, because the federal government had refused to insist on the original financing package negotiated between Coyne and Trans-Canada, 51-per-cent control of Trans-Canada passed to three U.S. companies – Tennessee Gas Transmission, Gulf Oil, and Continental Oil – and it would stay that way until additional shares were sold to the public. The control was won in exchange for the three companies' guarantee of payment for steel pipe orders which had to be made then if construction was to start before the end of 1956. U.S. control was personally approved by C. D. Howe. Yet the Trans-Canada group still turned to the federal government for financial assistance, and in fact Ottawa authorized loans for up to 90 per cent of the cost of the Alberta-Manitoba section of the pipeline, as well as undertaking to build the section from the Manitoba border to Kapuskasing, Ontario through a Crown corporation.

The whole affair generated what was probably the most frenzied and the angriest debate in Canadian parliamentary history. One session ran until 4:30 in the morning, an opposition MP was expelled from the Commons, the reputation of the Speaker of the House was destroyed, and closure was resorted to an unheard-of four times in a three-week period. Some 70 votes were needed, including 43 to appeal rulings of the Speaker or change House procedure. Royal assent was finally given on 7 June 1956, and the government's $80-million loan could be made available to Trans-Canada. On 27 October 1958, gas flowed all the way from Alberta to Montreal. Meanwhile, as public shares were issued, the company came under Canadian ownership and control. In 1957, more than 35,000 individual and corporate investors picked up the largest stock offering in Canadian history, indicating that Canadians were eager to invest in new enterprises. Moreover, the heavy placement of these shares in Canada was achieved over the objections of the Wall Street financial advisers of Trans-Canada's controlling group, who wanted half the public shares offered to U.S. investors.

Yet despite the shocking experience of the trans-Canada pipeline project and the publication of both the Gordon Report and its supporting study on energy issues, the Diefenbaker government, in office from 1957 to 1963, made few changes affecting the ownership of the oil and gas industry and adopted few policies to help Canadian-controlled companies. However it did appoint the Royal Commission on Energy, headed by Toronto industrialist Henry Borden, in 1957. One of the commission's main assignments was to resolve a dispute between the largely foreign-controlled oil majors and the much smaller Canadian independents over whether or not the oil pipeline system should be extended to Montreal so that the big refineries there could use Canadian crude instead of imports from Venezuela and other countries. The independents were anxious to find new markets. Production was running at less than 50 per cent of capacity; they needed cash flow to finance their growth. Led by Home Oil, they wanted the Montreal refineries owned by the oil majors to sign long-term contracts for western

Canadian oil just as they signed contracts with their foreign parent companies for oil from elsewhere. With such contracts in place, Home argued, a pipeline to Montreal could be financed.

The oil majors countered with such considerations as their investment in the Maine-to-Montreal pipeline and the design of their refineries, which were engineered to use imported oil and would require some modifications to handle the western Canadian crude. But the real conflict went much deeper. The majors did not want to displace highly profitable oil imports in eastern Canada with less profitable western Canadian oil. The concessions were running out on their huge Venezuelan reserves; the Venezuelan government, whose take was well above the government take in the Middle East, was demanding an increasing share of oil profits. "Accordingly," as one analyst has noted, "the multinationals were anxious to produce their Venezuelan oil as soon as possible while conditions were favourable. Since this oil was higher priced than Middle East oil, both at the source and at North American ports of entry, the multinationals preferred to route as much Venezuelan oil [as they could] to eastern Canada where they were able to maintain higher retail prices than in comparable regions of the U.S., such as New England."[24] And importing oil that they owned, rather than using Canadian oil that would have been subject to Alberta prorationing, allowed "the Jersey or Shell-controlled refineries in Montreal to be exclusively supplied from Jersey or Shell-controlled oil fields respectively, and to have much of this oil transported in company-owned tankers. In other words, more Jersey or Shell oil is sold for every barrel of oil imported by Imperial and Shell refineries in Montreal than if this oil originated from 'prorated' production in Alberta. This is because Shell and Imperial production in Alberta is 'diluted' by the proration formula which allocates 'production allowables' to all Alberta producers."[25]

While it was true that consumers in eastern Canada might have paid slightly more for their gasoline and other products if they used western Canadian oil, the proponents of the pipeline to Montreal argued as follows: "1. It was needed to restore Alberta oil activity since the province was producing at only 30 per cent of its capacity and one third of its drilling rigs were idle. 2. It would increase Canadian national security by eliminating the dependence of Montreal refineries on imported oil. 3. Construction of the pipeline would generate $300 million of orders for Ontario steel mills as well as thousands of new jobs in Canada. 4. Use of Canadian oil in Montreal would end a drain of $350 million a year in foreign exchange to pay for imported oil. 5. The creation of a new market for 250,000 barrels a day in Montreal would act as a strong incentive for new exploration and development in western Canada and lead to the discovery of new oil and gas reserves."[26] The pipeline supporters also claimed that there would in fact be no increase in consumer price.

However, in this confrontation between the oil majors and the Canadian independents, the majors won. The Royal Commission on Energy, in the second volume of its report, published in 1959, came down clearly on the side of the majors. The use of western Canadian oil in Montreal could lead to higher prices, would require government intervention in the oil industry, and might jeopardize the prospects of a continental energy policy, since the U.S. majors and the U.S. government opposed the displacement of Venezuelan oil in Montreal: "We mention the possibility of a continental oil policy not because we believe that it can necessarily be developed in the immediate future but because we feel that care should be taken to ensure that Canada, by its actions and commitments now, does not jeopardize the possible development of such a policy."[27] Instead of expanding the Canadian market for Canadian oil, the commission continued, Canadians should rely on the oil majors and the American government to create a growing U.S. market for Canadian oil. While there was a certain logic to this, it also meant that Canadian oil sales would depend on Washington's policy on imports, forcing Canada into the position of having to bargain for exemptions from U.S. quotas at the expense of other Canadian interests, as well as relying on the oil majors to facilitate those sales; moreover Canadian oil was subject to a duty of 10.5 cents a barrel as it entered the U.S. It seemed that Ottawa still found U.S. government intervention more tolerable than its own. Imperial had told the commission that a Montreal pipeline would require a Canadian protective tariff on oil and government guarantees of the pipeline bonds: "Neither of these measures was desirable, since both implied a greater measure of government control over the oil industry."[28] Not surprisingly, attitudes changed when it was in the industry's interest: by the mid-1970s, Imperial itself was seeking government participation to ensure the completion of the Syncrude tar sands project, and when the oil pipeline was eventually extended to Montreal in 1979, in the wake of the 1973-74 OPEC crisis, the industry had no hesitation in asking for government assistance, which it received.

The National Oil Policy announced by the Diefenbaker government in February 1961 left the eastern markets of Quebec and

Atlantic Canada to imported oil, reserved Canadian markets west of the Ottawa River for domestic oil, and told the oil majors to develop new markets for Canadian oil in the United States. Yet though the independents had lost this battle, there was a heightened awareness among Canadians of the ways in which the majors' power could override the national interest. Evidently there were two sets of rules: the United States, at the urging of its oil industry, could establish quotas as well as a tariff on oil imports, but the Canadian subsidiaries of the same companies could argue that these things would be bad for Canada. The majors' preferred supply patterns were simply aggravating a reduced-production predicament in Alberta that increased the likelihood of more takeovers of cash- and credit-poor Canadian independents. "The major companies," the energy commission had conceded, "because of their ability to reply on capital generated within the parent company's group, could withstand these difficulties for substantial periods of time. The smaller independent companies which have played a vital role in the growth of the Canadian oil industry, especially in the wildcat drilling phase, would undoubtedly lose ground to the major integrated companies. They have no large resources of working capital but depend, to a large extent, upon short-term credit from the banks. With prolonged marketing difficulties this source of credit could be denied them."[29]

It is not surprising, then, that the 1961 National Oil Policy was followed by one of the biggest takeover splurges in Canadian oil and gas history. Takeovers were nothing new; they had been one of the principal vehicles for the extension of the majors' control. Indeed, a subsequent study for the Economic Council of Canada noted that in the years 1945-61, about one third of all takeovers in the manufacturing sector were made by integrated oil companies, spending a total of $460 million to buy Canadian firms.[30] What was new was the sheer volume of early-'60s activity. In 1960, Shell Canada acquired North Star Oil, a refining and marketing company, and its exploration affiliate, Cree Oil of Canada, while Phillips Petroleum gained control of Pacific Petroleum and Westcoast Transmission, and Petrofina took over New Superior Oils of Canada. In 1961 there were a number of smaller takeovers: in one of these, Britain's Burmah Oil picked up 16 per cent of Great Plains Development with an option to acquire up to 30 per cent. But 1962 was the record-breaking year. Gulf Canada acquired Royalite Oil, Anglo-American Exploration, and Superior Propane; Shell Canada made the spectacular acquisition, already mentioned, of Canada's last remaining integrated firm, Canadian

Oil; Pacific Petroleum bought Bailey Shelburn Oil and Gas and the Canadian properties of Western Natural Gas; Canadian Superior took full control of the Calgary and Edmonton Corporation. In addition, British Petroleum's Triad Oil purchased Devon-Palmer Oils, Husky Oil purchased Wainwright Producers and Refineries and Canadian Kodiak Refineries, and Union Oil of Canada acquired Williamson Oil and Gas. In the following year, Gulf purchased the Purity 99 chain in western Canada, along with Shawinigan Chemicals in Quebec and smaller manufacturing operations such as Western Tire and Auto Supply and Gunning Ltd. Sun acquired 83 per cent of Great Canadian Oil Sands, Hudson's Bay Oil and Gas acquired Consolidated Mic Mac Oils and Security Freehold Petroleum, while Union Oil took over E. H. Vallat Ltd. In 1965, Standard Oil of Ohio took over Canadian Delhi, Aquitaine purchased Banff Oil, Great Plains (controlled by Burmah) took over Westburne Oil Development, and Imperial acquired Building Products Ltd., a major manufacturer.

In its summary for 1962, the *Canadian Annual Review* had reported: "At year end, rumours that the remaining independents might not survive as such for another year were run-of-the-mill conversation in Calgary. The paradox of the success of the National Oil Policy appeared to be that its production goals had been met by Canadian facilities about 70-per-cent controlled outside Canada."[31] As it turned out, the 70-per-cent foreign ownership estimate was low. The spate of 1962 takeovers moved one Calgary MP, Arthur Smith, to rise in the House that October to urge new tax incentives that would encourage greater Canadian participation in the takeover-ridden oil and gas industry. But in a later tax debate, opposition Liberal MP and future finance minister Edgar Benson opposed new tax incentives on the grounds that "the benefits from this legislation will go largely to foreign investors in this field rather than to Canadian citizens."[32] He complained that the industry paid too little in taxes as it was. New write-offs proposed by the Diefenbaker government would allow Canadians to deduct more for oil and gas investments, but, Benson argued, "foreign control and ownership of this industry has been increasing and this legislation, I submit, will do nothing to discourage foreign ownership and encourage Canadian ownership. In this particular type of industry you have to go into the business whole-heartedly and operate in a big way to make a success of oil and gas exploration and development. Permitting other Canadian interests and industries to dabble in this type of activity is no way to ensure the expansion of Canadian investment in this field." The industry received its tax incentives nonetheless, and takeovers of Canadian companies continued.

An opening for a change in Canadian policy on oil takeovers arose in 1962 at the time when Shell Canada gained control of Canadian Oil. Here was a move that was bound to touch a national nerve. As a 1961 company publication had pointed out, Canadian Oil Companies was as Canadian as its name: "An overwhelming 93 per cent of its shares are held by Canadian investors and the company is operated by Canadian personnel. Moreover it is the only major Canadian oil company that processes Canadian oil exclusively. And it is the only major Canadian-owned oil company with completely integrated facilities from oil fields to refineries to service stations."[33] Canadian Oil Companies had been incorporated in 1908 and U.S.-controlled until 1938: originally a refining-marketing company, it got into western Canadian oil exploration in 1955, and by 1962 had 55,000 barrels a day of refining capacity, 3,100 service stations, 5,000 barrels a day of oil production, and some petrochemicals facilities. At this point, however, it was becoming in a sense a victim of the National Oil Policy. Previously, it had supplied its Ontario refinery with imported oil, but when that source was excluded, Canadian Oil found itself with little of its own crude for its Ontario and Alberta refineries. Shell Canada, meanwhile, urgently needed an Ontario refinery to supply its service stations in that province, which could no longer be fed from the Montreal refinery. The takeover would mean that what Canadian-controlled presence remained in the industry would be significantly reduced. Opposition MPs tried to get the government to take action. However, when a British Columbia CCF member, H. W. Herridge, pushed the prime minister to "assure the House that he will urge the directors of the Canadian Oil Companies to put Canada first," Diefenbaker insisted that his government could do nothing: "It is beyond the jurisdiction of the government to act on his behalf, however desirous all Canadians are that ownership and management of our resources be in Canadian hands," and added that "any action suggested by the Hon. gentleman would be gratuitous on the part of the government."[34]

Yet as *Oilweek* magazine warned shortly afterwards: "The independents are disappearing at an alarming rate. What's the outlook? More mergers, more sales. And the fewer strong independents that are left, the more determined will be the bidding to acquire them. Why? Because the independents are in such good shape they make attractive assets to acquire, for one reason. Because of the increased difficulty of finding oil, for another."[35] In fact, *Oilweek* reported, Dome Petroleum, until it was refused a favourable tax ruling, had planned to sell almost all its reserves to Sinclair Canada, a subsidiary of the U.S.-based Sinclair Oil. Their growing revenues, coupled with the fact that the value of reserves in the ground was rising, made the independents attractive to the majors at the same time that low stock-market prices were making new financing more difficult for the independents. The majors were also anxious to pick up service-station chains and increase the markets for their refineries. By 1962, they had 95 per cent of the country's refining capacity.

Virtually the only government policy addressing itself to the foreign-ownership issue during the Diefenbaker years came in 1961 with the new land regulations for the Canadian North and Atlantic and Pacific offshore regions. While there were few restrictions on who could hold exploration permits, only Canadian-owned companies or foreign-controlled companies in which Canadians would have a chance to invest would be granted production leases. Though the Conservative government tried to sell this as an important step towards Canadian ownership, it seemed to have very little concrete significance, as any parent company listed on, say, the Toronto Stock Exchange could qualify, even if no shares in its Canadian subsidiary were made available to the Canadian public.

Almost the only company of any size to make shares available to Canadians, in fact, was Shell Canada, which announced in 1961 that it would become a publicly traded company. At the time, it was owned 50 per cent by Shell U.S., the other half belonging to a Royal Dutch/Shell holding company. As a U.S. Treasury official noted in 1962 – the U.S. Treasury had to approve the Shell plan for tax purposes: "For some years the policy of the Canadian government has been developing steadily in the direction of urging non-Canadian interests operating in Canada through subsidiary companies, particularly those engaged in the exploitation of Canadian natural resources such as oil and gas, to permit the Canadian citizens to participate in the equity investment and to a greater degree in the management of such Canadian enterprises. From time to time, Canadian government officials have urged that this policy be implemented by positive action. . . . Although obviously difficult to measure in terms of sales or income, it is felt that failure to comply with the emphatically announced policy of the Canadian government regarding the availability of equity participation to Canadian citizens in companies operating in Canada is, and may become increasingly, injurious to the company's business."[36] The method Shell chose to mitigate its non-compliance was highly unusual. Shell Oil of the United States, which already had public shareholders, distributed its 50 per cent of Shell Canada as a stock dividend to its shareholders. This meant that 65 per cent of the shares went to the majority shareholders, Royal Dutch/Shell, while 35 went to the public, mainly U.S. citizens and institutions. And the "emphatically announced Canadian policy" referred to by the U.S. treasury official had no impact at all on many U.S. majors in Canada, such as Standard Oil of California, Mobil, Amoco (Standard Oil of Indiana), and Standard Oil of Ohio.

In 1963, the Diefenbaker Conservatives were replaced by the Pearson Liberals. Almost immediately, the new government moved to curb foreign takeovers and force foreign-controlled companies to make 25 per cent of their shares available to Canadians. In his first budget the new finance minister – Walter Gordon, who had been chairman of the 1955-57 Royal Commission on Canada's Economic Prospects – introduced a tax of 30 per cent of the value of Canadian corporations taken over by non-residents. The same budget also introduced the concern that a corporation have "a degree of Canadian ownership" of about 25 per cent. Only those with "a degree of Canadian ownership" – a restriction that would clearly militate against the oil and gas industry – could benefit from accelerated depreciation under Canadian tax laws. At the same time, the withholding tax on dividends to foreign stockholders by oil and gas companies would be reduced from the normal 15 per cent to 10 per cent for those with 25 per cent or more Canadian ownership, while the same tax for other corporations would be raised to 20 per cent. All these provisions were withdrawn following a storm of protest rained on the government, not only by the multinationals themselves, but also by such public figures as Eric Kierans, then president of the Montreal Stock Exchange.

Gordon argued in defending his budget that 25-per-cent Canadian ownership was a necessity.[37] Foreign parents would be more likely to take Canadian views and interests into consideration if there were minority Canadian shareholders; net economic benefits from foreign direct investment would increase if Canadians shared in the growth from equity participation; there would be a broader and more diversified Canadian stock market, and foreign subsidiaries would have to publish annual reports on their financial activities. However, the Canadian investment and business community was opposed to Gordon's proposed methods and not especially sympathetic to his goals. With the withdrawal of his measure, the 1960s version of Canadianization was largely abandoned. Had Canadians been able to acquire 25 per cent of the oil and gas industry at that time, they would have paid a far lower price than they would have to pay in the 1980s, and become much better off in the process. One problem, no doubt, was that in the early 1960s only a minority of Canadian politicians or policy-makers understood the importance of oil and gas in the country's economy. There is some significance in the fact that it was not until 1966, almost two decades after the oil find at Leduc, that the Canadian government established the Department of Energy, Mines and Resources. Before that, responsibility for energy policy had always been divided between Industry, Trade and Commerce, Mines and Technical Surveys, and Northern Affairs and National Resources.

Defeated in its efforts to legislate greater Canadian ownership through tax amendments, the Pearson government formulated voluntary guidelines, a tactic much favoured by industry. The *Guiding Principles of Good Corporate Behaviour* were issued in 1966. These included the development of Canadian sources of supply, more research and development in Canada, greater use of Canadian management and directors, the issue of shares to Canadians, and the regular publication of financial information. They were largely ignored by the oil and gas industry. Such companies as Chevron Standard, Mobil, Amoco, Canada-Cities Service, and Texaco Exploration refused to publish information or sell shares to Canadians, and treated with indifference the requests for the fostering of Canadian suppliers and the implementing of research and development programs. The oil industry of the mid-1960s believed that it could safely dismiss such official statements of Canada's aspirations.

While the official guidelines were a failure, as guidelines almost invariably are, the Pearson government did manage to take one important step that had long-term significance for the Canadian oil and gas industry. On 12 December 1967, Ottawa announced that it was entering into partnership with 20 oil and mining companies to carry out joint exploration and drilling programs in the Arctic islands, one of the promising oil and gas areas of the frontier regions. This was the federal government's first real entry into the oil and gas business, although it was as a partner in a private company, Panarctic Oils, rather than through a Crown corporation. "The original government objectives . . . were to stimulate oil and gas exploration in Canada's Arctic islands and to maintain significant Canadian ownership and control over the development of Canada's largest remaining areas of undeveloped resources," a senior official has explained: "It was also realized that the program would create opportunities for northern residents as well as other Canadians, and would further the development of Canadian technology suitable to the northern terrain and climate."[38] The idea for Panarctic came from a prominent Alberta geologist, J. Cam Sproule, who saw the Arctic islands' potential and wanted to create a Canadian company to develop the archipelago's oil and gas resources. Without government support, the Canadian companies would have lacked the long-term investment capital needed in this pre-Prudhoe-Bay period, and been forced either to farm their land out to the majors directly or else surrender it to the Crown and make it available to the majors indirectly. This was the only area in the Canadian frontiers where Canadian-owned companies had a significant land position, and to maintain this the federal government took 45 per cent of the new company, Panarctic Oils, for an initial investment of $9 million. Without Panarctic, it is highly unlikely that an ongoing, Canadian-directed exploration program in the islands would have been kept up through the 1970s. And without Panarctic, it is unlikely that there would now be a strong element of Canadian ownership and control in Arctic development.

By the end of the 1960s, then, Canadians' awareness had grown sufficiently to support major policy changes in the coming 1970s. As *The Financial Post* observed in a 1969 editorial: "Clearly, time is running out as far as Canada's independence is concerned. The sweep of foreign (particularly United States) control of industry and resources in Canada is not matched in any other industrial country."[39] And as Jack Austin, a Vancouver lawyer who would become Ottawa's deputy energy minister the following year, told a 1969 Canadian Bar Association meeting: "In Quebec the philosophy is growing stronger that natural resources have a special relationship to the 'national patrimony.' Outsiders have exploited and continue to want to exploit this patrimony, but it must be protected, for it is the source of the wealth of the future – the nation's birthright. This concept will be more heard from across Canada."[40] And if further proof were needed that the oil majors would ride roughshod over Canadian interests, it came with the 1969 voyage of Exxon's *S.S. Manhattan* through the Canadian northwest passage, a test of the viability of using ice-breaking tankers to carry oil from Alaska's Prudhoe Bay to refineries on the U.S. Atlantic coast. Backed by the U.S. government, Exxon challenged Canadian claims to sovereignty in these waters, though it did eventually agree to accept Canadian observers on the vessel.

Following the voyage, Canada was denied access to research data collected in the experiment for a time.[41]

One sign that Ottawa's attitude towards foreign ownership of resource industries was turning around came with Prime Minister Trudeau's announcement in March of 1970 that the government would not allow the takeover of Denison Mines by Hudson's Bay Oil and Gas, a company controlled by Continental Oil (Conoco) in the United States. Trudeau told the House: "Last week the government of Canada learned that a substantial ownership interest in Canada's largest uranium mining company might be passing into non-Canadian hands. The government cannot delay making its position clear because it is understood the transaction may be close to completion." He went on to state: "Our reservations about this change of control of Canadian uranium resources are such that if necessary the government will introduce an amendment to the Atomic Energy Control Act, to take effect as of today, to prevent such a transaction."[42] And energy minister Joe Greene was soon introducing a broader policy that imposed a limit of 33 per cent on foreign ownership of Canadian uranium production capacity in new mines resulting from explorations then under way; foreign investors currently holding 50 per cent of more of a mining property, if they wished to reduce their interest, had to sell part of their holdings to Canadians so that foreign ownership would total no more than 33 per cent.

But it was the takeover bid for Home by Ashland Oil that really roused Parliament. On 18 February 1971 the Speaker of the Commons, responding to a motion by NDP member Tommy Douglas, permitted an emergency debate on the issue. Pointing to the size and value of Canada's oil and gas resources, Douglas reminded MPs: "This is not a renewable resource; it is a resource which once disposed of will be gone for all time. We are merely the trustees of this vast accumulation of wealth which nature has placed under our soil. The Canadian Parliament must decide whether or not in the development and sale of these vast quantities of oil and gas Canadians will get a piece of the action. Approximately 85 per cent of the oil and gas well production in this country is in the hands of foreign corporations, and 99 per cent of the oil refining is in the hands of foreign corporations." He went on to warn that "we will never get a piece of the action unless there are developed in Canada several major oil-producing companies. We have a number of independent producers and small companies, but we have never been able to develop a major company. One of the few companies which has any hope of becoming a major producer of oil is in the Home Oil Company of Calgary. That is why it is so important we consider this matter now.''

While MPs were definitely concerned, there were conflicting opinions on what should be done. Douglas wanted the Trudeau government to intervene and block the sale and then either bankroll a group of small Canadian companies to buy Home Oil or else have it purchased by Panarctic or a Crown corporation. The Conservatives, on the other hand, used the debate to attack government proposals for reducing oil industry tax incentives and urge additional tax incentives for Canadians to buy oil shares. Liberals were divided. One of their members, Robert Kaplan, argued that ''natural resource industries are the last that should be protected from foreign encroachment,'' and said he regretted Canadian public opinion that stressed domestic ownership of these industries: ''I deeply hope that no action will be taken which would lead international mining investors to steer around Canada. This country does not need, and cannot afford, such a policy.'' Other government members, Alastair Gillespie and Martin O'Connell among them, called for strong government action. Gillespie argued that resource industries were ''one of the first areas we should concern ourselves with when we come to formulating foreign ownership policies.'' They were a dominant part of the economy and represented one area where Canadians could establish their own multinationals. He proposed a rule limiting future foreign ownership to 50 per cent of any enterprise. And O'Connell contended: ''What concerns people is the thought that we might look back in ten years' time to realize that, by failing to take steps when we had the opportunity, we had gone so far in allowing control of our economy to slip away that we could not reverse the direction of events. This feeling finds its way into the debate on Home Oil, and it will find its way into debates on many other questions involving foreign takeovers, since people will see in each particular instance the general spectre of events running out of control, with machinery not yet in place and with a Parliament which does not seem to have the will to take the necessary action.'' O'Connell urged the government to consider setting up a Crown oil company and giving it preferential access to oil and gas lands in the far North and Canada's coastal offshore areas.

Another member entering the debate was Jack Horner, at the time a Conservative: ''I too am concerned about the amount of foreign ownership in Canada. I am concerned that the decisions with regard to our resources are not being made by Canadians. The power to make those decisions is being taken out of Canadian hands. These days we hear a great deal of discussion about the quality of life and the standard of living. What those two phrases really mean to me is that we must have some right, some ability, to make decisions that affect our own livelihood and well-being. Little by little, as the power to make these decisions slips into the hands of foreign corporations, so slips away the power that Canadians may enjoy in the years ahead to control the quality of their lives." And a Créditiste MP, André Fortin, noted that the proposed Home Oil takeover was no new problem: "For too long in Canada we have left to others the task of developing our own natural resources so that today, if we place the Home Oil problem in the overall picture, we realize that the situation has become very serious. Home Oil is a Canadian business in the process of becoming American. That is the tragedy, and it is not new. Slowly but surely, our leaders – if one can call them that since their leadership does not extend over much and since all our raw materials belong to foreigners – have let foreigners take over our basic industries. This vast country, which at one time belonged to us, does not belong to us now. We have become tenants."

What the Commons debate demonstrated, strongly and passionately, was that support existed in all four major political parties for policies to strengthen Canadian ownership and control in the oil and gas and other natural resource industries. A similar note was sounded in a series of speeches made in the early 1970s by energy minister Joe Greene and his new deputy, Jack Austin. Greene told the Independent Petroleum Association of America in Denver, Colorado: "I feel very confident that if, in America, some 70 per cent of your petroleum industry and some 60 per cent of your natural resources, and some 50 per cent of your manufacturing industry was owned by non-Americans, you would share an equal concern."[43] Canadians recognized, he said, that foreign capital had helped their country grow: "But Canadians are now determined that the time has come to take stock and to assume that a substantial portion of the future growth remains in Canadian hands." Failure to increase Canadian ownership, he said, would mean Canadians would lack the big corporations with head offices in Canada and that "such a country will become essentially a branch plant economy, with an attendant diminution of opportunity for its young people. I, for one, have come but lately to the conclusion that a growing degree of Canadian ownership in our own resources was essential to the maintenance of Canada as a free and viable and independent nation."

These were strong and blunt words from a Canadian cabinet

minister to an audience of U.S. oil men, accustomed to reassurances from Canadians about close relations between the two countries, but Greene kept up his campaign. The following month, he told the American Association of Petroleum Geologists that "the question arises whether a high degree of Canadian ownership in the oil industry might be feasible in a financial sense and at the same time assure a greater control and direction of our future in Canadian hands with international activity being developed through the establishment of multinational enterprises from a Canadian base. The United States, Britain, France, Holland, Belgium, Italy, and Japan, to name some principal examples, have over the years established companies – some private companies, others with government participation or control – which now operate as multinational enterprises. Must Canada be only the home of the branch plant? The challenge of the 1970s relating to oil supply activities should reach beyond the concerns of subsidiary companies to find and develop new reserves, to a larger concept which would see the Canadian resource base as the home of more effectively integrated corporations of national identity, some with multinational characteristics."[44] And in August of that year, Greene and Indian Affairs Minister Jean Chrétien announced guidelines for oil and gas pipelines in the Mackenzie Valley, under which "means by which Canadians will have a substantial opportunity for participating in the financing, engineering, construction, ownership, and management of northern pipelines will form an important element in Canadian government consideration of proposals for such pipelines."[45]

To the Vancouver Men's Canadian Club that winter, Greene described his December resources mission to Japan and the Japanese attitude to foreign investment. The Canadians on the mission, Greene said, "told them that we approved of the very high level of debt funds which they had employed as against the habits of other foreign investors in participating substantially in equity. We discussed with the Japanese the importance which they had given to domestic ownership of their essential industries, and compared the motives in examining our own goals for increasing Canadian ownership in the resource and energy industries while, at the same time, encouraging the flow of foreign capital to assist in the growth which is required."[46] Indications that Canada might consider a state oil company began to emerge in 1971, following Trudeau's 1970 approval of the study of a national oil company as part of the government's overall energy policy review. Jack Austin told the 1971 annual meeting of the Canadian Petroleum

Association that "when Canadians look abroad to foreign experience, they see that state control of foreign participation is the rule rather than the exception in most parts of the world. This is true in countries such as Australia and the United Kingdom, France and Japan, the Scandinavian countries and Italy – all of whom may be classified as industrial countries, comparable to Canada."[47] Moreover, Austin added, "Canadians are also bound to notice, in international business affairs, decisions such as the announcement by the Organization of Arab Petroleum Exporting Countries of the establishment of the Arab Tanker Company to operate their own tanker fleet and to engage in joint ventures through their General Petroleum Service Company in all oil exploration, refining, and petroleum product marketing. We are bound to be aware of the policies of France since the Second World War to achieve world oil prominence through state control of participation in the French marketplace and through state-organized and -controlled exploration in many parts of the world, including Canada." For the government, Austin said, what all this suggested was a review of its appropriate role – whether it should restrict itself to regulating activities and support for scientific research or whether it "should also establish a presence alongside of industry in several sectors of this vitally important part of the Canadian economy."

While Greene and Austin were sending out these unmistakable signals, reflecting in large part a changing public sense of the need for stiffer rules, within the government itself work was intensifying on the foreign-ownership review headed by revenue minister Herb Gray. As part of the process, a 1972 internal memorandum from the finance department reminded the government of the benefits of Canadian ownership. Reviewing the economic impact of a northern pipeline to carry gas from Alaska and the Canadian North to U.S. and Canadian markets, the memorandum spoke of the need to ensure that the line "will procure its goods, services, research, and development from Canadian sources as far as is economically possible, both in the operating as well as the construction phase."[48] But this was more likely to be done if the project were clearly controlled by Canadian investors: "Such additional benefits would not likely be forthcoming if Canadians were simply to achieve majority ownership, since this would not guarantee financial control by Canadians. The likelihood of financial control relates to the question of probable shareholder behaviour, since normally only a small proportion of total shareholders control corporate policies. In contrast to the possible behaviour of Canadian investors in the pipeline, most foreign investors (especi-

67

ally the American-controlled members of the pipeline consortium) will be interested in controlling the management of the pipeline. It is evident, therefore, that something beyond majority ownership by Canadians would be needed to guarantee Canadian financial control of the pipeline. . . . Financial control must be achieved in addition to majority ownership." Canadians had to be in a position to choose the senior executives and set the management policies, the finance department experts concluded, if Canadians were to get the maximum possible benefits from such a major project.

In 1971 the Canada Development Corporation had been set up to, among other things, increase Canadian participation in the oil and gas industry. In addition, 1973 saw the establishment of the Foreign Investment Review Agency to give government control over foreign takeovers – although as far as the oil and gas industry was concerned, the move came nearly twenty years too late to have any major impact. Nonetheless, the new agency could still be useful in terms of inhibiting new takeovers and controlling the diversification activities of the oil majors; and in addition, the legislation provided an opportunity for Canadians to buy back some oil and gas subsidiaries when there was a change in the ownership of the foreign parent. Also in 1973, energy minister Donald Macdonald published the government's two-volume review of energy policy. It dealt in terms of costs and benefits with foreign ownership of the oil and gas industry and set out some policy options, going on to spell out the arguments for and against the creation of a national oil corporation. While the study attempted to deal with both sides of these questions, their very inclusion in the review was a clear sign that the government was leaning towards action in this area.

Because the principal source of growth financing in the industry – 91.3-per-cent foreign-controlled as compared with 73.2 for coal and 22.5 per cent for uranium – was internally generated, including profits and tax write-offs, "a policy which deals only with capital entering Canada will not significantly change the ownership pattern nor cover what could be the largest source of capital for the growth of foreign-controlled investment in Canada."[49] The Canadian government could ban all foreign takeovers, then, block the entry of new foreign-controlled firms, and restrict the injection of new capital by the foreign parents, and the prevailing pattern of foreign ownership and control would still be left virtually unchanged. The review disclosed that the takeover of Canadian firms during the 1960s had meant a transfer of $253.6 million in assets at the date of acquisition; in 1970, these same assets were worth $572.8 million and accounted for 5.8 per cent of the assets of the foreign-controlled companies that dominated the industry. Looking at possible Canadian policies to increase domestic ownership and control, the energy policy study set out five possible approaches: Canadian ownership, say 51 per cent, in all companies in the oil and gas industry or in all new ventures; more joint ventures in the oil and gas industry, with Canadian companies or Crown corporations as partners; carried interests in oil and gas lands which would allow a public authority, say a national oil company, the right to a percentage interest in all oil or gas fields; public ownership of a major corporation in the oil and gas industry; or more extensive use of the FIRA review process for oil and gas investments. All these options, as it turned out, were to receive serious consideration.

On 6 December 1973, a dozen years after the government had rejected the bid of the Canadian oil independents for an oil pipeline into Montreal, Prime Minister Trudeau announced the abolition of the National Oil Policy with its Ottawa Valley line and the creation of a national market for Canadian oil in the interest of security of supply. In his remarks to the House of Commons, Trudeau reiterated the government's intention of ensuring early completion of the Montreal pipeline, which, he said, "is the single most urgent step toward the attainment of our national goals. Without a pipeline, eastern Canada will never be certain that it can meet its requirements should overseas supply be interrupted. Moreover, without a pipeline the government is unable to guarantee a market in Canada for Canadian oil at a level sufficient to ensure the development of the oil sands and other Canadian sources of supply."[50] In the same speech, Trudeau spelled out the plans for Petro-Canada, plans which were partly the result of heavy NDP pressure on his minority government. While it was not meant to replace the foreign-controlled oil companies, Trudeau said, "the government will, however, look to this corporation to contribute to an increased Canadian presence in petroleum exploration and development." One of its roles would be to bring smaller Canadian-controlled companies with modest resources into joint ventures and thus "ensure for Canadians a more significant role in the development of their own resources."

During the 1974 federal election campaign that followed, Trudeau again raised the issue of foreign ownership in such resource industries as oil and gas. "Resources are both the historic and modern basis of Canada's prosperity," he argued: "They are the jumping-off point for the continuing industrial development of Canada."[51] Because "our natural resources are the underpinning of our whole economy and are therefore of prime importance for Canadian ownership," his government's objective would be "that new major projects in the natural resource field should have at least 50 per cent and preferably 60 per cent Canadian equity ownership. As there are overlapping responsibilities for the development of Canada's natural resources shared by both the federal government and the provinces, we would hope to pursue this objective jointly with the provinces." The prime minister repeated his promise to set up Petro-Canada as a major Canadian-controlled corporation for the exploration and development of Canada's oil and gas resources. This was done in 1975. And in that year, Ottawa also issued its *New Principles for International Business*, voluntary guidelines for foreign subsidiaries. Like the 1966 guidelines, these stressed the need for research and development in Canada, the development of Canadian suppliers, regular publication of financial information, the opportunity for Canadians to buy shares in subsidiaries, and the development of a Canadian outlook in management. Also like the 1966 guidelines, they were generally ignored by the oil and gas industry.

Further indications of the Trudeau government's intentions were contained in its 1976 paper, *An Energy Strategy for Canada: Policies for Self-Reliance*, which stated that "in the elaboration of the strategy proposed for the next ten years, the government of Canada is committed to higher levels of Canadian content and participation in resource development."[52] The paper acknowledged that Canada would continue to need foreign capital, but, it added, "the Foreign Investment Review Agency will have the responsibility of determining that future screenable foreign investments are of significant benefit to Canada." In addition, greater Canadian content and participation would be aided by "legislation concerning oil and gas land regulations to be introduced to Parliament shortly which will facilitate greater Canadian participation in exploration and development of Canada Lands; the entry of Petro-Canada into exploration and development; uranium ownership policy under which foreign participation in new uranium developments is limited to 33 per cent; guidelines with regard to Canadian content in resources-related activities on Canada Lands, particularly with respect to engineering and project management at the development stage."

Yet what was most remarkable as the 1970s neared their end was that, despite all the Canadian concern expressed through that decade, the oil majors appeared not to have noticed. Nor had the Canadian Petroleum Association shifted from its negative view of

70

Canadian aspirations. Right up to the end of the decade, the attitude persisted in many of the major companies that if Ottawa went too far, executives could always be sent from the parent company to prod the Canadians back into line. In spite of the tens of millions of dollars they spent on opinion polling, political analysis, and public affairs in the 1970s, the oil majors failed to detect – or simply chose to ignore – that Canadians were no longer satisfied with a minor role in the development of their own natural resources. The National Energy Policy shock of 1980 was a direct result of industry indifference in the 1970s.

Notes

1. Department of Defence Production. "Confidential Report on the Petroleum Industry." March 1952.
2. Russell S. Uhler. "Oil and Gas Drilling Activity and Success by Selected Companies in Alberta." Calgary, Energy Resources Conservation Board, 1980.
3. Quoted in an unpublished history of Imperial Oil written by J. S. Ewing for the Harvard Business Foundation. Ewing had full access to Standard Oil and Imperial documents, but these were unfortunately destroyed after his study was done in the early 1950s. Many of the details of Imperial's early history, and hence of the pioneer development of the Canadian oil industry, are drawn from his study, a copy of which was made available by Imperial Oil.
4. John T. Saywell. "Through Famine to Fortune: the White Rose Story." Unpublished manuscript produced for Canadian Oil Companies, Toronto, 1958.
5. Saywell, "Through Famine to Fortune."
6. Ewing, history of Imperial Oil.
7. Saywell, "Through Famine to Fortune."
8. W. A. MacRae, in *Saturday Night*, Toronto, 15 and 22 March 1919.
9. G. C. Potter, in the *Evening Telegram*, Toronto, 16, 23, and 26 September 1919.
10. Quoted in D. H. Breen, "Anglo-American Rivalry and the Evolution of Canadian Petroleum Policy to 1930." *Canadian Historical Review*, LXII, 3 (September 1981).
11. Ewing, history of Imperial Oil.
12. Ewing, history of Imperial Oil.
13. James H. Gray. *Troublemaker!* Toronto, Macmillan, 1978.
14. President's Materials Policy Commission. *Resources for Freedom*. Washington 1952. For a review of Paley's implications for Canada, see Goodman, Bernard, *Industrial Materials in Canadian-American Relations*. Detroit, Wayne State University Press, 1961.
15. Royal Bank of Canada, Oil and Gas Department. Bulletin No. 13: "Oil Financing – the Bank's Role." Calgary, 15 March 1956.
16. John Davis. *Canadian Energy Prospects*. Royal Commission on Canada's Economic Prospects. Ottawa 1957.

17. Royal Commission on Canada's Economic Prospects. Final Report. Ottawa 1957.
18. In *Farm and Ranch Review*. Calgary, June 1951.
19. Quoted in Gray, *Troublemaker!*
20. A. Deane Nesbitt. *History of Trans-Canada Pipe Lines Ltd.* Montreal, n.d.
21. Quoted in Nesbitt, *History of Trans-Canada Pipe Lines.*
22. Quoted in Nesbitt, *History of Trans-Canada Pipe Lines.*
23. Nesbitt, *History of Trans-Canada Pipe Lines.*
24. J. G. Debanné. "Oil and Canadian Policy." In *The Energy Question*, vol. 2, E. W. Erickson and L. Waverman, eds. Toronto, University of Toronto Press, 1974.
25. Debanné, "Oil and Canadian Policy."
26. Gray, *Troublemaker!*
27. Royal Commission on Energy. Second Report. Ottawa 1959.
28. Alan R. Plotnick. *Petroleum: Canadian Markets and United States Foreign Trade Policy.* Seattle, University of Washington Press, 1964.
29. Royal Commission on Energy. Second Report.
30. Grant Reuber and Frank Roseman. *The Take-over of Canadian Firms 1945-61.* Ottawa, Economic Council of Canada, 1969.
31. *Canadian Annual Review 1962.* Toronto, University of Toronto Press, 1963.
32. House of Commons Debates, 9 November 1962.
33. Brochure published on the opening of Canadian Oil's new Alberta refinery, 20 June 1961.
34. House of Commons Debates, 3 October 1962.
35. "Will Independents Survive Take-Overs?" *Oilweek*, 8 October 1962.
36. Letter from Harold Swarty, Internal Revenue Service, U.S. Treasury, to Shell Oil Co., New York, 10 August 1962.
37. House of Commons Debates, 13 June 1963.
38. John A. Macdonald, deputy minister of Public Works, to the Fifth National Northern Development Conference, Edmonton, 5 November 1970.
39. *The Financial Post,* 19 July 1969.
40. Jack Austin, "Comments on the Legal Status of United States-Canadian Economic Relations in Natural Resource Sharing." Speech to the Canadian Economic Bar Association, Ottawa, 3 September 1969.
41. Ed. Dosman. *The National Interest: The Politics of Northern Development 1968-1975.* Toronto, McClelland and Stewart, 1975.
42. House of Commons Debate, 2 March 1970.
43. J. J. Greene, Minister of Energy, Mines and Resources, to the Independent Petroleum Association of America, Denver, 12 May 1970.
44. J. J. Greene to the American Association of Petroleum Geologists, Calgary, 22 June 1970.
45. Department of Indian Affairs and Northern Development. "Guidelines for the Construction of Northern Oil and Gas Pipelines." Ottawa, 13 August 1970.
46. J. J. Greene to the Vancouver Men's Canadian Club, 12 February 1971.
47. Jack Austin to the Canadian Petroleum Association, Calgary, 6 April 1971.
48. Department of Finance, "A Northern Gas Pipeline – Evaluation of the Impact on the National Economy." Ottawa, October 1972.

49. Department of Energy, Mines and Resources. *An Energy Policy for Canada – Phase 1,* vol. I. Ottawa 1973.
50. House of Commons Debates, 6 December 1973.
51. "Points for an Address by the Prime Minister on Industrial Development and Resources Policy," 28 June 1974.
52. Department of Energy, Mines and Resources. *An Energy Strategy for Canada: Policies for Self-Reliance.* Ottawa 1976.

Foreign Takeovers in Canada's Oil and Gas Industry 1950-1980

Year	Foreign-controlled Company	Canadian Company
1950	Imperial Oil	Aquila Petroleum
	Gulf Canada (British American Oil)	Anglo-Canadian Oils
1952	BP (Triad Oil)	Alton Oils
	BP (Triad Oil)	Atlantis Development Corporation
	Gulf Canada (British American Oil)	Union Oil of Canada (refinery assets)
	American Northland Oil	Wainwright Producers and Refiners
1953	BP	Triad Oil
	BP (Triad Oil)	Calwest Equities
	Petrofina	Norval Oil
	Petrofina	Dominion Oil
	Imperial Oil	Atlas Supply of Canada
	Husky Oil	Canadian Western Distributors
1954	Husky Oil	Moose Jaw Refineries (assets)
	Imperial Oil	Lowlands Exploration
	Petrofina	Calvan Consolidated Oil & Gas
	Petrofina	Dominion Oil
	Petrofina	Miller Oil
	Canadian Husky Oil	Riverlake Oils (assets)
	Canadian Husky Oil	Liberal Petroleum (assets)
	Canadian Husky Oil	Merit Oil
	Shell Investment	Harry Dwick
1955	Imperial Oil	Oval Natural Gas
	Texaco Canada	Norfolk Oil
	Petrofina	Graham Oil
	Petrofina	United Service Corporation
	Petrofina	Western Leaseholds
	Petrofina	Leasehold Securities
	Gulf Canada (British American Oil)	Great West Distributors
	Petrofina	Calvan Consolidated Oil & Gas
	Canadian Homestead Oils	West Territories Oils
1956	Imperial Oil	Kirkland Oil
	Imperial Oil	Chatlon Oil and Gas

73

Foreign Takeovers in Canada's Oil and Gas Industry 1950-1980

Year	Foreign-controlled Company	Canadian Company
1956	Imperial Oil	Eron Oil and Gas
	Texaco Canada	Regent Refining (Canada)
	Canadian Homestead Oils	Petcal (assets)
	Western Decalta Petroleum	Albermont Petroleum
	Castle Oil and Gas	B.C. Metal Mines
1957	Imperial Oil	Seaway Bunkers
	Canadian Homestead Oils	Pennant Drilling
	Sarcee Petroleums	Vanalta
	Sage Oil Co.	Vanlorne Oils
1958	Imperial Oil	Smiley Gas Conservation
	BP Canada	P.M. Fleming
	BP Canada	Barrington Petroleum Products
	BP Canada	Sunlight Oil
	Shell Investment	Associated Fuels
	Texaco Canada	Tolhurst Oil
	Western Decalta Petroleum	Amalgamated Oils
	Husky Oil	Liberal Petroleum
	United Canso Oil and Gas	Pan Western Oils
1959	Imperial Oil	Nottingham Gas
	Imperial Oil	Carnduff Gas
	Imperial Oil	James Murphy Fuel Oil
	Imperial Oil	Margeau & Robert Cie
	Imperial Oil	Monroe Ltée
	Hudson's Bay Oil and Gas	Rangeland Pipe Line Co.
	BP Canada	Cinq-Mars et Paquette
	Sarcee Petroleum	Highwood-Sarcee Oils
	Shell Canada	Canadian Eagle Oil
	Western States Petroleum	Canadian Western Oil
1960	Imperial Oil	L. H. Adam
	Shell Canada	North Star Oil
	Shell Canada	Peigan Oil of Canada
	Shell Canada	Cree Oil of Canada
	Phillips Petroleum	Pacific Petroleums
	Phillips Petroleum	Westcoast Transmission
	Petrofina	New Superior Oils of Canada
	Petrofina	Planketrol
	Petrofina	Joseph Elie
	BP Canada	J. W. Perkin
	BP Canada	St. Laurent Petroleum
	BP Canada	Desert Oil
	BP Canada	Northern Oil Co.
	Shell Canada	S. J. Coordon and Son
	Shell Canada	Gordon A. Ross
	Shell Canada	Abbotsford Wood and Coal
	Shell Canada	Coboconk Fuels
	Shell Canada	L. Wellington

74

Foreign Takeovers in Canada's Oil and Gas Industry 1950-1980

Year	Foreign-controlled Company	Canadian Company
1960	Western Decalta	Carleton Oils
	Western Decalta	Mazel Petroleum
1961	Shell Canada	Canadian Bishop Oil
	Hudson's Bay Oil and Gas	Mayfair Oil and Gas (1961)
	Imperial Oil	Porcupine Oil Co.
	Petrofina	Planet Oil
	Petrofina	Harvey O. Perry
	American Northland Oil	Travis Mud and Chemicals
	Canadian Delhi Oil	West Canadian Oil and Gas
	Castle Oil and Gas	Beaver Oil and Gas
	Husky Oil	Merit Oil
1962	Shell Canada	Canadian Oil Companies
	Gulf Canada	Royalite Oil Co.
	Gulf Canada	Anglo-American Exploration
	Pacific Petroleum	Bailey Selburn Oil and Gas
	Canadian Superior	Calgary and Edmonton Corporation
	Triad Oil (BP)	Devon-Palmer Oils
	Gulf Canada	Superior Propane
	Husky Oil	Wainwright Producers and Refineries
	Husky Oil	Canadian Kodiak Refineries
	Delhi-Taylor	Canadian Chieftain Petroleum
	Delhi-Taylor	Tidal Petroleum
	Union Oil of Canada	Williamson Oil and Gas
	Western Decalta Petroleum	Petrol Oil and Gas
	Wilshire Oil of Texas	Britalta Petroleums
1963	Texaco Canada	Elias Rogers
	Hudson's Bay Oil and Gas	Security Freehold Petroleums
	Hudson's Bay Oil and Gas	Consolidated Mic Mac Oils
	Union Oil of Canada	E. H. Vallat
	Gulf Canada	Purity 99 Oil
	Gulf Canada	Shawinigan Chemicals
	Gulf Canada	Western Tire and Auto Supply
	Gulf Canada	Gunning
	BP Canada	Paris Petroleum
	Sun Oil	Great Canadian Oil Sands
	Occidental Petroleum	Jefferson Lake Petrochemicals of Canada
	Western Decalta Petroleum	New Brunswick Oilfields
	Western Decalta Petroleum	South Brajean Petroleum
	Imperial Oil	Tecumseh Gas Storage
	Imperial Oil	Bourque Brothers
	Imperial Oil	Servacar
	Anlage Bank Zurich	Charter Oil
	Great Plains Development	Alida Oil

Foreign Takeovers in Canada's Oil and Gas Industry 1950-1980

Year	Foreign-controlled Company	Canadian Company
1963	Great Plains Development	B.O.C. Canada
	Great Plains Development	Lobitos Oilfields Canada
	Husky Oil	Wainwright Producers & Refiners (assets)
1964	Great Plains Development	Canada Oil Lands
	BP Canada	Gobles Gas and Oil
	BP Canada	Cities Service Oil – Eastern Canada (assets)
	BP Canada	Tidewater Canadian Oil
	Sage Oil	Marjack Oils
	Husky Oil	Sarcee Petroleum
	Imperial Oil	Building Products
	Aquitaine of Canada	Banff Oil
	Imperial Oil	Polybottle
1965	Great Plains Development	Westburne Oil
	Great Plains Development	Westburne Oil Development
	Richfield Oil	Candel International
	Union Oil of Canada	Pure Oil
	Sohio	Canadian Delhi Oil
	Permo Gas & Oil (Pan Ocean Oil)	New Continental Oil of Canada
	Western Equities	Camerina Petroleum
	BP	Lands of Canadian Kewanee
	Canadian Superior	Lands of Ross Security Assets & Ross Contract Assets
	Imperial Oil	Hall Fuel (1965)
1966	Consolidated Oil and Gas	Cold Lake Pipe Line
	Shell Canada	Bradfield Fertilizer Chemical
	Gulf Canada	Western GMC Truck Centre
	Shell Canada	Northland Boat Lines
	Shell Canada	Monarch Propane Gas
	Canadian Superior Oil	Calgary and Edmonton Corporation
	Husky Oil	Canada Western Distributors, Hartford Petroleum, High Development, Paul Guthrie Development, Stewart-Davis Oils
	Husky Oil	Fosca Oil
	Imperial Oil	Poli-Twine
1967	Superior Oil	McIntyre Porcupine Mines
	Shell Canada	Webster Group of Companies: Canadian Import, Liquifuels, Weaver Oil, Weaver Coal
	Hudson's Bay Oil and Gas	Blue Flame Propane
	Hudson's Bay Oil and Gas	Allied Propane
	Hudson's Bay Oil and Gas	Economy Propane

Foreign Takeovers in Canada's Oil and Gas Industry 1950-1980

Year	Foreign-controlled Company	Canadian Company
1967	French Petroleum Co. of Canada	Taurus Oil
	Angelus Petroleum (1965)	Norart Minerals
	Imperial Oil	Allied Heat and Fuel
1968	Imperial Oil	Poli-Twine Corp.
	Panoil	Lowe Petroleum Engineers
	Clark Canadian Petroleum	Amherst Canadian Oil
	Resource Ventures	Bralsaman Petroleums
	Gulf Canada	Anglo-Canadian Oils
1969	American Eagle Petroleums	Gull Oil and Gas
	American Eagle Petroleums	Penwa Oils
	Ashland Oil	W. B. Bennett Paving and Materials
	Bralorne Oil and Gas	Carleton Oil and Gas Development
	Great Basins Petroleum	Columbian Northland Exploration
	Manhattan Continental Development	Royal American Petroleum
	Manhattan Continental Development	Kodiak Petroleums
	Ultramar Canada	Gauthier Group
	Ashland Oil	White Hall Canadian Oil
	Ultramar Canada	Gérard Hébert
	Reserve Oil and Gas	Millsion Oil Development
	Great Basins Petroleum	Guyer Oil
	Spelman Prentice	Bluewater Oil and Gas
	Delhi International Oil	Blue Crown Petroleums
	Canadian Hydrocarbon	South Eastern Utilities
	Canadian Hydrocarbon	Golfe Oxygène
	Rainbow Pipe Line	Mitsue Pipeline
1970	Ashland Oil	Canadian Gridoil
	Lochaber Oil	Bueno Oils
	Mana Resources	Garrity and Baker Drilling
	Bralorne Oil and Gas	Junior Oils
	Canadian Reserve Oil and Gas	Mission Oil Development
	Canadian Reserve Oil and Gas	Pheasant Exploration Pheasant Petroleum
1971	BP Canada	Supertest Petroleum
	Imperial Oil	J. P. Papineau
	American Eagle Petroleum	Cenpet Exploration
	Pan Ocean Oil	Dynamic Petroleum Products, Permo Gas and Oil, New Continental Oil of Canada, Mill City Petroleum, Royal Canadian Ventures, Crusade

Foreign Takeovers in Canada's Oil and Gas Industry 1950-1980

Year	Foreign-controlled Company	Canadian Company
1971		Petroleum, Dynalta Oil and Gas, Consolidated East Coast Oil
1972	Petrofina	Arctic Islands Resources
1973	Murphy Oil	Bracell Petroleum
1974	Sun Oil	Forest Oil (assets)
1975	R. J. Adams Hudson's Bay Oil and Gas	Paloma Petroleum Sulphur (assets)
1976	BP Canada Total Petroleum Amoco Canada	BP Oil Lands Hanover Oil Golied Oil and Gas (assets)
1977	Canadian Superior	Alminex
1978	Shell Canada	Crow's Nest Industries
1979	Aquitaine Canada	Universal Gas

Chapter 3

The Nature of the Beast

By definition, the world-spanning oil multinationals march to the beat of their own corporate drummers. They are not and were never intended to be the servants of any interests other than their own. It should come as no surprise, then, that the directors and top executives of these huge enterprises have little sympathy with Canadian goals and aspirations, especially when these come into conflict with their corporate objectives. Nor should it come as any great surprise that they allow little room for independent decision making in their Canadian subsidiaries. The subsidiaries are simply operating arms of the parent companies. Head office is where policy gets made, budgets and investments set, top executives chosen for the Canadian subsidiary, research and development carried out, exploration priorities determined, and major contract awards decided. As corporations dealing in strategic or lifeblood materials for our societies, these multinationals are close-mouthed. Their role is both single-minded and pervasive. Yet occasionally, inadvertently, they reveal themselves in surprising ways, and in surprising places.

Little information is available, for example, on how local subsidiaries relate to their parent companies. But in Canada, one of the most telling examples of the decision-making power – or lack of it – enjoyed by the subsidiary of a multinational corporation dealing in oil or any other strategic commodity can be read in the records of a case that came before the 1978-79 session of the Alberta Supreme Court. In this particular case, Mobil Canada unsuccessfully sued Canadian Superior Oil and its new president, who had resigned his comparable position at Mobil, for breach of an employment contract. The effect of the courtroom testimony was to expose a Canadian subsidiary that was almost totally bereft of real independent existence. It transpired that Mobil's New York head office called the shots down to the pettiest detail, keeping

Mobil Canada on a tight rein even though corporate policy wished it that Canadians should think otherwise. In fact, Mobil's corporate affairs in Canada were run in a way that was deliberately misleading: there was no local option for the subsidiary. A December 1975 internal memo from Alex Massad, president of Mobil Exploration and Production, New York, defined the working relationship in these words: "As stated frequently, my three-part guideline is: 1. Maintain the image of Mobil Oil Canada as one company, under one head, to anyone viewing it from the outside. 2. Within Mobil Oil, understand certain segments of the affiliate will be the responsibility of and receive directives from managers outside MOCAN. 3. Minimize personnel assignments and cost of staff services to effect #1 and #2 above."[1] In other words, Mobil Canada was to pretend to be independent while in fact, various of its executives were reporting directly to U.S. head office instead of to the Canadian president. Massad did recognize that there could be problems and advised that supervisors and managers always be kept informed of what was happening: "In the event of disagreement, every effort should be made to prevent polarization."

In his Alberta court testimony, Arne Nielsen, who had been the president of Mobil Canada from early 1967 until he left to head Canadian Superior in November 1977, spelled out just how little authority he had exercised as president of a major Canadian subsidiary in the oil industry, and how Mobil's 1976 corporate reorganization had diminished the position of the Canadian chief executive even further. Before 1976, Mobil Canada's president reported to the executive vice-president for exploration and production of Mobil Oil Corporation, who reported in turn to the president of the North American division of Mobil Oil. After the change, effective on 1 January 1976, the president of Mobil Canada was relegated to four reporting steps below the president of the new Mobil Exploration and Production group in New York, reporting to a vice-president of operations, who reported to a senior vice-president, who reported to an executive vice-president, who reported to the president of the new worldwide exploration and production division. "From the time of the reorganization," Nielsen said, "I never again appeared before the executive committee. All of Canada's matters were no longer brought to the attention of the executive committee by those who knew them best. This was the Mobil Oil of Canada people of course. We would submit our material to the New York office and then it would be reworked in New York and then they would present it to the executive committee."[2] This involved a number of consequences for the Canadian subsidiary, as Nielsen explained in his testimony.

Q. What were they?

A. Well, the philosophy of the new organization was to de-emphasize functional responsibility. In so far as this was possible in an international corporation, there is a limit as to what can be done in this direction because international boundaries and national laws of countries in which affiliates are located have certain requirements. For example, Mobil Oil Canada had to remain Mobil Oil Canada as a corporate entity because this is the only way that Mobil could operate in Canada. On the other hand, the functions, the staff functions that reported directly to Mr. Massad were given a very large amount of authority. We were clearly advised that there should be free flow of information and there should be much stronger relationships established between those functional staff groups at the New York level with their Canadian counterparts. I will give a couple of examples. A good example is planning. I had a planning manager report to me. There also was a, I think he was a vice-president of planning in the New York office reporting to Mr. Massad. Very strong functional ties were established between those two people.

Q. At what time?

A. At the time of the reorganization, this was coincident with the reorganization, the same also occurred in the treasurer's department and in the comptroller's department and in the employee relations department.

Q. Would these [be] people that had previously been reporting to you and only to you?

A. These people were still reporting to me on the organization chart. Final recommendations still went through me but there were many projects that were developed between the New York functional groups and the Mobil Canada functional groups and the projects were frequently well advanced before I even was aware of them. Ultimately this recommendation would go through me. It did result in what I considered to be a much more difficult way of operating.

Q. Difficult for whom?

A. For me as president of Mobil Canada. I no longer felt that I had total control of the company as I had in the past.

81

Q. Were there any other changes resulting from this re-organization in late 1975?

A. Yes. In January 1976, I attended a personnel meeting in New York where more of the people were, the exploration people primarily were being more or less redistributed to fit into this new worldwide concept. At that time, I learned that somebody in New York had decided that Mobil Oil Canada had 35 too many geologists and geophysicists. I had never been apprised of this and no one had ever asked me. I had never been consulted in any way, shape, or form as to whether we had 35 too many, 20 too many, or just right, or whether we were short 20. I was told at that particular meeting that there were 35 too many. I was also advised that they were short of geologists and geophysicists in the newly expanded MEPSI, Mobil's exploration centre in Dallas, Texas. It was my responsibility to see to it that these people be transferred south. Now, this represented a goodly number of problems. First of all, they were essentially all Canadians who had been hired in Canada from Canadian universities to work for Mobil Oil Canada. Now let's recognize, when you go to work for a multinational corporation you accept the fact that you may have to be transferred elsewhere in the world. Certainly it would be within North America. . . . However, to be suddenly faced as an executive with telling 35 people, picking out the 35 people and telling them you move south or anywhere else, presented a major problem in management, particularly when I personally did not agree that we were 35 people short.

According to Nielsen, the Mobil head office in New York also, arbitrarily and without prior discussion, transferred a large part of Mobil Canada's frontier land holdings on the Atlantic offshore to MEPSI, and at the same time, a group of geologists and geophysicists on Mobil Canada's staff were to report directly to Dallas for supervision. Nielsen said that he had been "appalled, to say the least,"[3] at the transfer, effective 1 January 1976. He only learned about this major change in its operations at a Mobil budget meeting in Phoenix, Arizona, in October of 1975. Nielsen voiced his objections to Massad: "His reaction was that the decision had been made, that my responsibility was to see, in so far as I was concerned and Mobil Canada was concerned, that it worked. It was part of a worldwide organizational concept . . . he believed that Canada should participate in that worldwide concept and that is the way it was going to be period, which was in all, fairly typical of the way Mr. Massad did, when he made a decision.'' However, said Nielsen, Massad ''never really told me directly why it was good for Mobil Oil Canada.''

Nielsen also acknowledged a concern that the decision would reinforce public opposition to multinational oil companies: ''I personally was extremely concerned regarding the government and public relations in this regard. The multinational corporations in Canada, particularly the wholly-owned multinationals, have always had to defend their position in a foreign country, in a country like Canada. We know that the liberals and the left-wingers and so on in our society and many others are always after the multinational corporations. . . . It behooved the multinationals to be just as good a corporate citizen as they could be and in most cases they were. This action . . . I knew would be very very detrimental to the image of Mobil and also to the image of other multinationals, just because they were multinationals, if it were discovered that a part of our lands that were Mobil Oil Canada's lands were being run by, directly out of the United States when there was a corporate vehicle which could and had traditionally done it. As a result I managed to persuade I guess Mr. Massad, I presented him with the problem and he decided the way to handle it was that we would leave our internal organization charts the way they were, that is Mr. Brooks [Robert Brooks, supervisor of Mobil Canada's exploration staff in Calgary] and his group would continue to report through the exploration hierarchy and ostensibly to me so that from outside appearances, Mobil Oil Canada would appear still to be an entity. However, in fact he made it very clear that the people in my office who were doing work on these 25 million acres were in fact to report to Dallas and were to get their directions from Dallas.''[4]

There seemed to have been very little clear thinking involved in this transfer of land activities to Dallas. The original plan was that Dallas would take over the Grand Banks, where the Hibernia field is located, and the Scotian Shelf, including Sable Island, where natural gas had already been found. This scheme was abruptly changed, as Nielsen testified, after a meeting in Calgary: ''Mr. Massad decided that the Scotian Shelf would be left with Mobil Canada and that was because we were negotiating a farm-out with Petro-Canada. Mr. Massad could see that we were going to have a problem negotiating a deal with the federal government if the lands were going to be run and operated out of Dallas, so he made the decision right there on the spot that we would keep the Nova Scotia, the Shelf, but we had to make up for it by giving up something else instead. So he picked the Arctic islands, which is just about as far away from Dallas as you can get." When the responsibility for Mobil Canada's frontier lands moved to the Texas office, Nielsen ordered that any development plans for these lands cross his desk so that he would at least know what was going on. One reason for this was that he still had to deal with Ottawa on these lands. He soon found himself under fire from Massad for intervening. Nielsen asked what, specifically, Massad's criticism was. "That it was none of my business," Nielsen told the court.

As of 1 January 1978, jurisdiction over Mobil Canada's frontier lands was returned to the Canadian subsidiary – to a large extent, apparently, for political reasons. But Nielsen's efforts in fighting New York's changes resulted in his performance rating as president of Mobil Canada being downgraded for two consecutive years. A Mobil vice-president in New York, Nielsen testified, told him there was nothing wrong with his overall performance: "He just said that you showed a certain lack of co-operation during the reorganization, that is what his words were to me, you didn't really get your spirit into the thing." Executives who question the decisions of the parent company, then, put their careers on the line. At roughly the same time, the group rating and hence the minimum salaries of all Mobil Canada's senior officers were lowered, meaning that future replacements for these executives would fall into lower pay categories.

Control over Mobil Canada's spending, however, was the key lever wielded by New York. The budget, largely determined in New York, was strictly enforced. If the president of Mobil Canada found that he needed to go over budget in one area, for example in acquiring land, he had to get New York's approval first. In fact, New York was even pre-screening land bids. Although Nielsen was president of one of the largest corporations in Canada, virtually everything he did had to have prior approval, as shown by the following pre-trial exchange with H. K. Holland, a vice-president of Mobil Oil Corporation:[5]

Q. Was the president and general manager of Mobil Canada able to make charitable donations at his own discretion; that is, on behalf of Mobil Canada?
A. We have a budget for charitable donations.
Q. And he had to live within that budget?
A. Yes.

Q. What about membership in clubs? Was that at his discretion or was that approved by you?

A. That was a budget item also.

Q. And that means it had to be ultimately approved by you?

A. Endorsed.

Q. And I gather from time to time Mr. Nielsen complained to you about the time that it took to get decisions on these various budgetary items?

A. I would say there had been times that he complained, yes.

This tight control also emerged clearly as Holland was asked:

Q. When Mobil Canada would present its budget, part of that budget would be for the acquisition of lands and/or leases?

A. Yes.

Q. In Canada?

A. Yes.

Q. And there would be certain dollars allocated in that budget for those anticipated acquisitions?

A. Yes.

Q. I gather that the president of Mobil Canada would have authority to exceed that budgetary amount in the event that it was necessary to acquire those lands and leases?

A. No. . . . Pardon me, when I say no, I don't mean to be absolutely rigid, but a budget is a budget, and we attempt to work within the budget.

While initial work on the budget was done at Mobil Canada's Calgary head office, representatives from Mobil in New York would visit to review these plans, inform themselves of Mobil Canada's operations, and, according to Nielsen, "advise as to budget levels that may be considered."[6] The budget would then be submitted to New York, where it was reviewed by such company areas as exploration, planning, production, and land negotiation, as well as by the comptroller's office. No one from Mobil Canada participated in this phase. Afterwards, budgets were presented at Mobil's annual meeting of subsidiaries, regions, and divisions. Following this meeting, which was usually held in Phoenix, senior executives from Mobil in New York would present Mobil Canada's budget to the parent corporation's executive committee. By this process, Mobil New York retained a rigid control over Canadian exploration activities, as did the Dallas MEPSI group. In fact, exploration plans for the frontier regions, including the

Atlantic offshore and the Arctic islands, would originate in Dallas with some input from Mobil Canada. These projects were then passed for approval to Mobil Exploration and Production in New York.·

Not surprisingly, the parent company's tight restrictions on Mobil Canada's exploration spending in the mid-'70s created problems for its subsidiary with the Canadian government. For example, Mobil Canada wanted to drill in Hibernia in 1976, but Mobil New York was more interested in pursuing other plays, in Indonesia and west Africa. It may have been the right decision for Mobil, but it was the wrong decision for Canada. Had it been different, the rich Hibernia field might have been tapped several years sooner, and this would have meant that Canadians were getting its oil in the early '80s rather than some time after 1986. Federal officials felt even at the time that Mobil Canada was reinvesting too little of its sharply rising cash flow in the search for new domestic oil and gas supplies. In truth, the company in these years was busily and obediently funnelling capital down to New York: Mobil Canada actually had to petition its own head office for permission to spend more of its profits in Canada. And it was not only crucial exploration off Canada's east coast that head office was holding back. As Nielsen testified: "Mobil sat on its hands as far as western Canada was concerned, and it did not become active again until the year I left the company."

In addition to its budget, the parent company also controlled Mobil Canada's exploration strategy, a five-year plan that outlined a schedule of "geophysical operations, geographical data acquisitions, the timing of this work, the acquisition of lands, the drilling of wildcat wells, back-out points as to success or failure within the area, the follow-up appraisals."[7] According to Holland, this plan was a highly confidential document that included "Mobil Canada's assumptions as to the political and economic environment in Canada as they see it over the next five years or perhaps longer or shorter, depending on the issue. There are assumptions as to the tax structure that we may be looking at in Canada. It encompasses forecasts as to crude and natural gas prices. It forecasts energy demand, not only for the five-year period, but perhaps for ten or fifteen years. These are all what I refer to as assumptions; and we go through this procedure first in order to set the background on developing what we call our objectives." Holland went on to state: "Objectives are our specific plans and programs in detail over the forward five-year period. They encompass the end product of our objectives, they encompass the same things that I enumerated in the budget, the wildcat wells, the land acquisition programs, the geological programs, the same items that I mentioned earlier, except that in the budget we're only dealing for one year; in objectives, we deal for five years.''

In Mobil, parental control extended down to the smallest detail. As Nielsen told the Alberta Supreme Court, when he became president in 1967, he could authorize additional spending up to $500,000 on an item only if the money was already in the budget: "If it was not in the approved budget, no matter how small it was, I could not approve it." He had to contact New York. "There was a very strictly enforced authority level in every kind of category, all the way from drilling a wildcat well, buying land, and making farm-outs, all the way down to Petroleum Club membership and United Fund contributions."[8] While Nielsen did have the authority, initially for $500,000 and later for $1 million, "there were so many restrictions connected with it, though, so many modifications, in many cases it was meaningless. For example, a million-dollar authority to buy land is meaningless when your land budget is zero, like it was for three consecutive years." In late 1976 and 1977, there was some money for land, but it "was very limited in terms of the amount of money that had to be paid for acreage at the time." In fact "it was so small . . . that it was meaningless."

All these expenditure activities were laid out in a highly detailed manual produced by head office in New York. "You could look up every item of any type and you could find in there what my authority was as president of the company. It was different for so many different things, and I had no authority, really, beyond those authority levels without having to get some additional authority from the person to whom I reported in New York." Every year, Nielsen was sent a head count for Mobil Canada from New York, and he had to stay within that total. In addition, "we were not allowed to give speeches without having everything cleared through New York at that time." In fact, it began to look as if the only reason for Mobil Canada's existence as a separate company must be to meet Canadian legal or tax requirements. Donald MacWilliam, Mobil Canada's official representative in the case, was asked for evidence that there was any independence from New York. He replied: "Mobil Oil Canada Ltd., being a separate Canadian company, has its own secretary and secretary's department. It has its own office of general counsel, and it operates under and complies with the acts and regulations of the laws of Canada."[9] When the cross-examining lawyer asked if there was "anything else that occurs to you," MacWilliam answered: "Not at this point." Obviously, this was a branch plant in every sense of the word.

Imperial Oil's relationship with Exxon, which holds roughly 69.6 per cent of Imperial's shares, offers another view of parent-subsidiary interplay, one in which the Canadian subsidiary also has minority Canadian shareholders. There is no doubt that the existence of even a small group of Canadian shareholders can make a difference to the parent-subsidiary relationship, especially when shares in the subsidiary are traded publicly, as is the case with Imperial's. Not only must the subsidiary disclose a great deal more financial information to Canadians than, say, Mobil Canada, which files some information, or Chevron Standard, which files none, but the managers and directors also cannot altogether ignore the interests of these shareholders. Nonetheless, Exxon does have a considerable influence in Imperial's affairs, in particular on budgets, investment decisions, senior executive appointments, research and development activities, and oil imports. According to Imperial: "In general Exxon exercises the degree of interest in Imperial's affairs which might be expected of any prudent majority shareholder, but it is very sensitive to the widely held opinion in Canada that Canadian companies should shape their own destinies. The company's directors are Canadians and there is a substantial Canadian minority shareholder interest. Both companies recognize that Canadians must manage and be responsible for Imperial's operations."[10] Testifying before the Royal Commission on Corporate Concentration in 1976, the company insisted that "in most matters Imperial acts independently. For instance, it makes its own judgements on what market prices should be. There is no Exxon scrutiny of any external contracts. Dividend policies are established without consulting Exxon, and the company makes its own financing decisions. Imperial can and has acted responsively to Canadian law and Canadian wishes even when these are potentially in conflict with U.S. law and interests. There are no management fees or other management transfer charges."

On Exxon's June 1980 organization chart, however, the chairman of Imperial Oil, like the presidents of Esso Europe, Exxon Research and Engineering, and Esso Exploration, or Exxon vice-presidents for taxation, corporate planning, public affairs, or mining and synthetic fuels, reports to a designated senior vice-president of Exxon who is Imperial's liaison with the chairman and president of Exxon and a member of the multinational's powerful management committee. The Imperial chairman is one of 28 executives reporting to Exxon's senior vice-presidents. Moreover Exxon's interest in Imperial is far from passive. For example, it attempts to establish long-term investment guidelines for all its affiliates, identifying areas of high priority and goals for return on investment. In turn, the affiliates project their cash flow, draw up their budgets and investment plans, and tie these in with the parent company objectives.[11] As one of Exxon's 13 affiliated companies that produce oil and gas, a regional subsidiary similar to Esso Middle East or Exxon U.S.A., Imperial has three formal budget-investment meetings a year with its parent. The first, usually in February, deals with past and anticipated financial performance as well as operating details, including forecasts of oil needs. The next meeting takes place in April or May, occurs at the staff level, and includes the updating of Imperial's long-term programs. Exxon experts in oil and gas exploration, production, engineering, refinery operations, petrochemicals, and finance work closely with their Imperial counterparts. In some respects Exxon headquarters acts as a general auditing and advisory centre. The Exxon executives also form judgements as to the capability of people in the Exxon affiliates and decide whether the affiliates are properly staffed. The mid-year staff work between Imperial and Exxon results in an updated four- to five-year corporate plan along with details of the coming year's capital budget, which goes to the powerful eight-man management committee of Exxon, usually in November. It is up to this committee to approve Imperial's plans, or, to use the term employed by both Imperial and Exxon, "take exception to" Imperial's proposals. Through exchanges, in fact, Exxon has already exercised an important influence, and when Imperial's plans come before the management committee their spokesman is the senior Exxon vice-president who acts as permanent head-office contact man for everything that has to do with the Canadian operation.

While Imperial's minority shareholders give it greater autonomy than many other Exxon affiliates, everything of importance that Imperial does – such as a new rights issue to raise equity capital – is discussed with Exxon, which also receives monthly operating reports on production, sales, earnings, and the like. Exxon also exercises control over major increases in spending or new capital expenditures. As company president Jack Armstrong told the corporate concentration commission in 1976: "Anything under $5 million we don't even go near Exxon, anything over $5 million I think you would agree with me that if you owned 70 per cent of a company some place and they were investing something over $5 million you would be very interested in knowing what they were doing with your money, wouldn't you?"[12] In 1980, the ceiling was raised to $15 million – a large sum, but less than the cost of drilling a frontier well and less than the monthly escalation in costs of a tar sands plant.

Exxon also pays close attention to career development at Imperial, and this includes final approval of top executive appointments down to a level below that of vice-president. It has taken exception to proposed promotions in the past, and Imperial has abided by its opinions. As one Exxon official put it: "We review all people moves before they take place."[13] At the same time, Exxon plays an important development role for Imperial people. Again according to Armstrong: "I think we average somewhere between 65 to 70 people per year on either technical work or management work in Exxon, with the Exxon organization either in the United States or on foreign assignment, for the express purpose of training. All of our board of directors have been through this exercise anywhere from one to x number of years on foreign services."[14] One result of this is that senior management at Imperial tends to identify strongly with the multinational, and of course, since Exxon participates in Imperial promotions to senior management, aspiring executives will want to have good relationships with head-office people. Other fields of close, regular contact include global research needs, which are co-ordinated by the wholly-owned Exxon Research and Engineering.

Shell Canada, about 79-per-cent owned by the Royal Dutch/ Shell group, maintains that its controlling shareholder behaves as a passive investor. Its president, C. W. Daniel, told the Royal Commission on Corporate Concentration in 1976 that his was "an independent company, a company which is directed in Canada by a board of directors and is managed by residents of Canada for the benefit of all shareholders. . . . All Shell Canadian decisions are made in Canada by Canadians in the interests of Canadians. However it has not always been this way, but for many years we have had a steady program of Canadianization throughout the company and as and when Canadians were ready to take new responsibilities they were promoted to those responsibilities."[15] The Shell executive preached the gospel of the multinationals: "While any large and successful Canadian corporation has the capability of undertaking major development, taking risks, and advancing technology, this capability is increased if the corporation in question has worldwide corporate affiliations." Asked if Shell Canada, large and diversified as it is, would not be as well off if it were

100-per-cent Canadian-owned, Daniel answered: "I think we would not have the resources, let's not call them financial resources exclusively, we would not have the broad strengths that we do have, and let's say that if we are a company Canadian-owned with no affiliation of any kind, we would not have the call on the kind of help that we can get and do get. . . . I think, for example, if we are going to the market to finance a large tar sands project . . . or going into the offshore drilling business, whether we are borrowing money or getting ready to do the job, I think we will have much bigger advantages financially to get the money because the lenders are more inclined to think of us having broader technical resources than we might have here in Canada.''

While Shell says that it operates as an independent company in Canada, the controlling shareholder, Royal Dutch/Shell, looms ever large on the horizon, and many of Shell Canada's dealings are, not unnaturally, with other Shell affiliates, as in the company's historic importing relationship with Shell International Petroleum Co. Corporate senior management interchanges are common, as, for example, in 1980 the vice-president of finance for Shell Canada became assistant group comptroller with Shell International Petroleum Co. in London, while the finance manager of Shell Petroleum Development Co. of Nigeria moved to become vice-president of finance for Shell Canada. Similarly, Shell Canada in 1970 made a massive $250-million farm-out of its frontier and tar sands lands with Shell Explorer, a wholly-owned subsidiary of Shell Oil Co., Houston, instead of seeking out Canadian partners.

Shell Canada's claim of independence is based also on the fact that the parent company has only two directors on its board. Yet the two parent-company directors are also the two top executives of the parent group – the chairman and managing director of Shell Transport and Trading Company, London, and the president and managing director of Royal Dutch Petroleum, The Hague. These two would carry some considerable weight in any board meeting. Four other directors are Shell Canada senior executives, and the other six are Canadian academic or business figures who sit on the board at the company's invitation. According to one U.S. expert on corporate organization: "It is widely agreed among sophisticated observers of boards that, in the main: 1. Outsider directors are not invited to join the boards of major corporations to "run" the firms or decide on basic policy. 2. Outside directors are usually passive and do what managements want them to do. 3. Managements want boards to carry out certain limited functions, principally advising in areas of competence, solidifying relationships with important external constituencies, assuring the outside world by their presence that the organization is in good hands, and providing a standby for emergency use in a crisis.''[16] In other words, "the great majority of outside directors of large managerial companies play a limited, dependent and passive role that has remained essentially unchanged during the course of the twentieth century.''

There are differences in the degree of control exercised by the foreign parent. Companies such as Imperial and Shell, along with Gulf Canada, have a greater degree of autonomy than most, although they too must always be aware of the overriding interest of the dominant shareholder. Other companies operate virtually as outposts of their parent companies: Mobil is a good example of this. But there are other, more extreme cases, such as Standard Oil of California's Chevron Standard, Canada Cities-Service, Amerada Minerals, and Amoco Canada or, among the major integrated companies, Texaco Canada. Over the past twenty years many of Texaco Canada's top appointments have been parent-company executives assigned temporarily to Canada. Moreover until 1978, Texaco's exploration activities were conducted in Canada though a separate company, Texaco Exploration Canada, which was run out of White Plains, New York: almost all this company's senior officers were employees of Texaco Inc. in the United States and received their pay cheques from the parent company. In 1981, new presidents were named for Mobil and Amoco in Canada, both of them Americans from the parent company. And in many subsidiaries in Canada, a clear intimation of parent-company control has always been the absence of senior corporate and financial planning executives – functions that were reserved for head office. In the final analysis, despite their designation as "multinational," the oil majors are quite national in their outlook, drawing on prominent banking, political, and legal directors from their own country, so that in general, their boards reflect solely the interests of the country in which the parent companies are located. As of early 1982, no executive from a Canadian subsidiary was sitting on any of them, and in most cases Canadian executives were not even reporting directly to top management in their parents.

The goal of the oil multinationals has not only been to dominate Canadian exploration and development. In fact, several of them came here first to establish a captive market for their surplus oil supplies. Until the mid-'50s, Canada was almost entirely dependent on imported oil. Even after the arrival of the National Oil Policy in 1961, Quebec and Atlantic Canada remained dependent on imports, a situation that is still true to a marked degree today, even though Canada's oil pipeline has been extended to Montreal. By their domination, through market power and takeovers, of the refining and marketing of gasoline and other oil products, the multinationals were able to serve their parents' interests by forcing Canadians to pay high prices for imported oil until OPEC's intervention in 1973-74. In 1956, for example, Gulf, Imperial, Shell, and Texaco controlled 92 per cent of refining capacity in Quebec; in 1970, with the balance somewhat rearranged, the majors were still in control. Similarly, in 1956 Imperial controlled 99.3 per cent of refining capacity in the Maritime provinces; in 1970, Imperial, Irving (half-owned by Socal), and Texaco had 90 per cent of refining capacity in the region.

Control over supply confers control over pricing, and it was in view of the majors' preponderance in Canadian refining that the director of the Combines Investigation Branch of the Department of Consumer and Corporate Affairs came out in 1981 with the accusation that Canadians had been gouged in the years 1958-73 – the period he was investigating – for gasoline and other oil products.[17] The parent companies had forced their Canadian subsidiaries, he said, to buy their oil from the parent and have it delivered in parent-owned tankers, instead of letting the subsidiaries get the best price through independent negotiation on world markets. According to M. A. Adelman, one of the leading experts on the international oil trade: "Government difficulties in dealing with oil prices are shown in the taxation of refining profits earned by the local subsidiaries of the integrated companies. The higher the price at which crude is transferred to the local subsidiary, the less its profits. The transfer price set by the company itself has no public validity."[18] Thus, he has argued, "transfer prices from one to another division of the same corporate entity are simply bookkeeping notices to permit the corporation to minimize its total tax bill. There is no market without independence or freedom to bargain. No market, no price!"

International companies also use transfer prices to lower their taxes by pricing oil in such a way that the profit is taken in the country where the tax assessment is lowest. Hence the traditional use of so-called "tax havens," with the oil bought and resold through dummy trading corporations. And while both the Income Tax Act and the Customs Act attempted to curb the use of the transfer pricing for tax minimization – in other words, tried to ensure that the Canadian treasury was not cheated – there is little evidence that Revenue Canada officials have been particularly successful in detecting questionable manoeuvres. For much of the postwar period, in the absence of independent Canadian-controlled refiners dealing at arm's-length pricing in other countries and with most of the world's oil trade in the hands of the integrated multinationals, federal tax officials had few benchmarks for reviewing oil import prices. Certainly, the opportunity was there for overcharging Canadians on oil imports. In the period 1964-69, for example, 87 per cent of the imports of foreign-controlled oil companies in Canada came from their parents or affiliates. Similarly, though not to the same extent, opportunities existed when it came to exports of Canadian oil and gas to the United States for the manipulation of transfer pricing techniques to reduce taxes paid in Canada. In 1964-69, 64 per cent of exports from foreign-controlled oil and gas companies in Canada went to their parent companies or affiliates.[19]

Until OPEC pricing began in the early 1970s, the principal known price in world oil markets was the posted price. Neil Jacoby, a U.S. expert, has defined this as "a public offering price by the seller, f.o.b. port of origin, based on his assessment of the value of the petroleum to him, in terms of replacement and opportunity costs, and its value to buyers around the world. While the posted price is by its very nature the most visible to the public, the competitively significant price is the actual transaction price of oil delivered to refiners in the consuming countries."[20] But the transaction price varied from customer to customer. While the world oil prices declined steadily during the late 1950s and through the 1960s because of a surplus in world supply, the extent to which consumers benefited from lower prices depended on whether domestic refining operations were owned independently or as part of the multinationals' global enterprise. One thing is clear in this period, according to Jacoby: "These basic enlargements of the foreign crude oil supply led to reductions in the prices charged to non-affiliated refining companies." There were none in Canada. Moreover the strict controls on the importation of refined products such as gasoline was yet another factor making it easier for the oil majors to charge high transfer prices to their Canadian subsidiaries. This is borne out in research by a Canadian analyst, J. G. Debanné. While consumers in eastern Canada enjoyed lower prices than the Canadians who had to use Alberta and Saskatchewan oil, "surely Quebec and the Maritimes would have preferred still lower retail prices, comparable to those prevailing in

New England, which would have been possible if the bulk of crude oil imports were lower-priced Middle East oil or 'discounted' Venezuelan oil. Except for the occasional spot purchase by independents of lower priced crudes and products, the bulk of crude oil was purchased by the multinationals from Venezuela at the official posted prices rather than at discount prices, which were about 50 cents per barrel lower. This was to be expected, since the multinational refineries in eastern Canada bought crude from their respective affiliates in Venezuela, Colombia and the Caribbean."[21] What is surprising is that for so long there was no effective challenge to this policy. One of the first came from the Quebec government, which in 1970 established the Société Québécoise d'Initiatives Pétrolières (SOQUIP), the first publicly owned oil company in Canada. Its mandate included the purchase of foreign oil supplies for use in Quebec and the establishment of refining-marketing operations; however, neither step was taken.

The concern over transfer pricing was also being felt in Ottawa. In a 1971 confidential memo, the Department of Industry, Trade and Commerce said: "There is growing evidence that integrated companies exporting oil to eastern Canada have been charging artificially high transfer prices in order to reduce taxes paid in Canada and move taxable income to tax havens."[22] The memo referred to several recent studies. But for various reasons, one of them the usual unwillingness to offend the oil majors, the federal reaction was seen not in import pricing, but in export pricing. In September 1973, energy minister Donald Macdonald, acting on the advice of the National Energy Board, refused all oil export licences for the following month because the industry was charging its U.S. customers too little. Finally, in 1976, the federal government did propose measures to deal with transfer pricing and international conspiracies by multinational corporations in some proposed amendments to the Combines Investigation Act. They were never sanctioned by Parliament, but they drew fire from Imperial, which insisted that "international manipulation of transfer pricing would appear to be adequately supervised and deterred by provisions of other Canadian statutes relating to customs duties, dumping, and corporate income tax."[23] The subsequently published finding of Ottawa's anti-combines officials, however, seemed to prove quite the opposite.

While it was true that until the late 1950s there was very little difference between posted prices used by the oil multinationals and the arms-length price paid for oil in international markets, as independent producers entered the market, based in large part on Libyan production by independent companies, the gap between the two prices quickly widened. While the Middle East posted price was U.S. $1.70-U.S. $1.80 from the mid-'50s to about 1970, the arms-length price fell, to U.S. $1.60 in 1959 and, to Japanese refineries for example, U.S. $1.30 in 1967. Brazil, in the 1960s, was also paying as little as U.S. $1.30 a barrel.[24] Petrobras, the national oil company set up in 1953, found that it could buy oil on world markets well below prices the oil majors were charging their Brazilian refiners, and by 1964, the difference was so great that Brazil made Petrobras responsible for all imports, with the result that Brazilians were paying 20 to 25 per cent less for imported oil than Canada was. A Petro-Canada in the 1960s, operating its own refinery and negotiating arms-length supply contracts with oil producers, would almost certainly have been able to negotiate lower prices in a period of excess world supply. An alternative would have been a Canadian importing agency, handling all oil imports for domestic refineries. But the only support consumers had came from some independent service-station operators and jobbers, who, especially during the 1960s, were all too often regarded by government as troublemakers upsetting the National Oil Policy rather than as counterweights to the majors.

The extent to which Canadian subsidiaries paid high prices to boost parent-company profits was spelled out in corporate papers seized for the 1981 Bertrand investigation.[25] For example, documents from Sun Ltd., operators of the Sunoco chain in Canada, a wholly-owned subsidiary of the U.S.-based Sun Oil Company, stated that it was "to the benefit of the consolidated Sun organization for Sun Ltd. to pay a price as high as possible that is also acceptable to the Department of National Revenue." Another Sun document, dated 18 September 1970, explained why: "In summary, the answer is that tax dollars are saved in Canada, and therefore, for Sun Oil Co. overall, by this pricing method . . . for U.S. tax purposes, the parent company has a large foreign tax payment to use as a credit or deduction in computing U.S. taxes on consolidated results." The taxes were paid in the producing countries at special rates. Sun in Canada purchased its offshore oil from Sun International, a parent-company affiliate. But as Sun officials in Canada noted in a 1968 document: "The fact that Sun Ltd. is not free to purchase these crudes in the open market, of course, creates a sizeable penalty in crude costs for us." One Sun estimate calculated that it overpaid $5.6 million for imported oil, 41 cents a barrel, in 1968-70. Irving Oil complained in 1962 to Standard Oil of California that its supply contract no longer made sense, forcing overpayment by about $1.12 a barrel. A 1973 Imperial Oil document cited by Bertrand suggested a similar approach: "Past strategy has been to foster strong crude prices – both in the open market and to affiliates – since this contributed most to the total integrated profits as long as we had adequate equity crude resources." And when, in the 1960s and early '70s, Revenue Canada began to pry into transfer pricing, Sun Oil told itself that "we are ahead as long as the Canadian tax authorities recognize these high prices fully as costs, despite their basic unreality."

Reviewing Imperial's case, the Bertrand Report concluded that it "had little control over either the sources or the prices of its crude. Its freedom to choose the lowest-priced crude suitable for its refineries was substantially restricted by its parent corporation." Earlier, some little light had been cast on the Imperial-Exxon relationship in a 1975 trial resulting from a 1971 suit by Imperial Oil to wrest higher prices from Nova Scotia Light and Power. John Huffman, the company's manager in charge of oil imports, testified that "we may decide at Imperial, we may decide we want to get oil, and that is our decision, but whether or not the final decision is made that we are going to get that is not necessarily, particularly ours, Imperial's."[26] Asked who made the decision, Huffman replied: "That decision would be made by the people in charge of supplies for Exxon . . ." The official explained how, under "Jersey economics," supplies were dished out. Exxon affiliates such as Imperial would notify Exxon International Inc., the global oil trading company for Exxon, of their oil import needs, and producing companies would register what they had to sell. "Would somebody in Exxon make the decision on where it was most advantageous for the different subsidiaries to buy and sell?" Huffman was asked. "Yes," he answered. Imperial could propose, but Exxon disposed. And there was no Imperial representative in the supply group at Exxon's New York headquarters making those decisions. Even in cases when Imperial wanted to buy oil from an Exxon affiliate, say Esso Libya, it could not deal directly with the Libya subsidiary.

Q. But you could make your wishes known to "the group"?
A. Yes, sir.
Q. And the Libya company would make its position clear to "the group"?
A. Yes, it would.
Q. And "the group" would then make the decision?

A. Yes, I think that is fair and how it happens most of the time.

Little wonder then that Mr. Justice Hart of the Nova Scotia Supreme Court concluded that "even the senior officers of the plaintiff could not exercise control of their sources of supply but the ultimate decisions rested with Exxon Corporation who had to consider worldwide factors in determining economically the supply contracts of the plaintiff."[27]

The case also brought to light details of an Imperial tax-haven affiliate in Bermuda, Albury Ltd., which was set up in 1967 and operated until 1973. It negotiated supply contracts with Exxon International and, after a mark-up, resold the oil to its Imperial parent. In its first several years, it had profits of $35.2 million that were transferrable to Toronto free of Bermudan and Canadian taxes. In addition, Nova Scotia Light and Power charged, Albury arranged long-term shipping contracts with Exxon at high prices for which it was reimbursed by Imperial. "It was a complete wash," the Nova Scotia utility contended. Profits of Imperial's Building Products subsidiary in Canada were also routed through Bermuda, according to the Bertrand Report, to reduce Canadian taxes. As Imperial reported in its 1975 annual report, however, Revenue Canada had disallowed some of these claims and the company had earmarked $18 million for back taxes.

The Bertrand Report cited company documents concerning Exxon's takeover of all tanker operations from Imperial, which had earlier operated some of its own. What this meant, according to an 8 December 1971 Imperial document, was that "Esso Supply can assign any vessel to Imperial service at any time, which effectively gives them complete control of Imperial's supply and transportation operation. They have 100-per-cent control of the supply function."[28] The view was echoed in another Imperial document under the same date from the Albury manager in Bermuda: "It is becoming increasingly evident that New York are obtaining control of the supply and transportation functions in all Jersey affiliates worldwide including Imperial. . . . They now have complete control of our supplies and can force us to accept their decisions whether we agree with them or not."

In the early 1960s, Imperial complained to Exxon that it was paying about 36 cents a barrel more than its competitors; in the late 1960s it was paying roughly 30 cents a barrel extra, according to the Bertrand Report. Indeed, in its dealings with Exxon, Imperial frequently pointed out that its competitive position in

Canada was being eroded by the high prices it was forced to pay for Exxon's Venezuela crude, but its demands for price cuts were rejected. Nor was Imperial even guaranteed security of supply. In the winter of 1965-66, Imperial had at least three of its cargoes of crude oil diverted to Europe by Exxon, a practice that was repeated, according to Bertrand, in late 1966. More recently, in February 1979, Exxon International announced that it was reducing Imperial's shipments from Venezuela by 22 per cent or 25,000 barrels per day – a cutback that was later, after outcries from Canada, reduced to 9-10,000 barrels per day.

Bertrand uncovered the same situation at Texaco Canada. "Texaco's relationship with its parent illustrates the degree of control that was exercised over the operations of a Canadian subsidiary and the resulting high prices that were extracted from the Canadian firm. . . . From 1958 to 1970, Texaco paid prices for its crude oil which were not only higher than world market prices but which were also higher than the average paid by its 'competitors' in eastern Canada." In spite of anguished appeals to New York, the Canadian subsidiary was unable to get any price relief. Moreover, as the Bertrand Report pointed out, "at the same time, Texaco suffered from uncompetitive freight rates," which also raised its costs. Excessive tanker freight rates were often used in the oil industry to capture profits through tax-haven tanker fleets, thus reducing the taxes paid in importing countries. And like Imperial, Texaco found that total dependence on the parent company for crude supply did not guarantee security of supply. During the Mid-East War of 1967, Texaco Inc. told its Canadian subsidiary that despite its supply contract it would have to take U.S. Gulf Coast crude at a price more than 50 per cent higher. The subsidiary complained to New York that "should we pay more for our crude supply during this crisis, the advantage of this association will be questionable in the eyes of the Taxation Division, particularly in view of the fact that competitors are receiving crude at prices substantially the same as those prevailing prior to the Middle East crisis."[29]

Gulf has pursued a similar supply arrangement with its Canadian subsidiary. The basic policy has been to match the average price paid by the other major oil subsidiaries – no hint of competitive pricing here. Gulf's reaction to the OPEC moves of the early 1970s was to unveil a new corporate strategy of locating profit centres throughout its subsidiaries instead of relying heavily for profits on the sale of crude oil from the Middle East. One part of this new strategy involved "market-oriented" prices. As the Bertrand Report charged, however, this did not hold up in practice: "A distinction was drawn between regional companies (fully-owned subsidiaries) and affiliates such as the Canadian company (partially-owned subsidiaries)." Regional companies got priority plus lower prices; affiliates such as Gulf Canada, which had minority shareholders, had lower priority and paid higher prices. In 1972, Gulf Canada complained that "Gulf Eastern has been getting considerably lower prices than Gulf Canada, primarily on the philosophy that Gulf Canada is being treated as a third party and has been given the higher cost figures in the third-party range."[30] On the same grounds, Gulf Canada was also faced with higher tanker rates. Its parent's reply was that "when we deal with affiliates and third parties, we have an incentive to maximize the transportation charge and thereby Gulf's income." Gulf Canada did not have the privileges of a wholly-owned subsidiary and yet it lacked the freedom of an independent company. In fact, Gulf Oil Trading had to write Gulf Canada to make sure it behaved as a team player after Gulf Canada had protested its treatment under the new global corporate strategy: "I want to emphasize again that our one objective is to optimize the total Gulf Oil Corporation, and I know that in pursuit of this objective we are all pulling together . . . every member of our professional staffs around the world will recognize that he is part of this larger organization and that the health of the overall enterprise is what our organization is all about."

Shell Canada was not much better off. In fact, in 1971, the company noted that the price it was paying for crude was so well above prevailing fair market value that it could have trouble with Revenue Canada: "Shell Canada could have a tax exposure of $17 million for the period 1967 to 1970 under the present contract with CSV [a Shell company] as a result of known lower-cost crude purchases by other majors from Venezuelan sources for the Montreal Refining Orbit."[31] The Bertrand Report concluded: "In summary, apart from a brief episode in the early 1970s, Shell Canada was charged prices for its crude, for most years since the 1957 Suez crisis, that were higher than arms-length world market prices. Only in the early 1970s were the constraints imposed upon Shell's Canadian subsidiary weakened, and then because of the potential tax liability."

Because the industry is heavily foreign-controlled and highly concentrated, as Ottawa's 1973 energy policy review noted: "The Canadian unit within the international corporate structure is not free to optimize its results by whatever measure of corporate performance one might choose – profitability, sales level, etc."[32] For example, in obtaining imported oil for Quebec and the Atlantic provinces, "the Canadian subsidiary of a multinational firm would be expected to give some preference to the crude owned by its parent or affiliates elsewhere in the world. Indeed, it would be disadvantageous to the overall profitability of the multinational enterprise for a Canadian subsidiary to buy its inputs from a source other than an affiliated company if in doing so it were to pay a price which is lower than the one which it would be required to pay to the affiliated firm, but above the price at which the affiliate could sell to some other purchaser internationally. The Canadian subsidiary contributes to the overall profitability of the international operation as long as it contributes to the overhead of the global operation, even though the transaction might be sub-optimal from the viewpoint exclusively of the Canadian business operation."

A different but important concern about the oil multinationals has been their tendency, in spite of their huge size and resources in Canada's corporate world, to carry out much of their research and development in their parent companies' facilities. The 1973 analysis of the oil and gas industry published by the federal energy department cited data to show that research spending by the integrated oil companies had been $16 million in 1970, or about 0.04 per cent of their $4 billion in sales. Moreover, "much of the research and development which is undertaken in Canada by foreign-owned firms is integrated into its enterprise-wide program for R and D. As a result it would be less likely to relate directly to product innovation and development in Canada for purposes of production leading to exports of improved products."[33] In addition, not all the research budgets of oil major subsidiaries in Canada were actually spent in Canada. In 1966-71, for example, one third of the total went to parent companies or other oil firms abroad.

The National Energy Program unveiled on 28 October 1980 included the announcement that data gathering in this area would be one assignment of the proposed Petroleum Monitoring Agency: "On the technical side, Canada has a sophisticated talent base. Furthermore, many of the challenges of future energy developments are somewhat unique to Canada – oil sands development and operations in ice-infested frontier waters, for example. Technical services in these and other areas will have to be paid for by the value of the Canadian resources involved, regardless of which companies undertake the work, and it is only fair that the benefits of the activity and know-how associated with such efforts accrue to Canadians."[34] While government would have to increase its research spending to help meet Canada's future energy needs, industry would have to do much more as well: "Yet expenditures in Canada on research and development by the energy industry are low by international standards. This is particularly true for the oil and gas sector, where most of the research takes place in the home country of multinational companies. This practice must change."

Imperial is the multinational affiliate with the most extensive activity. As early as 1924, it set up a research department in Sarnia. In 1980, with a staff of 365, it was the largest oil research centre in Canada, although Petro-Canada was moving to replace Imperial as the leading spender in the industry. A second Imperial research facility in Calgary, established in 1955, had a staff of 220 by 1980. The company has a third research group in Montreal, operated as part of Building Products of Canada, with a staff of 25. Imperial researchers are working on four areas of specialization for Exxon: heavy crude oil recovery, lube-oil processing, polyvinyl chloride plastics, and lubricating base-oil quality. As stated by Imperial president J. G. Livingstone: "Our research agreements with Exxon specify that we may use the other's technology wherever it is applicable in the petroleum or chemical business. We share the cost of research of mutual interest to Exxon affiliates, but we are also free to do any research we feel is of specific interest in Imperial or has particular application in Canada. These agreements also provide for the licensing of technology and the fees from licensing are used to offset the costs of mutualized research. Our net payment to Exxon under these agreements was $6.3 million in 1979 and for this amount we gained access to research that cost $381 million."[35] Imperial's total research spending was $37 million in 1979. In 1975, the company spent about $30 million, with some $7 million going to Exxon.

Imperial may develop the technology, but it does not own it. Concern over the company's making independent commitments for third-party use of the fruits of its research labours prompted the circulation by Exxon head office of a letter from the multinational's research chief that set out Exxon's complete ownership of patents: "Patent rights in the field of the SRA (Standard Research Agreement) are vested in Exxon Research and Engineering Company (ER&E) itself or by an affiliate, and this is so whether or not the cost of the research in question is borne by ER&E. Each affiliate has a patent licence under the SRA to carry out petroleum or chemical operations for its own account. It has no power to grant patents rights of any kind to third parties. In appropriate situations, ER&E will license its patent rights for the common benefit of SRA parties."[36] Asked about Exxon research and development policy, Imperial's chairman, Jack Armstrong, told MPs in a 1981 hearing that "by and large that policy is still in effect." However, he contended, "I think the important thing in that policy is that every year Imperial has access to ten to fifteen times the amount of research that Imperial is conducting in this country – and I think we have the largest research program of any company in the industry at this time."[37] For example, the coking furnance technology used in the Syncrude tar sands project and planned for use in the Cold Lake project, a process called flexicoking, is Exxon technology.

This arrangement has a number of implications for Canada. It means that Imperial Oil research that is financed in part by tax or other incentives in Canada belongs ultimately to the U.S.-based parent corporation. Nor do minority shareholders of Imperial who helped to finance the research through their share of the company's reinvested earnings have ownership rights to the resulting technology. If Imperial were ever sold, its assets would not include the technology it had developed. And then the opportunities for Canadian technology exports might be lessened – for example, if Venezuelans wanted to purchase heavy oil recovery patents or tar sands technology developed in Canada, they might have to negotiate the sale or licensing agreement with Exxon. In fact, the Exxon letter was quite strict on this point: "Affiliates are not permitted by the terms of the SRA to disclose or license technical information of a confidential nature to any third party, with very minor exceptions in respect of disclosure to customers and contractors."[38]

Shell Canada has three research labs in Canada: one in Montreal, a second in Oakville, Ontario to deal with oil products and petrochemicals, and another in Calgary for on-the-spot work concerning tar sands and enhanced recovery from existing fields. At the same time, however, Shell Canada has a research agreement with Shell International Research and pays Shell Research fees for the information it uses. Shell Canada has argued that it is too small to carry out a much larger research role. "It has been estimated to maintain a research facility in our industry which is comprehensive and covers all aspects of the technologies required, would require a minimum facility of some $50 million of operating costs per annum, that any facility smaller than that would not have the critical means to cover all of these technological costs . . . although we are a large company we couldn't afford to spend $50 million a year on research alone and the only way we can get research on this comprehensive scale is one of two ways, either we subscribe to a research facility that does this for a number of companies such as the agreement we are in, and I believe other oil companies are likely doing similar things with other very large research facilities elsewhere, and the only alternative to that would be a single research facility for all our companies in Canada."[39]

Gulf Canada, which reported $31 million in research spending for 1979, has a research centre at Sheridan Park near Toronto concentrating on petrochemicals and such so-called specialty products as paving materials. It is also participating with Gulf Corp. as a half partner in research for process technology. Two of the programs are working on the production of petrochemicals from residual fuel oil and the direct conversion of natural gas into gasoline, diesel fuel, and petrochemicals. Other companies do even less here. For example, Texaco, one of the largest integrated oil and gas companies in Canada, spent just $12.5 million in 1980 and only $4.9 million in 1979. Mobil Oil Canada, one of the largest producing companies, does nothing. Its parent, Mobil Oil Corporation, reports that it "is engaged in research and related activities, principally in laboratories in the United States, France, Germany, Italy, the United Kingdom, and Japan. These activities include providing new technology in exploration and producing, in synfuels, in refining, and in the manufacture of fuels, lubricants, and chemicals; studies in fundamental sciences, research in environmental protection and product safety; and technical assistance to users of Mobil Oil products."[40] Missing from this 1980 list of $135 million in research spending was Canada. Similarly, Standard Oil Co. (Indiana) operates two major research facilities, one in Tulsa, Oklahoma, and the other in Naperville, Illinois; its 1980 research budget was $108.3 million U.S., but its large and profitable wholly-owned Canadian subsidiary, Amoco Petroleum Canada, has no research and development facility of its own. The same is true of Standard Oil of California and its principal Canadian subsidiary, Chevron Standard, Cities Service and Canada-Cities Service, and the other branch-plant operations in the oil industry.

In 1981, the Petroleum Monitoring Agency issued the first comprehensive outline of industry activity. Altogether, it spent $274 million on research in 1980, which amounted to 3 per cent of its internal cash flow, 1 per cent of revenues (minus royalties and sales and excise tax payments), or 6 per cent of net income.[41] This compared to spending in 1978 of $130 million or 13 per cent of the total by Canadian industry. In 1980, about three quarters or $203 million was spent internally by the companies, $123 million of this for pilot projects and other spending on tar sands and heavy oil commitments. Thus, tar sands and heavy oil represented about 45 per cent of all research spending by corporations using their own facilities and personnel. Another $63 million or 31 per cent of this spending was in the areas of oil and gas exploration, production, and refining. The other 25 per cent, or $67 million, consisted of payments to other companies, including $41 million to parent or affiliated companies mainly outside Canada and $22 million to unrelated companies in Canada or abroad. In their internal research, the oil and gas companies spent 4 per cent of their funds on coal activities, 2 per cent on conservation, 1 per cent on renewables such as solar energy, and 1 per cent on transportation and transmission, including pipelines. Interestingly, new initiatives have tended to come from Canadian-controlled companies. For example, since Canada is a gas-prone country, it may make a great deal of sense to use compressed natural gas – a cheaper and cleaner fuel – instead of gasoline in motor vehicles. This would also reduce Canada's dependence on imported oil. Yet here is an opportunity almost completely ignored by the oil multinationals in Canada, even though they control a large proportion of Canada's natural gas reserves. Instead, the move to introduce the technology into Canada was made by a small Calgary company, CNG Fuel Systems, while the first oil company to announce that its service stations would sell compressed natural gas was Nova-controlled Husky Oil.

Thus, the nature of the beast – neutral and briskly businesslike

R and D Spending in the Oil and Gas Industry

	1977	1978	1979	1980	1981
			$ millions		
Current Spending					
Canadian-controlled companies	9	10	26	41	54
Foreign-controlled companies	75	80	85	128	200
Total current spending	84	90	111	169	254
Current and Capital Spending					
Canadian-controlled companies	10	13	63	53	89
Foreign-controlled companies	97	123	147	180	281
Total current and capital	107	136	210	233	370

Source: Statistics Canada.

in conception, but in practice unfairly exploitive when it comes to the treatment of subject markets. These three examples – centralization of power at head office, subordination of Canadian interests to global economics, withholding of research and development activity – show why it is harmful to have Canada's important and dynamic oil and gas sector largely owned and controlled by these particular animals.

Notes

1. Mobil Oil Corporation, New York. Interoffice correspondence from Alex Massad to J. H. Hohler and H. K. Holland, Mobil Exploration and Production vice-presidents, entitled: "Organizational Concepts, Mobil Oil Canada." 1 December 1975.
2. Testimony of A. R. Nielsen, Alberta Supreme Court, Calgary, 16 January 1979.
3. Examination for discovery of A. R. Nielsen, 8 and 9 November 1978.
4. Testimony of A. R. Nielsen, 17 January 1979.
5. Examination for discovery of H. K. Holland, vice-president, Mobil Oil Corporation, 6, 7 November 1978.
6. Testimony of A. R. Nielsen.
7. Testimony of H. K. Holland, 15 January 1979.
8. Examination for discovery of A. R. Nielsen.
9. Examination for discovery of Donald MacWilliam, 7 and 8 November 1978.
10. Imperial Oil Limited. Submission to the Royal Commission on Corporate Concentration, 20 February 1976.
11. The description of the Exxon relationship is based in part on helpful interviews with K. J. Jamieson, former chairman of Exxon Corporation, and James F. Dean, a senior vice-president and director of Exxon and a member of Exxon's management committee, who for a number of years has been Imperial's overseer at Exxon.
12. Imperial Oil chairman Jack Armstrong to the Royal Commission on Corporate Concentration, Toronto, 6 May 1976.
13. Author's interview, New York, December 1980.
14. Imperial Oil chairman Jack Armstrong to the Royal Commission on Corporate Concentration, Toronto, 6 May 1976.
15. C. W. Daniel, president of Shell Canada, to the Royal Commission on Corporate Concentration, 20 January 1976.
16. Edward S. Herman. *Corporate Control, Corporate Power*. New York, Cambridge University Press, 1981.
17. Robert Bertrand, Director of Investigation and Research, Combines Investigation Act, Department of Consumer and Corporate Affairs. *The State of Competition in the Canadian Petroleum Industry*. Ottawa 1981. See especially volume III, *International Linkages: Canada and the World Petroleum Market*.
18. M. A. Adelman. *The World Petroleum Market*. Baltimore, Johns Hopkins University Press, 1972.
19. Department of Industry, Trade and Commerce. *Foreign-owned Subsidiaries in Canada*. Ottawa 1972.

20. Neil Jacoby. *Multinational Oil.* New York, Macmillan, 1974.
21. J. G. Debanné. "Oil and Canadian Policy." In *The Energy Question,* vol. 2, Edward W. Erikson and Leonard Waverman, eds. Toronto, University of Toronto Press, 1974.
22. Industry, Trade and Commerce memorandum on "Canada's Commercial Policy and Energy," attached to a 22 November 1971 letter from J. F. Grandy, deputy minister of Industry, Trade and Commerce, to Robert Howland, chairman of the National Energy Board.
23. Imperial Oil Limited. Brief to Consumer and Corporate Affairs concerning Phase 2 amendments to the Combines Investigation Act, December 1976.
24. John Blair. *The Control of Oil.* New York, Pantheon, 1977.
25. Bertrand, vol. III.
26. Testimony of John Huffman, Imperial Oil, to the Nova Scotia Supreme Court, Trial Division, Halifax, 19 February 1975.
27. *Imperial Oil Limited v. Nova Scotia Light and Power Co. Ltd.,* Nova Scotia Supreme Court, Trial Division, Hart, J., 2 May 1975. Dominion Law Reports, 62.
28. Bertrand, vol. III.
29. Texaco Canada document, 10 August 1967, in Bertrand, vol. III.
30. Gulf Canada documents, 2 August 1972 and 26 February 1973, in Bertrand, vol. III.
31. Shell document, 5 March 1971, in Bertrand, vol. III.
32. *An Energy Policy for Canada – Phase I.* (See Ch. 2 n. 49.)
33. *An Energy Policy for Canada – Phase I.*
34. Department of Energy, Mines and Resources. *National Energy Program.* Ottawa 1980.
35. J. G. Livingstone, president, Imperial Oil, at an Imperial Oil Research and Development seminar, Sarnia, 17 September 1980.
36. N. V. Hakala, president, Exxon Research and Engineering, to Standard Research Agreement affiliates, 4 March 1976.
37. J. A. Armstrong, chairman, Imperial Oil, to the House of Commons Committee on National Resources and Public Works, Ottawa, 2 February 1981.
38. Hakala letter.
39. D. W. Manzel, vice-president, Shell Canada, to the Royal Commission on Corporate Concentration, Toronto, 20 January 1976.
40. Mobil Oil Corporation Form 10-K and annual report. New York 1980.
41. Petroleum Monitoring Agency. *Canadian Petroleum Industry: 1980 Monitoring Survey.* Ottawa 1981.

Chapter 4

Money Machines

When you invent a money machine, the last thing you will want to do is let anyone else in on the action. One of the revelations that comes out of the story of Canada's oil and gas industry is how the multinational majors have made so much from so little actual investment. For despite their insistent claims that they have brought in vast amounts of capital to underwrite the development of Canada's resources, the fact is that the sums invested have been modest, the returns enormous, and the value of what they now control is truly staggering. Today's ten most important foreign-controlled oil companies in Canada – Imperial, Shell, Gulf, Texaco, Mobil, Amoco, Chevron, Canadian Superior, BP, and Suncor – had invested roughly $2.5 billion by the end of the 1970s. reaped over $4 billion in dividends and equity repatriation, and had in aggregate more than 80 per cent of the equity ownership in Canadian subsidiaries worth close to $50 billion.[1] By this time, they had also become highly diversified corporations with interests ranging from the exploitation and marketing of the resources themselves and the management of their sizeable reserves, as well as the extensive land holdings that will generate future reserves, to mining of coal, uranium, and metals, petrochemicals, real estate, and the manufacture of building products. And while their own original capital and expertise had clearly helped make this shining success possible, so had the people of Canada, through their accommodating banks and the tax incentives that provided more than half the working funds used by the Canadian subsidiaries for expansion. The financial profiles and growth patterns of these companies, pieced together with varying degrees of co-operation, are subject for fascination. They show us the giants' performance and their worth in the aftermath of the 1981 federal-provincial energy policy agreements.

The historian's words on the oldest and biggest of them all, Imperial, as it faced Standard's takeover challenge in 1898, have much to say about the story of the Canadian industry as a whole: "There could be little doubt in anyone's mind as to what would have happened in the event of a pitched battle . . . its opponents had the backing of an organization which had proven too big, too powerful, for any man or agency to defeat."[2] John D. Rockefeller's $315,884.16 got him 75 per cent of Imperial, into which Exxon's Canadian affiliates, with a value of about $450,000, were then merged. In the years up to 1907, the parent company collected about $650,000 in dividends, and in 1907 itself, with a cash surplus of $5 million in its bank accounts, Imperial declared a special dividend of $3 million, which the existing shareholders used to buy additional shares; Exxon picked up the shares others did not want, and increased its holding to 82.3 per cent. And in fact business was so good that Exxon picked up another $931,056 in dividends that year. The investment was off to a roaring and profitable start. Over the next 14 years, a period of aggressive expansion that made it a leading landowner in western Canada, Imperial pumped out a steady flow of dividends, as well as issuing new blocks of shares to its existing shareholders. Up to the end of 1921, Exxon had received more than $13 million in cash dividends, along with stock dividends (or cash to be used for stocks) with a par value of more than $4 million. In the same period, Exxon had invested a total of about $23 million in Imperial equity.

A 1921 share offering was the last by Imperial until 1951. In that 30-year period Exxon bought and sold Imperial shares on the market, though not in large numbers, in order to retain its majority ownership and control of the increasingly valuable enterprise. And in the meantime, its investment spewed forth a handsome flow of dividends – about $52 million cash during the 1920s, $177 million in the 1930s, and about $97 million in the 1940s, for a total dividend income in these years of $326 million. In fact Exxon was so insistent on high dividends – high profits, high dividends was Imperial's goal in this period – that Imperial actually lost ground in the market and maintained a level of investment so low that it became a matter of grave concern to the company's middle and senior executives. In the years 1921-39, Imperial paid out in dividends almost as much as it earned in profits, $320 as against $334 million, and during the 1930s, it actually paid out more. Imperial's historian lays the blame on Exxon's doorstep: "During the Depression, New York had indicated to Toronto its strong wish to have capital expenditures kept low and income high, and . . . this, even more than innate conservation on the part of Imperial's management, was the reason why the company had in many respects failed to keep pace with competitive developments. Eager to keep its shareholders as happy as possible during the hard years, Jersey Standard appears to have been perfectly willing to draw from its subsidiaries even more than their earnings, justifying such a policy, if any justification were needed, through the knowledge that the other Imperial shareholders were probably equally happy to receive handsome returns in years when money was scarce and hard to come by."[3] Imperial's capital and earned surplus declined from $111.5 million in 1929 to $49.9 million in 1930.

In the aftermath of World War II, Imperial was launched into a new era of growth with the discovery of oil at Leduc. In the period 1917-47, the company had spent about $25 million searching for oil and gas, or about one third of total industry spending in Canada. It accounted for about 90 per cent of spending in the Northwest Territories, about 80 per cent in Saskatchewan, and about 27 in Alberta. In 1947, according to Imperial data, it was by far the busiest explorer, accounting for about half the geological work, a third of the geophysical survey work, and half the wildcat drilling in the country. This effort paid off, of course, with Leduc and the even more important 1948 Redwater discovery. Because Exxon had squeezed out so much cash during the 1930s, however, Imperial now lacked the financial resources to maintain and expand its exploration and production activities while at the same time upgrading its refining and marketing operations, which had been allowed to run down. Even so, in 1948 Imperial paid out about 60 per cent of its profits, or about 40 per cent of its cash flow, in dividends. To raise new money, it sold off some of its assets, including its control of International Petroleum, a South American subsidiary, three Canadian producers – Royalite Oil, Foothills Oil and Gas, and Lowery Petroleums – and its interest in the big Viking-Kinsella natural gas field. Yet when still more was needed, Imperial found its scheme for a debenture issue blocked by Exxon, and it was told to hold its 1950 budget to 60 per cent of the 1949 figure. Eventually, Exxon relented, and allowed Imperial to raise enough money through a $50-million bond issue to meet its immediate needs, but the episode is a classic example of tight parental control.

In 1951, for the first time since 1921, Imperial sought more money from its shareholders. In rights offerings of that year and 1956, Exxon invested a further $101.5 million. The parent company now owned 21,787,800 Imperial shares, or 69.5 per cent of the total outstanding. During the 1950s and '60s, Exxon continued to buy small blocks of Imperial shares on the market to offset a dilution of its position from the issue of shares under stock option and employee benefit plans: 1956, however, was the last time Exxon invested new capital in Imperial, in spite of the company's massive growth, until 24 years later, in 1980. At the same time, the dividends kept flowing south, to the sum of $197 million in the 1950s, $390 million in the 1960s, and $717 million during the 1970s, for a total of $1.3 billion. In 1980, Exxon received another $140 million in dividends from Imperial. And during that year, to help finance Imperial's massive investment and diversification plans, a new rights offering was made, the largest in Canadian history. Exxon, to maintain its ownership level, paid out about $600 million in new investment in Imperial. At the end of 1980, it controlled one of the biggest corporations in Canada with a 69.6-per-cent stake that was probably worth about $7 billion. John D. Rockefeller had made a shrewd and cheap investment back in 1898.

Beginning in the late 1940s, in the wake of its big oil discoveries, Imperial strengthened its position in Canada by investing heavily in pipeline and other projects. Today it owns 32.8 per cent of Interprovincial Pipe Line, carrying oil from Edmonton to Montreal; 30 per cent of Alberta Products Pipe Line, which carries oil from Edmonton to Calgary (Gulf Canada owns 40 per cent, Texaco Canada 20 per cent, and Shell Canada 10 per cent); 32 per cent of Montreal Pipe Line, funnelling imported oil from Portland, Maine to Montreal (Texaco, Gulf, and Shell each own 16 per cent); 8.6 per cent of the Trans-Mountain Pipe Line Company bringing oil from Edmonton to Vancouver and the State of Washington; and 33.3 per cent of Rainbow Pipe Line, moving oil to Edmonton out of the Zama, Virgo, Rainbow, Nipisi, and Mitsue fields in northwestern Alberta (Mobil Oil Canada and Canterra Energy, a Canada Development Corporation subsidiary, each own one third).

In 1955, Imperial took a big step towards diversification as it branched out into petrochemicals. It cemented this move in 1964 by its takeover of the large Building Products of Canada, a building materials company, and followed up with the acquisition of several other companies, including Poli-Twine Corporation, Midwest Fibreboard, and Robbins Floor Products of Canada. In the 1950s and 1960s, Imperial was also taking over a large number of independent marketing and distribution companies. The 1970s saw further diversification, this time into mining, including the new tin operation in Nova Scotia. In 1980, Imperial purchased Byron Creek Collieries, an important coal producer in southeastern B.C., and the Granduc copper mine in the same province. The company also has a 50-per-cent stake in the big uranium discovery at Midwest Lake in northern Saskatchewan.

At the end of 1980, then, Imperial was clearly established as a highly diversified oil and gas company, still dominating oil production, refining, and marketing, but with major expansion plans in tar sands, petrochemicals, coal, uranium, and metals. It held the best immediate position in Alberta's tar sands, with 25 per cent of Syncrude Canada and ambitious plans for Canada's first underground or in situ tar sands project at Cold Lake, projects that will help replace its declining conventional reserves. It also had a promising oil position at Norman Wells in the Northwest Territories, with plans to connect these reserves to Edmonton with a new pipeline that could also be extended north to oil reserves in the Mackenzie Delta and Beaufort Sea. And it had significant land positions throughout the frontiers, as well as a newly acquired stake in Alberta's West Pembina oil play.

Its principal subsidiaries currently are Esso Resources Canada Ltd., formed in 1978 to manage all of its oil and gas exploration, tar sands activities, and coal operations; Building Products of Canada, which manufactures a wide range of materials in Quebec, Ontario, Manitoba, and Alberta; Devon Estates, a real estate investment company, and Champlain Oil Products, a distribution company. Other operating subsidiaries include Atlas Supply of Canada, E & F Ltd., F.A.F. Holdings Ltd., J. P. Papineau Ltée., and Margeau & Robert Cie Ltée. It owns 50 per cent of McRaine Properties, 50 per cent of Williamsport Properties, 11.3 per cent of Cuvier Mines, 25 per cent of Northward Developments, 16.1 per cent of Rare Earth Resources, 45.2 per cent of Redwater Water Disposal, 50 per cent of Tecumseh Gas Storage, and 70 per cent of Servacar Ltd. Through Imperial, Exxon controls one of the largest and most profitable corporations in Canada.

Exxon's great original rival in the battle for world oil domination was the Shell organization led by the bold and brilliant oil man Henri Deterding. Like players in a chess game, the top executives at Exxon and Shell plotted move and countermove to upstage and outmanoeuvre one another. The global contest reached Canada when, in 1911, Shell of Canada was incorporated in Ontario with an initial capital of $50,000. For the next 14 years, the company was financed by loans from the parent company. A separate company set up in British Columbia in 1913 was owned and managed by a Shell-owned U.S. affiliate. The war years, when the Royal Navy took over its Montreal distribution and storage facilities, also saw the beginning of Shell's notorious lobby, using British government access to Rideau Hall, for vast western oil concessions. In 1925 Shell Co. of Canada Ltd. was reincorporated as a federal company with a capital of $1 million; all 10,000 authorized common shares, at $100 par value, were taken up by the parent group through two different Royal Dutch/Shell affiliates, Anglo-Saxon Petroleum and Roxana Petroleum. Both these companies purchased an additional 15,000 shares at $100 par value in 1930, raising a further $3 million for the Canadian subsidiary. In the following year, the 50-per-cent interest held by Roxana was transferred to Shell Oil Co., the principal U.S. company in the Royal Dutch/Shell group, inaugurating a supervisory relationship that long persisted. The two parent companies acquired another 15,000 shares each in 1933 for $3 million, bringing the total equity investment by the Royal Dutch/Shell group in their principal Canadian subsidiary to $7 million. A further 10,000 shares at $100 each were purchased by the two parents in 1938, raising to $8 million or 80,000 common shares the total Royal Dutch/Shell holding in Shell Canada, and dividends totalling $2.6 million were paid in 1938-39. No further equity capital was invested by the parent until 1945, when Shell Canada issued $2 million in preferred shares to Shell Oil Co. in the United States to help pay the $2.1 million cost of acquiring Shell of B.C. In 1957, the company subdivided and converted each issued $100-par-value common share into 140 common shares of no par value, so that 5.6 million each were owned by Shell U.S. and Canadian Shell Ltd., a wholly-owned holding company of the Royal Dutch/Shell group which had taken up Anglo-Saxon's interest. The following month, each of Shell Canada's two shareholders acquired three million additional common shares in exchange for $48.2 million in Canadian assets they held. There were now 17.2 million common shares outstanding, and the Royal Dutch/Shell group had invested about $58 million in its Canadian subsidiary since 1911.

In September 1962, major changes took place in Shell Canada's capital structure so that it could become a publicly traded company with minority Canadian shareholders. First, some 100 preferred shares of $10,000 each, with one vote each, were sold to Shell Investments Ltd., a Canadian-based holding company wholly owned by the Royal Dutch/Shell group, which in turn owned 50 per cent of the outstanding common shares of Shell Canada. This was done to preserve the continuity of Shell

Canada's dividend payment record and ensure that its debt securities would continue to be eligible as investments by insurance and trust companies. The Shell U.S. holdings of 10,000 preferred shares that had been acquired back in 1945, plus 8.6 common shares valued at $28.1 million for this transaction ($3.27 a share), were reclassified into class A common shares with a declared value of $29.1 million. Next, the 10,000 preferred and 8.6 million common shares owned by Shell Investments Ltd. were reclassified into three million class B common shares valued at $29.1 million ($9.61 a share). Two separate classes of common shares were created to get around tax problems for American shareholders of Shell U.S., who were handed Shell Canada shares as stock dividends on the basis of one Shell Canada share for each five Shell U.S. shares held.

By this complex process, shareholders of Shell U.S., primarily Americans, became the first public shareholders of Shell Canada. A total of 35 per cent of these Shell Canada shares were distributed to public shareholders of Shell U.S., with the other 65 per cent going to the Royal Dutch/Shell group, the majority shareholder. This meant that 82.5 per cent of Shell Canada's shares were now owned by the parent company. At the same time that Shell Canada became a publicly traded company, the two parent companies forgave advances made since 1952 for the expansion of Shell Canada's refining and marketing operations, its 1960 acquisition of North Star Oil of Winnipeg, and for exploration and development purposes, the $232-million total being credited to Shell Canada's contributed surplus as part of the shareholders' equity in Shell Canada. The Royal Dutch/Shell investment in Canada was now $290 million, and it soon rose again, as the creation of Shell Canada as a public company coincided with the takeover bid for Canadian Oil by Shell Investments. In January 1963, Shell Canada purchased Canadian Oil from Shell Investments for $152 million by issuing 8.9 million additional class A common shares to the parent's holding company at the then market price of $17 per share. The issue of new class A shares to Shell Invesments raised Royal Dutch/Shell's ownership of Shell Canada to 87.3 per cent and its investment to just over $442 million. In all this period, Shell has never issued shares directly to Canadians, aside from stock options to employees, shares exchanged in takeovers, and a $250-million issue of preferred shares that will be redeemed by the company. The parent company's own dividend income from its Canadian subsidiary totalled $460 million to the end of 1980.

The group's record in Canada is confusing before 1950, since its

114

activities were run through a number of different corporate entities. Shell Oil Co., a U.S. subsidiary of the Royal Dutch/Shell group, began exploring in western Canada in 1939. During the early 1940s, it had some success in finding gas, but none in its search for oil. Shell got out of western exploration in 1946 but began again in 1950, after Imperial's successes. This exploration effort was financed directly by U.S. Shell and the parent Royal Dutch/Shell organization, but the Canadian company was busy expanding. In 1950, it absorbed Shell's B.C. operations. In 1952 it expanded into the petrochemical business, while in 1954 it took over Royal Dutch/Shell's holdings in Newfoundland. And in 1957, Shell Canada took over the exploration and production activities of the various Royal Dutch/Shell-owned firms operating in western Canada, a move that made it at last a fully integrated oil and gas company. During the 1960s Shell Canada also went on a takeover spree. In 1960 it acquired North Star Oil, the third largest refining and service station company in Western Canada; in 1962, in addition to Canadian Oil, it picked up Canadian Bishop, an Alberta oil and gas producer; in 1969 it acquired Canadian Fuel Oil Marketers, a large marketing and storage company operating in central Canada which would be resold to Ultramar Canada a decade later. From the 1950s to the 1970s, Shell Canada also purchased several hundred small service-station and fuel-oil distribution companies. In 1978, Shell Canada bought Crows Nest Industries for about $140 million; the company has large coal reserves at Line Creek in B.C., and Shell is putting in a mine there through a new subsidiary called Crows Nest Resources, which also has forest-product interests. In 1978 as well, Shell Canada acquired 52.7 per cent of Alphatext Ltd., an electronic office systems concern.

The principal Shell Canada subsidiaries at the end of 1980 were Shell Canada Resources, formed in 1976 to take charge of all oil, gas, tar sands, coal, and mineral activities; Beaver Service Centres, which owns and leases service stations to the parent company; Deep Sea Tankers, which owns vessels carrying gasoline and other products; Enviroglas, a 1977 company set up to manufacture fibreglass storage tanks, and Shell Canadian Tankers, a property management company. Other investments include 19.7 per cent of Handy Andy Inc., 8.6 per cent of Trans-Mountain Pipe Line, 16 per cent of Montreal Pipe Line, 12.8 per cent of Peace Pipe Line, 16.7 per cent of 204383 Enterprises Ltd., 45 per cent of Sun-Canadian Pipe Line, 33.3 per cent of INPG Inc., 50 per cent of Commercial Solids Pipe Line, 10 per cent of Canada Pipe Line, and 10 per cent of Alberta Products Pipe Line. Shell Canada also had important land interests in Canada's frontiers and was the lead company in the proposed Alsands tar sands project. A U.S.-owned Shell subsidiary, Shell Explorer, also owned significant tar sands and frontier land rights purchased from Shell Canada in 1970 for $250 million: Shell Oil in the United States thus became a 50-per-cent partner in Shell Canada's frontier and tar sands lands and would wield a significant influence in any decisions about their development.

Gulf Oil, though Pittsburgh head office and the original Mellon family investment go back to the early years of the twentieth century, was a relative latecomer to this country. It began exploring for oil and gas in western Canada in 1942-43 through a U.S. company, Gulf Research and Development. Operations there were soon taken over by Canadian Gulf Oil, which was owned in turn by the American International Fuel and Petroleum Corporation, a Delaware-based Gulf subsidiary. Canadian Gulf was started with a capital of $50,000 and its parent company met its ongoing financial requirements. It had a successful exploration record, with a major gas find at Pincher Creek in 1948, and important oil finds at Fenn-Big Valley in 1950-51, Westernore in 1952, and Boundary Lake in B.C. in 1955. It also held 8.7 per cent of Interprovincial Pipe Line, 7.1 per cent of Trans-Mountain Pipe Line, and at one point owned 10.3 per cent of the voting shares of Alberta Gas Trunk as well as 33 per cent of Trans-Canada Pipe Line. By the end of 1955, Canadian Gulf Oil owed Gulf Oil Corp. $132.5 million in advances and had an accumulated deficit of $22.4 million. It had paid no dividends but held important assets, including 300 million barrels of oil reserves and three trillion cubic feet of natural gas, as well as nine million net acres of land for exploration in western Canada. Because of the U.S. excess profits tax during the Korean War, the parent company had pumped millions of dollars into the Canadian exploration subsidiary. While this was investment, it was made with 18-cent dollars – had the money been kept as profits in the parent, it would have been taxed at 82 per cent. In the meantime, Canadian Gulf was earning no profits and accumulating losses which could save it from paying taxes when it did begin to earn.

Gulf Oil Corporation had also been acquiring shares in one of Canada's largest oil companies, British American. As well as being one of the country's leading oil refining and marketing companies, British American had, at the end of 1955, a U.S. subsidiary with 87 million barrels of oil reserves and 300 million cubic feet of natural gas reserves. The first investment in B-A was made in the 1940s, with the acquisition of 247,672 shares through a nominee. Gulf subsequently raised its holdings to 2,332,811 common shares, or 25.6 per cent – enough, according to B-A's president, to allow it to exercise effective control.[4] Gulf Oil did not appear on the registered list of B-A shareholders until May 1956, when its investment in the company stood at roughly $23 million. In that year, through an exchange of shares and aided by an accommodating change in federal tax policy, Gulf Oil merged B-A with Canadian Gulf, acquiring 59.8 per cent of the enlarged firm. In the reorganization, B-A "took over" Canadian Gulf, giving the impression that a Canadian-controlled company had swallowed a foreign-controlled one. This announcement "set off a flurry of public exultation on the editorial pages of Canadian newspapers. The deal, Canadians were told, marked a new high point in Canadian enterprise. Here was a Canadian company buying out a giant American company, just the reverse of what had been happening."[5] The fact is, however, that B-A paid for Canadian Gulf by issuing 8.3 million of its shares to the Pittsburgh giant, which thus ended up with just under 60 per cent of the fully integrated oil and gas company. The shares were assigned a value of $55.5 million, $6.66 a share. The tax policy change that facilitated the merger-takeover was the recognition of so-called successor rights that gave a buyer company access to the unused tax write-offs of its acquisition. Since Canadian Gulf came with extensive unused tax write-offs, B-A was able to slash its corporate income taxes by $29.7 million.[6]

The operation generated some debate. B-A was by far the largest majority Canadian-owned oil company, even though Gulf had been able to exercise effective control over corporate policy. At a special shareholder's meeting to sanction the merger, M. S. Beringer, B-A's president, acknowledged that "some of our shareholders have expressed concern that if the proposed transaction is consummated, approximately 59 per cent of the capital stock of British American will be owned by Gulf Oil Corporation, a United States company, and that as a result control of one of our largest Canadian companies will have passed to a United States corporation."[7] He contended that the company urgently needed access to new oil and gas reserves but could not have borrowed enough money to buy Canadian Gulf without taking on "a staggering mountain of debt," and this would have restricted its ability to pay dividends. Moreover, he doubted that Gulf Oil would have been willing to sell Canadian Gulf; this arrangement permitted B-A and its Canadian investors to share in the future appreciation and earning power of Canadian Gulf's oil and gas reserves. Gulf Oil was already in a position to control B-A, and if it needed more shares it could readily buy them on the market. Recognizing that sensitivities did exist, however, he went on to say that "a substantial offering" of new shares would be made to "permit greater Canadian participation in the ownership and development of the petroleum resources of Canada."

In 1956, a new 600,000-share B-A issue was sold to Canadians, marginally reducing Gulf's ownership. In 1958, an additional two million new shares were issued, the last time up to 1982 that the company now called Gulf Canada issued shares to Canadians, except in the course of takeover offers financed by an exchange of shares. Gulf took 58 per cent of the issue, investing $46.3 million and restoring its holding to 57.8 per cent. The parent company made an additional investment of about $56 million for 1.8 million shares in 1962, increasing Gulf's total investment in the Canadian company to $365 million and giving it 62.2-per-cent ownership. The parent continued to buy additional shares on the open market. Between 1962 and 1965, it picked up 1.2 million shares at an estimated cost of $45 million, and its ownership went up to 67.8 per cent. In 1966, Gulf acquired another 119,075 shares for $5 million, bringing its holding to 68.2 per cent of the total. Two years later, the subsidiary issued 644,485 of its shares to the U.S. parent, a transaction worth $25 million, in exchange for Gulf's one-third ownership of Shawinigan Chemicals and all the shares of Perkins Glue of Canada. Gulf Oil Corporation now had 15.6 million Gulf Canada shares, 68.9 per cent of the total. From 1956 to 1968 the U.S. parent company had increased its ownership of Gulf Canada from about 58 per cent to 68.9 per cent at a cost of $175 million, for a total investment of $440 million. Control also grew through exchange of share offers. For example, B-A issued its own shares to shareholders of Royalite Oil in 1962; Gulf was a leading shareholder of Royalite. In 1968 B-A shares were split two for one, and Gulf was the owner of 31 million of them. And the pattern has continued. In a complicated 1979 transaction, Gulf Canada purchased all the shares of a U.S. oil company, Amalgamated Bonanza Petroleum, for 1.6 million of its own shares with an aggregate value of $139 million plus $2 million in cash. Gulf Oil then delivered 1.6 million of its own Gulf Canada shares and $2 million in cash to Gulf Canada in exchange for Amalgamated Bonanza. Thus, by reducing its ownership of Gulf Canada from 68.3 per cent to 64.6 per cent and paying $2 million in cash, the parent now had a $141-million U.S. oil company. In 1980, Gulf Canada shares were split five for one, so that Gulf Oil's remaining 29.4 million shares became 147 million new shares. The parent company immediately sold ten million of these new shares for $267.5 million, reducing its holdings to 137 million shares or 60.23 per cent of the total. By the end of 1980, then, U.S. Gulf had reaped $406.5 million from its Gulf Canada investment, through this and the Amalgamated Bonanza deal, on top of the $477.4 million in dividends it had received since 1956 from Gulf Canada, for a total of $844 million on its investment of $440 million. And it still owned 60.2 per cent of Gulf Canada, which at the beginning of 1982 would be worth at least $4.5 billion. Like Exxon and Shell, Gulf had done pretty well on its Canadian investment.

As with its competitors, Gulf's growth in Canada was marked by an active takeover program. In 1956 it acquired the assets of Cashin Oils of Newfoundland. In 1962, it picked up Anglo-American Exploration, Royalite Oil, and Superior Propane. In 1963, it acquired the Purity 99 gas-station chain in western Canada, and through the 1960s and 1970s it absorbed a large number of independent service-station and fuel-oil companies. Two important distribution companies purchased in the mid-1960s were Western Tire and Auto Supply, resold to UAP Inc. of Montreal in 1975, and Gunning Oil, an Ontario company.

Gulf Canada has significant land holdings in western Canada and the frontiers, including 25 per cent of the Hibernia discovery off Newfoundland and 25 per cent of the Kopanoar and Koakoak discoveries in the Beaufort Sea; it also has 50 per cent of the North Issungnak play and 56.3 per cent of the Tarsuit play, as well as gas reserves of about 1.3 trillion cubic feet at Parsons Lake in the Mackenzie Delta. It is a 32.5-per-cent member of the Arctic Islands Exploration Group which owns the big Whitefish natural gas discovery and a subsequent oil find. In addition, it holds an 8.9-per-cent stake in the Alberta Syncrude tar sands plant and has a major position in Saskatchewan's heavy oil. While Gulf Canada may have some problems over the next few years in meeting oil needs for its own refineries, it is well placed to play an important role in almost every frontier project that will bring oil or gas to markets in the late 1980s and early 1990s.

Gulf Canada's principal subsidiaries are Commercial Alcohols, an ethanol producer it acquired in 1978; Econ Oil (1977) Ltd., a discount service-station chain; Gulf Canada Resources, a 1979 subsidiary set up to manage its exploration and development activities; James Comway Ltd., a 1980 acquisition; Servico, a retail operation; Superior Propane, a company directly and through three active subsidiaries marketing propane gas nationally and selling propane appliances; Gulf Realty, whose assets include a hotel, and Gulf Canada Products, which is responsible for refining-marketing operations. Other investments or interests of Gulf Canada include 100 per cent of Anhydrous Ammonia, 33.3 per cent of Canadian Helium, 33.3 per cent of Canada Systems Group, 25 per cent of Petromont and Co., a Quebec-based petrochemicals complex; 33.3 per cent of Trans-Canada Pipe Line, 8.6 per cent of Trans-Mountain Pipe Line, 7.1 per cent of Interprovincial Pipe Line, 16 per cent of Montreal Pipe Line, 12.7 per cent of Peace Pipe Line, 51 per cent of Western GMC Pontiac Buick Ltd., and 40 per cent of Alberta Products Pipe Line. Like the other oil majors, Gulf Canada is also putting more emphasis on coal and petrochemicals, and it has a 5.1-per-cent stake in the Rabbit Lake uranium mine in Saskatchewan. The parent Gulf Oil Corporation has a number of interests in Canada beyond Gulf Canada itself. Its Gulf Canada Minerals branch is active in uranium and other mineral exploration and has major uranium mining operations in Saskatchewan. Gulf Canada participates with Gulf Minerals in exploration programs. The Gulf Oil Corporation also owns 53 per cent of Kewanee Industries, active in chemical and gas production in Canada.

Texaco is another big U.S. oil company whose history dates back to the beginnings of the twentieth century. A ruthlessly run organization, it came to this country in the early 1930s, when the Texas Co. of Canada was established in western Canada as a distributor for parent-company oil. At roughly the same time, starting in 1936, Texaco took steps to acquire control of McColl-Frontenac Oil, then one of the largest Canadian-controlled oil refining and marketing companies, operating mainly in Ontario and Quebec. In 1938 it challenged McColl-Frontenac's board of directors after purchasing about 35 per cent of the company's shares on the open market, and, following an adjourned annual meeting, eventually succeeded in voting its own shares, plus others obtained in a bitter proxy fight, to oust the Canadian directors and management. Assuming that Texaco paid $10 a share – the average market price – for its 267,914 shares, its investment in McColl-Frontenac was only $2.7 million. While the Canadian board was defeated only after a prolonged struggle, the corporate version is quite different: "Being committed to the need for and the goal of continued growth, the key company directors felt it was time for McColl-Frontenac to become part of a larger worldwide organization which would have access to the capital needed for such expansion. Therefore, they encouraged investment by the Texas Co. in McColl-Frontenac shares."[8]

In 1939-40, under its new Texaco management, McColl-Frontenac acquired Empire Oil of Winnipeg and B.C. Fuel, as well as Texas Co. of Canada, making it one of Canada's largest refining-marketing companies. Texas of Canada, the wholly-owned subsidiary of Texaco, was acquired for $1.6 million, mainly in new McColl-Frontenac shares issued to the U.S. parent. This raised Texaco's ownership to 45.9 per cent of McColl-Frontenac for an investment of $4.2 million. In 1943, McColl-Frontenac set up a wholly-owned subsidiary, Red Indian Exploration and Development, to acquire land and look for oil and gas in Alberta. It acquired 20 per cent of Montreal Pipe Line and the Portland Pipe Line Company in 1946. In 1947 the common shares were split two for one, raising the number of shares outstanding to 1.8 million and the number held by Texaco to 827,000. In the period from 1938 to 1947, the parent company received common share dividends of $1.3 million on its $4.2-million Canadian investment. In the following year a rights offering was made to existing shareholders on the basis of one share for every two held, at $10 a share. Texaco exercised all its rights with an investment of $4.1 million, bringing its total investment in the company up to $8.3 million and its shareholding to about 48 per cent. At about the same time, Texaco acquired an additional 337,000 shares to raise its holdings to almost 60 per cent of McColl-Frontenac with an estimated additional investment of $3.4 million, bringing its total investment to $11.7 million and its shares to 1.6 million.

The 1948 issue was the last occasion when McColl-Frontenac or its successor Texaco Canada provided Canadians with an opportunity to participate in the company through the purchase of shares. From 1948 until 1978, when it was merged with Texaco Exploration, the company was able to finance all its growth from internal cash flow and intercorporate loans while paying an uninterrupted flow of dividends. Additional shares were issued in 1956-57 when McColl-Frontenac acquired Regent Refining (Canada), a small integrated oil company, in an exchange of shares offer. As Texaco had previously acquired control of Regent's parent Trinidad Oil, a British-owned company, the majority of McColl-Frontenac shares offered for Regent went to New York, raising Texaco ownership in McColl-Frontenac to 2.2 million shares or 68.2 per cent. The additional 630,000 McColl-Frontenac shares were worth about $12 million, bringing the Texaco investment in

McColl-Frontenac to some $26.5 million. From 1947 to 1966, the U.S. parent received about $50 million in dividends from its investment in Texaco Canada, as the subsidiary was renamed in 1959, bringing its total dividends since 1938 to about $51.3 million. In 1967, the stock was split three for one, with Texaco thus holding 6.6 million of the new 9.7 million shares outstanding. From 1967 until mid-1978, when Texaco Canada Ltd. was merged with Texaco Exploration Canada Ltd. to form Texaco Canada Inc., the New York parent received an additional $69 million in dividends from the Canadian company, raising its dividend income to about $121 million on its original equity investments of about $26.5 million in the company.

Texaco Exploration Canada, a wholly-owned subsidiary of U.S. Texaco, functioned as the company's key Canadian exploration arm until this merger. The company was formed in 1970 by consolidating the existing Texaco exploration companies in western Canada, Texaco Exploration Co., set up in 1949, and Seaboard Oil, set up in Canada at about the same time. Texaco Exploration Co. was the major owner of two of Canada's most important oil fields, Bonnie Glen and Wizard Lake. Texaco Exploration Canada was created with common share equity of just $1,000 as a wholly-owned subsidiary of Texaco Inc. to operate assets of other wholly-owned Texaco subsidiaries. The U.S. parent company "charged" its new subsidiary $39.9 million – $22.6 million in a demand note and $17.2 million in preferred shares – for the assets of its western Canada subsidiaries. The demand note was paid off and the preferred shares redeemed out of the new company's profits by the end of 1973. Texaco Exploration Canada also carried $140.7 million in contributed surplus on its books, later written down to $94.5 million, representing the unused tax write-offs of the two predecessor companies. Retained earnings rose from $50.1 million at the end of 1971 to $514.3 million at the end of 1977, while profits rose from $45.6 million in 1971 to $123.9 million in 1977. Yet while Texaco Exploration was highly profitable, it reinvested only 20 per cent of the funds available to it during 1971-77 in new exploration, development, and other investment activities – just $138.7 million of $694.2 million. In addition to repatriating capital of $39.9 million and paying common share dividends of $49.7 million to its parent company, it used its funds from Canadian oil and gas production to provide loans to its parent company and other Texaco affiliates. These included $293.5 million to Texaco Canada for its Nanticoke, Ontario, refinery, and loans and advances of $191.5 million to its parent or other affiliates. In early

122

1978 it carried this banker role a step further by providing funds to its U.S. parent for exploration equipment through a Bermuda company. Purchasing the inactive Oilship firm, it put up $166.5 million in equity capital and long-term loans from its Canadian oil and gas profits to buy drilling and other equipment from its parent and then lease this same equipment back to the parent for use in the U.S. In this way, Canadian oil and gas money financed exploration in the United States without a direct capital transfer to the parent company. And at the same time that Texaco Exploration was putting a freeze on its Canadian exploration activities – in 1976, for example, it invested $7 million in Canadian exploration and development out of funds available of $100 million – the oil and gas industry in Canada was lobbying hard for higher oil prices and new tax incentives on the grounds that companies lacked the funds to continue the search for oil and gas.

The 1978 merger had significant tax considerations attached to it. Under tax changes that had just come into effect, capital investment in refineries could be written off in two years: the $480-million Nanticoke refinery could be written off against Texaco Exploration's substantial profits if the two companies were merged. In 1977, Texaco Canada paid no corporate income tax while Texaco Exploration paid $105.6 million: in 1978, the combined income taxes paid by the new company were just $43.3 million, while deferred income taxes amounted to $98.2 million. The old Texaco Canada Ltd. shares were now replaced one for one by Texaco Canada Inc. shares, and U.S. Texaco received 6.6 million of them. In addition, 1,000 Texaco Exploration Canada shares were replaced by 20.4 million Texaco Canada Inc. common shares plus $170 million in preferred shares paying 7.5 per cent a year and $120 million in preferred shares paying 7.25 per cent a year. All these shares, common and preferred, were owned by Texaco of New York. In the new integrated company, then, Texaco New York held 17 million common shares or 89.9 per cent of the outstanding common share issue. It also held $290 million in Texaco Canada Inc. preferred shares. In the two years 1979-80, Texaco Inc. received $109.6 million in dividends from its reorganized Canadian operations. The parent company had invested a total of about $26.5 million in McColl-Frontenac from 1936 to 1957 and carried its exploration subsidiary in western Canada on an equity of just $1,000. From 1939 to 1978, it had received about $121 million in dividends from McColl-Frontenac; in 1970-77 it took about $50 million in dividends and $40 million in repatriated capital from its exploration subsidiary. In the two years 1979-80, it received almost $110 million in dividends from the new merged company, and at the same time owned 90 per cent of an operation worth well over $5 billion.

Texaco Canada is a highly conservative company whose main resource strength comes from just two oil fields. It is Canada's second largest oil producer, and while currently it produces little gas, it does hold extensive gas reserves and some good potential for new ones. Texaco has not done much work in the frontiers, and its land holdings are limited. It has also had a low reinvestment ratio. In the three years 1977-79, for example, it reinvested just 24.9 per cent of its upstream cash flow in exploration, as compared with 49.6 per cent for Imperial, 49.2 per cent for Shell, and 45 per cent for Gulf. Similarly, its total upstream investment averaged only 37 per cent of upstream cash flow, as compared with 98.7 per cent for Imperial, 85.9 per cent for Shell, and 85.4 per cent for Gulf. And its frontier investment averaged just 1.6 per cent of its upstream cash flow, when Imperial's was 17.6 per cent, Shell's 2.1, and Gulf's 16.3. Tight parental control has included head office executives, and since U.S. Texaco has been badly managed, the Canadian affiliate has suffered as well. U.S. corporate changes in 1980, however, have given Texaco Canada more freedom. "I have a great deal more authority to spend money and make decisions," according to Texaco Canada chairman Robert Sparks: "I'm not prepared to tell you how much I can spend without approval from New York . . . but there has been a considerable change in the past year or more."[9]

At the end of 1980, Texaco Canada Inc. had three operating subsidiaries in Canada. They were Great Eastern Oil and Import Ltd., 72.1-per-cent owned, which sells heating oil and services; Public Fuel Transmission Systems, which distributes heating fuel by pipeline to residential developments, and Texaco Canada Resources, set up in 1979 to own and manage all exploration and producing properties. Texaco Canada Resources itself had three operating subsidiaries, 214661 Resources Ltd., Société Acadienne de Recherches Pétrolières Ltée., and Green River Exploration. The company also owned a third of Trans-Northern Pipe Line and 16 per cent of Glen Park Gas Pipe Line. The parent Texaco Inc. also owned in Canada, separately from Texaco Canada Inc., 60 per cent of Cynthia Gas Gathering and 99.5 per cent of Texaco Chemicals Canada Ltd.

Like a number of the world's biggest oil companies, Mobil was formed from parts of John D. Rockefeller's Standard Oil Trust after it was dissolved by order of the U.S. Supreme Court in 1911.

Mobil Oil Canada is another oil industry giant to profit handsomely in Canada on the basis of a modest equity investment here. A wholly-owned subsidiary of Mobil Oil Corporation of New York, it was Canada's fourth largest oil producer and ninth largest gas producer in 1980. It has no refining or marketing operations in Canada, functioning here only as an exploration and production company. It has been a part of Canada's oil play since 1943, but until 1962 operated as a branch of a Delaware corporation created to carry on business in Canada and Libya. In 1962 a separate Canadian company, Socony Mobil Oil of Canada, was incorporated; its name was changed in 1966 to Mobil Oil of Canada and later to Mobil Oil Canada.

Mobil emerged quickly as one of the leaders: in 1953, with Texaco-owned Seaboard Oil, it found what has turned out to be Canada's most productive oil field to date, the Pembina field. Like most wholly-owned subsidiaries of U.S. oil majors, the company is secretive about its financial past. Public data are available, however, from 1967 onwards, and statements of that time reveal that shareholder's equity, in this case New York's equity, amounted to $157.5 million, including just $110,000 in common shares, plus $115 million in 5-per-cent redeemable preferred shares and $42.3 million in retained earnings on profits reinvested in the company. Considering the size of the company's interest in Canada and the fact that the preferred shares were a form of parental loan, the common share stake of just $110,000 is remarkably small. And it was in this period that Mobil Oil Canada began to repatriate capital. In 1969 a special $28.1 million dividend was paid on the common shares, and two years later the company paid a common stock dividend valued at $114.9 million. In 1971, it began redeeming the $115 million of preferred shares held by its parent, reducing the preferred outstanding to $90 million. By the end of 1974, Mobil New York had back the $115 million loaned to the Canadian subsidiary in the form of preferred shares. Its equity in Mobil Canada now consisted of 115 million $1-par-value common shares, valued at $115 million, and almost all of these shares had come from the $114.9 million common share dividend of 1971. Starting in 1976, Mobil Canada, which between 1973 and 1976 had paid out $8.7 million in dividends on these common shares, repatriated still more capital: it reduced the par value of these common shares in that year by 23 cents, yielding $26.5 million for its parent, in 1978 by another 42 cents, yielding another $40.3 million, and in 1979 by another 41 cents to just one cent a share, which sent a further $47.2 million down to new York. In addition to all this, Mobil Oil Canada also paid $125.4 million in dividends on the common shares, for a total pay-out to its parent company of $239.3 million in the four years 1976-79. In 1980, it paid another $29 million in dividends, raising the total to $268.3 million. Soaring profits meant that shareholder's equity in the company also soared, from $193.4 million in 1970 to $668.6 million in 1980. Retained earnings in 1971 were $4.9 million; in 1980 they were $667.4 million. The parent company's common equity stake at the end of 1980 was just $1 million, which gave it 100-percent control of a veritable money machine worth, at a conservative estimate, $5 billion.

While Mobil was making these large payments to its parent, it virtually stopped reinvesting its profits in new exploration and production in the 1970s. In some '70s years, in fact, it sent more money south than it reinvested in the search for oil and gas in Canada. From 1969 to 1979, Mobil Oil Canada put just over $380 million into exploration, development, and production. In the same period, it paid out about $420 million in preferred share redemptions, capital repatriation, and dividends. From $31.1 million in 1972, its Canadian exploration budget was slashed to $13.3 million in 1973, $16.2 million in 1974, $10 million in 1975, and $23.4 million in 1976. The company was arguing that it lacked funds for exploration in Hibernia and Sable Island when, to take 1979 as an example, its common share dividends were $87.4 million, or 64 per cent of Mobil's net income. And such practices had been drawing criticism. A 1972 study by the Department of Regional Economic Expansion complained that "the Atlantic offshore oil and gas play does not appear to rate as a high priority for the international oil companies,"[10] adding that the 190,000-square-mile area had been only sparsely drilled. Mobil, which held the lands where Sable Island gas and, later, Hibernia oil were located, called the report "grossly inaccurate."[11] In 1974, however, the subsidiary's president declared that Canada had "become a less desirable place for oil and gas investment than other parts of the world," and announced cutbacks. In November 1975, the company announced that it was suspending drilling off Newfoundland and Nova Scotia. Sable Island drilling was later resumed only because Petro-Canada farmed into Mobil's land; Hibernia was found only because Gulf and Chevron financed the exploration. Moreover, Mobil has provided no opportunity for Canadians to participate as shareholders in the Canadian operation. Mobil Oil Corp. chairman Rawleigh Warner did say in 1976 that "we are studying the possibility of increasing the Canadian content in ownership of Mobil Oil Canada Ltd.,''[12] but nothing had come of this by early 1982.

Mobil has obviously been a highly profitable subsidiary, generating lots of cash, and it has continued appeal to its New York head office because of its strong position in the frontier lands. It holds 28 per cent of the big Hibernia oil play, as well as much of the surrounding area; it has 40 per cent of Sable Island and 25 per cent of Parsons Lake in the Mackenzie Delta. Yet it has been able to establish these finds without using much of its own money, relying instead on the spending of other companies in farm-out arrangements. In the three years 1977-79, it reinvested only 72.2 per cent of its upstream cash flow in exploration and only 54 per cent of its upstream cash flow in exploration, well below the average for the larger oil and gas companies. Finally, Mobil has done little to develop research and other facilities in Canada: much of the analytical work on Hibernia, for example, was done in Houston.

Mobil Oil Canada owns 26.2 per cent of Nottingham Gas, 30.9 per cent of Petrogas Processing, 33.3 per cent of Rainbow Pipe Line, and 50 per cent of South Saskatchewan Pipe Line. Among other direct subsidiaries of the parent company, Mobil Energy Minerals Canada is a company set up in 1979 in Calgary to explore for, produce, and market uranium and other minerals; Mobil Chemical Canada was formed in 1971 to manufacture and sell paints and plastics in this country, and Mobil-GC Canada was established in 1979 originally to operate the Canadian properties of General Crude, a U.S. oil company acquired by Mobil. The Foreign Investment Review Agency, however, rejected Mobil's takeover of General Crude's Canadian assets, and these were put up for sale.

Standard Oil (Indiana) or Amoco, as it is usually called, is another spin-off from the Standard Oil trust of John D. Rockefeller that was broken up in 1911. It did not begin operating in Canada until 1948, through a branch of Stanolind Oil and Gas of Chicago, which changed its name to Pan American Petroleum in 1957 and functioned as a Western Hemisphere corporation under U.S. tax laws. In the same year, the company made its most important oil discovery to date, the South Swan Hills field. In 1969, the Canadian affiliate was incorporated as a Canadian company, Amoco Canada Petroleum, wholly owned by Standard of Indiana. In 1980 it was Canada's sixth largest oil producer, second largest gas producer, and one of the biggest landholders in western Canada.

According to the company, from 1948 to 1969 Standard of Indiana invested $400 million in cash, goods, or services in its Canadian operation. Assets subject to capital cost allowance were valued at cost, amounting to $97.7 million. When Amoco Canada was set up, Standard of Indiana received 9,766 common shares to reflect the value of these assets: the remaining $300 million, including the value of services the parent had supplied, were treated as a gift to the Canadian subsidiary and recorded on Amoco Canada's books as contributed surplus. From 1969 to 1972, the parent invested an additional $78 million in 10-per-cent redeemable preferred shares, and in 1975 it was issued another $20 million in preferred shares for the Canadian assets of Midwest Oil Production, bringing Standard of Indiana's total investment to about $500 million. The multinational's policy is that this $500-million investment must be repaid, and according to its 1980 annual report, all but $40 million of it had in fact gone back south. By the end of 1976, the Canadian subsidiary had redeemed the $78 million in preferred shares issued for the Canadian assets of Midwest Oil. In that same year, Amoco Canada issued its parent $223.7 million in preferred shares as a stock dividend, and by 1978 had redeemed these for cash. In 1978 it issued Indiana another $151.1-million stock dividend, again in the form of preferred shares. By the end of 1980, it had redeemed $48.6 million of these for cash and presumably would redeem the remainder as profits permitted. Indiana has now collected $375 million in preferred share dividends and a further $42.7 in dividends on preferred shares. It had recovered most of its investment by the end of 1980 and yet retained 100-percent ownership of one of Canada's largest oil and gas companies. Moreover, even though the subsidiary was repatriating several hundred million dollars to its parent, sharply rising profits and corporate cash flow resulting from higher prices and tax incentives allowed it to increase capital spending from $74 million in 1975 to $327 million in 1980, and boost retained earnings from $89 million in 1975 to $521 million in 1980. Not surprisingly, there was no move to bring in Canadian shareholders. In 1979 the company floated a $100-million debenture issue in Canada – the first time it had gone to the Canadian market. But this was a debt issue and thus kept ownership intact.

Amoco has strong potential for natural gas in western Canada, and has some promising tar sands and heavy oil interests as well – for example, a 10-per-cent interest in the proposed Alsands project. It has a weak land position, however, in the frontiers. The company is active in mineral exploration, with interests that include 50 per cent of a Detour Lake gold mine in northern Ontario.

Until the late 1970s, the company's repatriation program meant a low rate of investment, but in recent years this situation has improved. In 1979 it paid only 7.1 per cent of its net operating income to Indiana, and in 1977-79 was putting 60.3 per cent of its upstream cash flow back into exploration and 95.9 per cent into upstream investments of all kinds, though only 3.3 per cent went into frontier activities. Its parent's other wholly-owned Canadian ventures are Amoco Fabrics, which in 1979 acquired Thiokol Fabrics, and Amoco (Canada) Ltd., which prospects and explores for minerals and owns 11.9 per cent of Teshierpi Mines.

Yet another limb from the Rockefeller dismemberment of 1911, Standard of California, or Socal, has been described as the "right wing" of the U.S. oil industry, which is saying a lot. One observer of the company credits it with "a long history of aloofness and indifference to public opinion."[13] Such is clearly the case in Canada, where Socal's principal affiliate, Chevron Standard, will not make any of its financial details public.

Yet Socal is the seventh most important oil multinational operating in Canada. It became active here in 1935 when Standard Oil of British Columbia was set up as a wholly-owned subsidiary with an authorized capital of $250,000, and three existing west-coast companies – Dominion Oil, Fuel Oil Sales, and Metropolitan Holdings – were taken over as a marketing and distribution base for the company's new refinery, producing 2,000 barrels a day, that opened in Burnaby the same year. In 1938, the company began sending its exploration geologists to Alberta. By 1941 the search for oil had shifted the emphasis in Standard of B.C. away from refining-marketing, and the company had become a small Alberta producer with two oil wells and four gas wells. At the same time, two more west-coast companies, Island Pacific Oil and Signal Oil, were acquired and merged into Standard's distribution system. The responsibility for oil and gas in western Canada was transferred in 1944 to another Socal affiliate, California Standard, with offices in Calgary, and B.C. continued to operate as a refining-marketing company. In 1952, for $1.3 million, Standard of B.C. became an 8.6-per-cent shareholder in the new 715-mile Trans-Mountain Pipe Line running from Edmonton to British Columbia refineries and the U.S. border. Standard of B.C. built a new Burnaby refinery which developed a capacity of 18,000 barrels a day by 1955. In 1960 Standard of B.C. acquired 49 per cent of Irving Oil Co., which holds 62 per cent of the voting stock of Irving Oil Ltd. along with 18 per cent of Irving Oil Ltd. itself, giving Socal an outlet for its Aramco oil. Twenty years later, this was being carried on Standard's books as a $25.3-million investment, while the company's interest was given a value of $352 million.

In 1966, Socal created a new B.C. subsidiary, Chevron Canada, which took over the refining operations, distribution terminal, and bulk facilities of B.C. Standard the next year for $7.2 million. For its first ten years, Chevron Canada continued to be a relatively modest concern; shareholder's equity in 1975 consisted of just $1,000 in equity capital and less than $7 million in retained earnings. In 1976, however, the two subsidiaries merged, with Chevron issuing 335 shares of Socal in exchange for 24,999 shares of Standard of B.C. and recording its investment at the original $2.5 million cost to Socal. Standard of B.C. paid Chevron a special $25-million dividend and was wound up, its retained earnings of $83 million and contributed surplus of $29.8 million being transferred to Chevron's books. Chevron Canada now had shareholder's equity of $153.6 million: $2.5 million in equity capital, $29.8 million in contributed surplus, and $121.3 million in retained earnings. By the end of 1980, shareholder's equity had risen to $213.2 million, and in the four-year period, dividends of $52.8 million had been paid to the California parent. Chevron Canada was now the second largest refining-marketing company on Canada's west coast, with close to 350 service stations and 36,000 barrels a day of refining capacity. Irving Oil was the second largest marketing company in Atlantic Canada, with about 2,200 service stations, and the largest refining capacity, 250,000 barrels a day, in the region. Though Chevron had not emerged as a truly nationwide operation, a company document boasted that "you may see 'Chevron' in downtown Toronto one of these days."[14] The subsidiary also accounted for about 23 per cent of Socal's Canadian oil reserves and 5 per cent of its gas reserves, with land positions in both western Canada and the frontiers, though the actual exploration and development is done by Socal's own producing company in Canada. Chevron Canada interests also include an asphalt affiliate, Chevron Asphalt, and Furnace Oil Sales, a heating distributor established in 1962.

The Socal exploration and production company is Chevron Standard, a branch of a Delaware-incorporated subsidiary. By operating as a branch instead of a Canadian-incorporated company, Chevron Standard is able to conceal its financial affairs from Canadians; only companies with Canadian incorporation are required to publish financial statements. Under its earlier name of California Standard, the company began Canadian operations in

1944, taking over in Alberta and British Columbia from the California Company based in Denver, Vancouver-based Standard of B.C., and Dominion Oil of Calgary. California Standard took over the producing and land assets of Dominion Oil and, by the official account, "the California Standard Co. thus became solely responsible to Standard Oil of California for all exploration, development, and producing activities in Canada, a position which that company through its successor, Chevron Standard Ltd., still holds."[15] California Standard was renamed Chevron Standard in 1965. In 1980, Chevron Standard and Chevron Canada together were Canada's fourth largest oil producer, tenth largest gas producer, and had the sixth most valuable land holdings. Chevron Standard is a key player in Alberta's west Pembina oil field; it also holds 25 per cent of the big Hibernia oil field off Newfoundland, a field which Socal says it "believes to be the largest oil field found in North America since Prudhoe Bay."[16]

Little is known about Chevron Standard's financial performance, although the prime minister's aides named it as one of the companies Trudeau had in mind when, in the 1980 federal election campaign, he attacked foreign-controlled oil companies for shipping too much money out of Canada to their parents instead of stepping up oil and gas exploration in Canada. In the late 1970s, Chevron Standard had been reinvesting about 62 per cent of its cash flow from oil and gas production in exploration and development; the figure for Chevron Canada was about 38 per cent. According to Standard Oil of California financial reports, Chevron Standard's equity base is just $1 million U.S., based on 1,000 shares held by the parent at $1,000 each. In the three years 1978-80, Socal received $165 million U.S. in dividends from Chevron Standard and $54 million from Chevron Canada. Dividends to the parent company by the end of the 1970s represented about one third of Chevron Standard-Chevron Canada's net operating income, a proportion exceeded only by Mobil Canada.

In addition to its role as Socal's principal exploration and production arm in Canada, Chevron Standard owns 13.7 per cent of Cansulex, a company set up in 1962 to export sulphur, 33.3 per cent of Glen Park Gas Pipe Line, and 14.0 per cent of Sultran, a sulphur transportation company established in 1975. Socal also has a number of other wholly-owned subsidiaries in Canada, including Cornwallis Arctic Oils, an oil and gas exploration company in operation since 1960, Crest Exploration, a mining exploration and processing company with extensive interests in the Canadian North set up in 1962, and Chevron Investments and Services, a holding company set up in 1973. Another company, Chevron Chemical Canada, is a wholly-owned subsidiary of Chevron Chemical, another Socal affiliate, and was incorporated in Canada in 1954 to manufacture agricultural and industrial chemicals.

Superior, one of the most successful independent U.S. oil companies, began looking at western Canada in 1939, liked what it saw, and in 1943 established a wholly-owned Canadian company, Rio Bravo Oil, that was renamed Canadian Superior Oil of California in 1950 and Canadian Superior Oil in 1961. Its single biggest oil find came in 1949, in partnership with a group of other companies, when it discovered the Joarcam field in Alberta. In 1980, Canadian Superior was Canada's 13th largest oil producer and 11th largest gas producer.

Superior Oil set up the ancestor of Canadian Superior with a $1,000 equity investment; the parent provided additional cash as needed for exploration and development. In 1950, Superior acquired another 2.3 million shares in Canadian Superior in return for $2.3 million it had already advanced the Canadian subsidiary for exploration and development, and made a contribution of the remaining advances totalling $4.4 million. At the same time, Canadian Superior sold 2.2 million shares to the public at $11 per share, raising $23.7 million. This also established a value for Superior Oil's 51.7-per-cent interest of $25.3 million, as compared with the actual $6.7 million. Aside from small offerings of stock options to employees, no additional shares were issued until 1961 when a rights offering was made of 1.2 million shares at $1 per share. Superior Oil was entitled to purchase 616,200 of these shares, and so it put another $616,200 into its Canadian subsidiary, bringing its total investment to $8.3 million. This was the only other investment the company made in its Canadian subsidiary until 1979-80, when it paid $576.8 million U.S. to acquire the 50.37 per cent of Canadian Superior it didn't already own, making Canadian Superior again a wholly-owned subsidiary as it had been from 1943 to 1950. While Superior Oil had received no dividends from Canada, the huge increase in the value of its $8.3-million investment had made it a real winner. At the start of 1982, the company was worth well over $2 billion, a large oil and gas producer with important mining interests as well. The subsidiary had also made some important acquisitions, purchasing producing properties of Devon-Palmer Oils in Saskatchewan in 1962, and in 1965, taking over Calgary and Edmonton Corp., an important independent, as well as land holdings of Ross Security Assets and Ross Contract Assets. In 1977-78 it acquired Alminex, another important Canadian independent.

Yet the 1980 move to complete ownership could hardly have been worse timed. A year earlier, exercising full corporate control with its existing 49.6 per cent of Canadian Superior's stock, Superior Oil management had not been paying attention to the direction of Canadian policy. Then they were hit with the National Energy Program, increasing taxes and introducing preferential incentives for companies with Canadian ownership, "all of which," said Superior's 1980 annual report, "are counter to Canadian Superior's interests and its 37-year investment program in Canada." And at the very moment when it needed to be even better informed about Canada, Superior Oil dropped the president of its Canadian subsidiary from the parent board of directors.

Superior Oil has a poor reputation in the Canadian investment community because of its treatment of minority shareholders. This first became an issue in mid-1979 when it offered to buy the minority shares of Canadian Superior for $25 U.S. a share plus 0.229 Superior oil shares. Minority Canadian shareholders were advised by Gardiner, Watson, a Toronto investment house, that the offer, which worked out to $141 a share, was underpriced by 20 to 25 per cent. "Canadian Superior's intrinsic value, plus its growth potential is not adequately reflected in the Superior offer,"[17] Gardiner, Watson said; it calculated Canadian Superior's asset value at $257 per share for a total of $2.4 billion. Moreover, based on its land holdings and comparative success ratios for drilling in the United States and Canada, Canadian Superior held much greater potential than the U.S. parent: "There is little doubt that the Canadian Superior shareholder is giving up more potential growth opportunity than he is receiving. On the other hand the Superior Oil shareholder is clearly gaining if the proposed combination succeeds." In response to this, Superior Oil raised its dividends by 25 per cent, split its shares five for one to improve their marketability, and generally talked up the stock to make the offer look better. However, it did not improve the actual offer. Not surprisingly, the board of Canadian Superior recommended that minority shareholders accept, arguing it was "fair and reasonable."[18] In the end, Superior Oil succeeded in acquiring enough shares in Canadian Superior to allow it to take up those of the angry minority.

Superior Oil's second run-in with Canadian shareholders came with its effort to acquire 100 per cent of McIntyre Mines, an important coal producer and 37-per-cent owner of Falconbridge Nickel Mines. Superior had owned the biggest block of shares in McIntyre Mines since 1966. But after acquiring majority control in 1979 when it raised its stake from 44 to 53 per cent, it moved to acquire all of McIntyre and merge it with Canadian Superior. The

U.S. company had already angered minority shareholders in McIntyre by the way in which it had gained majority control. In December 1979, McIntyre had issued a rights offering at a price that was clearly above the market price of McIntyre shares, thus discouraging minority shareholders from exercising their rights. Superior had an option to buy all the unsold shares[19] with which it picked up 60 per cent of the offering and raised its McIntyre stake to 53 per cent. The following June, Superior offered the equivalent of $73.56 per share for the remaining 47 per cent, a low bid that so irritated Canada's investment community – one Toronto house, McLean, McCarthy, valued McIntyre shares at $116 – that a group threatened to take the case to the Ontario Securities Commission if the Superior Oil offer went ahead. In the meantime, a Canadian-controlled company, Brascan, made an offer equivalent to $94 per McIntyre share, which Superior Oil rejected. Brascan subsequently raised its offer to $110 per McIntyre share, which the multinational still rejected even though it was more than 50 per cent higher than Superior's own offer. The final result was that Superior, which refused to raise its underpriced offer to McIntyre minority shareholders or let anyone else buy control of the company, withdrew its offer, leaving McIntyre 53-per-cent controlled by Superior Oil. At the same time, though, the Superior-influenced Falconbridge board won shareholder approval at its 1979 annual meeting to buy up its own shares on the market. If Falconbridge were to go ahead and do this, McIntyre's 37 per cent of Falconbridge could at some point become greater than 50 per cent, meaning that Superior Oil would have unchallengeable control of both McIntyre and Falconbridge, an oil multinational with a proven record of indifference to corporate citizenship dominating two of the biggest mineral concerns in the country.

The Canadian activities of British Petroleum, one of the world's oldest oil companies that was taken over for strategic purposes by the U.K. government, really began in 1953, when it acquired a stake in Triad, an Alberta oil and gas exploration company. By the end of 1958, BP Exploration (Canada) had spent just under $20 million to acquire 50.2 per cent of the independent Calgary company. During the next 12 years the BP organization spent another $43 million to raise its stake in Triad to 65.9 per cent in 1970. The company was subsequently renamed BP Oil and Gas. When trading in the stock closed on 14 September 1972 as part of another corporate reorganization, BP's holding was 18 million BP Oil and Gas shares valued at $5.70 a share, for a total of $103 million.

In central Canada, meanwhile, BP moved through a separate

company to establish itself in the refining-marketing business as an outlet for its foreign oil. In 1955, it set up BP Oil, and up to 1958 invested a total of $10 million in equity, with no additional equity in the period up to 1971. In those years, the subsidiary moved aggressively to entrench its position in Quebec and Ontario. In 1960, it opened a major refinery in Montreal at a cost of $47.5 million. In 1964 BP's wholly-owned holding company, British Petroleum Co. of Canada, bought Cities Service Oil's refining, marketing, and other assets in Ontario and Quebec, including a refinery in Ontario. In the following year, BP's Canadian holding company acquired Saccor, a holding company for a group of Montreal oil firms that was owned by Cory Brothers, a British company. BP also acquired a 10-per-cent interest in the Montreal Pipe Line Co. Although no new equity was invested in BP Oil during this period, in 1969 BP's Canadian holding company – at that point called BP Canada Ltd. – and other affiliates forgave $42.2 million in outstanding loans, raising the capital contribution by the parent to $52.2 million up to the end of 1971.

In 1971 BP made a major acquisition, buying the biggest remaining Canadian-controlled marketing company, Supertest Petroleum of London, Ontario, for $57 million. Supertest had 1,417 service stations in Ontario and Quebec and oil and gas production in western Canada, along with tar sands holdings. In a complicated corporate reorganization, BP Canada Ltd., the BP holding company, acquired Supertest, then sold BP Oil Ltd. and its 65.9 per cent of BP Oil and Gas to Supertest in exchange for 13,150,600 new shares issued by Supertest. Supertest, renamed BP Canada Ltd., was then 79.8-per-cent owned by the British parent. BP in turn owned 65.9 per cent of BP Oil and Gas. In the following year, BP merged BP Oil and Gas into BP Canada. The parent company now owned 65.6 per cent of the reorganized subsidiary group. At the end of 1980, the parent company held 13.8 million of the 21.4 million common shares, or 64.5 per cent, of the renamed BP Canada Inc. Since 1973, BP Canada had been paying dividends that for the parent company added up to about $50 million by the end of 1980. The estimated value of the company at the end of 1980 was about $2 billion, with the parent company's interest worth about $1.4 billion. During the quarter century from its Canadian debut in the 1950s to the end of the 1970s, BP in Britain had made an equity investment of about $185 million in this country and forgiven debts of subsidiaries totalling about $42 million, for an investment of some $227 million.

Sun Oil, controlled by the right-wing Pew family of Philadelphia, first moved into Canada in 1919; in 1923 it incorporated Sun Oil Co. as its Canadian subsidiary, and was well on the road to becoming an important refining-marketing company. In 1935 it built its first Canadian refinery at Sarnia. In 1949 the parent company established a separate exploration and production company in western Canada, although its first oil well had actually been drilled at Amherst, N.S., in 1944. For many years, it operated with modest financial success, never offering shares to Canadians. Then, in 1954, the parent company chairman, Joseph N. Pew Jr., promised that the subsidiary would give Canadians a voice in management and a chance to own shares, announcing at a dedication ceremony for the new Sarnia refinery: "As Sun Oil Co. develops in its organization as a separate operation, we do not look forward to it remaining for ever as a subsidiary or daughter company to our parent Sun Oil Co. We confidently expect, before too many years have elapsed, that it will emerge as a sister organization with common ideals and philosophies, but nevertheless as completely independent."[20] Two years later, the parent company appointed the first president to reside in Canada and transferred the Canadian subsidiary's books to Canada, although it was not until 1964 that a Canadian was named president. In 1958, W. T. Askew, the chief Sun executive in Canada, reiterated the company's determination to make shares available to Canadians, although he added that a first step would have to be the integration of the refining-marketing operations and the exploration-production operations, which were then being run as separate entities.

In 1969 Sun Ltd. estimated its total investment in Canada in subsidiaries and affiliates, including $235 million in Great Canadian Oil Sands, as exceeding $400 million. It was not until 1974, however, that Sun moved to fully integrate the two branches in Sun Oil Co. Ltd., 100-per-cent owned by the parent company. A subsidiary, Sun Ltd., was set up to carry out exploration and production, while its tar sands operations continued to operate separately as Great Canadian Oil Sands, owned 96.1 per cent by Sun in Philadelphia. A new commitment to issue shares to Canadians came as a result of negotiations at that time with the Foreign Investment Review Agency over Sun's acquisition of Canadian oil and gas properties from Forest Oil. Subject to market conditions being favourable for its shares, Sun or its parent company would, in five to eight years after 26 November 1974, offer 20 to 30 per cent of Sun's shares for sale in Canada. Sun told its own employees in 1975 that "in the past we have never made enough profit to make it attractive for people to want to invest in our company.

Sun's goal is to make a stock offering to Canadians in the next two to five years."[21]

In 1978, the Philadelphia parent decided to merge Great Canadian Oil Sands with Sun Oil, and the result of this was, as it argued to the FIRA, that it could no longer honour its commitment to sell shares to Canadians by 1982. The new Sun Oil Co. (Suncor) had become significantly larger with the addition of the tar sands facility, so that a 20- to 30-per-cent offering would have to raise much more money from equity markets. In addition, and this was of critical importance to the parent company, "if the 1974 Sun undertaking to FIRA were to require the amalgamated corporation to sell a percentage of its equity in excess of 20 per cent, the amalgamation of Sun and GCOS would not constitute a tax-free reorganization under United States Tax law."[22] Under a new agreement negotiated with FIRA, either the Canadian subsidiary or the parent company was to make 15 to 20 per cent of its shares available to Canadians by the end of 1983 or else show why this could not be done. In 1979, Sun indicated that the first issue would be a secondary offering of shares held by the parent company, "based primarily on the desire of Sun Co. Inc. to receive a return of a portion of its capital investment in GCOS and the absence of a perceived need of the amalgamated corporation for equity financing during the foreseeable future."[23] What this indicated was that profits plus tax incentives were expected to enable Suncor to pursue an aggressive expansion program without a need for new investment capital, while Sun in the U.S. could comfortably repatriate much of its Canadian investment. The first Canadian participation came in a public mode when, in 1981, the Ontario Energy Corporation put up $650 million for 25 per cent of the subsidiary, a transaction that was not completed until Suncor had paid its parent a special cash dividend of $70 million. It remains to be seen, of course, what effect this minority Canadian ownership will have on the policies of the still Philadelphia-controlled giant, although the company has said it seeks 51-per-cent Canadian ownership.

What these brief profiles of the top ten oil and gas multinationals consistently reveal is a pattern of gigantic profit on modest investment, with Canadian subsidiaries that are so prolific at generating cash flow that they have little motive for seeking growth capital from the sale of shares. In these circumstances and in the absence of aggressive government policy, the possibility of increased Canadian ownership has been remote. Over the past decade or so, these companies have been able to withdraw something like $4 billion in dividends, redemption of preferred shares, and other forms of capital repatriation. At the same time, they have been left with investment stakes in subsidiaries that, in 1980-81, accounted for 60 per cent of oil production, 30 per cent of gas production, 90 per cent of refining capacity, and 71 per cent of the service-station network in Canada.

The pattern of modest investments, capital repatriations and soaring values was not confined to the larger oil companies. Amerada Minerals Corporation, the wholly-owned subsidiary of Amerada Hess Corporation, had a parent-company common equity investment in 1971 of just $3 million and preferred shares of $75 million. By the end of 1979 the preferred shares had been redeemed, $63 million in capital repatriated, and almost $37 million in dividends paid. And the Canadian subsidiary is now probably worth close to $800 million. Cities Service's wholly-owned subsidiary, Canada-Cities Service Ltd., had a parent-company common share investment of only $6 million, yet is probably worth about $1.3 billion.

At a very conservative estimate, the assets of the ten would bring the multinational parents a cool $40 billion. A significant proportion of this figure is accounted for by the reserves they hold. Looking at the size of their proven reserves of oil and gas, the anticipated rate of production, expected future prices, taxes, and inflation rates, it is possible to put a present value on these reserves. Assuming a 12-per-cent after-tax discount rate, the average value today of future production is about $2.85 per barrel of oil and 45 cents per 1000 cubic feet of natural gas. This means, for example,

The 1981 Value of Oil and Gas Reserves of the Top Ten Foreign-controlled Companies After the 1981 Federal-provincial Energy Pricing Agreements

	Oil Reserves (million bbls)	1981 value ($ millions)	Gas Reserves (bcf)	1981 value ($ millions)
Imperial	900	2,570	1,850	850
Shell	260	740	4,200	1,930
Gulf	310	890	2,450	1,130
Texaco	485	1,390	2,150	990
Mobil	280	800	2,900	1,330
Amoco	250	715	3,000	1,380
Chevron	280	800	1,400	640
Canadian Superior	150	430	2,250	1,040
BP	73	210	1,100	510
Suncor	46	130	354	160
Total	3,032	8,675	21,654	9,960

that Mobil Oil Canada's 280 million barrels of oil reserves are worth about $800 million and its 2.9 trillion cubic feet of gas reserves are worth about $1.3 billion.

Similarly, it is possible to put a present value on their undeveloped land. No one can know exactly what lies under each company's acreage, but using highly conservative values and recognizing that all this real estate is in oil- and gas-prone regions, it is reasonable to value undeveloped acreage in western Canada at $120 per acre, and undeveloped acreage in the Canada Lands at $20 per acre now that its known frontier oil will get world prices. Certainly, if a company was selling an interest in its land holdings, it would demand this as a minimum. And where discoveries have actually been made, a higher value can be used. Thus, Gulf Canada's 25-per-cent interest in Hibernia would be worth at least $1.3 billion, assuming at least one billion barrels of oil, while its 75-per-cent interest in the Parsons Lake gas discovery in the Canadian North, assuming 1.6 trillion cubic feet of gas at three cents per 1000 cubic feet, would be worth at least $35 million.

Undeveloped Land Positions of the Top Ten Foreign-controlled Companies at the End of 1980

	Western Provinces (million acres)	Value ($ millions)	Canada Lands* (million acres)	Value ($ millions)	Total Value ($ millions)
Imperial	3.5	420	23	460	880
Shell‡	6.0	720	17.4	350	1,070
Gulf	4.75	570	27.75	455	1,025
Texaco	2.0	240	7.9	160	400
Mobil	4.0	480	10	200	680
Amoco	7.4	890	6.8	136	1,026
Chevron	6	720	12	240	960
Cdn. Superior	3.7	440	3.2	60	500
BP	1.8	220	6.7	130	350
Suncor	0.71	85	11.4	228	313
Total	39.86	4,785	121.15	2,419	7,204

* Does not include the value of key discoveries in the Beaufort Sea, Mackenzie Delta and Atlantic offshore

‡ Does not include the value of Shell Explorer, a U.S. company owned by Royal Dutch/Shell

The valuation of downstream activities such as refineries and service stations is also quite straightforward. Refineries can be

valued in terms of their replacement cost – depending on age, between $3,420 and $4,000 per barrel of daily oil capacity. Thus, Imperial's 483,000 barrels per day of refining capacity would have a
value of about $1,650 million. Texaco's refining capacity is given a
higher value to reflect its more recent costs in the construction of
the Nanticoke refinery in Ontario. Gasoline stations vary widely in
value, but an average of $200,000 is used here.

Value of Refineries and Service Stations

	Refining Capacity (000 b/d)	Value ($ millions)	Service Stations (number)	Value ($ millions)	Total Value ($ millions)
Imperial	483	1,650	4,800	960	2,610
Shell	295	1,010	3,880	780	1,790
Gulf	305	1,220	2,700	540	1,760
Texaco	214	800	3,000	600	1,400
Chevron	35	110	450	90	200
Irving Oil*	250	855	2,190	430	1,285
BP	153	460	1,700	340	800
Suncor	90	310	870	175	485
Total	1,826	6,415	19,590	3,915	10,330

* Owned 50 per cent by Standard Oil of California, also the parent company for
  Chevron.

By adding together land, reserves, refining and service-station
assets, plus the value of tar sands, pipeline, coal, uranium, and
other investments, it is possible to arrive at a conservative asset
value for each of these companies. In the case of frontier discoveries where production can be reasonably assumed, this can be
done as well. For example, the present value of the Hibernia oil
discovery is put at $5 billion, giving Mobil a $1.4-billion stake
(28.1 per cent), Gulf Canada a $1.3-billion stake (25 per cent), and
Chevron Standard an $820-million stake (16.4 per cent). Similarly,
the Syncrude tar sands plant is valued at $4.5 billion. This makes
Imperial Oil's 25-per-cent interest worth just over $1.1 billion,
Gulf Canada's 8.9-per-cent stake worth about $400 million, and
Canada-Cities Service's 17.6-per-cent interest worth about $780
million.

The market value of these companies would undoubtedly be
higher. For example, the $650 million the Ontario Energy Cor-
poration paid for 25 per cent of Suncor suggests a market value of
$2.6 billion, always assuming that Ontario paid a realistic price. To

Asset Value $ Millions

	Upstream Oil	Upstream Gas	Land	Frontier Dis- coveries	Refining Mktg.	Other*	Lia- bilities	Total
Imperial	2,570	850	880	75	2,610	3,495	620	9,860
Gulf	890	1,130	1,025	1,335	1,760	1,490	315	7,315
Shell	740	1,930	1,070		1,790	1,260	650	6,140
Texaco	1,390	990	400	50	1,400	880	85	5,025
Mobil	800	1,330	680	1,615		390	10	4,805
Amoco	715	1,380	1,025			260	100	3,280
Chevron	800	640	960	820	200	125		3,545
Cdn. Superior	430	1,040	500			190	10	2,150
BP	210	510	350		800	235	70	2,035
Suncor	130	160	315		485	765	95	1,760
Total	8,675	9,960	7,205	3,895	9,045	9,090	1,955	45,915

* Includes tar sands, coal, uranium, metal minerals, pipeline investments, and working capital.

gain control of Suncor, Ontario would undoubtedly have had to pay more than $1.3 billion for 51 per cent. Control of corporate assets is often worth more than their replacement value if new owners feel they can increase the earning power of those assets. This is borne out by the three large takeovers that have occurred since the National Energy Program was brought in. Petro-Canada paid $1.5 billion to acquire 100 per cent of Petrofina Canada which, based on conservative estimates, before the 1981 pricing agreement, would have had an asset value of about $1.4 billion. Dome Petroleum negotiated the takeover of Hudson's Bay Oil and Gas, paying $1.8 billion for Conoco's 53 per cent which, again working from the conservative asset valuations then prevailing, was worth about $1.6 billion. What these figures indicate is the sheer size of the challenge laid down in the NEP of achieving 50-per-cent Canadian ownership of oil and gas production by 1990, along with Canadian control of a significant number of the larger integrated oil and gas firms and an early increase in the share of the oil and gas sector owned by the government of Canada. None of the principal Canadian companies – Petro-Canada, Dome Petroleum, Nova/Husky Oil, PanCanadian, Canterra, and Norcen – is as big as Imperial, Gulf, or Shell Canada. Based on the calculations by the Petroleum Monitoring Agency, the effect of takeovers in the first half of 1981 was to reduce foreign control by 1.1 percentage points for each $1 billion of takeover spending. That means there's a long way to go, and a lot of money to be spent, before 1990 rolls around.

Notes

1. The financial data in this chapter comes from many different sources, including company annual reports, 10-K filings of U.S. parent companies with the U.S. Securities and Exchange Commission, filings with the federal Department of Consumer and Corporate Affairs, corporate information contained in the various reports on individual companies published by *The Financial Post*'s Corporation Service, and from reports of the Petroleum Monitoring Agency.
2. The early financial history of Imperial comes from company records in Imperial's archives and the unpublished history of Imperial written by J. S. Ewing for the Harvard Business Foundation.
3. Ewing, history of Imperial Oil.
4. M. S. Beringer, president, British American Oil Co., to the Special General Meeting of Shareholders, Toronto, 18 May 1956.
5. James H. Gray. *Troublemaker!* Toronto, Macmillan, 1978.
6. Wood Gundy and Co. Ltd. "Prospective for the sale of 843,800 shares in The British American Oil Co." Toronto 1958.
7. Beringer to the B-A shareholders' meeting of 18 May 1956.
8. *History of Texaco Canada Inc.* Toronto, Texaco Canada Inc., n.d.
9. *Globe and Mail*, 22 June 1981.
10. Department of Regional Economic Expansion.
11. *Globe and Mail*, 9 September 1972.
12. *Globe and Mail*, 7 August 1976.
13. Milton Moskowitz, Michael Katz, and Robert Levering. *Everybody's Business: An Almanac.* San Francisco, Harper and Row, 1980.
14. Chevron Canada company history. Vancouver, 16 August 1976.
15. Chevron Standard Ltd. "Company Facts." Calgary, 9 December 1979.
16. Standard Oil of California 1980 10-K Statement to the U.S. Securities and Exchange Commission.
17. Robert Robinson. "An Assessment of the Superior Oil offer for Canadian Superior Oil Ltd." Toronto, Gardiner, Watson Ltd., September 1979.
18. *The Financial Post*, 8 September 1979.
19. *Business Week*, 15 September 1980.
20. Quoted in "Sun's $100-million Stake in Canada," in *Our Sun*, Philadelphia, Autumn 1958.
21. "Introduction to Sun Oil Co. Ltd." Company memorandum, Toronto 1975.
22. Management proxy circular and prospectus to the shareholders of Great Canadian Oil Sands Ltd., Edmonton, 27 July 1979.
23. Management circular to GCOS shareholders.

Foreign Ownership of Leading Oil Companies (1979)

	%
Alminex	100
Amerada Minerals of Canada	100
Amoco Canada Petroleum	100
Andarko Production	100
Aquitaine of Canada	78.8
BP Canada	67.9

142

Canada-Cities Service	100
Canadian Merrill	53.1
Canadian Occidental Petroleum	98.5
Canadian Reserve Oil and Gas	90.3
Canadian Superior Oil	100
Champlin Petroleum	—
CanDel Oil	95.6
Chevron Canada	100
Chevron Standard	100
Chieftain Development	60.9
Dome Petroleum	63.6
Francana Oil and Gas	57.2
General American Oils	100
Gulf Canada	70.4
Hudson's Bay Oil and Gas	64.6
Imperial Oil	75.7
Irving Oil	—
Kaiser Petroleum	61.3
Marathon Oil	99.7
Mobil Oil Canada	100
Murphy Oil	80.8
North Canadian Oils	50.2
Numac Oil and Gas	41.6
Paloma Petroleum	87
Pan Ocean Oil	100
Petrofina Canada	92.5
Ranger Oil	59
Shell Canda	74.2
Suncor	100
Sundance	100
Texaco Canada	90.9
Total Petroleum (North American)	83.1
Ultramar Canada	99.9
Union Oil Co. of Canada	87.1
United Canso Oil and Gas	50.1
Universal Gas	76.4
Uno-Tex	100
Wainoco Oil and Gas	100

Source: Mary E. MacGregor. ''Estimate and Analysis of Foreign Ownership Changes in Canadian Oil and Gas Production 1972–1979.'' Department of Economics, University of British Columbia, Vancouver 1981.

Chapter 5

Land Stakes

Land is a crucial asset for any oil company. Without land, in the form of exploration permits, production leases, or other rights, the company has nowhere to explore, generate profits from production, and build up a savings account of reserves on which to base and plan its future. Whoever controls the land, controls the industry. In Canada's case, provincial and federal governments that are the ultimate custodians of the country's natural resources have followed land policies which left the bulk of our oil and gas potential in the hands of multinationals. Had Alberta, Saskatchewan, and British Columbia, as well as Ottawa on federally-administered lands, taken steps in earlier decades, and especially in the critical, formative years of cheap and easy discovery of major western fields in the 1940s and '50s, to ensure a Canadian presence in the allocation of exploration and production rights, Canadians would not have been faced, as they were by 1970, with a situation in which almost all the country's proven oil and gas reserves were owned by foreign-controlled companies, companies which also held most of the country's best land for future exploration and production and thus the profits of that future. We were the inheritors of a situation in which rapid growth had been the only priority.

Canadians ought to have been inheritors in a much more positive sense. While in the United States, where nearly all these companies originate, most oil and gas rights adhere automatically to the owner of the surface land, in Canada these rights belong to the Crown. A farmer, for example, can do whatever he wants on the surface of his land – plant crops, install irrigation systems, lease pasture to other farmers, and so on – but he has no say about who can drill for oil and gas. There are some exceptions. In land grants to railways, the Hudson's Bay Company, and some early settlers in western Canada, mineral rights were included: these are known as freehold lands, and by far the largest holders in the West were the Canadian Pacific Railway, which sold much of its oil and gas rights to such companies as Imperial Oil, and the Bay, which used its land rights as equity in the big Hudson's Bay Oil and Gas Company that was controlled until mid-1981 by the giant U.S. Conoco Corporation. About 80 per cent of the oil- and gas-bearing land in western Canada, however, belongs to the Crown through provincial governments, and in the Canada Lands – the Yukon, Northwest Territories, Arctic islands, and offshore regions of the Pacific, far North, Hudson Bay, and the Atlantic – the oil and gas rights are under federal jurisdiction. These Canadian governments have never been involved in such outrageous give-aways as occurred many years ago in the Middle East, Mexico, or Venezuela, but they have also not been protective of long-term benefits for their people. Moreover the combination of U.S. and Canadian tax laws have given American enterprises a distinct edge over local independents. Land acquisition costs were not originally tax deductible in Canada, but wholly-owned U.S. firms operating here could claim land costs against their parent-company income; after 1962, land acquisition costs were made deductible, but, paradoxically, this left Canadian independents still at a disadvantage since they had low profit bases against which to write off, while the oil majors, with large profit bases, could easily afford to outbid them for land and carry out the minimum exploration work required under their permits. And on top of this, with markets for Canadian oil and gas severely limited in the 1950s and '60s, only the big oil companies could afford to look for oil and gas, find it, and sit on it. The sums involved have been substantial indeed. From the time of Imperial's big Leduc discovery up to 1980, the oil and gas industry spent just over $9 billion to acquire and retain land for exploration and production.

Oil and Gas Land Costs in Canada 1947-1980 ($ millions)

	1947-60	1961-70	1971-80	1947-80
Alberta	908.5	1,393.6	4,859.3	7,161.4
Saskatchewan	113.2	159.5	327.2	599.9
British Columbia	61.4	226.2	970.0	1,257.6
Manitoba	48.6	12.9	16.0	77.5
Canadian North	14.1	31.7	49.8	95.6
Offshore	—	17.0	473.4	490.4
Total	1,145.8	1,840.9	6,695.7	9,682.4

Source: *Oilweek*.

The real evolution of land policy in Canada dates back to Leduc and 1947. Leduc gave the industry a much-needed new lease on life when many companies had all but given up on western Canada, and it was followed by a wild land scramble, accompanied by growing criticism from small Canadian-owned companies that there was no land left in favourable areas for them to drill on. Almost all the land in the Leduc district, for example, was held by either Imperial Oil or Texaco-controlled McColl-Frontenac. As M. A. Dresser of Jersey Standard warned Imperial in mid-August of that year: "Some political writers now advocate restricting the size of reservations on the plains, restricting the amount of land to be selected, and restricting the operations of foreign companies in favour of Canadian companies. It will take a clever writer and good politician to present the facts of the situation to the people of Alberta in the proper light."[1] The industry must have found the writers and politicians it needed, because little was done in the years following to ensure a presence for Canadians. In spite of the fact that Alberta owned about 80 per cent of the potential oil and gas lands in the province, it failed to develop a strong domestically owned oil and gas industry. The land administration system was imported from the United States along with some of the people who ran it, who were heavily influenced by the oil majors. After its extreme suffering in the 1930s Depression, the Alberta government felt an urgent need to reduce the province's economic dependence on wheat and diversify its economy, as well as raise new provincial revenues, as rapidly as possible. While Alberta, and Saskatchewan, were anxious to develop their oil and gas, the Canadian West was not a big play by world standards; some provincial officials felt they had to practically give the land away. Until the mid-1970s, the oil companies had enormous influence in the setting of policy.[2]

Up to that time, Alberta's system of distributing oil and gas land rights was generally a two-stage process. Exploration permits, or reservations, were handed out on a first-come, first-served basis. There was a maximum size for reservations but no practical restriction on the number of reservations a company could hold. The legislation set a limit of two for any company at any one time, but companies could easily get around this by setting up strings of subsidiaries. Costs were cheap, and the land could be held for up to 6½ years. There was no restriction on country of ownership, not even a requirement for incorporation in Canada: companies and individuals simply had to register to do business in Alberta, a routine filing of a name with the provincial government. And the permits carried with them the exclusive right to apply for leases on the land where oil or gas was found. Leases applied to 50 per cent of the land, in renewable ten-year terms (21 years before 1962); the other 50 per cent reverted to the government as a Crown reserve, but any company could apply to have the Crown reserve put up for auction, with the land going to the highest bidder. The company that had made the find had a clear advantage in the bidding, for it alone would know what was likely to be produced. The province's failure to develop Crown reserves in some other way – for example by insisting that all the information be put on the table to make for better-informed bids, or creating a Crown corporation – meant that Albertans probably got much less than they could have for their oil and gas.[3] Though one purpose of the Crown reserve system was to give smaller Canadian companies a chance to get positions in proven land areas, this was not what happened. As James Gray of the *Western Oil Examiner* put it in an editorial of the mid-1950s: "Under the Canadian leasing system, the door of access to our oil and gas reserves is open only to the highest cash bidders. The American companies, who have grown enormously through development of their own resources, are able to pay millions of dollars, cash in advance, for Canadian mineral rights. Canadian independents, who are just as eager to develop these resources, are barred from the bidding because they lack the resources, because they have not yet had the time in which to grow and accumulate reserves. . . . It is imperative . . . that something be done to enable Canadian independents to gain access to our resources; not to the exclusion of foreign interests but in competition with them."[4] Alberta's policy of handing out permits to all comers, intended to spur development, had the effect of putting small companies under pressure they could not afford. To hold permits and leases, they had to do work. And the pressure grew with the system of prorationing or production sharing introduced in 1950, along with the application of the rule of capture, according to which anyone who could pump oil and gas out of the ground owned the resource, even if it came from under someone else's land. A study of the province's land system has concluded that "all these factors operate in the same direction, encouraging earlier investment in exploration and development than private enterprise would otherwise by willing to undertake."[5]

A team of three western economists looking at the question in 1976 explored the alternative, given the government's fundamental obligation to collect the maximum benefit for its people from these non-renewable oil and gas resources, of its employing "private enterprise to conduct exploration on its behalf, in exchange for cash payments, thus breaking the link between exploration and production rights. In effect, the position of the firm would be similar to that of the highway contractor. Of course, not all exploration need be handled in this way; it is desirable to utilize and harness the risk-taking capacities and expertise of the industry, rather than supplant it. Thus there will emerge some ideal mix of Crown-sponsored and industry-sponsored exploration."[6] They also argued that Alberta should have had public disclosure of all land bids for Crown reserves, as was the usual practice in the United States, rather than just the winning ones: "Suspicious economists, we would recommend research into the extent of lease competition between the large energy companies."

The province's prorationing policy also had the inadvertent effect of helping the oil majors, establishing a producers' cartel that eliminated price competition. While it allowed smaller Canadian companies access to markets, it was a costly way of helping them. Under the prorationing system, the monthly Canadian and export market need was calculated on the basis of submissions by the industry to the Alberta Oil and Gas Conservation Board, later renamed the Energy Resources Conservation Board; production was then assigned on a pro-rata basis to individual oil fields, and then within these fields to individual wells. It was introduced because, in the face of excess oil capacity, the majors were in the position of allocating production. In order to produce, a small company had to get a sales contract from one of the multinational subsidiaries. Unfortunately, in correcting one abuse, it created another, drilling competition. And in such a race, the big companies always have an edge over the small ones. Imperial, for example, drilled 286 production wells in Redwater, where it held a 50-per-cent interest, to keep up with the competition from 20 other companies with land in the other 50 per cent.[7] One critic pointed out that the board could instead have "taken steps to break the power of the integrated companies by requiring unitization of pools [the merging of interests in an oil pool so that it can be operated much more efficiently as a single unit] prior to production, by enforcing common purchaser agreements and, if necessary, by suggesting government entry into wellhead purchasing. It should also have suggested that the government curtail the allocation of exploration and production rights over Crown oil and gas resources while the problem of over-capacity persisted."[8] Moreover, the system forced Canadians to pay high prices. According to the same critic: "It is clear that the free market has had little to do with the determination of prices for both oil and gas during Alberta's production life. Government regulation has been significant. In the case of oil, the price has been affected by the system of market demand prorationing, the exclusion of foreign oil from Canadian markets west of the Ottawa Valley, and the United States oil import program.'' The price of oil was determined by the price prevailing in mid-west U.S. markets to which it was exported. But this was an artificial price, held above world levels by the imposition of import quotas. As economist Milton Moore has pointed out: "If the Alberta government had not borrowed the prorationing system from the United States and if the organization of the oil and gas industry had been less restrictive of competition, there might have been considerable price competition."[9]

In the early 1970s, with the election of the Conservative government of Peter Lougheed, there were moves to update Alberta's royalty and land policies. The maximum 16.7-per-cent royalty written into the leases and the law by Manning's Socreds was leaving the industry with too big a share of production revenues from oil and gas. A 1973 article by two University of Alberta economists noted that since 1962, the last time royalties had been reviewed, the price of a barrel of oil had risen by 93 cents (80 cents since 1970), while the cost of operating wells had declined by 6 cents a barrel.[10] In addition, "most of the Crown lands were put up for auction at a time when the current increases in petroleum and natural gas prices were not anticipated. Therefore the bids accepted did not capture the economic rents [the excess of returns over costs of production] generated by the current market situation." In fact, they argued, taking into account that Albertans consumed 11 per cent of their own oil and had to pay the higher prices at home, in 1972 they would get $35 million for the incremental revenues on the price increases since 1962, while the companies would get $357 million. Just based on the price increases up to early 1973, the average rate of return for the oil companies could reach 25 per cent. Moreover, 86 per cent of the dividends on retained earnings would go to foreigners, so that the price increases based on Alberta's traditional royalty system "are a transfer from Canadian consumers to the largely foreign-owned producers."

In 1972, the Lougheed government removed the maximum royalty commitment for all future leases. The problem was that over 75 per cent of Alberta's production was covered by the old restrictions, and even by 1976 at least half of Alberta oil production would be held under the Manning government's maximum royalty ceiling. "It will take as long as after 1980 before the situation can be reversed and the bulk of the production of crude oil be freed from the maximum royalty restrictions," the premier told his legislature.[11] And 63 per cent of the land would still be exempt from the higher royalties after 1981. Huge windfall gains would flow to the foreign-controlled oil companies and their non-resident shareholders. This led Alberta to propose a tax on reserves, something it could legally do. Such a tax would have the same effect as raising the maximum royalty rate to 23 per cent. The industry preferred a royalty increase to the reserves tax and the royalty rate was subsequently changed.

Lougheed was also concerned, however, about the declining level of activity in Alberta by the largest oil companies, which were rapidly turning to the far North following the 1969 oil discovery at Prudhoe Bay. The Mackenzie Delta and Beaufort Sea were the new active centres for exploration. In 1970, 30 oil companies had accounted for 95 per cent of royalties paid and held 50 per cent of net acreage in Alberta; they also drilled less than 28 per cent of the new wells in the province that year.[12] But to increase exploration in the province, Lougheed found that he had no alternative, since he did not favour the use of a Crown corporation, to providing yet more incentives for the industry. After 1976, companies wanting to explore on available land had to bid for two-year exploration licences (longer-term in some areas) by public tender. Leases were to be for five years, renewable, and cover the full area and depth explored, with no 50-per-cent reversion in the form of Crown reserves. Oil and gas below the depths drilled were not covered by the leases.[13] The new bidding system only reinforced the oil majors' advantage over the Canadian independents.

Given that Saskatchewan had elected North America's first socialist government in 1944, one that was heavily committed to a strong public presence in the resource industries, one might have expected that province to place more emphasis on Canadian ownership as well as land regulations that better protected the public interest. But the CCF government of Tommy Douglas turned out to be not much different in this respect from the Social Credit government of Ernest Manning. Both believed that the oil and gas industry was best left in the hands of the oil majors. The flavour, however, did vary considerably, as summed up in a 1949 "Report on Fuel Policy" prepared for Cabinet by the province's Economic and Advisory Planning Board.[14] The memorandum held that the government had a threefold responsibility to the public in administering oil or other natural resources: to develop resource wealth, raise the standard of living of the people, and promote economic stability through diversification; to prevent physical waste "for which the extractive industries generally, and the petroleum industry in particular, have been notoriously responsible," and to protect the consumer from price gouging. It was recognized that "the intensive program of exploration for petroleum now under way in Saskatchewan has been purchased at the cost of important concessions to the oil industry," but the oil majors were still seen as indispensable for the growth of a sector that was still in its infancy. During the 1930s, a number of gas fields had been developed in the province, and in 1940, Imperial Oil embarked on an important oil drilling program that, in spite of favourable structure, had hit only dry holes.

The new government's program of "orderly change to social ownership" was announced by resources minister J. L. Phelps soon after it took office.[15] While private industry would continue to play a role in resource development for some time to come, "eventually it is hoped to establish complete social ownership and management of key industries in the development of our resources." Not surprisingly, Imperial left Saskatchewan for Alberta in 1946, and the other majors became extremely reluctant to invest in the province. Faced with this situation, the Economic Advisory and Planning Board reviewed the government's policies and came to the following conclusions regarding oil: "(b) A program of exploration and development of these prospective resources is both necessary and desirable. (c) Although public development is preferred, the large financial commitment involved is too heavy a burden for the provincial government itself to assume at the present time. (d) For the same reason the straight alternative of a joint program with the co-operative movement alone is not feasible over any large area. (e) It is therefore necessary to encourage development by private capital and to define a policy which will at the same time safeguard the interests of the province as fully as possible."[16] Cabinet considered and rejected the idea of financing a government exploration program by levying an additional tax on gasoline and other petroleum products. The government had also offered to undertake an exploration program with the co-ops, but they decided that they should invest their money in the newly discovered Alberta Leduc field instead.[17] Saskatchewan had no wish to forgo its share of the excitement and investment that had followed the recent Alberta finds, and so Premier Douglas capitulated with a statement that his government was "desirous of encouraging mineral and petroleum exploration, development and production to the greatest possible extent," and "gives a firm undertaking that no steps will be taken to expropriate or socialize the mining or petroleum industry in the province."[18] The majors had won, and about 80 per cent of the province's land was soon held by foreign-controlled companies. The principal permit holders, as of 1 August 1949, were Sohio, with 9,027,852 acres, Tidewater Oil, with 8,750,000 acres, Husky Oil and Refining, with 2,646,660 acres, Albercan Oil, with 1,956,800 acres, Shell, with 1,674,080 acres, Western Prairie Exploration, with 1,000,000 acres, Lambton, with 1,000,000 acres, Battleford Petroleum, with 1,000,000 acres, B. F. Lundy, with 818,720 acres, and Husky-Phillips Petroleum, with 750,000 acres.[19]

While the province was obliged to rely on the oil majors for the bulk of development – and on their terms – the 1949 report did propose a Crown corporation to develop oil and gas resources on the Crown reserves, a recommendation that was echoed later in a comprehensive document from the province's Oil Policy Committee, headed by Tommy Shoyama. The June 1953 memorandum called for the creation of a Saskatchewan Crown corporation to explore on and produce oil and gas from the reserves, normally ranging from 40 to 60 per cent, that reverted to the government when companies converted exploration permits into leases. The committee did not want to get into the business of refining the oil and selling it through service stations, but it did want to make sure that the province captured more of the value of its oil and gas reserves, and calculated that by operating a Crown corporation the government could realize $500 million to $1 billion at 1953 prices.[20] One concern of Shoyama and his group was that 1951 land regulation changes allowed a company with a permit to choose which portion would revert, reducing the likelihood that the Crown would end up with favourable land. The key question, however, was what to do with these reserves. In Alberta, the government simply auctioned them off to the highest bidder. The Shoyama group went out of its way to emphasize that there was no obligation to follow the Alberta practice of selling Crown reserves back to private industry: "The only obligation which the government has with respect to Crown reserves, which are a 'privileged asset,' is to develop them by those methods that will maximize the total revenue to the public treasury from the province's oil reserves." The cost of exploration would have to be financed initially out of the provincial treasury to the tune of $10 million a year for an estimated four or five years, but once the program was under way it could operate on reinvested earnings.

The committee observed realistically that the province's economic well-being depended on its ability to sell its bonds in eastern Canada and the United States: "Some concern has therefore been expressed that a government policy of investing in oil might prejudice the success of the anticipated bond flotations. Several reasons have been cited. The conservative tradition of financial investment houses is well known, and a political reaction might be expected in the initial period, particularly in Canada. Further, if the private oil companies express an active hostility toward the policy, this hostility is likely to be transmitted to the capital sources through the close-knit relationships of the financial world. In a more general sense investment houses may argue that the policy is an 'unwise' one, which may have unfavourable effects upon the further influx of private investment capital into Saskatchewan, thereby impairing the continued economic development and future credit status of the province." And in fact, when in 1954 Saskatchewan farmed out two small parcels of Crown reserve land to Consumers' Co-op, even this small step drew cries of outrage from the Canadian Petroleum Association, which saw it as a first move into the oil business. There were dark warnings that the oil companies might move out of Saskatchewan, and Bay Street quickly joined in with its own threats. N. K. McKinnon of Harris and Partners wrote to Douglas that if his government extended this policy "there would be a number of corporations and institutions who would decline to buy Saskatchewan bonds as a protest to an apparently inequitable policy."[21] What the oil industry and the financial community were saying was that a provincial government did not have the right to do what it wanted with the Crown reserves that belonged to the people. While this was clearly an outrageous argument, Douglas bowed to pressure from the industry and the financial community. What had started as an experiment that could have led to a much stronger Canadian presence in the oil and gas industry – an example that might well have spilled over into Alberta – was all too easily abandoned.

In 1964, the newly elected Liberal government of Ross Thatcher, a harsh opponent of restrictions on foreign ownership and determined to make Saskatchewan North America's haven for free enterprise, introduced new incentives for oil and gas exploration. These incentives, one of which was a royalty-free period for deep wells, were largely based on CPA recommendations the Thatcher Liberals had endorsed while in opposition. "The government of

Saskatchewan believes there is no place in a developing country like Canada for narrow economic nationalism,'' Thatcher declared: ''Our government believes that measures which hinder American investment are harmful to Canada.''[22] The Thatcher regime was defeated in 1968, and the NDP government of Allan Blakeney took its place. Like Lougheed in Alberta, Blakeney sharply increased royalty revenues for oil and gas, but he also saw the pitfalls, telling the CPA in 1973 that it was hard to be optimistic about the future of oil production in Saskatchewan because ''the major oil companies prefer to explore for oil elsewhere in pursuit of their respective corporate objectives. This is borne out by the fact, so I'm told, that three quarters of our exploration wells over the past decade have been drilled by small independents rather than the majors. This disturbs us. Our geological people estimate that there is another billion barrels of oil awaiting discovery in Saskatchewan. But there is no concerted effort under way in the private sector to prove it up.''[23] He explained further: ''The oil industry revenue from Saskatchewan production of oil and gas is currently about $130 million per year. The resulting $100 million excess of revenue over expenditure for Saskatchewan is being used by the industry to finance its development elsewhere, particularly, it seems to us, in the Arctic islands and the Mackenzie Delta, as well as the North Sea and on the east coast.'' It was shortly afterwards that his government announced plans for the province's own oil company, Saskoil.

The 1950s and '60s had seen increasingly numerous expressions of concern at the way provincial land policies worked in favour of the multinationals and against Canadian enterprises. One of these had come from the Gordon Commission on Canada's Economic Prospects, which pointed out in its 1957 report: ''The granting of applications for mining rights, oil leases, and timber limits is the responsibility of the provinces under the Canadian constitution. With this in mind, the commission suggests that provincial governments might well consider requiring foreign applicants for such rights in future to incorporate under Canadian laws and to take in Canadian partners.''[24] The commission cited the fact that 70 per cent of the land under reservation or lease and close to 80 per cent of the proven oil reserves in the four western provinces, after a decade of exciting discoveries, were in the hands of corporations owned and controlled in the United States; if one added the other foreign companies, the figures went up to 85 to 90 per cent of the land and about 88 per cent of the proven reserves. ''At the present time,'' the commission's research showed, ''six of the largest internationally connected majors – Imperial Oil Ltd., California Standard Co., Shell Oil of Canada Ltd., the British American Oil Co. Ltd., Texaco Exploration Ltd., and Mobil Oil of Canada Ltd. – hold, between them, about 40 per cent of the gross acreage under reservation and lease in western Canada. They, at the same time, control about three quarters of the proven oil reserves in the country."[25] The commission was also informed that "in recent years high bidding in provincial government land sales has prohibited the smaller companies with limited capital resources from acquiring land in the more favourable oil and gas areas." This situation was unlikely to change so long as the provincial governments considered ownership and control to be irrelevant. While it was true that the total percentage of land held by the largest oil companies had declined, the research study pointed out, "the fact that they have been at once more active and more discerning, in so far as exploration and development are concerned, has its rewards." And *Oilweek* recorded a 1962 comment by the president of Western Decalta Petroleum on the group of companies sitting on two thirds of the western land: "The 14 major holders pay well in excess of $30 million annually on rentals. This is purely protective expenditure. Annual financial obligations of this magnitude in one province alone are an obvious reason why the major companies can afford to dominate the land picture."[26] To this day, neither British Columbia nor Alberta, nor even Saskatchewan, requires Canadian incorporation or Canadian shareholder participation in the exploration and production of oil and gas.

This ability to acquire and retain land was a clear advantage for the giants, as the list of discoveries overleaf demonstrates. Moreover, while the pace of discovery in western Canada had fallen off by the late 1960s, there was a continuing strong interest in acquiring and holding land. One reason for this was certainly the projected 1970s growth of exports. Another was the much lower cost of finding oil in Canada, 28 per cent lower in the West than the U.S. average: our excellent prospects kept land costs identical at 21 cents a barrel, but producing and royalty costs, for example, were $1.48 per barrel in the Canadian West as compared with $2.12 in the U.S.[27] And Canadian oil- and gas-prone regions had been much less intensively drilled. *Oilweek* calculated in 1970 that oil and associated natural gas liquids production would rise from 1.3 million barrels a day in 1969 to 3.3 million a day in 1979, while natural gas sales would rise from 4.3 billion cubic feet a day in 1969 to 11.5 billion a day in 1979. This meant, said *Oilweek*, that 21 billion barrels of new oil reserves would have to be found in the

Major Oil Field Discoveries[28]

Field	Province	Company	Date	Production to July 1, 1980 million barrels	Barrels/day First half 1980
Leduc	Alberta	Imperial	1947	357	10,000
Redwater	Alberta	Imperial	1948	704	90,000
Golden Spike	Alberta	Imperial	1944	219	8,000
Fenn-Big Valley	Alberta	Gulf	1950	210	48,000
Steelman	Sask.	Shell	1950	226	13,000
Wizard Lake	Alberta	Texaco	1951	228	5,000
Judy Creek	Alberta	Imperial	1951	321	53,000
Bonnie Glen	Alberta	Texaco	1952	344	74,000
Sturgeon Lake S.	Alberta	Amerada Minerals	1953	100	12,000
Pembina	Alberta	Mobil/Seaboard	1953	973	80,000
Boundary Lake	B.C.	Texaco	1954	135	15,000
Weyburn	Sask.	Gulf	1955	244	17,000
Swan Hills	Alberta	Home Oil	1957	531	72,000
Virginia Hills	Alberta	Home Oil	1957	106	12,000
Carson Creek N.	Alberta	Mobil	1958	94	21,000
Swan Hills S.	Alberta	Pan Canadian	1959	262	56,000
Mitsue	Alberta	Chevron	1964	188	41,000
Nipisi	Alberta	Chevron	1965	171	33,000
Rainbow	Alberta	Banff Oil Co.	1965	342	71,000

1970s as compared with 10 billion barrels proved up during the 1960s, and raw natural gas reserves of 85 billion cubic feet had to be found in the 1970s as compared with 38 trillion in the 1960s.[29] The magazine's optimism was based on National Energy Board and oil industry hopes for the future, embracing natural gas production from the Atlantic offshore region, oil from the Arctic islands and Atlantic offshore to displace imports in eastern Canada, and the completion of oil and gas pipelines from Alaska across Canada to carry U.S. and Canadian oil and gas into American markets. In the previous year, 1969, the CPA had estimated Canada's potential reserves at about 120 billion barrels of oil and 725 trillion cubic feet of gas. About 10 per cent had been discovered, almost all of it in western Canada. By the CPA's reckoning, about 25 per cent of Canada's potential lay in the western provinces and about 75 per cent – 90 billion barrels of oil and 550 trillion cubic feet of gas – in the frontiers. This optimism coming into the '70s was given added impetus by the 1969 major oil find in Alaska's Prudhoe Bay and Imperial's 1970 discovery of oil at Atkinson Point in the nearby Mackenzie Delta. And it was reflected in land payments, which in Alberta, for instance, soared from $1.4 billion in 1961-70 to $4.9 billion in 1971-80. This meant in turn that land costs per barrel of oil rose steadily through the 1970s, from 54 cents in 1971-75 to 60 cents in 1972-76 and $1.03 in 1975-79.[30] As in previous decades, the oil majors remained in the best position to bid for and sit on land. And as in previous decades, they had strong allies in the provincial land policies.

Disturbingly enough, federal policy on the Canada Lands – the vast regions of the far North, the Atlantic and Pacific offshore, and Hudson's Bay – has until recently been just as careless about Canadian content. This would seem to have been belied by the Diefenbaker government's 1960 declaration that Canada Lands oil and gas production licences would be granted only to Canadian-owned corporations or foreign-owned corporations listed on a Canadian stock exchange and thus giving Canadians an opportunity to invest in them. While this was the first time Canadian ownership had rated a mention in any Canadian land policy for resource rights, the measure was really of little practical importance. It did not force Mobil Canada or Chevron Standard to sell shares to Canadians; it simply meant that their parent companies had to be listed on a Canadian stock exchange. Canadians could already invest in these companies through foreign stock exchanges. And there was no pretence of imposing ownership rules on companies taking out exploration permits in the Lands; indeed the government said in the same announcement that it would extend the permits from nine to 12 years and double the first three-year permit term without increasing the deposit. Despite the innocuousness of all this, the CPA fired a telegram off to the government to claim that such ownership requirements would discourage investment and slow exploration and development.[31]

While the policy at that time was to accelerate development as part of Diefenbaker's northern vision, there was not much activity before the late 1960s. It was not until 1967 that Ottawa became a 45-per-cent partner in Panarctic Oils, a company set up to explore for oil and gas in the Arctic islands, having begun to realize that the majors had taken advantage of the cheap and easy terms of the Diefenbaker land policy to tie up most of the Canada Lands that were reckoned as having any potential. Canadian companies were simply not part of the country's exciting oil and gas frontiers. By the late 1960s, for example, some 50 firms had blanketed 300 million acres off the east coast with exploration permits, but Canadian-controlled holdings were virtually non-existent. The principal exploration groups in the late 1960s and early 1970s were Mobil Oil Canada on Sable Island, Shell Canada on the Scotian Shelf, Amoco-Imperial-Chevron Standard on the south Grand Banks, and Mobil-Gulf Canada on the east Grand Banks.

Concern about these land policies was coming to a head. Andrew Thompson, then a University of Alberta law professor, had told the Commons Committee on Indian Affairs and Northern Development in 1968 that the incentives offered in the federal oil and gas regulations were "substantially more generous than those offered in any other Canadian legislation, and more generous than those offered in many other parts of the world."[32] For example, a company with an 11-year exploration permit could convert it to lease for 42 years and thus own and operate an entire field: Mobil could have had 50 per cent of Hibernia on its own. The government could not ignore the problems. A confidential 1972 finance department study on the costs and benefits of a Mackenzie Valley pipeline pointed out that Canada would get only $75 million a year in tax and royalty revenues from the scheme, about $50 million from withholding tax revenues on dividends and interests paid to non-residents and only $23 million from Delta gas. The pipeline would not be paying a penny of corporate income tax for many years. By contrast, "in the case of Alaska, the state government will receive $300 million a year for the extraction and transportation of Arctic oil under recently enacted legislation, including: a supplementary profits tax on pipeline profits; a levy for the Alaskan Native Fund of 5 cents per barrel of oil; and a provision whereby the absolute royalty on oil production is inversely related to the price at the wellhead. Revenues of this magnitude will be far in excess of anything which the Canadian government would expect to receive from gas development in the Canadian North, under existing provisions."[33] The main beneficiaries of a northern gas pipeline would be three foreign-controlled oil companies – Imperial, Shell, and Gulf – who also happened to be important shareholders in the pipeline company. Canadians would get little in direct revenue from the exploitation of their gas resources, but they would be financing a good part of the operation through tax incentives, not to mention over $200 million in direct infrastructure spending.

The public whistle on Canada's land policies was finally blown in 1973 by the Canadian Arctic Resources Committee, an activist public-interest group backed by some of the top scientific and legal experts in the country. At an Ottawa conference, Andrew Thompson and Michael Crommelin of the University of British Columbia produced a devastating paper on the Canada Lands regulations. They charged that in 1961 the Diefenbaker government had given the industry "carte blanche, telling them to write the kind of regulations that would create incentive for northern development. As a result we have a resource 'give-away' unparalleled in any country in modern times."[34] In the first place, exploration permits were handed out on warmly generous terms that grew even warmer the more remote the location was. And they were generally granted for 12 years as compared with five years today in Norway, with a work requirement consisting of $2.70 an acre over the life of the permit, the only other cost being the $250 filing fee. This meant that in 1965, Mobil had been able to acquire 13 million acres in Hibernia – the most important oil discovery in North America since Prudhoe Bay – at a price of only $37,000.[35] Secondly, these exploration permits conferred sweeping privileges that included the exclusive right to a 21-year renewable production lease if oil or gas were found. If nothing had been found, the holder could still convert to a 21-year lease. Thus, land picked up by, say, Mobil in 1965 could be held under permit until 1977 and then under lease to 1998, with the automatic right to renew for another 21 years to 2019 if oil or gas had been discovered in commercial quantities by 1998. This clearly justified the use of the term, "give-away." In effect, Canada had handed over control of its resource wealth, including the pace of the development of that wealth, for up to 53 years.

A Crown reserve rule was included, similar to the one in the Alberta regulations, by which a company moving from exploration permit to lease had to surrender 50 per cent of its land. However, the federal regulations virtually gave the Crown reserves away instead of auctioning them off as Alberta had done. When a company had chosen its land for lease in the frontier, it had the right to take up the other half at a modestly higher royalty rate than the usual 5 or 10 per cent. This was peanuts compared to the $1.5 billion raised by Alberta in 1947-72 land auctions, and it looked even more insignificant next to the $900 million the State of Alaska got for 413,000 acres of Prudhoe Bay leases in 1969, or the $2.6 billion collected by the U.S. Treasury in 1972 from the sale of leases on 830,000 acres of the Louisiana coast.[36] The federal royalties of 5 per cent for the first three years and 10 per cent after that could be compared with the 16.7 per cent in the U.S. offshore and an effective 20 per cent in Alaska. Thompson and Crommelin pointed out that "the petroleum revenues forgone under the present system amount to hundreds of millions of dollars. They are of the order required to settle native claims and provide an economic base for the Yukon and Northwest Territories. In the Maritime provinces and Quebec they can mean economic resurgence."[37]

The arrangements were even more outrageous when viewed in the aftermath of the OPEC price increases of 1973. Countries like

Britain and Norway were giving much shorter exploration terms, and some even required a progressive surrendering of land: for example a company exploring for oil and gas in Australia had to surrender half its land under exploration permit after six years and then cut back each successive five years by 50 per cent of whatever it had left. The Canadian system was unique in the Western world in providing for no relinquishment of land. Instead, it turned over one of the potentially richest resource areas on the planet for $250 a permit, plus $1 an acre rental after the first 12 years and a modest royalty after the start of production. For the oil majors, this had to be one of the best deals since they walked into the Middle East and tied up its fabulous oil wealth for up to 99 years at a cost of next to nothing.

Yet for a time, there was a refusal in Ottawa to face up to the enormity of what had been done. Typical of the official attitude were 1964 remarks by resources minister Arthur Laing that the government role was "to assist in every way possible to search and explore for those minerals,"[38] and, concerning the high level of foreign ownership in the frontiers: "In a nation like Canada, with its fantastic expanse and enormously dispersed resources, it appears to me to be foolish to require risk capital to carry a passport."[39] It was only in 1970, after the Prudhoe Bay discovery, that the federal government revoked Oil and Gas Land Order No. 1-1961. This meant that it could now reclaim its right to the ownership and sale of Crown reserves. It also meant a freeze on new exploration permits, but since all but the most marginal land was already under permit, this was not so important. However, even these modest measures drew howls of outrage from the oil industry, which claimed a vested right to the additional land that would now become a Crown reserve.

The government then announced that it would redraft the regulations in consultation with the industry. Canadians were kept in the dark on the negotiations. The industry lobbied hard, however, and apparently succeeded in convincing officials that change should apply only to the marginal lands not yet under permit.[40] The oil executives seemed to be getting somewhere with the "evils of retroactivity" argument; companies would have the option to the remaining 50 per cent as they had had under the original regulations. Fortunately for Canadians, the oil industry continued to press for fatter concessions until the whole picture was changed by OPEC in 1973. In the following year, energy minister Donald Macdonald withdrew the government's proposals, which were never made public, and said that there would be a new round of drafting.

In any case, by this time about 90 per cent of the potential oil and gas acreage in the Canada Lands – 827 million acres out of 920 million, many of them picked up immediately after Prudhoe Bay – was under permit and thus subject to the old 1961 regulations. "In fact," Professor Thompson had pointed out, "the remaining acreage comprises the most marginal of the potential producing sediments, including large areas of Hudson Bay where exploration results have been disappointing, and offshore regions in water depths far beyond the limits of current technology."[41] As a senior Exxon executive has explained, the oil majors knew by the 1960s that from a strategic point of view they had to position themselves to deal with future shortages, and his company had "embarked on an expanding world exploration program. With the knowledge that this would be only a partial solution, we have concentrated on the offshore basins and the remote Arctic areas of the world where the possibility of great oil reserves still exists."[42] A similar outline was given by another Exxon executive as he listed what he called "Jersey's strengths" for the benefit of investment analysts: "Among our new prospects, Canada's Mackenzie Delta certainly deserves mention. Imperial has made significant discoveries in two separate areas and has stepped up its program of exploration to define its reserves."[43] Nor was the Exxon interest unique. Most major U.S. oil companies, in efforts to reassure Americans at the time of the mid-'70s oil crisis, made glowing reference to their holdings in Canada Lands.

It is not hard to see why the oil majors were anxious to secure strong positions in the four million square miles of the Canada Lands, perhaps the biggest unexplored region in the world, about half of it with oil and gas potential. Already in 1973, the Geological Survey of Canada had estimated potential recoverable oil reserves of 28 billion barrels in the far North and 50 billion barrels off Canada's east coast, as compared with remaining proved and potential recoverable reserves of 14.7 billion barrels in western Canada, and potential recoverable natural gas reserves of 342 trillion cubic feet in the far North and 326 trillion cubic feet off Canada's east coast, as against remaining proved and potential recoverable reserves of 95.4 trillion cubic feet in western Canada.[44] This large potential was confirmed in a special study for the U.S. Central Intelligence Agency, according to which the Canadian Arctic and offshore areas are among the most promising candidates for large future oil discoveries anywhere in the world.[45] In 1981, the federal energy department reported to Parliament that "in all of Canada Lands we expect to find about half of Canada's oil and two thirds of all of Canada's natural gas. Since exploration

began, we have discovered in Canada some 138 trillion cubic feet
of gas and 18 billion barrels of oil. We expect to find about the
same amount of oil as we have already found and about twice as
much gas."[46] While more than 100,000 wells had been drilled in
western Canada over the past 80 years or so, resulting in the discovery of 9,000 oil fields and 3,200 gas fields, only 1,100 wells had
been drilled in Canada Lands up to the end of 1980: "There are
hundreds of huge structures remaining to be tested and the expec-
tation is that some 85 per cent of Canada's undiscovered oil and
gas resources lie beneath the Canada Lands." The department
rated the three most promising areas of Canada Lands as the Mackenzie Delta-Beaufort Sea area, with potential recoverable resources of 112 trillion cubic feet of gas and 9.4 billion barrels of
oil, the east-coast offshore, with 72 trillion cubic feet of gas and
7.4 billion barrels of oil (although the department regards these
figures as conservative), and the Arctic islands, mainly the Sver-
drup Basin, with 87 trillion cubic feet of gas and 4.3 billion barrels
of oil. Not surprisingly, it is these areas that have been the most
heavily blanketed with exploration permits by the oil majors.

The department's 1973 energy policy review had foreseen coming high demand and a period of strong activity in exploration for
oil and gas, and added: "Most territory which is expected to yield
new oil and gas reserves is already under permit to firms doing exploration. If one examines the present distribution of these federal
and provincial permits and leases it can be determined that
Canadian-controlled firms only hold the rights to about 15 per
cent. Even though the areas where petroleum will ultimately be
discovered will establish the eventual degree of Canadian control,
it is obvious that unless significant changes occur at the production
lease stage, the degree of foreign control in the production area of
this industry can be expected to continue."[47] Though the oil majors held most of the land, however, they were slow to explore.
Mobil had obtained its Hibernia exploration permit in 1965, but
oil was not found until 1979, and it was found by Chevron Standard, working under a farm-in arrangement with an offshore drilling rig that was not being used elsewhere. Mobil itself spent only
$3 million on exploration until oil was found,[48] and had balked at a
1976 suggestion from Gulf, which had taken a part interest, that
another wildcat be drilled. In fact, Mobil seemed content to do the
minimal seismic work necessary to meet the work requirement of
its 12-year exploration permits. In 1977 Mobil and Gulf reduced
their holdings to six million acres, and Petro-Canada obtained 27
per cent of Hibernia under new back-in regulations. Mobil then

farmed out another 22 per cent to Chevron and 7 per cent to Gulf, reducing its stake to 28 per cent. Using the super-depletion tax incentive that paid most of the drilling costs, Chevron drilled the famous P-15 well that resulted in the Hibernia find. The Hibernia experience showed how, under the 1960-61 regulations, a company could tie up a potentially rich area because its foreign parent, in this instance Mobil Oil, had other priorities. The federal government was powerless to speed up activity except by offering tax write-offs by which the Canadian public paid more than 90 per cent of exploration costs. No other country had put itself in such a one-sided situation. As Petro-Canada chairman Bill Hopper pointed out in 1980, commenting on the east-coast "bargain basement" permits: "The multinational companies have accumulated excellent land positions on behalf of the shareholders, but have done precious little exploration on behalf of Canadians. And who can blame them? If you had a prospect in another country where the government is saying, 'Drill by the end of the year or lose your land,' and a prospect in Canada, complete with icebergs, where the government is saying, 'No problem, take 12 years and we'll still let you renew,' you know whose acreage is going to get drilled first."[49] If Canadians were to get the oil and Atlantic Canada the economic boost from greater drilling, land policies needed drastic change.

The first taste of change came in 1976 when energy minister Alastair Gillespie tabled a Green Paper on Canada Lands in the Commons.[50] Noting that most of the prospective areas for exploration were already held under permit, Gillespie said that "to institute meaningful changes in the existing system, it is necessary to amend substantially the terms and conditions of those permits, which currently contain commitments to lease and royalty conditions for periods exceeding 50 years."[51] The Green Paper abolished the 21-year leases and replaced them with provisional five-year leases for the entire permit area, which would be succeeded by production licences for ten-year renewable periods. There was to be a new progressive, incremental royalty, based on the profitability of each oil and gas field, and payable only after a company had recovered its investment, the 10-per-cent production royalty and income tax had been deducted, and an after-tax return of 25 per cent allowed. The Green Paper proposed much tougher work requirements and higher annual rentals on leases – $2.50 an acre instead of $1 – that could be offset against any exploration work done. Other changes included specific requirements for Canadian goods and services in the granting of special renewal permits and new exploration agreements. The government also planned to acquire new powers to order drilling and farm-outs on lands held under permit where it was dissatisfied with the pace of private industry exploration, and also to order production.

But what drew the hottest industry reaction was the decision to give Petro-Canada preferences and require 25-per-cent Canadian participation in all production leases. The new national oil and gas corporation would be allowed, for a one-year period, to take permits on areas not already taken up, and in addition, for a seven-year period, to acquire up to 25 per cent of any land surrendered to the Crown on the termination of permits or conversion to production. At the same time, when companies applied for special renewals on the expiry of their existing 12-year exploration permits, but only in areas where no discoveries had been made, Petro-Canada was to have the option of acquiring an interest of up to 25 per cent, depending on existing Canadian participation in the permit lands. For each percentage point of net Canadian equity below 25 per cent, Petro-Canada's interest could be increased by the same amount until it reached 25 per cent. If Canadian participation was 35 per cent or more, Petro-Canada would have no right to participate. At the same time, there was no requirement that Petro-Canada pay back a share of past exploration costs, mainly on the grounds that tax write-offs had financed almost all the cost of previous exploration. "There are really two motivations for these preferential provisions for Petro-Canada," according to Donald Crosby, the top Canada Lands official: "The primary motivation is, very simply, to enable Petro-Canada to achieve a catch-up position with the rest of the industry. Petro-Canada is a Johnny-come-lately in this field and the idea is to help it become a more or less equal partner with the other industry participants as soon as possible."[53] The other, he said, was "that of spurring oil and gas exploration." The federal government was clearly frustrated that oil and gas companies were sitting on vast acreages of Canada's potentially richest oil and gas lands and using the 1960-61 regulations to excuse a snail's-pace exploration effort; in return for its preference, Petro-Canada would have to meet the tougher work requirements of the new regulations. On the proposed right to require 25-per-cent participation for production licences, the energy minister told Parliament that "only about one third of existing permits are now held by parties or groups of parties having a level of Canadian ownership which would meet this requirement. This provision will help strengthen the Canadian presence in an industry at present more than 90-per-cent foreign-owned."[53]

The Petro-Canada provisions were widely attacked, in part because the industry did not want to see the Crown corporation become a strong presence. And industry executives worried about meeting the 25-per-cent Canadian participation requirement. Jack Armstrong, president of Imperial Oil, said that his company would have problems, with its Canadian ownership between 21 and 23 per cent.[54] Companies like Mobil, Chevron, and Amoco, of course, had none. The industry took the line that the government could not make retroactive changes. Having set out the terms and conditions for permits and leases in 1960-61, it had to live with them even if they did represent a massive resource give-away. At most, the oil giants might go along with changes in the rules for land no one had yet taken up, the land with the least promising potential. As Crosby pointed out, however, "although perhaps only a quarter of our continental margin is presently covered by permits, nevertheless this represents the bulk of the prospective area from the standpoint of technology as it exists today. Thus, if we are going to have a new regime, to make it meaningful there has to be retroactive legislation so as to be able to bring into line the terms and conditions of the contracts already covering extensive offshore areas."[55]

The changes in the Canada Oil and Gas Land Regulations unveiled in 1976 came into effect on 17 August 1977, and Gillespie announced at that time that the government would start processing lease applications and issuing new exploration rights on a selective basis. A new petroleum and gas bill was introduced in Parliament on 20 December 1977, but never passed. Nonetheless, the scene was set for the even stronger policies that were brought down on 28 October 1980 as part of the National Energy Program. By that time, there was a higher level of Canadian participation in Canada Lands, in large part because of the preferential position granted Petro-Canada in 1977 and also because the oil majors were surrendering the least promising areas to the Crown. Of 290 million acres held under exploration permits in the frontiers, 38 per cent of 110 million acres was held by Canadian-controlled companies, with Petro-Canada accounting for 60 per cent of the Canadian presence and Dome Petroleum for 15 per cent: other Canadian interests were marginal, and almost none were in the most immediately promising areas of Hibernia, Sable Island, and the Beaufort Sea. The main other Canadian presence was Panarctic Oils in the Arctic islands.

The new Canada Lands legislation of 1982 has brought in sweeping changes. These include the replacement of exploration permits by new exploration agreements which have to be negotiated by the government and the existing permit holders, and which have much stiffer work requirements, along with a 25-per-cent carried interest to be exercised by Petro-Canada or another designated Crown corporation. This will give Canadians a 25-per-cent stake in every oil and gas field found in the Canada Lands, with the carried interest being convertible to a working interest at any time before costly development spending begins. Other new requirements include at least 50-per-cent Canadian ownership of any production from Canada Lands; a requirement that companies seeking exploration and development rights ensure a high level of Canadian content, including industrial spin-offs, research and development, and the use of Canadian services in such areas as engineering and project management; and a reintroduction of the progressive incremental royalty first proposed in 1976 to be added on to the 10-per-cent basic royalty and based on the profitability of individual fields. Other changes allow the federal government to issue drilling and production orders and even to designate Petro-Canada as the operator of an exploration or development program where private companies are dragging their heels. The old leniency, as the NEP put it in 1980, "is no longer appropriate, especially in the context of Canada's energy security goals."[56] At the same time, the government said, in return for the 25-per-cent back-in for Petro-Canada or other Crown corporations, the Canadian public would not take a free ride. In the past, it had paid 90 per cent or more of drilling costs, even for 100-per-cent foreign-controlled companies: in future it would be paying up to 72 cents of every exploration dollar for foreign-controlled firms and up to 93 cents for firms at least 75-per-cent Canadian-owned and -controlled.

Some of the sharpest criticism of the new land system focused on its retroactive character and the fact that no compensation was offered for the 25-per-cent Crown back-in. The oil industry, with the federal Conservatives, argued the provisions should only apply to new land being released for exploration or land where no discovery had been made. This would have exempted all the principal areas where production was likely to begin during the 1980s and early 1990s – for example, Hibernia off Newfoundland, Sable Island off Nova Scotia, the Mackenzie Delta and Beaufort Sea, and the Arctic islands. However, while the retroactive back-in might be a last-ditch way of amending a clearly unacceptable situation, it was perfectly legal. "The Canadian constitution does not prohibit expropriation without compensation,"[57] a leading resources law expert pointed out. The government's action could be seen as being like a massive change in taxation or royalty rates.

On the compensation issue, energy minister Marc Lalonde argued initially that the 25-per-cent back-in for the Crown, and thus probably for Petro-Canada, represented a return to the long-suffering taxpayer: "For years now the Canadian taxpayer has been in fact paying the bulk of the oil and gas exploration expenditures made in the frontier regions. Some $4.5 billion to $5 billion has been spent to date in oil and gas development activities in the frontier regions. It is fair to say, and in fact I believe that it is conservative to say, that some $3 billion has been footed by the Canadian taxpayer. Indeed, not uncommonly more than 90 per cent of every exploration dollar has been covered through the contribution of the Canadian taxpayer. How then can anybody say that the 25-per-cent Crown share is 'expropriation without compensation'?"[58] He added that in future there would be a minimum 25-per-cent federal incentive grant, so the taxpayer would clearly be paying his way; and beyond the direct grant, "the income tax rules continue to provide substantial indirect subsidies. For many companies, the after-tax, after-grant cost of frontier exploration is greatly reduced as a result of the National Energy Program. Canadian companies will have a net exploration cost as low as seven cents on the dollar. For others, the cash cost of a dollar expended on Canadian Lands exploration will be no more than 28 cents."[59] The foreign-owned oil industry was still going to get remarkably generous treatment from the Canadian public. Under the new legislation, in spite of the 25-per-cent back-in, companies would retain access to all the land held under exploration permits. As Lalonde put it: "Under the current regime, holders of exploration rights are required to return to the Crown at least 50 per cent of their acreage which in certain cases could involve up to 30 per cent of their discoveries, prior to obtaining production rights. I do not understand the argument of those who say that the current regime's provisions for return of acreage does not in fact pose a burden for explorers. If this were so, why have explorers in several cases opted for special renewal permits on their entire acreage, thereby accepting a 25-per-cent Petro-Canada back-in? They did not choose to move directly to lease, yielding 50 per cent of their acreage but avoiding a Petro-Canada back-in. Under Bill C-48, holders of exploration rights will not face this dilemma. They will be allowed to retain production rights to the entire area of an oil or gas field." The loss of land was a much less significant problem than the industry, with its scare talk of confiscation and nationalization, made it seem. In Norway, the state oil company has a 50-per-cent carried interest and makes no contribution to exploration costs. In Canada as in Norway, the state would pay its share of the much costlier development stage in oil and gas fields.

According to Rowland Harrison, executive director of the Canadian Institute for Resources Law, it was "wrong to think of the 25-per-cent reservation provision as a confiscation of the investment. . . . It is a withdrawal of 25 per cent of the land area that might have previously been taken through permit to lease. . . . What it has done is change the terms and conditions of the system so now only 75 per cent of the land might proceed to production. In fact, in some situations under the previous system only 50 per cent or less would proceed to production."[60] In other words, Harrison testified before the Commons resources committee, "under the old system, in most cases, the lease would be a lease for 50 per cent of less of the total area so it seems to me to be wrong to say the he [the operator] had a lease of the whole area. What the permittee had under the former system was a right to explore the whole area and convert up to 50 per cent of that area to a lease and he did not know which area until the conversion point came. Instead of that, now what he has is the right to retain the whole area but subject to the 25-per-cent reservation." Nonetheless, Lalonde eventually offered the industry ex gratia payments consisting of 25 per cent of the geological, geophysical, and drilling expenditures made up to the end of 1980 for any oil or gas discovery declared as significant before the end of 1982. The government would pay 25 per cent of the qualifying expenditures, escalated at 15 per cent a year to reflect inflation to the end of 1980, out of the 25-per-cent Crown claim on future production. While it was easy to see the politics behind this concession – the result of intense pressure from Washington and London as well as the oil industry, Wall Street, and Bay Street – it was still painful and costly for the Canadian public.

The Progressive Incremental Royalty first bruited in 1976 and later brought in as part of the National Energy Program has the advantage of being based not on the physical value of production but on costs and profitability: it "provides for participation in 'surplus' profits on the very rich fields while it leaves the marginally economic pools untouched."[61] The federal energy department estimates that there are 25 to 30 major oil and gas fields in Canada Lands to which the profit-related royalty will apply, generating billions of dollars in future revenues.[62] Even though the new royalty system will mean extra money for the public treasury, however, it still leaves the industry in a highly favourable position: the effective exploration cost to companies in Canada Lands will range from seven to 20 cents of their own money for each dollar they invest, while through tax incentives 150 to 175 per cent of development costs will be recovered before a profit tax is levied. Moreover, companies are assured of a 25-per-cent rate of return on their depreciated investment, and still retain 60 per cent of the extra profits on more profitable fields. And given that the world price for oil will prevail in the frontier areas, profits should not be hard to make.

The requirement for 50-per-cent Canadian participation at the production stage, plus the availability of grants of up to 80 per cent of exploration costs and 20 per cent of development costs for Canadian-owned companies, should accelerate Canadian participation in the Canada Lands. In fact, this has already begun to happen. The stiffer work requirements could have the same effect. As *Business Week* has pointed out, they come as a blow to the multinationals: "These companies will have little choice but to farm out the lands to Canadian companies."[63] From the New York perspective of *Business Week*, this seemed to be a bad thing.

For all the physical difficulties posed by the Canada Lands environment, the future looks bright indeed. Though the cost of drilling exploration wells is much higher in the far North and the Atlantic offshore than it is in western Canada, the size of the probable find per well will also be much higher. According to one set of estimates from the Geological Survey, the average gas find per exploration well in the 1980s will be 1.6 billion cubic feet (bcf) of gas in western Canada, compared to 133 bcf per well in the east coast, 190 bcf per well in the Arctic islands, and 386.7 bcf per well in the Mackenzie Delta-Beaufort Sea area.[64] Similarly, the average oil find per exploration well in the 1980s will be 118,000 barrels in western Canada, 4 million barrels in the Arctic islands, 16 million barrels in the east coast, and 32 million barrels in the Mackenzie Delta-Beaufort Sea. Admittedly, the Canada Lands finds will in many instances require new technology and skills, and some of what is found will be too expensive to produce at today's world prices. Even so, however, the Geological Survey expects significant finds during the 1980s: in the Mackenzie Delta-Beaufort Sea area, 2.4 to 2.6 billion barrels of oil and 20 to 31 billion cubic feet of gas; and in the Arctic islands, 0.4 to 0.5 billion barrels of oil and 19 to 32 trillion cubic feet of gas.[65] The Survey's estimate of total potential recoverable reserves are: Mackenzie Delta-Beaufort Sea, 112 to 147 tcf of gas and 9.4 to 12.3 billion barrels of oil, Atlantic offshore, 72 to 125 tcf of gas and 7.4 to 13 billion barrels of oil, and in the Arctic islands, 87 to 138 tcf of gas and 4.3 to 7.6 billion barrels of oil. And in the words of D. F. Sherwin, a leading federal geologist, "if we are going to find giant fields in Canada, ones that are going to be produced relatively efficiently and at low cost and high productivity, then we must look in the frontier regions."[66] Under new legislation with strong Canadian participation requirements, Canadian companies will play an important role in this development.

It is a misfortune that provincial and federal land policies over the past thirty-five years turned Canada's richest oil and gas lands over to industry at low cost and on easy terms. The give-away simply set the stage for domination by the larger companies with the strongest financial resources. In Canada's case, this meant the foreign-controlled oil multinationals. Had the provinces and Ottawa pursued pro-Canadian land policies in the past, Canadians would have been spared the necessary cost of billions of dollars to buy their way back into their own inheritance.

Land Acreage Interests in Canada Lands

East-coast Offshore	
	Net Acres (millions)
Gulf	13.03
Shell Canada/Shell Explorer (U.S.)	12.56
Imperial	8.69
Mobil	7.90
BP	5.83
Texaco	4.82
Chevron Canada/Chevron Standard	4.66
Aquitaine of Canada	4.07
Total Eastcan/Total Petroleum (NA)	3.10
Suncor	2.25
AGIP Canada	2.23
Amoco	1.80
Amerada Minerals	1.58
Total foreign-controlled (84 per cent)	77.18
Petro-Canada	10.12
Dome Petroleum	1.74
Total Canadian-controlled (16 per cent)	14.94
(100 per cent)	92.12

West-coast Offshore	
Shell Canada/Shell Explorer (U.S.)	12.28
Chevron Standard	2.93
Union Oil	.11
Total foreign-controlled (97 per cent)	15.32
Total Canadian-controlled (3 per cent)	.44
Total (100 per cent)	15.76

170

Hudson Bay

Mobil	.50
Aquitaine of Canada	.21
Pan Ocean Oil (Canada)	.21
Petrofina	.04
Total foreign (23 per cent)	.96
Sogepet	1.88
Canadian Homestead Oils	.67
Teck Corp.	.67
Petro-Canada	.33
Total Canadian-controlled (77 per cent)	3.3
Total	4.26

Northwest Territories and Arctic Offshore

Aquitaine Canada	16.97
Suncor	14.00
Imperial	11.92
Gulf	6.38
Hudson's Bay Oil and Gas	5.29
Canadian Superior	4.03
Amoco	3.84
Phillips Petroleum	3.80
Texaco	3.25
Shell Canada/Shell Resources (U.S.)	3.44
Hunt Brothers	3.86
Magnorth Petroleum	2.41
Mobil	1.64
Butley Resources	1.21
Chevron Canada	1.1
Union Oil	1.07
Murphy Oil	1.04
BP Canada/BP Oil and Gas	.71
Total foreign-controlled (78 per cent)	184.18
Panarctic Oils	18.80
Dome Petroleum	14.31*
Petro-Canada	9.55
Westcoast Petroleum	1.33
Norcen	.94
Pan Canadian	.78
Total Canadian-controlled (22 per cent)	52
Total (100 per cent)	236.18

* Lands controlled under Fina but about 65-per-cent foreign-owned.

All Canada Lands

Total foreign-controlled (80 per cent)	277.64
Total Canadian-controlled (20 per cent)	70.68
Total (100 per cent)	348.32

Source: Department of Energy, Mines and Resources, 7 October 1980.

Oil and Gas Expenditures on Canada Lands – Estimated ($ millions)

Atlantic Offshore

Labrador Group	$250
BP et al.	$ 40
Petro-Canada (excluding share of Labrador Group)	$170
Chevron	$ 70
Shell et al.	$110
Amoco et al.	$120
Mobil et al.	$140
Texaco	$ 25
Esso	$ 50
Others	$100
Total	$1,075

Arctic Islands

Panarctic	$550
Others	$200
Total	$750

Mackenzie-Beaufort

Dome et al.	$900
Imperial	$300
Gulf et al.	$200
Shell	$150
Others	$100
Total	$165

Eastern Arctic Offshore

Imperial	$ 40
Aquitaine et al.	$ 60
Others	$ 50
Total	$150

Hudson Bay

Aquitaine et al.	$ 35
Others	$ 5
Total	$ 40

Pacific Offshore

Shell	$ 28
Others	$ 2
Total	$ 30

Grand Total:	$4,695

Source: Department of Energy, Mines and Resources, 1981.

172

Initial Oil in Place Discovered in Alberta in Exploratory Wells
(million cubic metres) 1946-1979

Imperial	638.1
Mobil	1,327.2
Gulf	253.7
Chevron	229.3
Texaco	320.5
Hudson Bay Oil and Gas	156.3
Shell	65.3
Amoco	9.7
Total above (61 per cent)	3,000.4
Total all companies (100 per cent)	4,916.4

Initial Gas in Place Discovered in Alberta in Exploratory Wells
(billion cubic metres) 1946-1979

Imperial	127.6
Mobil	222.0
Gulf	156.3
Chevron	131.3
Texaco	75.2
Hudson Bay Oil and Gas	244.8
Shell	302.4
Amoco	124.1
Total above (52 per cent)	1,383.7
Total all companies	2,670.0

Source: Russell S. Uhler. *Oil and Gas Drilling Activity and Success by Selected Companies in Alberta.* Calgary, Energy Resources Conservation Board, 1980.

Notes

1. Quoted in J. S. Ewing, unpublished history of Imperial Oil. Imperial Oil archives.
2. For a discussion of Alberta and Saskatchewan land policies in the 1940s and 1950s, see John Richards and Larry Pratt, *Prairie Capitalism.* Toronto, McClelland and Stewart, 1980.
3. Michael Crommelin. "Government Management of Oil and Gas in Alberta." *Alberta Law Review*, XIII.
4. Quoted in James H. Gray, *Troublemaker!* Toronto, Macmillan, 1978.
5. Crommelin, "Government Management."
6. Michael Crommelin, Peter H. Pearse and Anthony Scott. "Management of Oil and Gas Resources in Alberta: An Economic Evaluation of Public Policy." Vancouver, University of British Columbia, Department of Economics Discussion Paper No. 76-19, June 1976.
7. Crommelin, "Government Management."
8. Quoted in Crommelin, "Government Management," from Dasher, "Effect of the National Oil Policy on the Ontario Refining Industry." Montreal, unpublished thesis for McGill University, 1968.

9. Milton Moore, University of British Columbia, to the Canadian Arctic Resources Committee Conference, Ottawa, 23 March 1973.

10. Frank Roseman and Bruce Wilkinson. "Who Benefits? The Alberta Energy Price Increases." *Canadian Forum*, June-July 1973.

11. Alberta Legislature Debates, 17 April 1972.

12. Government of Alberta. Position Paper: "Tentative Natural Resources Plan for the Government of Alberta." Edmonton 1972.

13. Alberta Department of Energy and Natural Resources. "Summary of Alberta Legislation: Petroleum and Natural Gas." Edmonton, 31 December 1977.

14. B. Sufrin. Economic Advisory and Planning Board, Government of Saskatchewan. "Report on Fuel Policy." Regina, November 1949.

15. Saskatchewan Department of Natural Resources. "The Natural Resources of Saskatchewan." Foreword by the Hon. J. L. Phelps. Regina 1945. Quoted by Sufrin.

16. Sufrin, "Report on Fuel Policy."

17. Sufrin, "Report on Fuel Policy."

18. Quoted in Richards and Pratt, *Prairie Capitalism*.

19. Saskatchewan Department of Natural Resources. Mines Branch report. Regina 1949.

20. "Interim Report of the Oil Policy Committee on Government Policy for the Development of Crown Reserves." Regina, June 1953.

21. Quoted in Richards and Pratt, *Prairie Capitalism*.

22. Quoted in *Canadian Annual Review 1965*. Toronto, University of Toronto Press, 1966.

23. Allan Blakeney, Premier of Saskatchewan, to the Saskatchewan Division, Canadian Petroleum Association, Regina, 11 January 1973.

24. Royal Commission on Canada's Economic Prospects. Final Report. Ottawa 1957.

25. John Davis. *Canadian Energy Prospects*. Royal Commission on Canada's Economic Prospects. Ottawa 1957.

26. *Oilweek*, 8 October 1962.

27. *Oilweek*, 19 February 1973.

28. Production data from *Oil and Gas Journal*, 29 December 1980.

29. *Oilweek*, 23 February 1970.

30. *Oilweek*, various editions.

31. *Canadian Annual Review 1961*. Toronto, University of Toronto Press, 1962.

32. Andrew Thompson, University of Alberta, to the House of Commons Committee on Indian Affairs and Northern Development, 6 December 1968.

33. Department of Finance. "A Northern Gas Pipeline – Evaluation of the Impact on the National Economy." Ottawa 1972.

34. Andrew Thompson and Michael Crommelin. "Canada's Petroleum Leasing Policy, A Cornucopia for Whom?" Ottawa, Canadian Arctic Resources Committee, 22 March 1973.

35. *Business Week*, 13 October 1980.

36. Thompson and Crommelin, "Canada's Petroleum Leasing Policy."

37. Thompson and Crommelin, "Canada's Petroleum Leasing Policy."

38. *Canadian Annual Review 1964*. Toronto, University of Toronto Press, 1965.

39. *Canadian Annual Review 1964*.

40. *Oilweek*, 9 October 1972.
41. Thompson and Crommelin, "Canada's Petroleum Leasing Policy."
42. T. D. Barrow, senior vice-president and director, Exxon Corp. to the Esso Research Club, Watchung, N.J., 17 January 1973.
43. G. T. Piercy, senior vice-president and director, Exxon Inc., to the Boston Security Analysts Society, 24 April 1972.
44. Department of Energy, Mines and Resources. *An Energy Policy for Canada - Phase 1.* Ottawa 1973.
45. Richard Nehrins. *Giant Oil Fields and World Oil Resources, A Study for the Economic Research Office of the Central Intelligence Agency.* San Francisco, Rand Corporation, 1978.
46. D. F. Sherwin, Department of Energy, Mines and Resources, to the House of Commons Committee on National Resources and Public Works, Ottawa, 10 February 1981.
47. *An Energy Policy for Canada - Phase I.*
48. "Mobil's Successful Exploration." *Business Week,* 13 October 1980.
49. W. H. Hopper to the Atlantic Provinces Economic Council, 29 Sept. 1980.
50. Department of Energy, Mines and Resources. "Statement of Policy: Proposed Petroleum and Natural Gas Act and New Canada Oil and Gas Land Regulations." Ottawa, May 1976.
51. Alastair Gillespie, Minister of Energy, Mines and Resources. "Notes for a Statement on tabling Statement of Policy: Proposed Petroleum and Natural Gas Act and New Canada Oil and Gas Land Regulations." Ottawa, 19 May 1976.
52. Donald Crosby, director, Resource Management and Conservation Branch, Department of Energy, Mines and Resources, at Dalhousie University, Halifax, 24-26 February 1977.
53. Gillespie, "Notes for a Statement."
54. *Globe and Mail*, 5 June 1976.
55. Crosby, Dalhousie speech.
56. Department of Energy, Mines and Resources. *National Energy Program.* Ottawa 1980.
57. Rowland Harrison, executive director, Canadian Institute for Resources Law. "The Legal Character of Petroleum Licences." *Canadian Bar Review*, 1980.
58. Marc Lalonde, Minister of Energy, Mines and Resources, to the House of Commons Committee on National Resources and Public Works, 20 January 1981.
59. Marc Lalonde to the House of Commons Committee on National Resources and Public Works, 14 May 1981.
60. Rowland Harrison, executive director, Canadian Institute for Resources Law, to the House of Commons Committee on National Resources and Public Works, Ottawa, 5 February 1981.
61. Submission of Dr. T. S. Tuschak, Department of Energy, Mines and Resources, to the House of Commons Committee on National Resources and Public Works, Ottawa, 10 February 1981.
62. Tuschak submission.
63. *Business Week,* 16 March 1981.
64. R. M. Procter, P. J. Lee, and D. N. Skibo. "Canada's Conventional Oil and Gas Resources." Calgary, Geological Survey of Canada, 1981.
65. Procter et al., "Canada's Conventional Oil and Gas Resources."
66. Sherwin to the Commons resources committee.

Chapter 6

The Write-off Game

The American, British, and European investors who own and control so much of Canada's oil and gas industry have good reason to be grateful to the Canadian people. It is unlikely, in fact, that any other major nation has ever operated a tax system so helpful to corporations from other countries. And tax systems are factors of critical importance in the growth of businesses, especially when they eliminate much of the risk. The fewer of its own dollars a company has to put up out of profits, new sales of shares, or increases in long-term debt, and the more it can recycle by taking advantage of tax measures that eliminate or defer taxes on corporate income, the better its chances of making money. For the gas and oil industry in Canada, these measures have included the accelerated write-off of exploration and, until 1974, development expenses, so-called depletion allowances, accelerated depreciation, investment credits, and automatic and other write-offs. The generosity of Canada's tax system has enabled the oil and gas industry to rely much less on borrowed money or the sale of ownership in the form of shares to finance its growth than has been the case for the corporate world as a whole. In the early 1970s, for example, close to 85 per cent of the oil and gas industry's funds were generated from profits and tax benefits. Most industries are fortunate indeed if they can find half their spending money in this way. Moreover, because they owned the majority of the producing oil and gas fields, and thus the biggest share of operating income, the subsidiaries of the multinationals have been able to squeeze much more of their spending power from these profits and tax incentives than the Canadian-controlled companies have.

This has been demonstrated in dramatic form with data collected by the Petroleum Monitoring Agency, the new federal watchdog body that has been playing a vital role in tracking the financial and investment performance of the oil and gas business.

In the two years 1979-80, foreign-controlled firms raised 73 per cent of their funds from profits and tax benefits, while Canadian-controlled companies raised only 44 per cent of their money from these sources and had to borrow heavily at rising interest rates to stay in the game. Thus the subsidiaries needed to raise only 27 per cent of their money through loans or selling ownership through shares; the figure for the Canadian-controlled sector was 56 per cent. And of the internal cash flow generated in those years, tax policy provided 39 per cent of the total for the foreign-controlled group and only 26 per cent for the Canadians.[1] Similarly, in the years 1971-79, internally generated money accounted for up to 90 per cent of the total sum available to the major foreign-controlled oil companies, as compared with a peak percentage of 60 for the larger Canadian-controlled firms.[2] Especially in a time of high interest rates and weak stock markets, companies with strong internal cash flow have a decided edge on the ones that have to depend on debt and equity markets.

Another way of judging the importance of tax provisions is to see how they reduce the cost to an oil company of making a capital expenditure or acquisition. In Canada's case, tax provisions not only slashed real costs in this area, but have also had the effect of making after-tax costs generally cheaper for foreign-controlled concerns. This is because tax incentives can be used only by companies that are earning profits and therefore paying current tax. Smaller Canadian firms have not had enough taxable income against which to write off expenditures. Until the arrival of the National Energy Program in 1980, a company that was in a position to take full advantage of Canadian tax incentives, for every dollar of investment, needed to spend only 37 cents of its own money on exploration, 46 cents on development, 48 cents on tar sands projects, 41 cents on enhanced recovery, and a minimal 6 cents on the costs of Canada Lands wells over $5 million. The figures for a Canadian-owned concern having to wait to write its spending off against future profits, according to the federal energy department,[3] ran to 60 cents and higher – even above the average for manufacturing in Canada of 55 cents for every invested dollar. These differences in after-tax costs for the same dollar of investment meant that in bidding for land, in takeovers, and in contemplating risky new ventures, a foreign-controlled company enjoyed a clear advantage over most Canadian-controlled ones. It could afford to bid high and think big, courtesy of the Canadian taxpayer.

The important role of the tax system in financing its growth explains why the oil and gas industry has been able to boast that it reinvests more than it earns. The giants have used this fact repeatedly to make Canadians think that they were doing something unusual, sacrificing dividends and pouring fresh capital into the country's drive to achieve energy self-sufficiency. However, such boasts are extremely misleading. According to the Petroleum Monitoring Agency, the foreign-controlled integrated oil companies and foreign-controlled senior producers had after-tax net income or profits in 1980 of $3.2 billion, and spent $4.8 billion on exploration and development and other capital investments. But this does not mean that the companies had to borrow the rest, or give up paying dividends. For when tax benefits were combined with profits, these companies had a $6.4-billion cash flow, and reinvested just 76 per cent of the funds available to them. They were still able to pay 1980 dividends of $652 million or 20 per cent of profits, chiefly to corporate and individual shareholders outside Canada, as well as repatriate $92 million in capital and increase their working capital in this country by about $2 billion.[4]

Why have Canadians been willing to accept such a generous tax system for so long, a system that in 1979 left the oil and gas industry with a 19-per-cent net return as compared with only 12 per cent for the rest of the private sector? To a large extent, Canada's politicians and government officials have been intimidated by the industry's arguments, restricted in their options because they have believed that only the big international companies had the knowledge and money to develop the country's reserves. In governments lacking the expertise to cross-question oil executives and anxious to see as much growth as soon as possible, the dispensing of tax favours has rarely been questioned. Any feature of the tax system that eroded their competitive advantage, moreover, has come under bitter attack by the giants. For example, the favourable treatment of co-operatives in Canadian tax law was strongly opposed by companies like Imperial when the western Consumers' Co-op Refineries moved into the field in the 1930s. Imperial executives working in Ottawa during World War II lobbied hard and successfully for a reduction in tax benefits to co-operatives, but the company was still complaining in the 1960s that the government had not gone far enough.

It was only after the fourfold OPEC hike of 1973, as the price Canadians were paying began to rise sharply, that concern really emerged about the inadequate taxation of the oil and gas industry. Without a tax change, the industry seemed likely to capture tens of billions of dollars in windfall profits. It became a matter of some urgency for governments to ensure that the companies gave up at

least a part of this bonanza. And the high level of foreign ownership made it even more imperative. According to University of
Alberta economist Bruce Wilkinson, 86 per cent of the haul would
leave the country.[5] By the late 1970s and early '80s, the debate had
shifted to focus on maximizing public revenue from the industry,
and eliminating the bias in the tax system in favour of the multinationals and against the much smaller Canadian-controlled companies. An esoteric term – economic rent – entered the country's
political vocabulary. It is what the economist uses to describe excess profit in an enterprise – in the case of oil and gas, the return
beyond what is necessary to find and produce the fuel and give investors enough profit to keep them interested. The goal of tax
policy became to capture as much as possible of this economic rent
for Canadians. Thus, the period from the late 1960s to the early
'80s saw a radical shift in tax policy as far as oil and gas were
concerned. The industry found itself unable to defend its privileged tax position, although it did not suffer a total loss, while
government, for the first time, was putting the public interest
ahead of the industry's interest. From now on the industry's position would be roughly similar to its position in other countries of
the world, and it would have to operate like any other industry,
selling shares or borrowing money through bank loans and corporate bond issues. Gone, it was hoped, were the days when, as
happened in 1978, a huge corporation like Shell Canada could
earn $230 million in profits and pay nothing in corporate income
tax on a consolidated basis.

One way of seeing how the tax system could be used to reduce an
oil or gas company's effective tax rate in pre-NEP days is to trace
what happened to a typical barrel of oil under different company
investment strategies. The Alberta wellhead price of our barrel of
oil is $20. Deducting the 40-per-cent provincial royalty plus $2 in
operating costs, we are left with $10 as the pre-tax money available
to the companies. The first outfit, Company A, follows a no-rein-
vestment policy. Like the others, it is liable for federal and provincial corporate taxes on its $18 of net operating revenues, the price
of the barrel minus its costs. It deducts 25 per cent of $18, or $4.50,
as its federal resource allowance, leaving $13.50 that is subject to
the 36-per-cent federal tax rate. There is now $5.14 left of the
original $10 available before taxes. However, it must also pay a
provincial corporate tax on its pre-tax $10. Assuming that A is an
Alberta company paying at 11 per cent, a further $1.10 comes off,
leaving A with $4.04 and an effective tax rate of 59.6 per cent.

Company B decides to take full advantage of the generous write-offs in the tax system and reinvests every penny of its pre-tax $10 in exploration. Such spending qualifies for a 100-per-cent write-off plus an earned depletion, automatic before 1972, of one third; B can deduct 133 per cent of its exploration spending, or $13.30. Like A, it qualifies for the federal resource allowance of 25 per cent of its net operating profit of $18, or $4.50, which has already reduced its potential taxable income to $13.50. From this, B proceeds to deduct the $13.30, leaving just 20 cents subject to federal tax. It owes Ottawa 7 cents. There is no Alberta corporate income tax to be paid since the deduction of the $8 Alberta royalty, $2 for costs, and the $13.30 for reinvestment adds up to $23.30, more than the price of the barrel of oil. Company B has been able to reduce its effective tax rate to .07 per cent. And by spending the $10 on exploration, the company could get back $5.89 through write-offs.

Company C has a different strategy again. Of the $10 in potential cash from the $20 barrel of oil, it decides to reinvest $6, spending half of this exploring for new oil and half developing an already discovered field. The 133-per-cent write-off applies, then, to $3. Of the $3 spent for development, 30 per cent could be written off as declining balance in the first year for a tax deduction of 90 cents, so C's write-off comes to a total of $4.90. Now C goes back to its $18 in net operating income and lops off the 25-per-cent resource allowance, leaving $13.50, from which the $4.90 is taken away before it calculates its federal tax: at 36 per cent of the remaining $8.60, this comes to $3.10, and C has $6.90. Alberta corporate income tax comes to 56 cents, for a total corporate income tax liability of $3.66 at an effective tax rate of 36.7 per cent. Of the $6 C put into exploration and development, $2.30 came from tax incentives. The total government take from the three companies, including provincial royalties, was $13.96 for A, or 78 per cent of its $18 net operating income from our barrel, reduced to $8.07 or 45 per cent for B because of exploration spending, and a median figure for Company C of $11.66, or 65 per cent.

The financing of exploration provides one example of how tax incentives reduced costs for oil and gas companies. Here is how the pre-NEP tax system cut company costs for a $1-million exploration effort. The full tax saving on earned depletion of one third of its $1 million of exploration spending, or $333,333, is deducted along with its immediate tax write-off of 100 per cent of its exploration spending, for total tax write-offs of $1.3 million. If the company is taxed at the 50-per-cent corporate rate, its taxes are reduced by $665,000. The after-tax cost to the company of $1 million of exploration spending is $335,000.

The Syncrude tar sands project can also be used to show how the game was played. Assuming, for the sake of simplicity, that it was built in one year, all the companies benefited the same way, and all the spending was subject to the most favourable capital cost allowance, here is how the tax system reduced the cost to the investor. The total bill for Syncrude was $2.2 billion. From this, a 7.5-per-cent investment tax credit of $165 million was deducted immediately, leaving $2,035 million. Capital cost allowance, which is 30 per cent of capital costs, assuming a 50-per-cent tax rate, meant a further reduction of $305 million, to $1,730 million. From this would be deducted the full tax saving on earned depletion allowance of 33.3 per cent, or $678.3 million. If this was taxed at 50 per cent, we can deduct $339 million, for a remaining cost of $1,391 million. But the company still had $1,424.5 million in capital cost allowance to be claimed in future years. To give this a present value, suppose we cut it in half to discount inflation. Taxed at 50 per cent, the $712.25 million was worth another $356 million. The actual project cost to the companies was $1,035 million; the cost to the Canadian taxpayer has been $1,165 million. Thus, 47 cents of each investment dollar came from the companies' own money, compared to 53 cents from tax incentives. And our example does not include research and development and other write-offs available to the companies; nor has it taken into account $300 million spent for a power plant, $100 million paid for a pipeline, and another $100 million for housing. After the federal, Alberta, and Ontario governments became partners, the private-sector share of the whole project was to be $1.54 billion; tax write-offs reduced that by a significant amount. In fact, when all the dust had settled, governments had come up with $660 million in investment capital, close to $700 million in tax write-offs, a $300-million power plant, a $100-million pipeline, $100 million for housing, and $200 million in loans to the oil companies, for a total of over $2 billion. And the massive public spending for associated research and infrastructure, manpower training and other social costs, is piled on top of this. Moreover Syncrude was set up as a flow-through joint venture that would never have taxable profits. The companies in Syncrude paid all its bills and received a share of production according to the percentage they owned. This meant that write-offs from other investments could be made against the future profits earned in each company on its Syncrude oil. And in addition, Alberta royalties on Syncrude production can be deducted in computing federal taxes, which is not the case with conventional oil and gas. While federal taxpayers had made a substantial contribution through the tax system to Syncrude's success, it was hard to see how they would ever reap their fair share of the benefits.

While Canada's willingness to grant special tax treatment to the oil and gas industry dates back to 1916, the year of the first depletion allowance, it was during the emergency years of World War II that the groundwork was laid for the system which prevailed until 1980. The fast write-off of exploration and development costs and the automatic one-third depletion allowance became a permanent part of the tax system in the 1949 budget. Right from the outset, the system was especially advantageous for big integrated oil companies, which could claim their exploration and development write-offs and depletion allowances against refining and marketing profits the small producers did not have. At the same time, two postwar moves by the United States increased the existing bias in that country's tax laws in favour of foreign oil and gas exploration and development, according to a research paper produced in 1956 for the Royal Commission on Canada's Economic Prospects.[6] First, the United States dropped its wartime excess profits tax at the end of 1945, two years before Canada did. This swelled the cash flow and retained earnings of U.S. corporations significantly, giving them funds to invest elsewhere. Secondly, at the time of the Korean War, the U.S. reintroduced an excess profits tax which was in force from 1950 to the end of 1953. U.S. companies were encouraged to invest abroad, spending what were in effect only 18-cent dollars, and any losses in exploration and development could be written off against profits made at home. The study found that in comparable circumstances, allowable depletion for U.S. tax purposes would amount to $3.7 million, while Canadian depletion allowances for an integrated oil major would be $1.8 million, and only $1.5 million for an independent exploration and production company. Defending the preferences planned for his new Crown corporation in 1977, Petro-Canada chairman Maurice Strong noted that most of the complaints came from foreign-controlled companies whose dominant position had been greatly facilitated by the fact that many of them could write costs of exploration in Canada off against their United States income. He stressed the foreign exploration write-off as having been "a special advantage not available to Canadians. It is certainly not one for which foreign companies should be blamed, but the advantages they gained over Canadian companies during a crucial period in the development of Canada's industry were far more important than any special advantage the government is considering now for Petro-Canada and to some extent for other Canadian companies in the proposed new federal land regulations."[7]

In the United States, oil companies could take their one-third automatic depletion before deducting exploration and other costs, whereas in Canada the one-third depletion allowance was taken after exploration costs had been deducted. Imperial Oil argued that Canadian tax law should be made the same as the U.S. law to equalize the situation. "In addition to this feature," the company told the Gordon Commission in 1955, "a United States oil operator may carry on business in Canada and, during the earlier stages of development (which could last for a considerable time) by a combination of U.S. and Canadian income tax laws as presently framed, obtain a definite tax advantage over the Canadian operators, whereby the U.S. company would have more dollars available for further investment than would a similar Canadian company."[8]

Even the left-wing CCF government in Saskatchewan campaigned in favour of greater concessions to the industry. In 1956 the Saskatchewan Department of Mineral Resources issued a pamphlet, written by a Toronto tax lawyer, that pushed for additional tax incentives. The minister, J. H. Brocklebank, proclaimed in his introduction that "as Canadians, we could not but wish that Canadian capital took a larger part of the development of our mineral resources," and went on to identify the main reason why Canadians were hanging back on investing in oil and gas as the fact that "foreign investment in Saskatchewan has been stimulated at the outset by tax policies, the counterpart of which we do not have in Canada . . . the Canadian individual and the Canadian company are denied the opportunity to compete on equal terms with foreign counterparts."[9] The publication urged that individuals, acting alone or in partnership or syndicate, be allowed to deduct up to $25,000 a year in oil and gas exploration costs, including land acquisitions, against all other forms of income, that mining companies and syndicates be allowed to offset oil drilling and other expenses against mining income, and that the price of oil and gas exploration rights be fully deductible for tax purposes.

In its 1957 final report, the Gordon Commission agreed that American corporations had a definite edge: "To this extent the United States government may be said to be encouraging a worldwide search for oil by United States citizens and United States oil companies . . . as a result of which great discoveries have been made and great developments have occurred in many parts of the world, including Canada, which otherwise would not have happened or, at least, would not have happened nearly so quickly."[10] This did not mean, however, that Canadian tax policy had to become equally generous: "While we have a vital interest in the development of the oil and gas industry in this country, we have a vital interest in the development of many other industries as well. It would be an unwise practice for Canada to start favouring one industry over others through tax concessions merely because this is being done in the United States for reasons which, in that country, may be perfectly valid.'' The commission's counter-proposal was for special concessions for oil and gas companies with Canadian shareholders, coupled with the recommendation, also received in complete silence, that governments redesign their land policies to make an assured place for Canadian participation.

The majors' lobby continued successful. Even the Cold War was used to justify greater tax incentives. In 1960, for example, Imperial's president raised the spectre of a threatening Soviet Union overtaking the West: "We must ask whether Russia handicaps its industry with the formidable list of non-engineering and non-commercial obstacles which face Western enterprise. We know, for example, that the Russians are not prejudiced against the size of farming units. It seems that, for the time being at least, Russian industry enjoys greater incentives than does industry in the West. One is reminded of the remark of Dr. Wernher von Braun that, as a scientist, he experienced no lack of freedom under Nazi rule."[11] Heavy taxation was one of the ways in which initiative had been deadened in Canada by contrast to the rapid progress and enterprise of the Soviets. The oil industry, in particular, was heavily taxed, the company president claimed. "In the mid-twentieth century, hostility to profits and capital is out of step. Mr. Khrushchev himself has said that he is out to beat the Western world on an economic basis. Today, it is more clear than ever that the only way one economy can outstrip another is in the generation and productive use of capital."

Later, the U.S.-controlled giants even tried to argue that, since American taxpayers had helped develop Canada's oil industry, the U.S. should continue to get a bargain on our oil. As Canadian trade expert Rodney de C. Grey has explained it: "There is a view in Washington that the Canadian oil and gas industry was in a sense created by U.S. financial resources and that this situation should give rise to certain rights. This outlook, in fact, has been expressed by experienced senior U.S. officials."[12] In 1973, the Nixon administration put pressure on the oil majors to have their subsidiaries lobby against Ottawa's plan to charge Americans the world price by means of an oil export tax. In November of that year, Canadian Petroleum Association president John Poyen accused Ottawa of taking "undue advantage" of the U.S. need for oil imports, calling the plan "deplorable" and predicting "some retaliatory action from the United States."[13] Later that year, the CPA president was still siding with Americans who thought they should pay less for oil from Canada than they did for purchases from other countries: "I am very concerned that the United States may take massive retaliatory action against Canada because they are pushed to the brink of retaliation, and I don't blame them."[14]

Further changes made in the Income Tax Act in 1962 allowed an oil or gas company to deduct land acquisition costs fully and immediately. This measure clearly favoured the multinationals with the big profits against which to claim write-offs. The same year, however, also saw the establishment of the Royal Commission on Taxation, under the chairmanship of Kenneth Carter, that would subject the concessions to tough economic analysis and ultimately make a finding that they had little justification, economic or social. In its report,[15] the Carter Commission rehearsed the five key arguments that were used to justify special tax treatment for the oil and gas industry. The first was an argument for accounting neutrality: in determining taxable income, all the costs of producing that income should be deductible at some point. The oil and gas industry held that because of the uncertainty about when it would get the return on its investment, it should be allowed to deduct its costs as rapidly as possible through early write-offs that would put it on a footing with other industries. It also used the old argument of risk. The Carter Commission's reaction to this was that "the probability of loss on a single exploratory venture is very high indeed. Whether the probability of loss from such an isolated venture is greater than the probability of loss from a single research experiment by a manufacturing firm, say, in the chemicals or electronics industry, is a moot point." Moreover, most oil and gas companies minimized their risk by spreading their exploration dollars among different areas, frequently in joint projects in which many companies had partial interests. "The greater the diversification, the more stable and predictable the percentage of successful ventures," the commission held: "To focus attention on the undeniably high risk attached to a particular exploratory venture grossly overstates the degree of risk" from investments in the oil and gas industry relative to other industries, especially when exploration costs could be written off by the big companies against production income.

The oil and gas industry contended further that the capital market was biased against risk taking. The Carter Commission was unable to find proof, however, that financial markets were demanding a risk premium for oil and gas investments. The oil majors seemed to be able to raise capital at the rates paid by other big industries: financing problems were more likely to occur for smaller, Canadian-controlled companies that lacked production income for the write-off game and could not spread their risk around. New tax concessions across the board would be an inefficient way of solving this situation, since most of the benefits would be wasted on the majors. (Since the early 1970s, in fact, the financial markets have had an insatiable appetite for oil and gas securities.) The multinationals also held that the tax system discriminated against the oil and gas industry because it was heavily dependent on equity capital and therefore had to raise prices, or else reduce investment, if it was to maintain after-tax rates of return comparable to those in other industries. To this, the Carter Commission retorted that other countries imposed corporate income taxes on oil and gas production, and that other industries in Canada were more capital-intensive than oil and gas and just as heavily dependent on equity financing. Moreover, "it would be inconceivable to grant tax concessions to all corporations that are unable to shift the corporation tax through short-run price increases."

Finally, industry spokesmen had told the commission that increased investment in oil and gas generated social and economic benefits, and for this reason should be encouraged. The withdrawal of tax concessions would mean less foreign direct investment and an emigration of Canadian capital. Among the benefits alleged were jobs, the maintenance of Canada's resources base and Canada's position as an important resource nation, exports, self-sufficiency, the attraction of outside money, stimulus for industrial development because of assured energy supplies, regional prosperity, and encouragement of Canadian ownership in oil and gas.

Most of these claims were rejected by the commission. Its report suggested that there were better ways to deal with unemployment, if there was a problem, than through tax concessions to big business. The key question when it came to maintaining a resource base was whether the additional cost was warranted as against other uses to which the labour and capital could have been part. Carter noted that oil and gas reserves were already adequate, and that oil production in Alberta was running at less than 50 per cent of capacity. In addition, the report questioned the benefit to Canada of giving tax concessions by preference to industries that export: "Canadians should specialize in producing the goods and services in which they have a comparative advantage and not necessarily the goods that have displaced imports in the past." Special subsidies through the tax system would divert skills and capital from doing other things, and therefore fewer other things would be produced. Canadians could end up much worse off for having given excessive incentives to an industry such as oil and gas.

On the issue of foreign investment, the Carter Commission flatly rejected the argument that because the United States offered substantial tax concessions to the oil and gas companies, Canada should offer similar incentives to attract foreign investment. For one thing, "a substantial proportion of foreign direct investment in Canada is probably related to considerations other than the after-tax rate of return to parent corporations. The security of sources of supply, investment in a politically stable country near the United States market, and the maintenance of a share of the market are clearly significant factors in the decision to invest in Canada." Since tax concessions were not a major factor in oil and gas investment in Canada, even bigger ones would only have the effect of shifting more of the tax burden for public services to other Canadian businesses and individuals. When it came to attracting outside money, "aside from instances where assured foreign markets or specialized foreign technology are involved, Canada can and should adopt general policies to control the inflow of foreign capital and should eschew industry concessions that could substantially reduce the net benefits from such foreign investments." The commission also rejected the view that reduced incentives would encourage Canadians to shift oil and gas investments to other countries, citing other, non-tax considerations.

The Carter Commission rejected the claim that the major integrated international oil companies still had a special advantage in Canada stemming from U.S. tax law, one frequently heard from by companies seeking additional concessions. It did agree that making the depletion allowance more generous would help some Canadian-controlled oil and gas companies. By the same stroke, however, Canadian tax concessions would be increased for U.S. subsidiaries here, and the result would be less tax paid in Canada and more paid in the United States. In the event that public encouragement of oil and gas exploration was needed, it should take the form of subsidies or grants rather than tax concessions: the cost of subsidies is out in the open for the public to see, and can be more efficient than tax concessions. (This Carter suggestion was eventually taken up in with the NEP's Petroleum Incentives Program of direct exploration grants.) Of all the tax concessions available to the oil industry, the Carter Commission found, depletion was the costliest and least efficient. It benefited only a few big companies with established incomes: in 1964, for example, three oil companies and five mining companies accounted for 85 per cent of the $150 million of depletion claimed by such companies for that year. What the depletion allowance did was give the oil and gas industry an automatic exemption: "In general, this provision can be said to reduce the effective rate of corporate tax by one third." The depletion allowance bore no relation to the cost of finding the oil and gas, but was based on whatever the oil and gas could be sold for. Nor was it a replacement for depreciation: companies could write off their investments in exploration, development, and production through other generous tax provisions. Abandoning depletion allowances would enable the government to cut taxes across the board for all businesses.

Having demolished oil and gas industry arguments for special treatment, the Carter Commission concluded that it should be taxed just as other industries were. The prospecting and exploration costs of an oil company were similar to the research and development costs of a manufacturer and should be eligible for the 100-per-cent immediate write-off, a provision that should be left unchanged. Development drilling and other development costs to bring oil and gas fields to the production stage were similar to the manufacturer's inventory costs, and should be subject to a 20- to 30-per-cent capital cost allowance to be written off over a period of years, rather than immediately, as was then the case. Property or land rights were similar to the patents, copyrights, and brand-name goodwill of manufacturers and should be written off over time as a percentage of revenues rather than immediately, as had been possible since 1962. The result would be to raise the cash flow of the independents with modest production income by 5 to 10 per cent. The oil majors would be the hardest hit, a fact that no doubt explained their strong reaction to the Carter Report, as well as their intensive and eventually successful campaign to ensure that its main proposals were not adopted. It was also true that foreign shareholders in Canadian oil and gas companies would not be as well off – and the major shareholders were companies such as Exxon, Gulf, Shell, Texaco, Standard Oil of California, Mobil, Standard Oil of Indiana, British Petroleum, and Phillips. "This is an unfortunate but inescapable result of removing an inefficient concession," Carter concluded: "Unless we are willing to accept the existing tax system as immutable, we must also accept undesired windfall gains and losses. They are the inescapable concomitants of change."

Ottawa's initial response to all this came with its 1970 White Paper, "Proposals for Tax Reform," issued by finance minister Edgar Benson. While the proposals would have meant some loss of incentives for the oil and gas industry, they fell far short of Carter's recommendation that oil and gas be treated like any other business. Industry lobbying had had some effect, for, as the White Paper announced, "the government has concluded that special rules are still needed for the mineral industry but that they should be revised substantially to ensure that really profitable projects bear a fair share of the burden of taxation. It is recognized that the exploration for and development of mines and oil and gas deposits involve more than the usual industrial risks and the scale of these risks is quite uncertain in most cases. Consequently, special arrangements are desirable to ensure that the costs of exploration and development may be charged for tax purposes as early as possible in order that taxes will only apply when it is clear that a project will be profitable."[16] Evidently the Trudeau government accepted the oil industry argument that a major oil company drilling for oil and gas was in a much riskier position, than, say, a struggling auto-parts company attempting to stay in business by developing new products that had to compete directly against the products of large U.S. companies. Nor was there any attempt to encourage Canadian ownership in the oil and gas industry, for all the brave speeches being made at about this time by energy minister Greene and his deputy, Jack Austin.

Even the depletion allowance was retained by the Trudeau government. The give-away, of which the multinationals were the principal beneficiaries, would total over $1 billion from the mid-1960s to the late 1970s. As Benson's own White Paper acknowledged, the measure originated in the days when companies were unable to write off the costs of acquiring and developing oil and gas lands. By the early 1960s, all these costs were covered by other tax provisions: depletion was simply the icing on the cake, an additional bonus that helped oil and gas companies report higher profits to their shareholders. Benson did redesign this tax feature somewhat. Instead of getting it automatically, companies would have to earn it by spending on new exploration and development; for every $3 a company spent, it could claim $1 in earned depletion, reducing its taxable income by up to one third of production profits. And the price of buying land rights could no longer be included in earned depletion. To mitigate the horror of these changes, the government offered generous transitional arrangements: companies could continue reducing their taxable income from production activities by one third, under the old rules, until the end of 1975. At the same time, they would be able to use that period to accumulate a bank of earned depletion to be claimed beginning in 1976. The old disadvantage under which most Canadian-controlled companies operated, then, was still there. They could, of course, carry their unused depletion allowances forward as a credit to be used in future years, but their need was comparable cash flow now.

The White Paper contained little that echoed Carter. The immediate write-off of exploration and development expenses was continued, so that, in effect, no taxes were paid until all of a company's costs were recovered. However, anodine as it was, the White Paper was even attacked by the oil and gas industry as a barrier to Canadianization. "I can see no reason whatsoever for a non-resident owner to provide the means whereby Canadians could participate in the growth potential of the Canadian petroleum industry," commented a Amoco Canada executive, claiming that "there is no true incentive in most instances for a non-resident owner to make shares available to Canadians."[17] And Gulf Canada's president argued: "The oil industry does not ask for subsidies, for government aid, or for government participation. All we ask is the opportunity for the successful explorer to enjoy a reasonable profit from his risky venture. . . . I submit that now is not the time to squeeze the goose that lays the golden eggs, nor to ask the goose to move over so that the government can try its luck, as continuing indications of government interest in greater oil industry involvement might suggest."[18]

To hear the oil industry tell it, you would have thought it made virtually no money at all. At the time of the 1970 tax reform debate, industry spokesmen held that they were still in a deficit position on the western fields. Amoco made this statement: "Some $14 billion have been invested in our industry in western Canada during the period 1947 through 1969; the gross revenue received from this investment by industry during this same period is approximately $12½ billion."[19] In 1974 an Imperial executive was still insisting that "there is no better illustration of lead times and risk than the fact that even today, more than twenty-five years after Leduc was discovered, the exploration and production phase of the Canadian oil industry has spent more than it has received in revenues. In total, the net deficit is still about $1 billion."[20] By 1981, this "deficit" had been raised to $62 billion by one industry spokesman, who calculated total investment in exploration and development at $43 billion, the cumulative value of prime-rate interest on all past investments at $59 billion, and then set this against a net industry revenue of $40 billion.[21]

These arguments were extremely misleading. The investment figure included the large share that came from tax concessions. The calculations ignored the valuable resources owned in the ground that could generate more than $100 billion in cash flow in the years ahead. The oil men preserved a monolithic solidarity, and they were widely believed. For one thing, they had vanishingly few credible opponents like the Texas oil economist who found Canada's immediate write-off for all exploration and development spending excessively generous: "It does not seem necessary to allow deductions for productive capital outlays as incurred. It may be observed that provision for full expensing of exploration and development costs can result in no current income tax liability, perhaps indefinitely for a growing company, despite the earning of substantial net income according to internal accounts – a result which is at odds with the government's stated aim of assuring that really profitable projects bear a fair share of the burden of taxation."[22] In his view, Canadian write-off provisions were "considerably more generous than the comparable practice in the United States," and he noted the obvious point that "a relatively light burden of taxation for one industry means a relatively heavy one for other industries."

In the period following the so-called reform, tax policy in Canada continued to reflect the ongoing conflict between the desire to have the industry pay a more responsible level of taxes and the desire to accelerate exploration and development by incentives. Meanwhile, criticism of the government give-away slowly grew. W. D. Gainer and T. L. Powrie, two University of Alberta economists, asked in 1975: "Does the oil industry require large net earnings as a major source of financing new exploration and development programs? A civil servant employed by an imaginary oil-rich province once told his minister that, in view of a local housing shortage, he was requesting a very large salary increase to permit him to save enough to finance the construction of several houses that he could then let. The minister agreed that more housing was urgently needed, but refused the request while encouraging the man to investigate the market for mortgage money. By the same implied principle one can suggest that no industry has an inherent right to or need of extra net earnings merely because it will use them in desirable ways. In the case of oil exploration, the

191

riskiness of the investments does raise problems with outside financing. But even so, if the problems are worth overcoming, the government as landlord need not give away potential revenue to augment private retained earnings; instead, it can collect the revenue and lend it back to private firms, directly or via conventional capital markets, thereby providing for the financing of new developments without dissipating its wealth."[23]

More telling criticism was heard from Douglas Hartle, a former senior treasury board official teaching public policy in the University of Toronto, who suggested that, in fact, "the joint venture arrangements prevalent in the petroleum industry allow a pooling of risk that cannot usually be achieved in most non-resource industries."[24] Because earned depletion could be applied only against resource profits, it was harder for new companies to enter the business, a circumstance that "sustains and strengthens the cartelized, foreign-dominated petroleum industry structure." However, "perhaps the most decisive evidence that the major petroleum corporations face no cash shortage is the recent spate of acquisitions. The major internationals have been acquiring control of other corporations, many of which are outside the energy sector. If the tax-royalty regime were judged to be inhospitable, the exploration and mineral rights sold by [Alberta] would be zero. In fact, prices received have rocketed upwards. This suggests that the industry finds them exceedingly comfortable at present, given projected oil prices. If the corporations were anxious to invest more in oil and gas but were cash poor, they would not be diversifying. The argument for the withdrawal of the federal earned depletion allowance on future conventional oil and gas exploration and development therefore seems unassailable." Hartle warned that "foreign-owned corporations are able to expand in Canada in the petroleum industry and elsewhere by virtue of the Canadian corporate taxes forgone. The Canadian taxpayer is making a gift of Canadian assets to non-residents." Hartle's counter-proposal was that the government lend money on riskier projects through a contingent repayment loan scheme. For example, in a tar sands project, it could loan $5 for every $1 invested by the shareholders, and not charge interest until the cumulative after-tax income reached the sum invested by the shareholders. Normal interest rates would then be charged and the loan repaid over a reasonable period of time. No move towards true change could fail to raise an outcry, Hartle predicted, perhaps on the basis of his own experience in government: "It can be expected that the petroleum industry will threaten to withdraw exploration and development expenditures from Canada in the face of a tightening of the current tax regime. The industry would be less than rational – and in the face of any tightening current tax regime, it is rational in terms of its own game – not to spend a great deal of money to persuade, cajole, frighten, and threaten Canadians. The stakes are large.''

Increasing oil prices, with huge benefits flowing to foreign shareholders, eventually bred concern even in such bodies as the Economic Council of Canada, which called in its 1979 annual review, *Two Cheers for the Eighties*, for a full re-evaluation of federal and provincial tax incentives to the oil and gas industry. The council, which brings together a number of prominent business, academic, and other public figures, noted that Ottawa's upgrading of tax incentives in the 1970s had occurred ''at considerable cost to government treasuries and to most Canadian taxpayers.''[25] The government had had several years to see how they worked, and in any case, projected oil and gas price increases should reduce the need for them. If oil prices increased by $4 per barrel a year to 1985, with natural gas keeping in step, oil revenues would rise by $15 billion and gas revenues by $11 billion in that period. Of this $26-billion increase, about $10 billion would go to the oil and gas industry under the current tax and royalty system. While the industry should be allowed to keep some of this money, the council said, more of it should go to finance energy conservation and other needs in Canada. Moreover, it admitted, ''there is also a major issue with respect to the transfer of income and wealth to non-resident owners of multinational energy companies.''

The most telling description of how tax concessions were reinforcing high foreign-ownership levels came, in 1979, from the Department of Energy, Mines and Resources.[26] As the department reported, the incentives gave strong encouragement for reinvestment of a company's cash flow, as did the provision in the tax regulations that, to a large extent, tax write-offs had to be made against resource income: ''This feature tends to encourage the investment of funds in the industry, but at the same time, it tends to reinforce concentration tendencies in an industry which is dominated both in ownership and control by non-Canadians.'' It proceeded to reveal the real-cost figures cited at the beginning of this chapter. And these figures did not include whatever available provincial incentives might further reduce net costs. With these added in, when Imperial offered $175 million to earn a 15-per-cent interest in Canadian Hunter lands, it spent about $58 million of its own money; the remainder came from the Canadian taxpayer.

Companies with little or no resource income were at a clear disadvantage, the federal study found. "The existing firm with the ability to make an immediate write-off can afford to make a higher bonus bid [for land] than a potential new entrant, and thus it tends to retain and strengthen its land position. It can also afford to offer better terms on a farm-in, since its after-tax exploration cost is lower. . . . The overall tendency thus is to promote an intensification of the current industry structure and ownership pattern. All other things being equal, the current system favours the large established company. In the Canadian context, this means – for the most part – the foreign-controlled element of the industry."

As the energy officials pointed out, with prices rising sharply in the 1970s, the oil industry was accumulating a vast money flow that would allow it to dwarf other industries in the economy. Net operating income had been $885 million in 1970; by 1978 it was $4.1 billion. In the five years of higher oil prices from 1974 to 1978, oil and gas industry cash flow, the money available for reinvestment, payment of dividends, takeovers, or diversification, totalled $15.5 billion as compared with $7.1 billion in the previous eight years. While the industry's share of net operating income was declining, from a high 69.3 per cent in 1970 to 44.2 per cent in 1978, rising oil and gas prices from resources found at low cost many years earlier were now more than offsetting rising royalties, taxes and other costs. The energy department estimated 1979-80 cash flow for the industry at another $11.5 billion; in 1985 alone, assuming a $2-a-year price increase per barrel of oil, it would generate a cash flow of $11.6 billion, and this would rise by 1990 to $19.2 billion. This flow of funds in the industry could easily lead to spending on questionable projects simply because the money was available, and "some of these revenues could also be diverted to increased dividend payments and other capital repayments which, because of the large foreign ownership of the industry, could have a substantial negative impact on Canada's balance of payments. Even if not repatriated, the funds remaining in Canada will have been largely transferred to foreign control, and may, as is the trend, be used to diversify into other sectors. Thus, even if they are reinvested in Canada, a future claim has been created which will ultimately represent a call on income generated in Canada." The energy department worried too that rising cash flow could lead to even greater concentration in the petroleum industry, already one of the most concentrated sectors in Canada: "As profits increase, it becomes increasingly attractive financially to acquire additional reserves and land positions, as well as associated tax credits and write-offs, through takeovers of smaller exploration and producing companies. There may also be an acceleration of the present trend toward diversification into other resource industries, resulting in large multi-resource conglomerates." In fact, even the big oil companies acknowledged privately that rising prices under the then prevailing tax system would result in profits that would be hard to defend, although they tended to see this as a future rather than a current problem. For example, an internal Imperial Oil memo, written in October 1979, had this to say: "It has been suggested that, under current revenue-sharing rules and price increases of $4 per barrel per year, industry may receive more funds than deserved as a return on past investments or more than can be effectively spent on new supply. To the extent this may become a problem, it will not arise before the late 1980s. The time to solve that problem will be in 1985."[27] Imperial said that this would not be an immediate problem because it assumed that the industry should continue to finance the bulk of its investments out of internally generated funds: "Should the industry, in a later period, not have enough energy investment opportunities then tax structures or incentives could be re-examined."

The paradox of the 1970s was that while the role of the tax system as an instrument of public policy, including the costs and benefits of different tax policies, came to be more clearly understood by politicians and the public, the system of reform launched by Carter and continued in a modest form in the 1970 White Paper seemed to go into reverse gear as the decade progressed. In spite of the reform efforts, concluded a study by the Canadian Energy Research Institute, "it is likely . . . that the numerous tax and royalty changes introduced during the period 1974-78 have left the tax position of a majority of the oil and gas producers unchanged or provided them with increased incentives relative to their pre-1971 standing."[28] The new range of tax incentives geared to supply included super-depletion, generous capital cost allowances for tar sands plants, and an increasingly valuable investment tax credit. They were in part the fruit of constant lobbying by the industry, which, even in the post-OPEC world, continued to portray itself as one of uniquely high risks. Texaco's president went as far as to claim in 1976 that the government should, as a matter of national priority, "return to the oil companies – which, after all, made the investment and took the risks – the major portion of increases in domestic crude oil prices," and "reduce, on a gradual basis if necessary, the excessively high level of taxes and royalties, and provide incentives that will encourage the oil companies to plow back the funds so generated into the exploration and development and downstream facilities wherever they are most needed."[29] While he spoke, his company's sister Texaco Exploration was busy diverting millions of its dollars out of the country to help its parent finance exploration and development in the United States. And in 1977, the chairman of Imperial Oil was complaining about the lack of incentives for people to invest in the oil and gas industry: "We badly need to create a new climate for the resource industries in Canada – a climate far more encouraging to investment than we have at present. We do not have in this country a set of policies to make resource investment attractive to either the corporate or the individual investor."[30] Or as company president James Livingstone put it, "as in all activity, the carrot works much better than the stick. In fact, Livingstone's Law of Economics says, 'The pace of economic activity varies directly with the size of the carrot.' "[31] Two years later, the company again called for tax policies "that provide investors with sufficient incentive to put their money into increasingly high-risk projects."[32] According to Imperial, "so-called government development incentives can more properly be regarded as investments, which can pay handsome dividends. Governments are too astute to engage in giving away and, in the final analysis, all incentives are based on a hard-headed appraisal of the ultimate pay-off."[33]

The price hikes of the 1970s did inspire some official moves to increase tax revenues, but profits still continued their rapid rise. In the five years 1970-79, oil and gas companies claimed $4.5 billion in depletion, which meant that their taxes were reduced by more than $2 billion. In the same period, they claimed $15.8 billion in exploration and development write-offs, much of this representing deferred taxation or interest-free loans from the public which might never be repaid or else repaid in future dollars with significantly less real value. Reserves for future income taxes – the industry's accumulated deferred income tax liability – rose from $604 million in 1970 to $5.6 billion in 1979. Tax incentives allowed the oil and gas industry to make much greater use of deferred taxes than other industries as a source of capital employed in the business. Overall, the oil and gas industry accounted for about 17 per cent of the capital employed by non-financial corporations, but about 30 per cent of deferred taxes. What this meant was that whereas manufacturing companies used deferred income taxes for an average of 6.8 per cent of the capital they employed in 1978-79, and non-financial corporations used 7.2 per cent, the oil and gas producing companies relied on deferred taxes for 12.7 per cent of the capital they used in their businesses, and integrated oil companies relied on deferred taxes for 12.5 per cent of the capital they employed. At the end of 1979, the corporations had accumulated $6.7 billion in unclaimed exploration and development expenses that they could use to lower their taxes in future years.[34] And while the industry was happy to use the tax system to enrich its coffers, it was a real cheapskate when it came to supporting worthy causes in Canada. The oil exploration and production companies, led by Mobil Canada, Amoco, Chevron Standard, Hudson's Bay Oil and Gas, and Canada-Cities Service, made donations of only $3.5 million to Canadian charities, universities, amateur sport, cultural organizations, hospitals, and other deductible institutions in spite of book profits after tax of $2.8 billion. Although their book profits after taxes had risen by $1.3 billion from 1978, their donations to the Canadian community rose by only $1.1 million. This was due in part to the fact that many foreign head offices forbade their Canadian subsidiaries to make more than token contributions. The integrated oil companies, led by Imperial Oil, Gulf Canada, Shell Canada, and Texaco Canada, made donations of $6 million in 1979, when book profits after taxes were $1.7 billion. While profits had gone up by almost $750 million over 1978, donations increased by only $600,000. Though the oil and gas production and integrated companies accounted for 20 per cent of book profits after taxes in non-financial industries in 1979, they accounted for only 8 per cent of donations to tax-deductible causes.

The result of the new supply-oriented tax incentives of the late '70s was, according to University of British Columbia economist John Helliwell, that tax incentives were inefficiently high for tar sands projects and frontier exploration. In the case of the Syncrude project, he argued in 1979, if production volumes and operating costs were maintained and with current and expected world oil prices, the net economic rents would have a present value in end-of-1980 dollars of $10 billion. More than 80 per cent of this would go to Alberta, and the rest to the private oil companies in the project. "The federal government, even with its equity interest, will find itself with negative economic rents. If the same tax incentives, or better, are made available to the next plant, and if the federal government does not have an equity interest, the federal government's position is likely to be even worse. If the next plant is assumed to have the same real costs as Syncrude, but if the ownership is entirely private, the $10.7 billion net rents would be divided as +$6.6 billion for Alberta, +$4.9 billion for the private owners, and – $700 million for the federal government.''[35] Yet the federal government would, through tax concessions, pay a large part of the costs.

The super-depletion provisions for wells costing more than $5 million was described by Helliwell as a "perverse form of negative taxation" because it could mean that investors were actually getting tax rebates on their investments, "giving rise to the possibility that the taxpayers are putting up more than 100 per cent of the cost of the well, while getting only a small claim on the profits from any eventual production." The incentive also said, in effect, the more expensive the well the better, thus encouraging high-cost activities over lower-cost exploration. "Under these circumstances it is hard to see how there can be any limit to the amount of taxpayers' money that would be invested in the Beaufort Sea." From an economic point of view, super-depletion made no sense at all, since it favoured one area of exploration over other possible sources of new supply. "If eventual production of frontier crude is to be at or near world prices, then there is no case for tax subsidies based on higher frontier costs. If development there cannot take place at costs less than the expected world price of crude oil, it is too costly to be part of Canada's least-cost plan of self-sufficiency, and obviously does not provide the basis for profitable exports. Now that world oil prices have taken a new large jump upwards, frontier oil developments may be able to stand on their own profitability if the push to the frontier is not to leap over less costly alternatives. Frontier natural gas developments are even less worthy of special tax treatment, as there have always been actual and potential stocks of much less expensive non-frontier gas more than sufficient to meet Canadian requirements until the end of the century. Thus if frontier natural gas has any early prospect, it is as an export commodity, and there is no efficiency or security argument in favour of tax subsidies for energy exports."

In the context of the past history of oil and gas taxation, the National Energy Program represented a sharp and overdue turnaround in public policy. As the NEP noted, while the federal corporate tax rate was 36 per cent – to which must be added a provincial corporate tax rate of 11 to 25 per cent, depending on the province – the effective rate since 1974 had been about 10 per cent, or less than one third of the nominal rate.[36] Clearly, the industry was not paying its fair share of taxes. This was in a situation with an industry more than 80-per-cent foreign-controlled and exporting large volumes of capital when Canada needed huge new investments to develop fresh energy supplies. And as Canada's ambassador pointed out to the U.S. National Energy Resources Organization, "the problem was compounded by a tax incentive system that favoured the growth and concentration of established firms already benefiting to a much greater degree than they had originally anticipated. As the value of foreign-owned firms grew, the opportunities for significant Canadian participation were steadily slipping away."[37] Tax reform was essential if Canadians were to have a reasonable chance of increasing their ownership and control of the oil and gas industry.

As a result of the National Energy Program, modified by 1981 agreements with the producing provinces, this tax system has now been significantly revised. Key measures include a Petroleum and Gas Revenue Tax or a windfall profits tax of effectively 12 per cent of net oil and gas production revenue before any deductions for exploration, development, or depletion are made, along with an additional Incremental Oil Revenue Tax on old oil of 50 per cent on the excess of price over a defined base after the deduction of national crown royalties. Earned depletion for domestic exploration spending outside the Canada Lands was to be phased out by the end of 1984, while earned depletion on development spending was to be eliminated immediately. Earned depletion would be retained on the basis of $1 for each $3 spent for exploration spending on Canada Lands as well as for tar sands, heavy oil upgrading, and enhanced recovery projects, but would be limited to 25 per cent of resource income. At the same time, new exploration incentives introduced under the Petroleum Incentives Program favoured Canadian-controlled companies and did not depend on a company's existing profitability. Grants instead of tax write-offs would be used. A company with 0- to 75-per-cent Canadian ownership and control would get a grant for 10 per cent (15 per cent in 1984 and later) of its exploration spending on provincial lands, and 10 per cent of its development spending on provincial lands or investments in tar sands, heavy oil upgrading, or tertiary projects; on Canada Lands it would get a grant equal to 25 per cent of its exploration spending but nothing for its development spending. A company with 50- to 75-per-cent Canadian ownership and control would receive a grant for 10 per cent (15 per cent beginning in 1984) of its exploration spending on provincial lands, and 10 per cent of its development spending on provincial lands or investments in tar sands, heavy oil upgrading, or tertiary projects. It would get a grant equal to 45 per cent of its exploration spending (50 per cent in 1984 and later) and 10 per cent of its development spending on Canada Lands. A company that was 75-per-cent or more Canadian-owned would get a grant for 35 per cent of its exploration spending and 30 per cent of its development spending on provincial lands and 20 per cent of its investment on tar sands plants, heavy oil upgrading, and tertiary oil projects, as well as 80 per cent of its Canada Lands exploration costs and 20 per cent of its Canada Lands development costs.

Not surprisingly, the new tax system was bitterly attacked by the oil majors, even though the eventual agreements with the oil-producing provinces provided for a much more rapid increase in oil and gas prices, plus a generous incentive price for new oil that was found. The result, according to J. G. Stabback, senior vice-president of the Royal Bank's Global Energy and Minerals Group in Calgary, was that "oil production activity appears to provide reasonably healthy returns to industry."[38] Based on the bank's analysis, "internal rates of return in excess of 20 per cent were generated. Although the returns in the oil and gas sector do not look extremely impressive in today's environment of high inflation and interest rates, over a somewhat longer term they may be more attractive. In particular, if inflation slows to 10 per cent or slightly less in 1983 as our forecast suggests, a 20-per-cent rate of return will look quite attractive, except for higher-risk frontier areas." One reason why the industry did not like the new regime, Stabback suggested, was that it had still not recovered from the loss of the high expectations it had developed during the short-lived Joe Clark government of 1979-80. The Conservatives "would have pushed all oil very quickly to 85 per cent of world levels, with the prospect of much higher cash flows for the industry," according to Stabback, so that the oil majors "may still be longing for what might have been. This sense may be intensified by the realization that this is a once-only opportunity to benefit from oil prices increasing sharply to world levels." Another problem, from the industry's viewpoint, was that the "federal government evidently feels the oil industry should rely to a greater extent on external financing."

The industry still had fairly generous incentives. According to Joel Bell, executive vice-president of Petro-Canada, a non-Canadian company (0 to 50%) will have to put up 53 cents of its own money for every $1 of exploration spending in western Canada and 40 cents in the Canada Lands. A Canadian company (75 per cent plus) will have to put up 34 cents of its own money for every $1 of exploration spending in western Canada and only 11 cents in the Canada Lands. Companies finding new oil in western Canada, according to Bell, would get roughly the same value as companies operating in the United States: "Canada, however, is a less intensively explored basin so that the size of prospects being pursued tends to be larger – something which would make the project economies superior in Canada if the land costs do not absorb the difference."[39] In addition, he argued, Canada offered royalty and other forms of tax relief so that "the economies in Canada from oil will be at least as good as, and most often superior to, the scene in the United States – the place which is supposed to be the most favourable in the world at the present time." Bell also insisted that the discoveries at Hibernia were still more profitable under the Canadian than they would be under the U.S. fiscal regime, even for foreign investors; and if Hibernia were a smaller field, the Canadian fiscal regime would be even more favourable in relation to the U.S. regime. Canadians have been, and even under the NEP continue to be, generous supporters of the oil multinationals, providing much of the funding and carrying much of the risk.

Deferred Income Taxes ($ millions)

Company	Increase in 1980	Outstanding at end of 1980
Imperial Oil	136	881
Gulf Canada	60	443
Texaco Canada	39	385
Shell Canada	30	337
Amoco Canada	78	314
Mobil Canada	34	120
Canadian Superior	38	100
Suncor	77	252
BP Canada	17	96
Total	509	2,928

Source: Company annual reports.

Taxation of the Petroleum and Natural Gas Industries ($ Millions)

	1970	1971	1972	1973	1974	1975	1976	1977	1978	1979
Book profit before taxes	1,032.6	1,216.7	1,365.8	2,086.8	3,101.3	3,717.7	4,043.1	4,686.5	5,474.8	8,783.7
Taxable income	398.0	516.1	567.6	898.8	2,212.2	3,459.9	2,553.2	3,118.6	2,853.6	3,770.5
Corporate income taxes paid	200.0	246.7	261.1	433.2	925.0	1,235.2	1,062.6	1,294.1	1,169.7	1,490.4
Corporate income taxes deferred	N/A	80.6	86.8	175.7	359.3	410.1	493.0	612.5	867.4	1,335.0
Tax credits					349.2	739.5	333.1	411.4	378.8	575.8
Canadian exploration and development expense	685.3	865.9	902.3	1,174.2	1,287.1	1,140.8	1,391.0	2,027.4	2,585.6	3,770.5
Depletion allowance	83.0	126.8	159.5	260.7	525.7	573.7	437.8	553.5	699.1	1,092.5
Total claimed for tax purposes	768.3	992.7	1,062.2	1,435.0	1,812.8	1,714.5	1,828.1	2,580.9	3,284.7	4,808.8
Amount written off in company books	409.5	500.5	593.4	763.1	816.0	810.5	1,006.1	1,185.4	1,427.5	1,967.4
Difference	358.8	492.2	468.8	671.9	996.7	904.0	823.0	1,395.6	1,857.2	2,841.4
Reserve for future income taxes (accumulated deferred taxes)	603.8	676.5	767.1	1,047.4	1,962.0	2,369.1	2,868.6	3,505.4	4,308.3	5,613.4
Taxes paid as % of book profits	19%	20%	19%	21%	30%	33%	26%	28%	21%	17%
Taxes paid as % of taxable income	50%	48%	46%	48%	42%	36%	42%	41%	41%	40%
Share of pre-tax book profits of all non-financial corporations	17%	16%	17%	17%	19%	24%	26%	28%	26%	29%
Taxes paid as % of book profits by all non-financial corporations	40%	39%	37.4%	31.5%	33.7%	37.5%	36.1%	33.5%	30%	27%

Source: Statistics Canada Corporation Taxation Statistics. 61-208.

The Role of the Tax System in Generating Oil Industry Investment Funds[1] ($ Millions)

	After-tax profits	Exploration and development write-offs	Depreciation	Depletion allowance	Write-offs, amortization	Deferred income taxes	Total Internal cash flow	Profit as % of internal cash flow	Internal cash flow as % of total cash flow
1980	3,867[2]	1,387	678	384	178	1,021	7,515	51%	68%
1979	3,075	1,007	611	315	110	887	6,006	51%	67%
1978	1,973	698	521	221	144	591	4,148	48%	68%
1977	1,814	577	477	194	159	410	3,631	50%	76%
1976	1,457	396	463	181	114	320	2,931	50%	73%
1975	1,483	285	402	154	86	291	2,698	55%	73%
1974	1,337	275	369	146	89	302	2,518	53%	83%
1973	1,072	233	346	132	71	202	2,055	52%	83%
1972	683	213	310	111	55	134	1,505	45%	79%
1971	561[3]	157	284	91	51	106	1,251	45%	78%

[1] Based on the top 30-plus companies; in 1980 they accounted for 78 per cent of the total internal cash flow of the oil and gas industry.
[2] 75% of the $39 billion in after-tax profits accrued to foreign-controlled oil and gas companies.
[3] 89% of the $561 million in after-tax profits accrued to foreign-controlled oil and gas companies.

Source: Petroleum Monitoring Agency, 1981.

203

Notes

1. Petroleum Monitoring Agency. *Canadian Petroleum Industry: 1980 Monitoring Survey.* Ottawa 1981.
2. Department of Energy, Mines and Resources. *Taxation and Revenue Sharing.* Ottawa, November 1979.
3. *Taxation and Revenue Sharing.*
4. *Canadian Petroleum Industry: 1980 Monitoring Survey.*
5. Bruce Wilkinson, University of Alberta, to the Canadian Tax Foundation, Montreal, November 1980.
6. J. Grant Glassco. *Certain Aspects of Taxation Relative to Investment in Canada by Non-Residents.* Royal Commission on Canada's Economic Prospects, Ottawa 1956.
7. Maurice Strong, chairman of Petro-Canada, to the Canadian Club, Toronto, 18 April 1977.
8. Imperial Oil Limited. "Prospects for Canada's Oil Industry 1955-1980." Brief to the Royal Commission on Canada's Economic Prospects, December 1955.
9. John G. McDonald. "Income Tax Incentives for Canadian Mineral Development." Saskatchewan Department of Mineral Resources, Regina 1956.
10. Royal Commission on Canada's Economic Prospects. Final Report. Ottawa 1957.
11. W. O. Twaits, president, Imperial Oil Limited, to the Atlantic Tax Conference, Halifax, 14 June 1960.
12. Rodney de C. Grey. "Trade Policy in the 1980s: An Agenda for Canadian-U.S. Relations." C. D. Howe Institute, Montreal 1981.
13. Toronto *Star*, 2 November 1973.
14. Toronto *Star*, 28 December 1973.
15. Royal Commission on Taxation. Report, vol. 4. Ottawa 1966.
16. Department of Finance. "Proposals for Tax Reform." Ottawa 1970.
17. K. C. Little, Amoco Canada Petroleum, to the Canadian Tax Foundation, Montreal, 23-25 March 1970.
18. Jerry McAfee, president, Gulf Canada, to the Fifth National Northern Development Conference, Edmonton, 4 November 1970.
19. K. C. Little to the Canadian Tax Foundation.
20. R. G. Reid, president, Imperial Oil Limited, to the Institute of Chartered Accountants of Ontario, Toronto, 4 October 1974.
21. J .P. Gallagher, chairman, Dome Petroleum, to the Canadian Institute of Mining and Metallurgy, Calgary, 5 May 1981.
22. Stephen L. McDonald, Department of Economics, University of Texas, to the Canadian Tax Foundation, Montreal, 23-25 March 1970.
23. W. D. Gainer and T. L. Powrie, Department of Economics, University of Alberta. "Public Revenue from Canadian Crude Oil Production." *Canadian Public Policy*, Winter 1975.
24. D. G. Hartle. *Energy Policies for the 1980s.* Toronto, Ontario Economic Council, 1980, vol. 2.
25. Economic Council of Canada. *Two Cheers for the Eighties.* Ottawa 1979.
26. Department of Energy, Mines and Resources. *Taxation and Revenue Sharing.* Ottawa, November 1979.
27. Imperial Oil Ltd. "A Summary of Current Public Discussions of Crude Oil Price Increases and Revenue Sharing." Toronto, October 1979.

28. W. B. Friedenberg, Z. C. Slagorsky, and A. J. Walsh. "Government Incentives in Canada's Petroleum Industry." Calgary, Canadian Energy Research Institute, 1980.

29. R. W. Sparks, president, Texaco Canada, to the Annual General Meeting of Shareholders, Toronto, 23 April 1976.

30. J. A. Armstrong, chairman, Imperial Oil Ltd., to the Men's Canadian Club of Winnipeg, 22 February 1977.

31. J. G. Livingstone, president, Imperial Oil Ltd., to Simon Fraser University MBA Alumni, Vancouver, 22 October 1979.

32. J. A. Armstrong, chairman, Imperial Oil Ltd., to the 14th World Gas Conference, Toronto, 29 May 1979.

33. J. A. Armstrong, chairman, Imperial Oil Ltd., to the Annual General Meeting of Shareholders, Toronto, 24 April 1973.

34. Statistics Canada. "Corporation Taxation Statistics 1979" and for earlier years. Ottawa 1982.

35. John F. Helliwell, University of British Columbia, to the Canadian Tax Foundation, Toronto, 26 November 1979.

36. Department of Energy, Mines and Resources. *The National Energy Program*. Ottawa 1980.

37. Peter Towe, Canadian ambassador to the United States, to the National Energy Resources organization, Washington, 21 October 1981.

38. J. G. Stabback, Royal Bank of Canada, to the *Financial Post* Energy Conference, Calgary, 27 October 1981.

39. Joel Bell, Petro-Canada vice-president, to the Fifth International Energy Forum, Mexico City, 12 November 1981.

Chapter 7

The Sands

Few countries can boast the ace in the hole we Canadians have in the majestic deposits of tar sands, or oil sands, that lie north of Edmonton in Alberta. The sticky mixture of thick oil and sand, much of it buried deep beneath the surface, is more difficult and much more expensive to tap than conventional oil: in 1980 dollars, a tar sands project would cost $50,000 per daily barrel of oil production as compared with $3,000 for a conventional Alberta field or $30,000 in the expensive new fields off our Atlantic coast. In a world where supply could well become a more important factor than price, however, the sheer immensity of these deposits, which rival in size the reserves of Saudi Arabia, as well as their known availability even with current or in-reach technology, makes them an energy bank that can buy out our dependence on imported oil and help secure a margin of freedom for Canada and its friends from OPEC's domination in world oil markets.

In the years ahead, there will be growing pressure to tap these resources. Indeed, a 1981 report by the Paris-based International Energy Agency – representing 21 industrial nations, including Canada, that banded together after the 1973-74 oil crisis – pointed to Canada's tar sands as one source that could make the industrial world much more energy self-reliant by the end of the century. Were that to happen, it would be logical for Canadians to control the play and make sure that Canadian engineers, manufacturers, and technologists were in the forefront of development. That, unhappily, has not been the story so far. While Canadians have learned some lessons from the sorry experience with the country's conventional oil and gas reserves, the sands stand as another monument to failed Canadian policy. Even though the original process for the separation of oil from the sands was developed in Canada by Canadians, lax Alberta land policies in the 1950s and

1960s let the multinationals tie up the most promising deposits at small cost, while much of the technology in the projects built so far has been developed and manufactured outside, in the United States for the upgrading process and Europe for the extraction or mining machinery, and engineering and project management have been directed from the U.S. Canadians were providing the tax incentives and other subsidies while the benefits, including the early financial returns, flowed out of the country to the oil majors and their global suppliers and engineers.

Fortunately, policies are changing: not only has the Canadianization of the oil industry, while still at an early stage, meant that some important land holdings are now in the hands of Canadian-controlled companies, but government investment in research and development, notably in Alberta, and growing pressure on the oil multinationals to use Canadian engineering companies and develop more technology through Canadian manufacturing companies, along with planned Alberta and Petro-Canada equity participation in future projects, all suggest that the potential for much greater Canadian benefits exists.

So far, two major installations have been built. Great Canadian Oil Sands, controlled by U.S. Sun Oil, opened the first truly commercial plant in 1967. Beginning at 45,000 barrels a day, its capacity was expanded in 1980-81 to 63,000 barrels a day. The second big plant, the Syncrude plant, came into production in 1978 with a capacity of 125,000 barrels a day. Syncrude is owned 25 per cent by Imperial Oil, 17 per cent by Petro-Canada, 16.8 per cent by the Alberta government, 13.2 per cent by Canada-Cities Service, 10 per cent by Alberta Energy Corp., 9 per cent by Gulf Canada, 5 per cent by Dome Petroleum, and 4 per cent by PanCanadian. Both these installations are surface mining or open pit operations on accessible deposits in the Athabasca region of Alberta. Much of the resource, however, can be extracted only by an underground or in situ recovery process, for example by injecting steam or other forms of heat into the ground and pumping out the released heavy oil. The two big projects most likely to come on stream next are Shell's Alsands, using traditional surface technology, and Imperial's Cold Lake, where in situ technology will be used for the first time.

The best and most recent estimate of the wealth of this tar sands bank comes from the province's Energy Resources Conservation Board, which has calculated the potential oil reserves recoverable by surface mining operations at 6 billion cubic metres (37.8 billion barrels), or roughly four times the remaining potential for

Alberta's conventional crude oil and liquids, while the in situ or underground potential of deeply buried tar sands is reckoned at 24 billion cubic metres (151 billion barrels).[1] Altogether, the sands represent about 95 per cent of Alberta's ultimate potential recoverable oil reserves. The total ultimate potential, of course, is much higher. The tar sands in place are estimated at 200 billion cubic metres (1,260 billion barrels) of which 25 billion cubic metres (157 billion barrels), as technology develops, may be recoverable by surface mining, while 175 billion cubic metres (1,100 billion barrels) will require in situ recovery. The ultimate total recoverable from established tar sands reserves is 40 billion cubic metres (252 billion barrels). Moreover, the Alberta energy board expects that tar sands will account for nearly 65 per cent of Alberta's total oil production capacity by the end of the 1990s as compared with 10 per cent in 1980, with productive capacity increasing sevenfold from 23,080 cubic metres (144,740 barrels a day) in 1980 to 160,000 cubic metres a day (1 million barrels a day) in 1999. The board "agrees with the industry consensus that bitumen synthetic crude is potentially the principal source of replenishment supply and is capable of offsetting the now rapid decline in conventional crude production." However, these striking figures came with the warning that, for instance, "much better in situ recovery methods than proposed for the initial production operations at Esso Cold Lake would have to be developed in order for in situ production to reach its projected dominant position in the synthetic crude supply position."

The National Energy Board is equally optimistic.[2] With 8 per cent of Canada's oil production capacity in 1980, the tar sands may account for about 47 per cent of Canada's oil production capacity by 1995. The energy agency anticipates that tar sands production will climb from the current 128,000 barrels a day to 736,000 barrels a day in 1995, an almost sixfold increase in production. By the latter date, the tar sands will have replaced western Canada's conventional oil fields as the country's principal source of oil, and when the year 2000 rolls around they "could be supplying more than half of our domestic production" from all fields in Canada, including the east coast and the Beaufort Sea. According to the NEB, the late 1990s will also see a tar sands petrochemicals project producing ethylene. In all, some half dozen new plants are expected before the end of the century, with major expansion of the existing Syncrude operation.

Knowledge of the tar sands dates back more than two and a half centuries, to the days of early exploration in the Canadian West.[3]

In 1719, Henry Kelsey of the Hudson's Bay Company was given a lump of oil sand bitumen by Indians who had travelled the Athabasca River. In 1778, the colourful trader Peter Pond built what is said to have been the first European dwelling in Alberta near the modern Fort McMurray, the centre of tar sands activity. Pond noted the Indians' use of the local tarry substance to caulk their canoes and cure some ailments. A decade later, the explorer Alexander Mackenzie travelled along the Athabasca and saw tar oozing from the river's banks. His diary recorded the existence of "some bituminous fountain, into which a pole of twenty feet long may be inserted without the least resistance. The bitumen is in a fluid state, and when mixed with gum or a resinous substance collected from the spruce fir, serves to gum the canoes. In its heated state it emits a smell like that of sea-coal. The banks of the river, which are very elevated, discover veins of the same bituminous quality."[4]

The early days of Confederation saw the beginnings of commercial interest in the sands, from both serious geologists and seat-of-the-pants speculators and adventurers. Analysing the Athabasca sands in 1882-84, Dr. Robert Bell of the Geological Survey of Canada suggested that they contained oil in commercial quantities which could be freighted up the river to Lake Athabasca and then carried by pipeline to Churchill Harbour on Hudson Bay, to be taken to market for use in roofing, paving, lubrication, and the manufacture of paraffin and asphalt tiles. During the 1890s, the Geological Survey began an exploratory drilling program that continued into the 1920s. After 1900, various entrepreneurs launched their own drilling programs. Imperial sank its first wells in tar sands country in 1917, and in 1919, T. O. Bosworth, who became the company's chief geologist, told an Edmonton public meeting: "In the district of McMurray on the Athabasca river we have the largest natural exposure of oil in the world. It is interesting to consider the amount of oil in this territory. For this purpose we will suppose the area to be 15,000 square miles, the average thickness 50 feet, and the average yield to be ten gallons per ton. A simple calculation gives the result as 30,000 million barrels of oil. This is an immense quantity – it is 600 times the world's annual production."[5]

One of the key figures in early tar sands development was Dr. Sidney C. Ells of the Geological Survey of Canada, who in 1913, as a young man fresh in the field, produced the first detailed federal report on the potential of the Athabasca tar sands. After a half century of tireless promotion, Dr. Ells was an honoured guest at the official opening of the Great Canadian Oil Sands plant in

1967. A second important figure was Karl Adolf Clark, a young scientist with Alberta's Scientific and Industrial Research Council, later the Alberta Research Council, who developed a process for separating out the gooey oil by the application of hot water. In 1923, he and another tar sands pioneer, Sidney M. Blair, built the first hot-water separation system in the basement of the University of Alberta power plant. A larger plant was set up in the Edmonton rail yards in 1924 and continued operation until 1929. In 1928, Dr. Clark patented the Canadian-designed and Canadian-financed hot-water separation process that is used in the commercial plants of today. And the early commercial history of the sands is dotted with personalities as well. One of them, Robert C. Fitzsimmons, set up the International Bitumount Co. in 1927 and ran a small tar sands plant that operated until 1942, producing oil and asphalt. In financial difficulty, Fitzsimmons was progressively squeezed out, and later blamed the shaky condition of tar sands development on the oil majors which, he claimed, wanted to delay tar sands development until they had used up other established reserves.[6]

The wartime need for oil fanned Alberta and federal government interest in tar sands development, and the oil majors began to be more active as well. In 1945, Clark advised the Alberta government to build and operate a commercial plant itself. The idea was turned down by the Social Credit government of Ernest Manning,[7] which elected to construct a demonstration pilot instead, and in 1950, issued a positive study by Clark's old partner, Blair, on the commercial feasibility of tar sands extraction. The first real step, however, was to make the tar sands land available to the oil industry. In September of 1951, the Manning government invited top executives from the international oil companies to the first Oil Sands Conference at the Edmonton campus of the University of Alberta and announced attractive leasing terms, making available all the province's accumulated taxpayer-financed research and guaranteeing extremely low royalty rates on production. Mines minister Nathan Tanner assured industry delegates that his government would neither participate in tar sands development nor retain a Crown reserve in explored land that companies wished to lease. He also promised renewable 21-year leases, with a maximum royalty of 10 per cent of raw production during the first 21 years. "The Alberta government is desirous of doing all that is reasonably possible to encourage the orderly development of the enormous oil sands deposits in the interest of the people of the province and Canada as a whole, and, further, the security of this continent," he said.[8] At the same time, Alberta was "opposed to monopoly of any kind, whether it be the government, a company, or a group of companies. We feel that only through individual enterprise where we have good wholesome competition can development go forward as it should go forward, and we are determined to see that that same competition, individual free enterprise as you refer to it, is carried on and our natural resources developed under that program."

Yet these policies had the opposite effect, centralizing control of tar sands resources in the hands of a small number of oil majors who had acquired most of their leases by the end of 1961, when the province's terms had become even easier. And Alberta also abandoned its enterprising role in the development of tar sands technology. It came as no surprise, then, nearly a quarter century later, to find the province reporting that "the vast amounts of capital and the technical expertise required to develop oil sands properties generally have been available only from major oil companies; hence, few of the smaller, independent companies have acquired oil sands leases."[9] The situation had developed over a period of some 15 years, starting in 1960, when the number of leases jumped from 17 to 31, covering about 718,000 acres as compared with the 238,000 under lease in 1959. By 1973 the numbers had soared, with 145 leases covering 4.3 million acres. Ten companies – Imperial, Atlantic Richfield, Canada-Cities Service, Texaco, Shell, Mobil, Amoco, Sun, Petrofina, and Union Oil, all of them foreign-controlled – owned about 80 per cent of the play.

1973 Ownership of Alberta Tar Sands

Company	Net Acres Under Lease
Imperial	686,140
Atlantic Richfield	577,054
Canada-Cities Service	492,648
Texaco Exploration	455,436
Shell	425,349
Mobil Oil	279,387
Amoco Petroleum	177,927
Sun Oil	172,937
Petrofina	113,752
Union Oil	102,907
Total of top ten (80 per cent of land)	3,483,537
Total all companies	4,381,055

Source: "Alberta Oil Sands Facts and Figures." Department of Mines and Minerals, Edmonton, 1974.

The domination of the tar sands land by the oil majors was not surprising. They had the financial resources which allowed them to hold land for long periods of time. The Alberta government, for its part, bent over backwards to entice the oil majors in, believing they were the only ones capable of developing the tar sands. There were no provisions in Alberta's tar sands leasing policy for Canadian ownership; nor were there meaningful restrictions on how much land any one company could hold under lease. Instead, easy terms were offered, starting in 1951, and when these failed to attract development, even easier terms were offered at the start of the 1960s.

These multinationals were sitting on reserves whose strategic value became even clearer in the early 1970s, as the U.S. industry tried to reassure the American public that it had the means to avoid shortages. In 1972, the industry's National Petroleum Council prepared a detailed outlook report which predicted that by the year 2000, "under favourable circumstances, these [tar sands] hydrocarbon resources in Canada could contribute slightly over 5 million barrels per day or about 10 quadrillion BTUs to U.S. energy supplies. (This assumes that 25 per cent of projected Canadian tar sands production is utilized in that country and 75 per cent is exported to the United States.)"[10] The majors continued to reinforce their positions on tar sands land, and at the end of 1978 leases totalled 5.6 million acres, with about 80 per cent still foreign-controlled, a share that would have been well over 90 per cent had it not been for Petro-Canada's acquisition of Atlantic Richfield Canada, a major leaseholder. In its report on tar sands land holdings at the end of 1978, Alberta's Department of Energy and Natural Resources noted that the major oil companies in recent years had "tended to be more selective in their holdings by retaining higher grade lands."[11] In other words, the best land had been taken. The most recent data from Edmonton shows that eight major companies, seven of them foreign-controlled, accounted for 67 per cent of land held under lease in April 1981.

And this ownership of tar sands leases by foreign-controlled oil companies had, in the words of Robert Blair, chairman of Nova, "stalemated" tar sands development by early 1982 as "the original holders mostly won't sell at less than a very large mark-up because of the intrinsic value of the resource, but won't proceed either because they don't trust the net economics apparently available to the petroleum industry at this stage."[12] Yet, Blair said, "an excellent price/tax/royalties regime is now in place for that development."

Who Owns the Alberta Tar Sands

Company	Net acres owned under lease	Prospecting permits held
Petro-Canada Exploration	780,134	14,320
Esso Resources Canada	674,407	14,560
Texaco Canada Resources	511,742	41,760
Canada-Cities Service	473,677	14,800
Gulf Canada Resources	340,250	60,000
Shell Canada Resources		
Shell Explorer	348,265	—
Mobil	287,610	—
Amoco Canada Petroleum	240,647	76,160
Total – Eight Major Companies	3,655,732	221,600
All other companies	1,807,193	550,460
Total	5,472,925	772,060

Source: Alberta Department of Energy and Natural Resources, April 1981.

With the background of U.S. strategic supply, this should logically have translated into accelerated development. Yet acceleration has been slow. For again, we are dealing with the nature of the multinational beast. Even Imperial Oil, which has a modest degree of autonomy, had to persuade a reluctant Exxon in the early 1960s that it should begin development work in the tar sands. Exxon did not see the need for a project, and was unwilling to approve the early investment. Imperial had to do a strong selling job in New York. In this case it was successful; but suppose it had not been. Failure would almost certainly have meant delay for the Syncrude tar sands project, the biggest to date. For strong and continuous development commitments are required, even for the surface mining operations in the Athabasca Wabiskaw-McMurray sands where the soil and other overburden is 150 feet or less. The commitments for in situ recovery on the portions of Wabiskaw-McMurray where deposits are 2,500 feet and more beneath the ground, as is the case with all of Cold Lake, Peace River Bluesky-Bullhead, and Wabasca, will have to be even more gigantic. Imperial's is a cautionary tale.

The picture had an added complication when, in 1960, with applications before it from Great Canadian Oil Sands, Shell, and a consortium led by Imperial, the Alberta government decided to approve only the Great Canadian plant. With much of its conventional oil already shut in by weak markets, the province was afraid at the time that this development would hurt existing producers. And there was an added irony in the fact that GCOS, soon to be

Sun-controlled, was the inheritor of the old Fitzsimmons leases. It was a difficult birth before the plant finally opened in 1967, a development watched closely by the industry, and by then, improved conditions as well as the installation's performance encouraged other companies to pick up additional leases; new plant applications began appearing in the early 1970s as the shortage spectre made tar sands investment more and more attractive.

The beginning of that decade, however, also saw a change of government in Alberta and the arrival of a new, young premier, Peter Lougheed, whose Progressive Conservatives replaced the weary Social Credit government that had managed the province's oil and gas resources with a distinctly pro-multinational flavour since 1935. Shortly after it came to office, the Lougheed government asked some of its senior civil servants to prepare a tar sands development strategy for consideration by Cabinet. In August 1972, the Conservation and Utilization Committee made up of officials from almost every government department delivered an initial confidential study.[13] There were two remarkable things about the report. In the first place, it came out and said that Albertans had not benefited as they should have from conventional oil and gas development. Secondly, it argued that Alberta should adopt a strategy for the tar sands that included special emphasis on Canadian ownership, the use of Canadian engineering, design, and other services, and the linking of sands activities to an industrial strategy under which Canadian companies would own much of the technology and produce most of the equipment required. Alberta had two choices: "We can continue the policies of the conventional crude oil developments, creating tremendous and unregulated growth and development resulting in short-term benefits accruing to the province as well as the long-term costs arising from exported energy, technology, job opportunities and environmental damages, in addition to the depletion of non-renewable resources," or "we can regulate the orderly growth and development of the bituminous tar sands for the ultimate benefit of Alberta and Canada in order that Canadian technology will be expanded, Alberta will find beneficial and satisfying employment within its diversified economy, and our environment will be protected and enhanced for future use." The second approach, termed "imperative," in addition to opening the way for a "tar sands technology . . . developed, shaped, and influenced by Canadians for the benefit of Canadians," would probably also require greater Canadian ownership and control of companies working the deposits. "The tar sands offer a unique opportunity to change

214

the historical trend of ever-increasing foreign control of non-renewable resource development in Canada. Here is a reserve of the greatest magnitude which does not require highly speculative investment to find and prove. The worldwide demand for petroleum will be so compelling within the near future that it should be Alberta's objective to increase Canadian equity participation in the resource developments."

The officials suggested that the Alberta government consider entering the field itself through an Alberta Resource Development Corporation which would also tap provincial savings, and that the government canvass such other possible sources of Canadian capital as the recently created Canada Development Corporation. They also urged the Lougheed government to make the Alberta Research Council, which had developed the original extraction and separation technology, the central tar sands research agency in the province, and consider imposing a special research and development levy on all leaseholders to help finance development. Left to their own devices, the senior officials said, the multinationals would develop the tar sands just as they had developed Alberta's conventional oil reserves, without any real interest in ensuring benefits to Canadians, as "corporate policy . . . does not consider questions such as Canadian economic sovereignty." The report pointed out that in tar sands operations, "often the construction and operating equipment is manufactured outside of Canada. Many of the senior staff positions, both in design, construction, and operations, are filled by non-Canadians. Much of the synthetic crude is planned to be pipelined out of the region or out of Alberta for processing." And in addition to Canadianizing the projects themselves, Alberta should see that they provided opportunities for small business. For example, Sun Oil owned the employee housing development in the Great Canadian Oil Sands project at Fort McMurray: if housing projects of this sort were owned by Canadians instead of big oil companies, "the profits from housing Alberta residents would accrue in Alberta and Canada rather than in other countries."

The Lougheed Cabinet was warned that "the multinational corporations will vigorously oppose the primary and economic objectives because [they] will diminish their control and consequently minimize their profits. Alberta must stand firm in the conviction that the tar sands make up approximately one third of the known world petroleum reserves." This warning arrived just as the Alberta government began negotiation on the big Syncrude project, planned to be three times the size of the earlier GCOS development, which was 100-per-cent foreign-controlled by Imperial, Canada-Cities Service, Atlantic Richfield, and Gulf. The project arrived pre-packaged from the U.S., and the consortium was demanding a wide range of concessions and public subsidies from both levels of government. One Albertan who flung his hands in the air in amazement at all this was veteran oil writer James Gray. He produced his own list of questions to be answered before such projects were approved: "How can Canadian participation in equity financing be enforced? How can Canadian control be exercised over policy decisions? How can the employment of Canadian design and consulting engineers and architects be insisted upon? How can the operation of the projects in Canadian national and economic interests be guaranteed?"[14] These questions were not being asked seriously, but "if this were France, Mexico, or many other countries, there would be no problem about equity participation. The government would say: 'Go get yourself a French (or Mexican) partner on a 50-50 basis and then we will talk business.' In Japan the American companies might have to give up 85 per cent of the equity to Japanese partners."

In its 1973 deal with Syncrude, the Lougheed government did insist on 20-per-cent Canadian participation through the newly created Alberta Energy Corporation, owned half by the provincial government and half by private citizens. This participation was for investment purposes alone, however, and not as a lever for influencing Syncrude's operation. Exxon would still develop the technology, through a variety of agreements with Exxon Research and Engineering in the United States for which Exxon would be paid, while Bechtel engineers in California would do much of the critical "learning curve" engineering work. Lougheed agreed to join the companies to press Ottawa for all kinds of generous tax concessions. Federal finance minister John Turner met their requests in large measure, a compliance which, as shown by later analysis, made the federal government a net loser on the project.[15]

The Syncrude package was renegotiated in 1975 after Atlantic Richfield's exit. Arco's action followed the doubling of cost estimates by Bechtel engineers in late 1974 and a decision by the U.S Export-Import Bank not to approve a request by Atlantic Richfield that it finance U.S.-made equipment to be used in the project. The issues were resolved at the famous 3 February 1975 meeting in a Winnipeg hotel, where Imperial, Canada-Cities Service, and Gulf Canada executives, with Alberta Premier Peter Lougheed, Ontario Premier William Davis, and federal energy minister Donald Macdonald, negotiated an arrangement under which the three governments would become equity partners in the Syncrude project, Ottawa for $300 million, Alberta for $200 million, and Ontario for $100 million. In the new consortium, Imperial increased its participation by 1.25 per cent to 31.25 per cent, Gulf raised its share by 6.75 per cent to 16.75 per cent, and Cities Service reduced its commitment by 8 per cent to 22 per cent; Ottawa took 15, Alberta 10, and Ontario 5 per cent. Alberta retained an option for 20 per cent of the shares since, as part of the financing, that province agreed to loan Gulf and Cities Service each $100 million that could be converted into shares. On paper, then, what had started out as a 100-per-cent foreign-controlled project might now end up a government-controlled one. However, there was very little deliberate policy in all this; the situation came about as the result of ad hoc negotiations which were carried out in such a way that the new shareholders were not able to use their participation to increase Canadian benefits significantly. Though Syncrude executives were later heard to boast that the project had a very high level of Canadian content, much of this was simply window dressing. Syncrude spokesman Murray Blakely acknowledged that purchases labelled as Canadian, such as the mammoth Japanese bulldozers for the project, were so listed because they had been purchased through a Canadian supplier. "Apparently none of the government partners questioned this practice," a *Canadian Business* writer has commented.[16]

Even for new projects to be built through the 1980s, we still have no clear policies on Canadian ownership and content. Yet, as a study commissioned by the Science Council of Canada warned in 1974, "an issue of considerable concern is whether the centre of expertise related to oil sands/processing technology will develop and reside in Canada or whether it will reside primarily in the United States. . . . Oil sands technology may be of special importance to Canada. Because the first significant application of this technology is in Canada, Canadian design and supply industry groups have the potential of becoming leaders in the application of this technology to deposits in Canada and other parts of the world."[17] The study pointed out: "At the present time a large part of the design expertise and equipment supply capacity resides outside Canada. The prime engineering and managing contractor of Syncrude (as was the case for GCOS) is Canadian Bechtel Ltd., a subsidiary of Bechtel Engineering headquartered in San Francisco. In addition Syncrude, who has designed the plant with Bechtel, draws on the expertise of the member companies of the consortium: Canada-Cities Service, Atlantic Richfield Canada, Imperial

Oil, and Gulf Canada. Most of this input is from parent-company personnel in the U.S. For example, the upgrading process to be used by Syncrude was tested in Exxon's pilot plant installations in Baton Rouge, La., and Avon, California, in conjunction with Exxon Research and Engineering staff; also, Syncrude has adopted the patented fluid coking technology developed by Exxon Research and Engineering as the first stage in its bitumen upgrading process." Moreover, as the Science Council study made clear, "so long as the prime engineering and contracting companies are American (or other non-Canadian) and the major developers are subsidiaries of foreign-based (usually U.S.) multinational oil companies, the tendency will be for oil sands technological expertise to continue to grow outside of this country." Because Bechtel built the first tar sands plant, GCOS, it was well placed to get the contract for Syncrude, and as a result of this, it is to be a key contractor for the third such plant, Alsands. The Petro-Canada/Nova project will be the first to put a Canadian firm in charge of engineering and construction. Meanwhile, in the first in situ development, Imperial Oil's Cold Lake project, the subsidiary of another big U.S. engineering and construction firm, Fluor of Irvine, California, has been picked as the manager. Imperial has defended its choice by saying that "to reach 'priority one' [a successful project] a firm with worldwide experience in megaprojects in the process industries was needed, and there aren't any in Canada. So Fluor Canada Ltd. has been hired as lead contractor – 'the quarterback' – to work with four Canadian-owned companies, Cana Construction Co. Ltd., Delta Projects Ltd., Lavalin Services Inc. and SNC/FW Ltd. . . . By working with Fluor, the Canadian members of the joint venture should gain valuable additional experience."[18] The U.S. firm, however, will have a competitive edge when the next in situ plant is built. The Science Council report concluded: "Not until Canadian capital controls an oil sands undertaking will Canadian firms be favourably considered for the primary engineering responsibilities, and then only if one of sufficient size and reputation exists."

Canadians should also be concerned at the slow growth of major manufacturing industries here to supply heavy equipment for tar sands projects. The Science Council study found that "most of the mining equipment used in oil sands projects, ranging from the relatively common 150-ton trucks and front-end loaders to the huge and specialized bucket-wheel excavators and drag lines, is of foreign manufacture. Also, a large proportion of the pressure vessels and boilers is supplied from outside Canada. This will con-

tinue in the future in the absence of government direction."[19]
Shell's Alsands project will spend 75 per cent of its $330-million
mining equipment budget outside Canada. The proportion has not
improved since Syncrude. Considering the fact that tar sands will
be developed on a large scale over the next half century in Canada,
Venezuela, the United States, parts of Africa, and other parts of
the world, this country should be carving out its own areas of advanced industrial expertise. Moreover many of the items needed in
tar sands operations are related to equipment for mining or petrochemicals and refining industries, all of them important development areas for the years ahead. At the same time, while it may
have been true that only a company the size of Bechtel could
handle the Syncrude project at the time, what has to concern
Canadians is, first, that so little effort was made to give Canadian
engineering companies a joint venture role, and thus bring them
along in the learning process, and secondly, that the entire international credit goes to Bechtel in the U.S., even when Canadian subcontractors did play a role. Moreover, as Barry Beale has observed, "with a large share of engineering design performed by
non-Canadian engineers, it is not surprising that Canadian manufacturing capabilities were not readily recognized or used."[20] In
some instances, for example mining equipment for tar sands
plants, the development of technology and equipment can fit into
the broader strategy already announced by Herb Gray, Minister of
Industry, Trade and Commerce, for increasing Canadian content
in that sector.

Alsands, already cited for its procurement policy, seems to have
taken an extraordinarily indifferent line in a number of other
respects. Alberta's Energy Resources Conservation Board has
voiced a number of criticisms of its application. Alsands had apparently understated its profitability by underestimating future oil
prices and excluding much of the tar sands resource that would be
available for processing. In addition, the Shell-led group would be
wasting precious oil by its proposal to locate the plant itself,
together with much of a mammoth tailings pond, right on top of
accessible tar sands, making inaccessible 12 years of supply. The
board was particularly critical, however, of the lack of research
and development carried out by the Alsands group.[21] The process
by which the oil was to be separated was the Clark Hot Water Process that had been used in the Suncor and Syncrude plants as well.
Though the Clark process was commercially proven, the Alberta
board had noted in 1974 and again in 1975 that it had still had environmental problems, with large water requirements that had

resulted in relatively large losses of oil, and "expressed its belief that plants coming on steam by or after the mid-1980s would have ample lead time for development of [better] technology." Here was the Shell-led Alsands group admitting that its research efforts had been "small," even though the 1974 board report pointing to the need for more research had been in response to an earlier tar sands plant application by Shell itself. As far as the board was concerned, "operators contemplating bitumen resource developments have a clear responsibility to go beyond merely reviewing the current status of process technology and actively participate in research leading to improvements. The applicant's contention that research commitments cannot be made before project approval is given by regulatory agencies is wholly untenable."

Fortunately, as a result of a far-sighted move by the Alberta government, much more research and development is under way in the tar sands. In 1974, the Alberta Oil Sands Technology and Research Authority was set up in Edmonton. With $250 million in funding at the end of 1980, AOSTRA has become one of the most important energy research bodies in Canada and, for tar sands and heavy oil, in the world. It has stimulated a considerable amount of in situ, heavy oil, and enhanced recovery research and development in Canada. It also obtains and owns patents and technology, is the sole licensing agent in Canada for new technology it develops, and owns with partner companies the licensing of technology outside Canada. Engaged in numerous joint pilot-plant projects with oil companies, it has also developed research and development exchanges and agreements with Venezuela's national oil company and the U.S. Department of Energy; Petro-Canada and the federal energy department are also participating in these exchanges. Without a body like AOSTRA, Venezuela and other countries with similar tar sands or heavy oil deposits would likely have to negotiate technology sales with the foreign parents of Canadian-based tar sands facilities. One reputed reason for AOSTRA's establishment, in fact, was the anger of some Albertans in the early 1970s when Venezuelans trying to negotiate access to oil sands technology in Canada were told that they would have to deal with parent companies in the United States. With the advent of Petro-Canada, there has been another important Canadian research presence on the tar sands scene; in 1981, the company was involved in a whole range of pilot projects in Alberta as well as operating laboratory facilities in Calgary.

Whether the domination of the tar sands by the oil multinationals can be turned around will depend to a great extent on the determination of the Alberta and federal governments. While the oil industry now accepts some degree of Canadian participation in new plants, partly because of high costs but also as a sponge to now recognized Canadian sensibilities, the majors are far from ready to give up much of their decision-making power in such projects. Frank Spragins, a former Imperial Oil executive and the first president of Syncrude, made the industry point in 1974: "It is quite possible, in time, that the Canadian government, alone or in conjunction with industry, could develop the tar sands under exclusively Canadian ownership; but it is widely recognized that this would take some time, perhaps as much as one decade longer than development of the tar sands in association with multinational corporations, and during this time, Canadian energy needs could escalate to unmanageable proportions."[22] Projects must be developed "with all possible speed," he said, "if Canada is to avert a serious chronic fuels shortage in the late 1970s which could increase to major proportions during the 1980s." Nor is the industry necessarily happy about accepting public participation in tar sands projects as a substitute for public risk sharing through tax concessions. In 1979 Fraser Allen, president of Amoco Canada and CPA chairman, referred to government participation as "nationalization of risk," and argued that "if government intervention is a result of what is perceived by investors as a poor likelihood of adequate return, it would seem more desirable to make the fiscal climate attractive through modification of government take."[23] The preferred route, as Allen spelled it out, would be to boost industry profits from conventional oil reserves so that companies have the money to spend. Fortunately, some Canadians feel otherwise. According to Joe Fitzgerald, a veteran Alberta oil man and the GCOS representative in Edmonton during the construction of the first commercial tar sands plant: "There can be no doubt that it would be preferable to see the crude oil of the Athabasca entirely under Canadian control; the economy of this country would undoubtedly benefit from broader involvement by Canadian interests in resource recovery. Neither can there be any doubt that politically and socially there are countless arguments against continental integration of the United States and Canada."[24]

The oil majors today are pushing development of the tar sands, providing incentives are there. But this can mean there is no time to devise other methods of development, seek out Canadian ownership options, and promote Canadian engineering firms and manufacturing suppliers to handle these projects. During the first Syncrude negotiations, the consortium stressed that Canada had to act or see the tar sands opportunity disappear; U.S. shale oil and nuclear power would make them an anachronism unless the plant was put up quickly.[25] The same message has come from the CPA, whose chairman stated flatly in 1979 that "plants have to be built at the average of one every two years."[26] Two Esso Resources spokesmen told a 1980 conference that "the most reasonable strategy for Canada is to reduce – and hopefully eliminate – the oil deficit by conservation and rapid development of the oil sands where the challenge is not discovery, but recovery."[27] "Canada's oil sands alone could conceivably produce as much as four to five times the amount of crude oil Canada currently imports every day," Imperial announced in 1981: "We have the technology and expertise in the petroleum industry right now to build more of the oil sands plants we need. Our resources could support ten to fifteen plants the size of the two we have in operation today."[28] And a Shell Canada executive has added another reason for haste that is critical to the oil industry itself: development of the sands, he said, would "guarantee continued utilization of the large pipeline system in Canada."[29] The oil pipeline system in Canada is controlled, of course, by the same majors who dominate the tar sands; reduced use of the pipeline would cut their profits.

The pace of future tar sands development is far from clear at this point. It will be influenced by the need to establish long-term fiscal conditions, uncertainties about future supplies from Canada's frontiers, pressures of international circumstances, and the rate of improvement in technology and in overcoming environmental problems. What does seem clear is that Canadian majority ownership in this development is desirable, and among those arguing for equity rather than the kind of participation we have had up to now is University of Alberta economist Bruce Wilkinson: "It is questionable whether at any time public funds should be lent to foreign companies for them to reap much higher returns via the guarantee of world prices for production. Any public funds involved might as well go in with equity as opposed to debt participation so that it is Canadians who gain the benefits as oil prices continue to rise."[30] Indeed, since the oil majors are demanding assured high rates of return on tar sands projects in addition to substantial tax concessions, it may also be worth considering whether the projects should be operated on a utility basis with regulated rates of return. In many respects, a tar sands project is not much different from a nuclear power plant or a hydro-electric or thermal power plant; it is hard to see why sands projects should have to be assured a much higher rate of return. This approach might discourage some of the oil majors, but as the demand for tar sands oil grew, other corporations, public or public-private joint ventures, could acquire the land positions and develop the resource. Would there really be much difference between, say, an Alberta agency using Alberta Heritage and Savings Trust Fund money to operate a tar sands plant on a utility basis, perhaps in partnership with Petro-Canada, the Ontario Energy Corporation, or other public energy companies, and Ontario Hydro operating a big nuclear power plant, or Hydro-Québec running the massive James Bay power project? The principle of public energy management is well established in the Canadian experience. At the same time, it would be useful if the federal finance department were to publish an assessment of rates of return on existing tar sands projects, based on the new pricing agreement with Alberta, so that the public would be better informed on the value of tax incentives and assured prices for these projects.

Secondly, we need a much more coherent industrial benefits program for the tar sands. While the Alberta government monitors projects to ensure that Alberta and Canadian companies have opportunities to participate, the results so far have been disappointing. Moral suasion has produced minimal results. It would make much more sense to identify key areas of new technology and ensure that these products are developed and manufactured in Canada, preferably by Canadian firms or through joint ventures between Canadian firms and foreign ones. As has been suggested by some Albertans, the province's Heritage Savings and Trust Fund could invest some of its resources as equity capital in Canadian companies trying to provide machinery and equipment for tar sands projects. In the third place, we need continued research and development to overcome the environmental difficulties associated with tar sands projects and reduce the high costs of sands development. More research is also needed to see whether we can build smaller plants that would provide greater participation opportunities for independent Canadian companies. AOSTRA and a Canadian company, Umatac Industrial Processes Ltd., are already working in this area, and a breakthrough could open the field to firms shut out by the multi-billion-dollar costs of the current large-scale projects. And finally, the time has come for Alberta to review its tar sands land policies just as the federal government has overhauled its Canada Lands regulations for the far North and offshore regions. It does not make sense to continue to allow a handful of oil multinationals which picked up the bulk of the best tar sands lands under 21-year renewable leases in the 1950s and

1960s to continue to sit on these deposits and determine – or, as is often the case, have their foreign head offices determine – when and on what terms they might be willing to get moving.

With proper Canadian management, the tar sands can provide one answer to our own future energy needs and allow Canadians to make a positive contribution to the world's energy picture. But it is also important that Canadians gain financial, technology, manufacturing and skills benefits from tar sands development, so that tar sands projects help raise our standard of living. Tar sands development under Canadian management should also be used to improve Canada's trade and technology ties with other countries such as Venezuela. In this way, tar sands development would provide far-reaching benefits and opportunities for Canadians.

Prospective Tar Sands Plants

Project	Sponsor	Investment (1980 $ millions)	Construction phase
Alsands Project	Shell Canada	7,900	1982-1989
Cold Lake in situ	Esso Resources	5,900 (initial cost)	1984-1990
Peace River in situ	Shell Canada	5,400	1987-1994
Canstar	Petro-Canada and Husky Oil	5,000	1985-1989
Sandalta	Gulf Canada	4,000	1986-1993

Source: "Major Capital Projects Inventory, October, 1981." Office of Industrial and Regional Benefits. Department of Industry, Trade and Commerce, Ottawa. Dates revised.

Notes

1. Alberta Energy Resources Conservation Board. "Report 81-B, Estimates of Ultimate Potential and Forecasts of Alternative Productive Capacity of Alberta's Crude Oil and Equivalent." Calgary 1981.
2. National Energy Board. *Canadian Energy Supply and Demand 1980-2000.* Ottawa 1981.
3. A number of books describe the history of the tar sands. One is *Oil in Canada West* by George de Mille, privately printed in Calgary, 1970. Another is *Black Gold with Grit*, by J. Joseph Fitzgerald: Gray's Publishing, Sidney, B.C., 1978.
4. De Mille, *Oil in Canada West.*
5. De Mille, *Oil in Canada West.*
6. R. C. Fitzsimmons. "The Truth about Alberta Tar Sands." Pamphlet, 1953.
7. Larry Pratt. *The Tar Sands.* Edmonton, Hurtig, 1976.
8. Athabasca Oil Sands Conference Proceedings. Edmonton, Government of Alberta, September 1951.

9. Alberta Department of Mines and Minerals. "Alberta Oil Sands Facts and Figures, 1974." Edmonton 1974.
10. National Petroleum Council. *The U.S. Energy Outlook*. Washington 1972.
11. Alberta Department of Energy and Natural Resources. "Alberta Oil Sands Facts and Figures, 1978." Edmonton 1979.
12. Robert Blair to the Men's Canadian Club, Ottawa, 12 Jan. 1982.
13. "Report of the Conservation and Utilization Committee of the Alberta Government of the Executive Council on Fort McMurray and an Athabasca Tar Sands Development Strategy." Edmonton 1972.
14. James Gray, in the *Ottawa Citizen*, 26 April 1973.
15. John Helliwell and Gerry May. "Taxes, Royalties, and Equity Participation as Alternative Methods of Dividing Resource Revenues: The Syncrude Example." In *Natural Resource Revenues*, Anthony Scott ed. Vancouver, University of British Columbia Press, 1975.
16. Robert Bott. "Was Syncrude Worth It?" *Canadian Business*, February 1978.
17. "Decision-Making in the North: Oil Sands Case Study." Prepared for the Science Council of Canada by Canadian Resources Ltd., Vancouver, 1974.
18. *Imperial Oil Review*, 3 November 1980.
19. "Decision-Making in the North."
20. Barry Beale. *Energy and Industry*. Toronto, James Lorimer, 1980.
21. Alberta Energy Resources Conservation Board. Applications 780724 and 790191. Calgary, December 1979.
22. Frank Spragins, president, Syncrude Canada. "A Techno-Political Assessment of the Potential of the Alberta Tar Sands." World Energy Conference, Detroit 1974.
23. Fraser Allen. "Canadian Experience in Financing Oil Sands." IV International Colloquium on Petroleum Economics, Groupe de recherche en économie de l'énergie (GREEN). Laval University, Quebec, 30 October 1979.
24. Fitzgerald, *Black Gold with Grit*.
25. Pratt, *The Tar Sands*.
26. Allen, "Canadian Experience in Financing Oil Sands."
27. G. E. Courtnage and J. F. C. De Souza, Esso Resources Co. Ltd. Edited version of a paper on Cold Lake originally presented at the 1980 Congress on the Future for Petroleum in the Pacific Region sponsored by the Australian Institute of Petroleum, Sydney, 14-17 September 1980. *Oil and Gas Journal,* 29 December 1980.
28. M. G. Handford, Imperial Oil, to the National Association of Fleet Administrators, Toronto, 12 May 1981.
29. Jack Threet, vice-president, Exploration and Development, Shell Canada, to the Montreal Conference on International Investing, 20-21 November 1973.
30. Bruce Wilkinson, University of Alberta, to the Canadian Tax Foundation, Montreal, November 1980.

Chapter 8

Canadian Content

Oil and gas projects over the next twenty-five years promise to give Canadians unparalleled opportunities for creating new jobs and industries in all parts of the country. Not only should there be more jobs, but these should also be better jobs calling for highly productive and well-paid skills. And many projects will be requiring new or improved technologies as well as new industries. Moreover, much of this activity could enhance Canada's global reputation as a nation of highly skilled people and advanced-technology industries, an exporter of techniques and skills. While the potential spin-offs from oil and gas development will of course be no panacea for Canada's overall economic problems, they could help give Canadians a chance to make the transition from a branch-plant economy plagued by weak industries to a more in-dependent one, far better equipped to compete in a tumultuous and ever-changing world economy.

Will this happen? Will Canadians get the spin-offs from oil and gas development – industries, jobs, technology – that they should expect? In other countries, there would be little doubt of this. Japan would have an industrial policy to make sure that it hap-pened. Without a detailed strategy, such U.S. legislation as the Buy American law for big, federally financed projects and the Jones Act, which requires the use of American-made and -owned shipping to service offshore drilling rigs, would still reinforce the strong tendency of a largely U.S.-owned oil industry to use domestic engineering companies and industrial suppliers. Britain and Norway have adopted policies to ensure that their own in-dustry captures major benefits from such development.

The history is not particularly reassuring, however, as far as Canada goes. According to the 1981 Major Project Task Force report, Canadians missed out in the big resource boom of the mid-dle to late 1950s, and "this was particularly true in the oil and gas sector."[1] Canada's rapid resource development in that decade gave openings to U.S. and European engineers and manufacturers for the generation of new skills, technology, and products. After the 1950s experience, in the words of the task force, "Canadians became concerned that, as a result of the established linkages associated with foreign investment, they were not being adequately involved in the large projects being proposed and undertaken in this country." In other words, Canadians came to see that they would be excluded even from consideration when contracts were being handed out. And in fact, many of these contracts were even led by the parent-company head office, not the Canadian subsidiary.

Direct spin-offs to bring Canadian industry into the development of resource projects were what most concerned the Major Projects Task Force. And here, ownership has clearly made a difference: "In examining Canadian strengths in the development and application of technology, one finds that industrial sectors such as electric power generation and transmission, steel, transportation, and communications have grown up with a high level of participation by Canadian-owned firms." Where a major industry has had a high level of Canadian ownership, there have been significant spin-offs. Where the level of Canadian ownership has been low, as in oil and gas, there have been far fewer industrial and other spin-offs available to Canadians.

While Canadian content in resource projects only really emerged as an issue during the 1970s – further proof that Canada has been rich in resources but poor in policies – we can find an example of earlier sensitivity on this question in the late 1940s, when Imperial Oil put together the Interprovincial pipeline project to move oil from western Canada to U.S. and Ontario markets. One of the biggest projects in Canadian history, it was designed and engineered through Imperial at offices in Tulsa, Oklahoma; U.S. engineers and draftsmen moved to Canada temporarily to oversee its completion. Early on, the U.S. engineering giant, Bechtel Corp., had aired a competing scheme to own, build, and operate an oil pipeline from Edmonton to the Great Lakes. According to an Imperial internal report: "The feeling at the moment is against foreign capital . . . and we are quite confident that any move to turn over the entire project to an American group without reference to a Canadian group as sponsors would be received very critically by the financial people here and certainly by the government officials in the finance department in Ottawa."[2] In 1949, Interprovincial's executive vice-president, L. F. Kahle, met with senior Alberta government officials who were concerned about lack of Canadian content in the project, and especially the decision to rely mainly on U.S. contractors in construction. He told them that "a number of Canadian contractors had been considered and among them, Fred Mannix was associated with the successful bidders on the 20-inch section of the line between Edmonton and Regina."[3] Canadians, then, would participate as junior partners in just one portion of the line. Kahle also recorded officials' concern about the number of jobs going to non-residents: "We gave an opinion that more than 50 per cent of the labour employed on the line would be Canadian, but that this was not binding or a definite figure. We also pointed out that the benefits to be derived by the economy of western Canada are not so much in the amount of money spent or the labour employed in building the line, but in the continuous flow of revenues which would result from providing an outlet for the crude producible in this area." The same day, Kahle met with Nathan Tanner, Alberta Minister of Mines and Minerals, to explain why U.S. contractors had been chosen, and "Mr. Tanner seemed to completely understand our position that we had to get competent and reliable contractors on this work in order to complete the project on time and he agreed that the prime objective was to get the pipeline in."[4] Kahle pointed out that Canadian companies had been invited to bid and that a number of them had formed partnerships with U.S. firms to get access to existing know-how and equipment, but he did not explain why all of them had been rejected. Still, "Mr. Tanner expressed the view that since they had all been given adequate consideration, they should have no complaint." The principal contracts went to three U.S. companies, Canadian Bechtel, Williams Brothers, and Anderson Brothers. There was little other pressure for Canadian content, beyond a letter from C. D. Howe, Minister of Trade and Commerce, to Imperial Oil president G. L. Stewart, hoping that "Canadian requirements for pipelines will be obtained from Canadian sources wherever possible. Our balance of payments situation is becoming more difficult each month."[5]

While the federal government was optimistic about the oil and gas potential of western Canada, it saw few opportunities in the early 1950s for processing these resources, for example into petrochemicals, or creating spin-off engineering and manufacturing industries to serve oil and gas exploration, development, and production. There was a resigned attitude with regard to boosting Canadian content or increasing Canadian benefits from oil and gas. Instead, policy-makers took the view that Canadians were lucky just to have the resources plus whatever tax and royalty benefits these might generate. U.S. industry was the main beneficiary of resources development, the Department of Defence Production reported in a confidential 1952 study: "Roughly 60 cents out of every dollar going into exploration and development has been going directly to United States machinery and equipment manufacturers. Practically all of the oil-well drilling machinery, as well as the seismograph trucks, bulldozers, ditch-digging machinery, and specially equipped vehicles required to carry out magnetometer and gravity-meter surveys, have had to be imported. Shipments from the United States of oil-well drilling machinery alone have amounted to over one hundred million dollars since 1946."[6] While there could be greater use of Canadian labour and raw materials, as well as greater use of standard industrial equipment such as steel pipes and pumps supplied by Canadian manufacturers, new technology would be left to non-Canadians. "New techniques and machinery are continually being developed for purposes of exploration by companies who are international specialists in such matters. In addition, the more elaborate type of investment project associated particularly with developments in the petrochemical and refining fields are beyond the capacity of Canadian contractors, who will therefore in the main carry out the more modest tasks involved in such projects. Although these contributions made by foreign specialists are essential to the carrying out of the Canadian oil investment program, it should be noted that the Canadian operators whose experience and know-how would enable them to perform tasks in the United States similar to those they carry out in Canada are prohibited, largely due to high tariffs on equipment and special licensing agreements." Although Ottawa acknowledged that Canadians were not getting all the industrial benefits they might, there appeared to be scant inclination to do anything about the situation.

In 1957, a special study on the outlook for Canadian energy up to 1980, prepared for the Gordon Commission on Canada's Economic Prospects, again drew attention to the lack of Canadian industrial benefits from oil and gas development: "One of the most significant characteristics of the energy program is its import content. Many of the specialized engineering services and much of the machinery and equipment employed by the oil and gas industries will continue to be purchased elsewhere."[7] Although the study projected a massive increase in oil and gas exploration, development, and production spending – including refineries, oil and gas pipelines, and gas processing plants – from $505 million in

1955 to between $2.5 and $3 billion a year (1955 dollars) by 1980, it made no specific recommendation on how Canadian content was to be increased.

James Gray, editor of the *Western Oil Examiner*, was one of the few at the time who saw this as a national issue. Noting that Alberta's Energy Resource Conservation Board relied on U.S. engineers and geologists as expert witnesses for its hearings, he asked why Canadian engineers and geologists could not be used. They had the expertise and were the people who handled many of the oil and gas industry projects in Canada. "One reason why the big American firms get so much work is because the New York brokers who finance pipelines with other people's money demand reports from engineers in whom they have confidence. To butter up the brokers, Canadian companies naturally employ the big name outfits because it gets them around one hurdle. But to the extent that this militates against the establishment of a thoroughly competent reservoir of engineering consultants in Canada, it is against the best interests of Canada and the oil industry . . . the more use that is made of foreign firms the less work there will be for our local engineers, the less chance there is for them to grow into the large and prosperous consulting practices."[8]

Moreover, when efforts were made to bolster Canadian content, most foreign-controlled companies simply ignored them. In 1966, for example, Ottawa sent all the multinationals a letter spelling out guidelines for good corporate citizenship. These included: "(6) In matters of procurement, to search out and develop economic sources of supply in Canada; (7) To develop as an integral part of the Canadian operation wherever practicable, the technological research and design capability necessary to enable the company to pursue appropriate product development programs so as to take full advantage of market opportunities domestically and abroad."[9] The plea fell on deaf ears. There was little effort to expand Canadian industrial opportunities in the oil and gas industry. Until 1975, for instance, according to the Canadian Association of Oil Well Drilling Contractors, the Canadian share in western drilling rigs was about zero per cent.[10] An analysis by the Ontario Ministry of Industry and Tourism of Canadian refinery construction between 1966 and 1971 showed that only about 6 per cent of the work, with a total value of $971 million, was engineered in Canada: "The oil industry is a highly integrated one, largely controlled in the U.S., and major oil companies have apparently concluded that it would not be profitable to decentralize into Canada the technical design work involved in the construction of refineries. Therefore, it appears that much of the design and engineering work, particularly for large projects, is conducted in the U.S. by both the oil company and the engineering contractor it hires. No such detailed examination of the petrochemical and chemical and other process industries has been carried out, but it appears that these are also areas in which a high proportion of engineering services are imported."[11] The study showed that Canadian-controlled engineering firms got between 20 and 35 per cent of their Canadian business from foreign-controlled companies in Canada, while foreign-controlled engineering firms got between 50 and 95 per cent of their business from foreign-controlled companies in Canada. Another study carried out at this time by the Association of Professional Engineers of Ontario concluded that the reputation of an engineering firm with the foreign parent company was critical: ". . . the subsidiaries 'purchase' the parent companies' 'know-how' in relying on experts known to the parent companies. The motivations then are related to group economics, group control, and group expertise."[12]

The early 1970s was a time of heightening awareness among Canadians of opportunities lost. In 1973, the Science Council of Canada reviewed trade journals and working papers from various government departments on the practices of multinational corporations. It highlighted the concern that "Canadian-controlled engineering, geological, and advertising consultants have often been unsuccessful in bidding on large projects in Canada in cases where financing is to be obtained in other countries, especially the United States. Institutions providing financing rely heavily upon feasibility and design studies and accept the work of consultants from their own countries more readily than that of Canada."[13] Another concern reported was that "the high degree of foreign control of the Canadian oil and gas industry leads to an outcome where nearly all technical and scientific information is sent via computer tape to research centres such as Houston, Texas, where research based upon it is undertaken. In this field little basic geological research is undertaken in Canada and Canadians who wish to advance in this field are required to leave Canada." The Science Council noted other possible areas where benefits had been lost to Canada because of high foreign ownership: management development, research and development, associated industries, related advertising, public relations, and management and engineering consulting services.

In 1970, the federal government had taken one of its first steps towards imposing Canadian content rules on the oil and gas industry. At the time, industry proposals for oil and gas pipelines from Alaska and the Mackenzie Delta were taking shape in corporate boardrooms. The Delta Oil Project (Gulf, Shell, Imperial, Interprovincial Pipeline, and Trans-Mountain Pipe Line) was reviewing the feasibility of an oil line, while Canadian Arctic Gas Pipeline (Exxon, Imperial Oil, BP/Sohio, Shell, Gulf, Atlantic Richfield, and Canadian Superior) was looking at gas pipeline prospects. It was clear that industry intended both of these to be very much under the thumb of the oil majors, and this prompted the fear in Ottawa that Canadians would be left on the sidelines as far as industrial benefits went. For this reason, 1970 guidelines issued by federal ministers Joe Greene of Energy, Mines and Resources and Jean Chrétien of Indian Affairs and Northern Development stressed that "means by which Canadians will have a substantial opportunity for participating in the financing, engineering, construction, ownership, and management of northern pipelines will form an important element in Canadian government consideration of proposals for such pipelines."[14] What this meant, as energy minister Donald Macdonald was to explain at a 1973 meeting with Canadian Arctic Gas executives, was that "the onus will be on the companies to buy Canadian or show why they can't."[15] Special emphasis, Macdonald said, would be placed on maximum Canadian engineering and design, as this was the route for acquiring new technology and know-how: "This is the new area of expertise and we should finance the development of this expertise in Canada." Although Canadian engineering firms formed groups to bid for pipeline contracts, the oil majors favoured the U.S. Bechtel or Williams Brothers, and Canadian Arctic Gas eventually picked a consortium that did include Canadian participation, but was effectively controlled by Williams.

In 1972, Cabinet approved a directive stressing that there must be Canadian content in any major development project on Canada Lands in the far North and Atlantic offshore. But as a confidential finance department study pointed out, calling for Canadian content in something like a northern pipeline was one thing, and achieving it was quite another. The National Energy Board, under Section 44 of the National Energy Board Act, could take Canadian content into account on projects such as pipelines: "Nevertheless, existing procedures for receiving information on supplies before and after contracts are entered into are inadequate to ensure that any particular level of Canadian content is achieved. In view of the magnitude of this project and the likely high level of foreign participation under any set of guidelines, the government may find it necessary to initiate procedures which would ensure that Canadian industries, in practice as well as in theory, obtain a fair chance to compete as pipeline suppliers."[16] In fact, the finance officials concluded, without Canadian ownership and control of the pipeline plus identification by the Department of Industry, Trade and Commerce of specific industries that should use this as a chance to expand their expertise and benefit from special treatment, Canadian content would get little more than lip service. This was one reason why the alternative pipeline proposal for a pipeline – the Foothills project led by Alberta Gas Trunk, now Nova – eventually edged out the competing Canadian Arctic Gas project dominated by the oil majors. It was Canadian-controlled, much more attuned to Canadian aspirations, and had a proven record of Canadian content.

In the meantime, in 1974, the federal government set up its Advisory Committee on Canadian Content in Oil and Gas Operations on Canada Lands as a watchdog to see that the objectives for Canadian industrial spin-offs from resource development in the North and Atlantic offshore were met. Yet the oil industry still appeared oblivious. For example, in May 1975, Imperial Oil chose a U.S. company, Fluor Corp., to build a major gas processing plant in the Mackenzie Delta. In a critical letter to Imperial chairman Jack Armstrong, the Minister of Indian Affairs and Northern Development, Judd Buchanan, said that it was "appropriate" for Imperial to review its decision. Buchanan expressed concern that Imperial Oil did not "fully appreciate the importance that the government places on Canadian participation in resources activities in Canada."[17] He wrote further: "We also question your belief that Canadian companies do not possess the degree of competence required to perform the engineering services called for in the Fluor contract. We were surprised, since at this moment the Canadian government is assisting in efforts by MONNAX (Montreal Engineering and Mannix) to export a gas gathering plant, of the very type required by you, to the Soviet Union. Furthermore, we have been informed by you and other experts that, with some exceptions, basically no new techniques have to be developed to perform this task. Finally, while you have advised this department and the Advisory Committee on Canadian Content that you expect to achieve 85-per-cent Canadian content in the overall project, you now indicate that of the 700,000 man hours of engineering work arising from the Fluor contract, only about one third would be contributed by Canadians." Buchanan reminded Imperial Oil that the government was "particularly concerned that Canada's project management and engineering service capability be developed with emphasis on the technological and innovative participation of Canadians." Through the letter, which was made public, Buchanan reminded the oil and gas industry that there was "a growing Canadian concern with respect to the level and nature of Canadian participation in the development of Canadian resources. If what is judged to be a reasonable level of Canadian participation cannot be achieved through voluntary co-operation, it will be necessary to consider establishing regulations to enforce the government's objectives." Following this, the minister announced in the House of Commons that the government had clarified its policy "in the key area of engineering and project management by setting an objective that such services must be carried out by firms which are beneficially owned or controlled by Canadians (or else performed or serviced by Canadians) unless it is clearly demonstrated that there is no potentially competitive firm. Even should it be necessary to contract abroad for such services, the government would wish that the foreign contractor place as much of the job in Canada as possible. It is apparent that up to 90 per cent of the work could be performed in Canada under most circumstances." Yet Gulf Canada also chose a U.S. firm for its gas processing plant in the Mackenzie Delta.

In the meantime, Buchanan had also sent a letter informing the oil and gas industry of the formation of the Advisory Committee on Industrial Benefits for Natural Resources Development (ACIB) as the successor to the more informal Advisory Committee on Canadian Content. The new committee consisted of representatives from several government departments, including Industry, Trade and Commerce, Indian Affairs and Northern Development, Energy, Mines and Resources, Employment and Immigration, and Transport. The Minister laid down five objectives: "increasing sourcing of equipment and services in Canada, emphasizing those with a substantial level of technological and innovative input by Canadians with a view to encouraging the growth and establishment of firms in Canada with independent, ongoing capabilities; the supply of these services and equipment on a fair and internationally competitive basis; increased participation of firms beneficially owned and controlled by Canadians; encouraging industrial activity in disparate regions of Canada; encouraging resource companies to rationalize their sourcing by purchasing in Canada for their worldwide operations."[18] Buchanan told the industry that he expected companies to contact either his department or Energy, Mines and Resources in the early planning stages of any resource activity being contemplated for Canada Lands. Subsequently, in 1976, Shell Canada awarded a contract for its Delta gas processing plant to a Canadian-led engineering consortium, MHG (Montreal Engineering, with majority ownership, and Humphreys of Glasgow, Britain). Its technology even turned out to be superior to that developed by U.S. firms for Imperial and Gulf.

While the processing plants in the Mackenzie Delta are now on hold until a pipeline to bring the gas out has been approved, the government's experience with the northern gas pipeline and such related facilities as the design and construction of gas processing plants taught it the importance of clear-cut requirements for Canadian content as well as the advantages of having a Canadian-controlled company in charge of a major northern line. The later Northern Pipeline Act (1978), administered by the Northern Pipeline Agency, shows how Canadian content can be given legislative backing in a major project, and no doubt reflects federal concern at the ineffectiveness of voluntary guidelines. Under Section 10 of the Act, the company, Foothills (Yukon) Ltd., must develop a purchasing policy ensuring that:

(i) Canadians have a fair and competive opportunity to participate in the supply of goods and services to the pipelines.

(ii) The level of Canadian content is maximized so far as practicable with respect to the origin of products, services, and their constituent components.

(iii) Maximum advantage is taken of opportunities provided by the pipeline to establish and expand suppliers in Canada that can make a long-term contribution to the Canadian industrial base.

(iv) Maximum advantage is taken of opportunities provided by the pipeline to foster research, development, and technological activities in Canada.[19]

As a result, Canadians are reaping noticeable industrial benefits from the Alaska Highway pipeline project, in both Canadian-owned companies and subsidiaries of foreign-controlled manufacturing companies that have won world product mandates from their parent firms for research, design, engineering, manufacturing, and international sales. Canadian steel pipe makers have developed new Arctic-grade steel. Turbine compressor units to push the gas through the pipeline are being built in Canada, as are many of the pipe fittings.[20] Canadians are handling the line's engineering and project management.

At the same time, other Canadian companies have moved aggressively in recent years into the manufacture of conventional drilling equipment. While in the nineteenth century, Canadians designed equipment that was used in many other parts of the world, prospects for a Canadian industry died off as exploration declined in the years before 1914. Although the industry might have been expected to bounce back with the massive late-1940s and '50s increase in exploration and development drilling, it did not: instead, rigs were imported from the United States. As recently as the mid-1970s, Canadian content in this industry was close to nil; today, however, between 70 and 80 per cent of drilling-rig costs flows back to Canadian-based companies. Some Canadian concerns, an example being Dreco, now enjoy worldwide reputations.

By contrast, refining and gas-processing plant technology and construction has remained largely in the hands of foreign corporations. Refining capacity increased more than threefold in the years 1947-60 and more than doubled again between 1960 and 1975, but with only limited Canadian participation. Canadian engineers were not employed to design and build refineries. It is true that, for a time, Canadian companies had little capacity to take on refining projects. But this situation has changed in recent years, and there is no reason why in future, Canadian firms should not play an important role in the upgrading technology for heavy oil and tar sands oil and the construction of gas processing plants.

The Alberta officials who briefed Premier Lougheed and his Cabinet in 1972 were concerned to enlist state support for the breaking of this cycle of dependence, and they were especially insistent that Canadians corner the engineering jobs and manufacturing business from the new plants.[21] A similar concern was voiced in a 1976 brief to the federal government from the Association of Consulting Engineers of Canada, urging new Canadian guidelines to secure our own engineers a leading role in oil and gas development. There was nothing wrong with the track record of Canadian engineers in sectors where they had grown along with industry; but, said the association, "this is unfortunately not the case in industries like oil and gas which appeared in a major way in Canada after the last world war and which continued to rely for process engineering and project management mainly on foreign engineers."[22] The technology for the oil and gas industry, including oil and petrochemical refining and natural gas processing, was developed mainly in the United States, and "to date, there has been no efficient method whereby the management of process technology can be transferred to Canadian groups. In fact the reverse is true . . . engineering of the facilities and management of construction generally goes to the firms which are regularly operating with the majors. You either belong to the 'Houston Club' or you don't.'' Millions of dollars in engineering profits were flowing out of Canada: looking at the operations of some of the major U.S. engineering firms active in the Canadian oil and gas industry in 1973-74, the Association of Consulting Engineers identified revenues of about $500 million, and even assuming a modest return of 10 per cent, this still put a round sum in outside hands. Canadian engineers were developing a global reputation for their performance in such industries as hydro-electricity, mining, pulp and paper, and railways, where there were Canadian-owned companies, but not in oil and gas, which was foreign-controlled. Moreover, while Canada allowed a steady flow of engineering work from Canadian oil and gas projects to flow freely across the border to U.S. engineering centres, the United States imposed a tariff of 4 per cent on the value of engineering work done in Canada for American clients.

The engineers asked for government regulation to offset the bias in the industry: "The development of a process technology-oriented engineering industry commences with the involvement of that industry in the development of these new technologies. Unless the Canadian engineer is caught with enthusiasm of the actual 'doing' of the development of new process technology, he will normally be on the sidelines, looking in, as foreign specialists apply their know-how in design and construction of both new and repetitive process technologies." There must be a major effort to develop resource technology in Canada, and "this should be recognized as particularly important in resource industries that are owned mainly by non-Canadians. It is becoming apparent more and more that ownership of technology and expertise is probably as important as the ownership of means of production. Engineering firms are no doubt the unique and privileged vehicles for acquiring and maintaining technological know-how in Canada."

The difficulty Canadian companies encountered in getting a fair share of contracts, especially for projects requiring new technology, was also spelled out in a 1978 industry-labour task force report on the ocean industry. "American service and equipment supply companies, as a result of pioneering oil and gas exploration in the Gulf of Mexico, dominate many aspects of the world's offshore hydrocarbon operations. These companies over the years have established close working relations with the major oil companies, resulting in a petroleum infrastructure in both technical and financial fields."[23] Canadian companies lacked both the U.S. companies' experience and their special relationships with the foreign-controlled oil giants. Moreover, the ocean industry group complained, "while the current Canadian government position encourages exploration as fully as possible, there is no legislation requiring foreign oil companies to utilize Canadian expertise when operating in Canadian waters." The conditions Ottawa then attached to the issuing of exploration permits did little to encourage oil companies and their service contractors to use Canadian goods and services, while the federal Advisory Committee on Industrial Benefits could employ only moral suasion and public pressure. The task force concluded: "Canada risks being dependent upon foreign operations not only for the primary production of its resources but also for most of the ancillary goods and services which might otherwise provide the most important direct impact upon the local economy."

The ocean industry study noted that while the industry might grow tenfold during the 1980s, this growth was dependent on strict regulations for a high level of Canadian technological content, recognition that the industry would have a difficult time raising equity financing without an encouraging tax environment, and government programs to ensure that adequate research and development were carried out, especially in the area of new offshore technology. It urged the establishment of a Canadian Ocean Technology Research Authority, with $100 million in federal funds plus money from private industry, to conduct research and development projects, with the resulting technology to be Canadian-owned.

By the late 1970s the federal government had learned a number of important lessons about the business habits of these foreign-controlled companies as well as the effectiveness of its voluntary guidelines. It concluded that laws or regulations were needed for Canadians to get a fair share of the work on their own resource projects, and it had also discovered that other countries already had stiff domestic requirements for key sectors of their economies. Finally, the government recognized the crucial role of the engineering and project management firms, U.S.-owned companies such as Bechtel, Fluor, Williams Bros., and Pullman-Kellogg, which were the oil companies' usual choices for the big projects. It was they who developed much of the technology needed to exploit Canadian resources, frequently at their U.S. parent facilities, and chose the major industrial suppliers for projects, again frequently choosing foreign ones with whom they had working relationships instead of developing Canadian alternatives.

In December 1978, as a further measure to stress Canadian content, the federal government, following meetings with provincial industry ministers, appointed the Major Projects Task Force, a group of 80 business and labour leaders along with representatives from eight provincial governments – Alberta and Prince Edward Island having refused to participate. The task force was co-chaired by Robert Blair of Nova and Shirley Carr, a vice-president of the Canadian Labour Congress. The group's program was to review all projects costing more than $100 million, aside from property and real estate developments, likely to be built up to the year 2000, and study their needs in manpower, technology, project management, engineering, procurement and construction services, manufactured imports, and financing; its goal was to recommend ways, based on these needs, to secure the greatest possible industrial benefit for Canada. While some $440 billion in projects from all sectors of the economy were dealt with, those in oil and gas accounted for a large proportion of the total, as did petrochemicals and coal and uranium mining, other areas where the oil majors are leading investors.

In its 1981 report, the task force confirmed that in the oil and gas industry, including refining, Canadians had derived inadequate industrial benefits, which translated into fewer jobs, less opportunity to develop technology and know-how, and less wealth for the country. For example, although Canada is one of the world's largest potential users of tar sands in situ technology, "until recently Canadian firms have not been involved in its development. Most work in these areas has been carried out by foreign-controlled companies, with Canada providing the 'test-bench'."[24] But this had to change, the task force said, and went on to spell out important areas in which Canadian know-how, jobs, and industries could be developed. These included tertiary recovery, the western tar sands, where the sheer size of operations "should make Canada a world leader in mining technology," and frontier developments. In the North, the task force found reason for optimism: "To date, technological developments in these fields have had a strong degree of involvement by Canadian firms. Dome Petroleum has built up a world-class team of naval architects and engineers. A consortium of Canadian firms operating as the Arctic Pilot Project is developing a liquefied natural gas transportation scheme from the Arctic islands to southern Canada. Special attention is being given on this project to the development of Canadian technology. As well, Canadian firms sponsoring the Polar Gas Project have developed and tested procedures for laying pipelines through ice." The striking feature of all these projects was that they were being directed by Canadian-controlled oil and gas companies.

Along Canada's east coast, the story is quite different, as the task force found: "To date, there has been little 'Canadian' technical participation. . . . Canadian coastal waters provide some of the most challenging deep-water areas in the world and it makes sense for Canadian technology to develop in this area." The lack of Canadian leverage in areas such as Mobil Oil's Hibernia field, even with Petro-Canada as a minority partner, has been borne out by other research. According to a Toronto engineering consultant: "Participation at this level provides some information on how the project is developing but absolutely no leverage in the important procurement decisions for the project. These decisions are left to Mobil's head office in New York."[25] The British in the early 1970s were getting only 25 to 30 per cent of the equipment and service business associated with North Sea oil and gas development; as a result of direct government intervention to deal with a situation the British found to be unacceptable, however, this content was raised to over 75 per cent by the late 1970s. "Currently Canada stands in a worse position than the U.K. did in 1972," finance minister Allan MacEachen has commented: "About 85 per cent of the goods and services used in Canada's offshore activities are imported, and duty free at that."[26] The Major Projects Task Force insisted that there was no time to lose: "The lesser developed countries of the world are assimilating more and more of the 'mature' technologies. Canada will therefore have to make efforts to stay at the leading edge of technology in selected fields of endeavour in order to enhance or even maintain our competitive position in the world. Domestic economic activity alone will make Canada a major consumer of various types of technology. The question to be answered then, is 'To what extent can Canadians afford to continue to rely on the importation of technology that is required for Canadian economic and industrial development?' "[27]

However, the Canadian drive to capture a large share of economic spinoffs will not be easy: "With limited offshore exploration experience and no domestic field development and production experience, Canadian participation will be severely challenged by the experience of the foreign firms."[28] In 1979, for example, only 35 per cent of the $190 million spent off Canada's east coast went to companies based in Canada. Not only have U.S. companies much longer experience in offshore activities, but the British and Norwegians also have had a good decade to hone their skills, while the Japanese as well are now active in offshore exploration and production equipment and services. Much of the development of new technology will be site-specific, so that Canadians will pay for it through the prices they pay for subsequent oil and gas production. And as James Stanford, a Petro-Canada vice-president, has pointed out, it takes a determined effort to secure long-term industrial benefits. While both the British and Norwegians, for example, have pursued high domestic-content policies in North Sea oil and gas projects, the results were not identical: "Much of the spin-off activity generated in the U.K. was in low-technology areas, such as in the construction of platform-building facilities, module construction, and direct supplies to platforms and rigs. In contrast, the Norwegians built a capacity to compete worldwide in several areas of specialty, such as in rig design, ownership and operations, and in platform and equipment design."[29] The result of this is that Britain has lost many of the long-term benefits she might have gained. In the case of offshore rigs, for example, Norway in the space of a decade set up a world-scale industry four to five times the size of the British one.

Clear government policies are obviously needed both on ownership and on spin-offs. Most importantly, according to the Major Projects Task Force, "governments must take a lead role and must demonstrate an unfailing commitment to the support of Canadian firms."[30] As the task force saw it: "Large and sustained demands in Canada and abroad over the next ten to 20 years will create a substantial market for management, engineering, procurement, and construction services. Canada will represent one of the world's larger markets for such skills. These factors combine to provide a major opportunity for Canadian firms to develop a world-scale capability in design, in process technology development, in project control systems and procedures, and in the management of large projects." What this means, the task force added, is that "the traditional reluctance of the Canadian subsidiaries of foreign-based multinational enterprises to employ Canadian-owned firms on their Canadian projects must be addressed."

The National Energy Program of 1980 attempted to impose realistically stiff rules on energy projects, especially in the Canadian North and Atlantic offshore. The new Canada Lands legislation, in its first draft, gave the federal government much greater scope for achieving these goals. Since the Major Projects Task Force has identified $74.7 billion of spending for frontier exploration and development over the next 20 years, this is obviously important. Under new Canadian legislation covering these areas, companies exploring for oil and natural gas had to have an exploration agreement with the federal government. One of the things companies had to do, according to the first draft of this legislation, was "submit a plan satisfactory to the Minister [of Energy, Mines and Resources] for the employment of Canadians and the use of Canadian goods and services in carrying out their work program."[31] Similarly, companies seeking production licences also had to "submit a plan satisfactory to the Minister for the employment of Canadians and the use of Canadian goods and services in the work or activity."[32] This intention was also expressed in the National Energy Program, with its promise of "strict requirements for use of Canadian goods and services in exploration, development, and production programs on the Canada Lands, and in major non-conventional oil projects."[33] The reason was obvious: "Energy-related investments will have spin-off effects that will stimulate the overall level of economic activity and foster rapid growth of businesses across the country, providing goods and services to the energy industry. One of the most promising areas in this respect is the Atlantic offshore. There, a projected multi-billion-dollar petroleum investment surge could, with the framework established by the program, revolutionize the industrial and employment outlook of the region." Moreover, it was argued, "many of the challenges of future energy developments are somewhat unique to Canada – oil sands development and operations in ice-infested frontier waters, for example. Technical advances in these and other areas will have to be paid for by the value of the Canadian resources involved, regardless of which companies undertake the work, and it is only fair that the benefits of the activity and know-how associated with such efforts accrue to Canadians."

What Canada was clearly doing was belatedly following such examples as those of Britain and Norway in the North Sea. Yet as we noted at the beginning of this book, the NEP called up a storm of protest, some of it coming through U.S. and E.E.C. diplomatic channels. There was an obvious odour of sponsorship about all this. And yet the diplomatic pressure did have some effect, mellowing official statements and evidently moving Ottawa to water down its Canadian content requirements. The amended version of the Canada Lands regulation stated only that companies had to show that they had given Canadian companies an opportunity to bid. The tone of tough government pushing for Canadian content was gone. Industry, Trade and Commerce Minister Herb Gray has set up an office of Industrial and Regional Benefits to ensure that Canadians knew about the opportunities, formed a government committee on Industrial and Regional Benefits to devise ways to ensure that Canadians pursued potential openings, and promised guidelines on Canadian content for all projects of $100 million or more. But the federal government has not so far responded to a Major Projects Task Force recommendation that companies making megaproject investments set aside 3 per cent of the total cost of the project as a premium to help the development of Canadian suppliers.

If Canada were Japan, there would be much less controversy over a policy to capture industrial benefits. The Japanese would team up a major planning body of government and industry to foster new high-technology businesses. But several factors have worked against a more assertive Canadian policy. These include the traditional reluctance of government to play a planning role, the opposition of the oil majors to government intervention in support of Canadian content, and the narrow vision of many provincial governments that support provincial content in projects but are unwilling to help develop a broader Canadian content. With this provincial attitude, it is hard to see how Canadians can reap all the potential industrial benefits.

A Canadian content program that really works will have to include some kind of central procurement and industrial benefits office that compiles data on all coming projects, identifies areas of industry opportunity for Canada, seeks out Canadian companies to participate, obtains advance notice from industry of all major contracts for goods or services such as engineering of more than, say, $500,000, and demands explanations when orders are placed outside Canada. At the same time, key areas of new technology to be developed in Canada should be identified – tar sands or frontier oil and gas development, for example – and every possible step taken to ensure that a Canadian supplier becomes available. This is the kind of policy that can be pursued as part of an activist industrial strategy. In the same vein, there should be strict monitoring of Canadian content in resource development and an annual report on what the oil and gas industry is actually doing to upgrade this content. The procurement office would, as the Major Projects Task Force proposed, ensure Canadian access to managerial, professional, technical, and skilled jobs in the planning, engineering, construction, and operation of big projects, and the selection of Canadian-controlled firms for key action roles in the learning curve of new technology and skills. Where Canadian firms cannot be found to play the leading role, they would still have joint-venture opportunities to acquire technology. The program's success, though, would depend very heavily on provincial cooperation for such areas as tar sands and heavy oil. There is a precedent for such an agency in the British Offshore Supplies Office for North Sea oil and gas.

It would also be worth having the Canadian Petroleum Association and the Independent Petroleum Association of Canada negotiate, with federal and provincial governments, a procurement code that spells out the procedures industry should follow, in awarding contracts, to strengthen Canadian content and secure commitments for research and development. Industrial oil companies would be expected to abide by the procurement code as a condition of membership in industry associations. The oil majors were willing to do something similar in Britain, and there is no reason why they shouldn't do the same thing here; they are largely the same companies.

In tandem with this, the national procurement office could, as engineering consultant Barry Beale has suggested,[34] establish a "Made in Canada" label. This would, of course, require a clear definition of Canadian content. While the oil and gas industry has preferred to use the simple but misleading definition that identifies as Canadian anything obtained from Canadian sources, including importing agents, the only definition that makes sense, as Beale pointed out, is one that deducts the cost of imported components from the total of the manufactured goods and permits a "Made in Canada" stamp only when there is a high level of Canadian content, say 60 or 70 per cent. This approach is not without its difficulties, but it is the one to work on.

A special effort is also needed to expand the role of Canadian engineering, procurement, construction, and design in major projects. This is a critical step for Canadian content, since it is the project engineering company that determines which companies develop technology, supply computer software and other services and designs, and manufacture important components and systems. The disappointment with Imperial Oil's decision to make Fluor the principal engineering firm on the Cold Lake in situ plant lies in the fact that much of the new technology engineering will be done in Irvine, California, and Fluor, rather than a Canadian engineering company, will become a world leader in the in situ technology, just as Bechtel has in tar sands mining technology. But the necessary bootstrap effort is being seen now on the Canadian private side, where a growing number of firms are bringing in foreign partners to fill gaps and achieve a transfer of technology in

Canada. These include such major companies as SNC, Lavalin, Simons Engineering, and Acres. Associated Engineering Services of Edmonton is another example: two years ago, it formed a joint corporate enterprise with Pullman-Kellogg of Calgary, under Canadian control, to develop the expertise to build petrochemical and tar sands plants. Similarly, a Vancouver-based firm, Wright Engineering, has formed a partnership which it controls, Wright-Technip, with the French engineering company Technip. The agreement provides for technology transfer to Canada in such key areas as natural gas liquefaction.

The importance of a country's having its own major engineering firms was spelled out in a report of Britain's Monopolies and Mergers Commission opposing the takeover of the country's largest such company, Davy Ltd., by the U.S. oil and gas giant, Enserch Corp.[35] The existence of an engineering firm capable of managing megaprojects, said the departments of Trade and Industry in their submissions to the commission, is "exceptionally important. Significant employment and technological benefits flow from the existence of a thriving industry capable of undertaking the design and construction of major capital projects overseas, as well as from the associated subcontracting business." Implicit in this statement is the assumption that a British engineering company managing a megaproject will make sure work flows back to British manufacturers and subcontractors. The commission itself quoted unpublished E.E.C. research stressing that one important reason why a country would want a major domestic engineering contractor is that it will bring in orders for manufacturers. The E.E.C. calculated that every design engineer on a project can mean six domestic manufacturing jobs. According to Davy Ltd., British engineering contractors working around the world would buy over 90 per cent of their equipment from British sources, as compared to U.S. contractors in Britain who were reported to place 60 per cent of their orders in that country.

The Foreign Review Investment Agency can also be used to promote joint ventures instead of opening Canada's doors to wholly-owned subsidiaries of foreign-controlled engineering companies anxious to participate in offshore drilling and production projects. For example, the review agency has negotiated a new 50-50 joint venture between Dominion Bridge of Montreal and McDermott Inc. of New Orleans, to be based in Calgary. McDermott is one of the larger companies in the world designing, constructing, and installing offshore drilling and production platforms, and installing deep underwater oil and gas pipelines. In announcing FIRA approval, industry minister Herb Gray said that the partnership had agreed to ensure a high level of Canadian content in the operation, hire Canadians for all jobs, including managerial and professional, whenever they are available, train Canadians in all aspects of the new business, and guarantee that five of the seven members of the executive committee controlling the partnership will be resident Canadians; that any new engineering designs or technology required for Canada's cold-water and ice conditions will be developed and owned by the partnership for commercial sale in Canada and other countries, and that any special products required for the application of that technology will be fabricated and exported from Canada. At the same time, McDermott's facility for offshore design technology will be transferred to the partnership's engineering office. According to Gray: "Overall, the ownership structure, the transfer of technology, Canadian participation in every aspect and at every level of the firm's activities, sourcing commitments, and the establishment of a Canadian-based firm in an industry which has been dominated by foreign-based firms, all add up to very considerable benefit for Canada."[36]

One pitfall for Canadian companies is lack of capital, especially risk capital. Companies eager to develop new technology must invest heavily in research and development and wait a long time before they can generate profits. Many Canadian companies that might become active players in energy projects simply do not have the financial resources to do so. While the oil and gas industry can help by actively encouraging the growth of domestic suppliers, and government can help by requiring a high level of Canadian content and pushing product standardization to reduce the numbers of different products, the problem of adequate financial resources remains a critical one. For research and development in the frontiers, the federal government could establish a research authority modelled after the Alberta Oil Sands Technology and Research Authority, to work with Canadian companies and share research and development costs. In addition, the federal government, with the Alberta Heritage Savings and Trust Fund or provincial governments, could provide equity and debt capital if private financial markets are unable to do so.

While there may be a tendency to assume, for example, that British and Norwegian companies have already developed all the needed technology for the Atlantic offshore, a detailed scrutiny of technological needs still reveals broad opportunities for Canadians. In Beale's view, future offshore requirements "will place Canadian firms in an ideal position to develop platforms compatible with moving ice environments, to improve drilling techniques and to extend drilling capacity to deeper water. With the international trend toward deep-water drilling, Canadians may quickly find themselves faced with an opportunity at the leading edge of an exportable technology."[37] Offshore production facilities present a yet greater challenge, but spending is even greater, perhaps seven to eight times more than in exploration. Canadian companies are inexperienced here, so there will be enormous pressure to use production platforms made abroad: however, there should be stress on joint ventures so that technology is transferred to Canada. At the same time, Canadian conditions will lead to depth requirements greater than the thousand feet of water encountered in the North Sea. Beale tells us that "as drilling programs find fields at depths greater than this, or as production systems are required in more hostile environments, Canada will again be in a position to develop novel technology. Man-made islands on the frontiers and floating platforms capable of evading ice-floes along the east coast will be examples of meeting the technical challenges that a unique Canadian environment poses. If the climate for innovation is right, there is little reason for Canadian firms not to develop the technology. With the drilling and production platforms costing an estimated 40 to 50 per cent of total development costs, developing indigenous technology and equipment supply capability is obviously desirable."[38]

Yet just as important if not actually more important than other policies for ensuring Canadian benefit from oil and gas projects is encouragement of Canadian ownership in the oil and gas industry itself. Canadian-controlled companies are demonstrating a strong commitment to Canadian content. Nova's procurement policy and that of Husky Oil, which it controls, put strong emphasis on Canadian suppliers. According to Nova president Robert Pierce: "We prefer and endeavour strenuously to deal with companies that are Canadian-owned. Our principal corporate reason for seeking to strengthen Canadian ownership and control is that it makes good sense. Our companies want long-standing, well-established supplier relationships and plant facilities."[39] Nova also, however, places a good deal of emphasis on finding suppliers who are reinvesting in their own businesses and upgrading their skills and technology, rather than simply seeking out ways to make Canadian content numbers look good. In the Foothills Pipeline project, Pierce stresses what he calls long-term industrial benefit for Canada, reflecting Nova's own industrial strategy: "To us, this concept means an ongoing contribution to the Canadian industrial base which enhances the ability of Canadian firms to compete internationally as a source of goods and services.'' Prospective suppliers are asked to what extent they foster the growth of existing domestic firms and the establishment of new Canadian-based enterprises; how much Canadian technological and innovative input there is in the goods and services they supply; and how their company works to increase the level of beneficial ownership and control by Canadians in Canada-based enterprises. "Even with 30 years' experience in exploration and development behind us,'' Pierce argues, "Canadian firms have not generally had responsibility for large national or international projects, principally because our industry is owned by foreigners who naturally depend to a large extent on their own country's resources.'' One sign that Nova/Husky will play a larger direct role in boosting Canadian content is Husky's 1979 purchase of Can Ocean Resources Ltd., formerly Lockheed Petroleum Services, a company set up in 1969 to develop offshore exploration and production technology. Husky, with Bow Valley Industries, expects to spend $300 million on two semi-submersible drilling rigs to be built by Saint John Shipbuilding and Dry Dock. This would be a major shot in the arm for Atlantic industry and the Canadian presence in offshore drilling.

Dome Petroleum, through its Canmar Resources, has built up its first-rate group of naval architects and engineers to develop a huge fleet of Arctic ice-breaking oil tankers, ice-breaker supply vessels, drill ships, and dredges to operate out of the Beaufort Sea. The company is planning construction of a world-scale shipyard, with an initial investment of $250 million, that will launch 200,000-ton ice-strengthened crude-oil tankers, costing $175 million each, to move oil from the Arctic. It could become the largest shipyard in North America, and would have nearly twice the capacity of all Canada's existing shipyards put together. At the same time, Dome is planning the construction of two of four LNG tankers needed to carry the gas from a west-coast port to Japan. A B.C. shipyard, Burrard Yarrows, is also developing new skills in ice-breaking technology, building an ice-breaker supply vessel for Dome that will be a scaled-down prototype of ice-breaker tankers planned for crude oil and LNG. The kind of $8-billion program that Dome suggests could materialize in the 1980s would represent a large new market for Canadian steel workers, and opportunities for many kinds of new technology in radar, navigation controls, micro-electronics, and telecommunications.

Dome acquired Davie Shipbuilding of Lauzon, Quebec, in 1981, and employed Graham Day, a Canadian who had been hired by the British government in 1975 to run British Shipbuilders, to superintend its shipbuilding operations. Dome's suggested shipping requirements through the 1980s are huge. They include the four LNG tankers to ship liquefied gas to Japan from British Columbia, up to twenty-five ice-strengthened crude-oil tankers, five more Arctic drilling ships, five large oil storage bays, 16 Arctic supply ships, 22 supply ships for offshore activities in the North, shipping to accommodate crews and supplies, and four class-10 ice-breakers.

Petro-Canada has a strong Canadian-oriented procurement policy. With Bawden Drilling, it will fund on a 50-50 basis the construction of a $125-million semi-submersible drilling rig to be built in a Canadian shipyard. This could be just the first in an offshore drilling fleet operation led by the national oil company. Its Canstar tar sands project in partnership with Nova will be completely Canadian. The Arctic Pilot Project to bring gas out of the islands will strongly emphasize Canadian content. Although the liquefaction process itself is French, developed by Technip, the detail engineering work may go to Vancouver's Wright-Technip partnership. Up to fifteen ice-breaking LNG tankers, costing $300 million each, may also be required, providing significant opportunities for Canadian shipyards, as will the highly sophisticated floating barge system on which the Arctic LNG plant and its control and loading systems will be based.

While the Canadian-controlled oil and gas companies are clearly moving to develop Canadian suppliers and engineers, the behaviour of the multinationals is much more uneven. The biggest companies, such as Imperial and Shell, are certainly being pushed to do more, and Imperial has expanded its program of grooming Canadian suppliers. More of this is likely to happen as such Canadian-controlled companies as Nova/Husky, Dome, and Petro-Canada show that it can be done. In mid-1981, Gulf Canada announced plans to build and operate its own drilling system for the exploration of the Beaufort Sea at a capital cost of $675 million. Two drilling vessels were to be acquired that would allow Gulf to extend the drilling season to at least 180 days, compared to the 100 to 110 days then available for conventional drilling. The plan also called for two ice-breakers, two ice-strengthened supply vessels, and a new shore base in the North. In spite of Gulf's statement that Canadian suppliers had been invited to bid, the first major contract, $190 million for the hulls of the two drilling vessels, was awarded to Japanese shipyards in September 1981. "These new drilling systems will, in effect, introduce a second-generation technology to frontier exploration," said the president of Gulf Canada.[40] However, it remained to be seen how much of Gulf's new-generation technology would be developed here.

The range of requirements is breathtaking: mining and materials-handling equipment, process control and other computer systems, pressure vessels, compressors, heavy construction equipment, telecommunications and satellite services for offshore drilling and production platforms, ice-breaking oil and LNG tankers, sophisticated Arctic barge systems, all types of instrumentation, electronic navigation equipment, environmental protection technology, plus all the equipment and know-how that will generate the capacity to produce these goods and services.

And dollar figures on future projects are enormous. The Major Projects Task Force calculated that the years 1980-2000 would produce $181 billion in new oil and gas and petrochemicals projects: $78.2 billion in oil and gas exploration and development, $42.7 billion in tar sands and heavy oil projects, $31.6 billion in oil and gas pipelines, and $28.5 billion in processing, refining and petrochemicals facilities. According to engineering analyst Beale, the years up to 1990 are likely to see $133.8 billion of oil and gas industry spending in 1980 dollars. While on the surface of Beale's estimate, Canadian opportunities look heady – about $30 billion or almost 70 per cent of the manufacturing content – based on past ex-

Oil and Gas 1980-1990 Manufacturing Opportunities (1980 billions of dollars)

(A) Reliable Estimates	Spending	Equipment share		Canadian content	
		%	$	%	$
Refineries	5.0	44	2.2	60	1.3
Pipelines	17.4	35	6.1	90	5.5
Tar Sands	21.4	40	8.6	75	6.6
	43.8	39	16.9	79	13.4
(B) Speculative Estimates	Spending	Equipment share		Canadian content	
		%	$	%	$
Oil and Gas Exploration and Development					
Western Canada	42.0	24	10.1	80	8.1
Frontier/Offshore	48.0	34	16.3	50	8.2
	90.0	29	26.4	62	16.3
Total (A + B)	133.8	32%	43.3	69%	29.7

Source: Barry Beale, *Energy and Industry.*

perience, much of the new technology will be contained in the imported 30 per cent. Canadians may provide the steel, cement, and work boots but the refining, engineering, the micro-electronic control systems, compressors, and valves could well be imported. The challenge is to make sure that Canadians get the chance to develop those new skills, technologies, and industries Canada's oil and gas resources will generate. If Canadians don't get them, someone else will.

Major Oil and Gas Industry Projects 1980-2000

Total reported projects $192 billion

1. Exploration and development $75.9 billion

Owner/Sponsor	Project	Location	Estimated Capital Cost ($ millions)	Const. Period From/To
Petro-Canada	Sour Gas Plant	Fort St. John, B.C.	250	
Esso Resources	CO_2 Miscible Flood	Judy Creek – Swan Hills Area, Alberta	500	1982-85 +
Gulf Canada	Gas Processing Plant	Hanlon Area, Alberta	200	1981-83
Esso Resources	Offshore Exploration	Offshore Nfld.	250	1980-85
Mobil et al.	Hibernia Development	Grand Banks, Nfld.	8 000	1983-92
	Sable Island Development	Sable Island, N.S.	1 000	1980-85
Labrador Group (Petro-Canada)	Exploration Program	Offshore Labrador	500-1 000	1980-90
Shell/Texaco	Gander Block Exploration	400 km N.E. of St. John's, Nfld.	1 500	1981-85
Dome Canmar	Oil Development – Offshore	Beaufort Sea	25 000	1981-92
Dome	Beaufort Sea gas	Beaufort Sea	23 000	1982-90
Esso Resources	Beaufort Sea Expl. & Dev.	Beaufort Sea	300	1980-85
	Taglu Gas Plant	Richards Island	2 000	1980-95
	Norman Wells Expansion	Norman Wells, NWT	400	1981-84
Gulf Canada	Parsons Lake gas plant	80 km from Inuvik	300	1985-90
Panarctic	Arctic Islands gas development	Arctic Islands	10 000	1990-96
Shell Canada Resources	Niglintgak gas plant	Mackenzie Delta	200	1985-90
Unknown	Offshore oil and gas development	Eastern Arctic	2 000	1990-91

Major Oil and Gas Industry Projects 1980-2000

2. Pipelines $31.6 billion

Owner/Sponsor	Project	Location	Estimated Capital Cost ($ millions)	Const. Period From/To
Mobil et al.	Atlantic Gas Pipeline	Sable Island to Mainland, N.S.	935	1983-84
Unknown	Oil Pipeline	From Grand Banks Region to Nfld.	250	
Amoco	Products Pipeline	Nova Scotia/Quebec	140	1982-83
Dome Petroleum	Cochin Pipeline Looping	Alberta and Saskatchewan	125	1982
Foothills Pipe Lines	Alaska Gas Pipeline	Alaska/Yukon Border to Southern Canada/US Border	8 365	1980-85
Interprovincial Pipe Line	Norman Wells Oil Pipeline	Norman Wells, NWT to Zama Lake, Alberta	365	1981-83
Polar Gas	Gas Pipeline	Melville Island to Longlac, Ont.	12 300	1989-94
TQ & M Pipeline	Gas Pipeline and Gas Dist.	Montreal to Quebec and Maritimes	2 285	1981-84
Trans-Canada Pipelines	Bypass Gas Line Looping & Compression	North Bay to Montreal Saskatchewan, Manitoba and Ontario	200 360	1982/83-84 1980-81
Trans-Mountain Pipe Line	New Oil Pipeline	Port Angeles to Edmonton	750	1981-83
Unknown	Municipal Gas Dist. Systems	Quebec and Maritimes	1 200	1981-2000
Unknown	Coal Slurry Pipeline	Hinton Region of Alberta to Pacific Coast	1 000	1983-85
B.C. Hydro	Gas Pipeline to Vancouver Island and Gas Dist.	From Mainland South of Vancouver to Vancouver Island	230	
Trans-Mountain Pipe	Coal Slurry Pipeline	B.C.	200	
Westcoast Transmission	Gas Transmission Sulphur Scrubbing Plant Pipeline Looping	Williams Lake to Comox Dawson Creek, B.C.	185 125 150	1983-85
Foothills Pipe Lines	Dempster Gas Lateral	Mackenzie Delta to Whitehorse	2 475	1985-89

3. Processing & Petrochemicals $24.6 billion

B.C. Hydro	Coal Liquefaction	Hat Creek, B.C.	5 000	1983-90
Dome Petroleum	LNG Plant	British Columbia	1 400	-85
Dome/Westcoast/ CanOxy/Mitsubishi	Ethylene & Two Derivative Plants	Fort St. John Region and Coast, B.C.	2 000	-85

252

Major Oil and Gas Industry Projects 1980-2000

Owner/Sponsor	Project	Location	Estimated Capital Cost ($ millions)	Const. Period From/To
Ocelot Industries Ltd.	Methanol Plant	Kitimat, B.C.	140	1980-81
Westcoast Transmission	Methanol Plant	Kitimat, B.C.	175	1981-82
Westcoast/Petrocan/ Mitsui	LNG Plant	British Columbia	1 500	1982-85
Unknown	Ammonia Plant	Northeast B.C.	200	1981-82
Alberta Energy Co.	Synthetic Nat. Gas Plant	Bruderheim	140	-82
Alberta Energy/ DuPont	Linear Polyethylene Plant	Edmonton Area	200	1981-84
Alberta Energy/Esso	Benzene Plant	13 km N.E. of Fort Sask., Alberta	225	1981-84
Alberta Energy/Esso Chemical (Petalta)	Ethylbenzene/Styrene Plant	Bruderheim, Alberta	300	1981-84
Alberta Gas Chemicals	Methanol Plan Expansion	Medicine Hat, Alberta	130	1979-82
Alberta Gas Ethylene	Ethylene II	Joffre, Alberta	375	1981-83
	Ethylene III	Joffre, Alberta	590	1983-85
AOSTRA	Synth. Oil Upgrading Plant		200	
City of Medicine Hat	Coal Gasification Pilot Plant	Medicine Hat Region, Alberta	200	1990s
Esso Chemical Canada	Ammonia/Urea Fert. Plant and Plant Expansion	Redwater, Alberta	345	1980-82
Gulf Canada	Refinery Expansion	Edmonton, Alberta	100	1980-83
Imperial Oil	Refinery Expansion	Edmonton, Alberta	185	1981-84
Nova/Shell	Styrene Plant	Scotford, Alberta	160	-84
	Linear Low Density Polyethylene Plant	Joffre, Alberta	250	-84
Petro-Canada	Heavy Oil Upgrading	Hardisty, Alberta	800	1983-84
Shell	Benzene Refinery	Fort Sask., Alberta	195	1981-84
Shell/Husky	Synthetic Oil Refinery	Fort Sask., Alberta	420	1980-84
Turbo Resources	Refinery	Balzac, Alberta	140	1980-82
Various with Fed./ Prov. Govt.	Coal Gasification/	Alberta	1 800	1988-94
	Liquefaction Coal Petrochemicals	Alberta	2 000	1988-96
Various	Styrene Derivatives	Alberta	2 000	
Husky et al.	Heavy Oil Upgrading	Lloydminster, Sask.	1 000	1981-86
Ocelot/Potash Corp.	Ammonia and Fertilizer		300	
Esso Chemical	Low Density Polyethylene	Sarnia, Ontario	100	1981-83
Mobil	Polypropylene	Ontario	100	1984-87

Major Oil and Gas Industry Projects 1980-2000

Owner/Sponsor	Project	Location	Estimated Capital Cost ($ millions)	Const. Period From/To
Petrosar/Suncor	Residual Oil Upgrading	Sarnia, Ontario	500	1983-85/86
Unknown	Gas Cracker Expansion	Ontario	105	1981-83
Gulf Canada	Refinery – Modernization and Upgrading	Montreal	100	1981-83
Gulf Canada et al.	Heavy Fuel Oil Upgrader	Montreal	1 500	1982-83
Petromont Inc./Gulf/ Union Carbide/Govt. of Quebec	Olefins Plant – Expansion	Varennes, Quebec	500	1981-85
Ultramar – Golden Eagle Refinery	Cat. Cracker for Resid. Oil	Quebec City	150	1980-82
Unknown	Vinyl Chloride Monomer	Quebec	100	1988-90
Various	Downstream Derivatives, Varennes Expansion	Quebec	500	1983-87
Petro-Canada	Refinery Reactivation	Come-by-Chance, Nfld.	200	
Unknown	Ammonia Plant	Nfld.	200	1981-82
Unknown	Methanol Plant	Nfld.	100	1981-82

4. Mining Projects	$6.6 billion			
BP	Coal Mine	Sukunka – Northeast B.C.	400	uncertain
Esso Resources	Molybdenum Mine	Trout Lake, B.C.	200	1983-84
	Copper/Zinc Mine	Kutcho Creek, B.C.	180	1985-88
Petro-Canada	Monkman Pass Coal B.C.		500	
Shell Canada	Line Creek Coal	Near Fernie, B.C.	180	1979-82
Consolidated Coal (Continental Oil Co.)	Open Pit Coal Mine	Nordegg, Alberta	150	
Esso Resources	Open Pit Coal Mine	Judy Creek, Alberta	345	1982-84
Fording/Petro-Canada	Thermal Coal Mine	Lethbridge, Alberta	100	
Gregg River Resources	Open Pit Met. Coal	Coal Branch, Alberta	185	1982-83
Luscar (Superior Oil)	Thermal Mines Exp.	Coal Valley, Alberta	250	1982-83
McIntyre Mines (Superior Oil)	Met. Coal Mine	Near Grande Cache, Alberta	100	
Petro-Canada	Kipp Underground Coal Mine	Near Lethbridge, Alberta	200	1984
Petrofina	Thermal Coal Mine	Near Shaughnessy, Alberta	150	

Major Oil and Gas Industry Projects 1980-2000

Owner/Sponsor	Project	Location	Estimated Capital Cost ($ millions)	Const. Period From/To
Shell	Gleichen Mine	Gleichen, Alberta	200	
Union Oil/Rescon	Open Pit Coal Mine	Obed, Alberta	400	1981-83
Unknown	Underground Coal Mine	Ram River, Alberta	400	
Unknown	Underground Coal Mine	Grassy Mountain, Alberta	400	
Canadian Occidental	Uranium Mine & Mill	McLean Lake, Sask.	300	
Esso et al	Uranium Mine & Mill	Midwest Lake, Sask.	300	
Cyprus Anvil (HBOE)	Lead/Zinc/Silver	Faro, Yukon	240	1980-86
Hudson's Bay Oil & Gas	Lead, Zinc	Tom Claims, Yukon	250	
	Lead, Zinc	Howard Pass, Yukon	250	
	Lead, Zinc, Tungsten Silver	McMillan Pass, Yukon	250	
	Lead, Zinc, Silver, Tungsten	Jason, Yukon	250	

	5. Tar Sands and Heavy Oil	$42.7 billion		
Esso Resources	Cold Lake In – Situ Oil Sands	Cold Lake	7 000	1981-89
Gulf Canada	Sundalta Oil Sands Mining	Fort McMurray Region	10 000	1986-90
Nova/Petro-Canada	Oil Sands Mining	Fort McMurray	10 000	1985-90
Shell Canada et al.	Peace River In – Situ	Peace River	5 000	1985-92
	Alsands Project	Fort McMurray	7 200	1980-87
Suncor	Oil Sands Plant Exp.	Fort McMurray	185	-81
Syncrude	Plant Exp. - 3rd. Train	Fort McMurray	1 500	1984-86
Unknown	Combustion Pilot Plant	Cold Lake	100	1985-87
Husky	Enhanced Oil Recovery	Lloydminster	1 750	1980-2000

	6. Other Projects	$10.6 billion		
Arctic Pilot Project	Liquefied natural gas	Melville Island to Eastern Canada	2 500	1981-86
Dome Petroleum	4 LNG Tankers (125 000 m³ capacity)		1 400	-85
Petro-Canada	Semi-sub. Drilling Rig		100	
Unknown	Class 10 Tankers and Barges		4 320 2 255	

Source: "Major Capital Project Inventory." Office of Industrial and Regional Benefits, Department of Industry, Trade and Commerce. Ottawa, October 1981.

Notes

1. "Major Canadian Projects, Major Canadian Opportunities. A Report by the Consultative Task Force on Industrial and Regional Benefits from Major Canadian Projects." Ottawa 1981.
2. Undated memorandum, probably 1949, in the Imperial Oil archives.
3. L. F. Kahle to Imperial Oil, 2 November 1949. Imperial Oil archives.
4. L. F. Kahle letter.
5. C. D. Howe to Imperial president G. L. Stewart, undated. Imperial Oil archives, Toronto.
6. Department of Defence Production. "Confidential Report on the Petroleum Industry." Ottawa 1952.
7. John Davis. *Canadian Energy Prospects*. Royal Commission on Canada's Economic Prospects. Ottawa 1957.
8. *Western Oil Examiner*, February 1958.
9. Robert Winters, Minister of Trade and Commerce. *Guiding Principles of Good Corporate Behaviour*. Ottawa, 31 March 1966.
10. Barry Beale. *Energy and Industry*. A Canadian Institute for Economic Policy Study. Toronto, James Lorimer, 1980.
11. Kates, Peat, Marwick and Co. *Foreign Ownership: Architecture and Engineering Consulting*. A study for the Select Committee on Economic and Cultural Nationalism of the Legislative Assembly of the Province of Ontario. Toronto, October 1973.
12. Association of Professional Engineers of Ontario. "Canadian Engineering for Canadian Engineers." Cited in Kates, Peat, Marwick.
13. A. J. Cordell. "Resources: Implications of Ownership." In *Essays on Aspects of Resource Policy*. Ottawa, Science Council of Canada, 1973.
14. Jean Chrétien to Ottawa press conference, 13 August 1970.
15. Donald Macdonald, 23 June 1973.
16. Department of Finance. *Northern Gas Pipeline: Evaluation of the Impact on the National Economy*. Ottawa, October 1972.
17. Judd Buchanan to Imperial chairman Jack Armstrong, July 1975.
18. Judd Buchanan, letter to the oil and gas companies, 16 September 1975.
19. *Northern Pipelines Act* (1978).
20. Robert Irvine. "The Alaska Highway Gas Pipeline: Not Your Everyday Shopping List." *Foreign Investment Review*, Spring 1981.
21. "Report of the Conservation and Utilization Committee of the Alberta Government for the Executive Council on Fort McMurray and on Athabasca Tar Sands Development Strategy." Edmonton 1972.
22. Association of Consulting Engineers of Canada. "Brief on Canadian Engineering and Project Management in Hydrocarbon Related Projects, to the Inter-Departmental Committee on Industrial Benefits from Canada's Resources Development." Ottawa, 23 June 1976.
23. Department of Industry, Trade and Commerce. "A Report by the Sector Task Force on the Canadian Ocean Industry." Ottawa 1978.
24. Major Projects Task Force, report.
25. Quoted in Beale, *Energy and Industry*.
26. Allan MacEachen to Offshore Canada, a *Financial Post* Conference, Halifax, 23 June 1981.
27. Major Projects Task Force, report.
28. Beale, *Energy and Industry*.
29. James Stanford to Offshore Canada, a *Financial Post* Conference, Halifax, 22 June 1981.

30. Major Projects Tax Force, report.
31. *Oil and Gas Production and Conservation Act*, s. 10(3).
32. *Oil and Gas Production and Conservation Act*, s. 3.2(2).
33. Department of Energy, Mines and Resources. *The National Energy Program*. Ottawa 1980.
34. Beale, *Energy and Industry*.
35. The Monopolies and Mergers Commission. "Enserch Corporation and Davy Corporation Limited: A Report on the Proposed Merger." London, HMSO, 1981.
36. Foreign Investment Review Agency. Press release, 8 April 1981.
37. Beale, *Energy and Industry*.
38. *Energy and Industry*.
39. Robert Pierce, president, Nova, to the Ecole des Hautes Etudes Commerciales, Montreal, 3 June 1980.
40. John Stoik, president, Gulf Canada, to Offshore Canada, a *Financial Post* Conference, Halifax, 22 June 1981.

Chapter 9

Maple Leaf Oil

Public enterprise, as Herschel Hardin has pointed out in *A Nation Unaware*, is "one of the most vibrant expressions of the Canadian character."[1] Public enterprise has for more than a century been one of our most important nation-building tools. We have used it for everything from railways and airlines to public power, broadcasting, and such science-based activities as nuclear technology, chemicals, and aerospace. And in the process of making the oil and gas sector work for the maximum benefit of Canadians, no single move has been as crucial as the creation of Petro-Canada as a public resource enterprise in 1975. The shock of Petro-Canada was not that it was set up, but that it took so long.

As related in an earlier chapter, concern about foreign control of the resource has been accompanied periodically in Canada by calls for public ownership. On the other side, multinational oil and gas companies have feared, not only competition, but also the knowledge and expertise that would go along with active public participation. It took the Depression of the 1930s, however, to bring the industry under the kind of critical review that could develop into a threat of nationalization. The issue was, appropriately enough to that decade, pricing: a Commons committee looked at the question and other inquiries or royal commissions were appointed in British Columbia, Saskatchewan, and Alberta. Price controls were imposed in B.C., Nova Scotia, and New Brunswick because of high industry profits, while Saskatchewan encouraged its co-operative movement to open its own refining and marketing system, Consumers' Co-op. Ontario's Premier Mitch Hepburn is reported to have made life so uncomfortable for the oil industry that Imperial at one point considered moving its head office to another province.

It was in Newfoundland, however, that the issue really came to a head.[2] Imperial had acquired the Newfoundland operations of

Standard Oil of New York in 1921 for $210,000, giving it a profitable monopoly on the island. Profits in 1929 were six cents a gallon as compared with 1.8 cents in the previous few years, and even during the early 1930s, the company earned a return of about 25 per cent on a depreciated investment of $288,000. Though Newfoundland increased gasoline taxes to reduce Imperial's profits, the company had little inclination to cut prices to more reasonable levels. One reason for this was that, since much of the final distribution of gasoline and other products was in the hands of local merchant families, it was felt that they would pocket any price cut themselves: as Imperial's public affairs director, Victor Ross, wrote to a senior company executive, Newfoundland "has a ruling class which is admittedly corrupt."

Meanwhile, the economic crisis was snowballing. The island had to cover a large government deficit in 1931 by borrowing in international markets. In 1932, its position deteriorated even further, and it was unable to borrow more money; there were riots in St. John's and the prime minister almost lost his life. At this point, the British treasury stepped in to review Newfoundland's situation and recommended, among other things, that the government take over Imperial's interests. If there was to be a monopoly, the argument went, it should be a government monopoly. This caused panic at Imperial. "If Newfoundland establishes a government monopoly in oil it will be undoubtedly successful for the first year or so at least," Ross wrote to G. H. Smith, an American executive representing Standard's interests in the company: "It will be the first instance of government ownership of a private industry on this continent. If it is even seemingly successful, as it will be, the example is almost certain to be followed by the Province of Quebec and possibly the Prairie Provinces . . . and they could be profitably engaged in the business until political graft proved their experiment a failure, by which time we would be out of business ourselves." Imperial applied strong pressure to keep the government out. It persuaded R. B. Bennett's government in Ottawa to make representations to the British treasury, Canadian banks to lobby through their British banking connections, and the St. John's business community, whose big profits were threatened, to campaign hard as well. The effort worked, and Imperial, in return for concessions that included an annual payment for exclusive rights in Newfoundland and the purchase of $1.75 million's worth of the island's 5.5-per-cent bonds, retained its monopoly until Newfoundland joined Canada in 1949.

Aside from the 1930s flurry, however, there was no great move for government participation in the oil industry until the 1970s. The issue did arise, of course, from time to time. In a debate on gasoline taxation during World War II, Richard Hanson, the Conservative leader in the House, asked the finance minister: "Has the minister or the government ever given consideration to the nationalization of the oil business in Canada? That is a big problem, and I do not wish to start a discussion of it tonight except to say that other countries have nationalized universally consumed products, and that the time may come when we shall have to give consideration to that in this country. If it could be done here, it would yield huge sums to the federal treasury without adding one cent to the cost to the consumer."[3] For a brief period during the war, in fact, the federal government did operate an oil company, Wartime Oils, to encourage exploration, but it was not particularly successful; it was wound up in 1945 and its 21 producing wells placed under the management of Ottawa mines officials.

The spectre of government participation hovered nearer as the industry moved into really significant exploration activity in Alberta and Saskatchewan. There were already signs that Venezuela might follow Mexico in nationalizing its industry. And the oil majors were hardly likely to be comforted by the election of the Co-operative Commonwealth Federation as North America's first socialist government in Saskatchewan in 1944. The general climate and the perception of the industry as an economic kingpin were such, however, that party resolutions calling for a public presence in oil and gas died in their tracks. Premier Douglas was notifying companies individually in the late '40s that "the province will stand by all agreements it enters into and it has no intention of either expropriating or socializing the oil industry."[4] One trade magazine, *Oil in Canada*, was moved to report the relief in the industry that the Douglas government had scotched "the rash talk of 'confiscation' or 'nationalization' of oil and gas by certain of its members."[5]

Even so, the growing scale of development required public concessions in various forms, and some mode of government participation was virtually inevitable even in the view of industry executives. The promoters of the trans-Canada pipeline negotiated government assistance in 1954-55, and there was talk at the time that the entire project should be publicly owned. The Borden energy commission was soon telling the government of John Diefenbaker that in oil and gas, "pertinent decisions may be made without reference to the best national interests of Canada. Surely, in these circumstances, it is a proper function of government to intervene to ensure that, to the maximum extent possible, the national interests of Canada are protected."[6] The commission had been particularly disturbed to find that B.C. gas was being exported to the U.S. at give-away prices. One result of its report was the establishment in 1959 of the regulatory National Energy Board. The 1961 National Oil Policy that carved the country into domestic and import fiefdoms followed as a clear case of the kind of government intervention the majors could support. On the other hand, the creation of Panarctic Oils in 1967 ushered in a more direct government role, a joint venture with 45-per-cent federal participation. "The major integrated oil companies did not accord to the Arctic islands an important priority for development at the time," it was reported in the 1973 federal paper, *An Energy Policy for Canada*: "By 1967, it became clear to the government of Canada that unless the government played a financial role in launching a major exploration program, there would be no serious efforts in the Arctic islands for some years."[7]

In 1970, the Vancouver resources lawyer Jack Austin was made deputy energy minister by Prime Minister Trudeau. In a discussion about Austin's job that took place in March of that year, Trudeau expressed concern about the government's lack of knowledge of the oil industry, and asked Austin to conduct a sweeping review of Canada's energy situation that would help the government devise more effective energy policies. Austin asked whether the review could include the option of a national oil company, and Trudeau said that it could. In the review, Bill Hopper, a Canadian oil expert working at the Boston consulting firm of Arthur D. Little, was commissioned to analyse the experience of other countries with such enterprises. Later that year, energy minister Joe Greene was dropping public hints about the creation of a national company, noting that other governments had them, including some that were active in Canada: "Must Canada be the only home of branch plants?"[8]

While Ottawa was considering the possible role of a national oil company, a number of provinces began to set up their own. Quebec's Société Québécoise d'Initiatives Pétrolières (SOQUIP) was established in 1970 to explore for oil and gas in the Gulf of St. Lawrence; its exploration activities were later extended to the Atlantic offshore and other parts of Canada. Saskatchewan, which might have been expected to pioneer in public resources enterprise under the CCF, was cowed by the violent reaction in industry and financial circles to its experimental farm-out of some Crown reserves to Consumers' Co-op without the usual competitive bidding process. The episode, described in an earlier chapter, seemed to close that particular case fairly conclusively. It was almost another twenty years before a new NDP government in Saskatchewan finally got into the oil and gas business. In 1971, Imperial Oil announced the shut-down of small and out-dated refineries in Regina, while Gulf cancelled a Saskatoon refinery and Husky Oil closed another in Moose Jaw. In December of that year, an NDP convention adopted a resolution urging that the government establish "an integrated oil company run as a Crown corporation." It was not until April 1973, however, that Saskatchewan Premier Allan Blakeney at last followed through and introduced legislation setting up Saskoil, a company with a mandate to explore for, produce, refine, market, transport, and trade in oil and natural gas. So far, Saskoil has concentrated much of its activity on the province's abundant heavy oil reserves. It holds 25 per cent of a proposed heavy oil upgrading plant in Saskatchewan, with Husky Oil also holding 25, Gulf Canada 20, and Petro-Canada and Shell Canada each holding 15 per cent. It also owns, with Petro-Canada and Gulf as partners, one third of the Saskatchewan Heavy Oil Project (SHOP) to develop these reserves in the province. By the mid-1980s, Saskoil expects to have assets of $1 billion as compared with $200 million at the beginning of the 1980s.[9]

In 1973 too, the Alberta government of Peter Lougheed announced its plan for an Alberta Energy Corporation. The idea arose during negotiation of the terms for the building of the Syncrude tar sands plant. As part of the deal, AEC would have an option to buy 20 per cent of Syncrude. The company, its ownership split between the Alberta government and the Canadian public, came into being in 1975. It has grown rapidly, undertaking forestry, petrochemicals, and oil and gas exploration projects; the provincial government, however, has so far remained a passive investor. Other provinces that now have their own energy corporations are British Columbia, with its B.C. Petroleum Corporation, and Ontario, with the Ontario Energy Corporation, which has a 25-per-cent interest in Suncor. The most recent entries are Newfoundland and Nova Scotia. In 1980, the Newfoundland Petroleum Corporation was set up to acquire a 40-per-cent interest in all offshore oil and gas finds. Its success in this, however, will depend on Newfoundland's ability to demonstrate jurisdiction in the Atlantic offshore oil and gas fields. Nova Scotia now has a similar corporation.

While Ottawa was studying the idea, then, the provinces were breaking the ice on a much smaller scale. And events were pushing the federal authorities inexorably towards reality. Canada was by now one of the few important oil producers in the world to lack a national oil company. Noting the presence of such public enterprises in a wide range of countries that included Britain, France, Italy, and Norway, *An Energy Policy for Canada* pointed out that among the benefits Canadians would get from having their own would be the "pride, satisfaction, and confidence of owning a portion of the petroleum industry operating in Canada"; increased knowledge for government policy-makers of how the industry works; better information on how to collect windfall profits from oil and gas development; some control over prices, if the oil company controlled large enough reserves; encouragement for refining or upgrading oil and gas instead of exporting it in its unprocessed state; more research and development in Canada; more jobs in Canada, since the company's head office would be here; greater Canadian manufacturing and engineering content in oil and gas projects; help for the development of other Canadian industries; stimulation of regional development, and direct negotiation with the governments and national oil corporations of other countries to ensure an adequate supply of oil imports and expanded opportunities for Canadian exports in exchange for the oil.[10] However, the federal policy statement also set down the arguments against having a national oil corporation. These were listed as the high cost of setting it up; the difficulty of gaining a significant market share in competition with the oil multinationals; the long delay in and large expense of acquiring sufficient land positions for exploration; the danger that the oil multinationals, in reaction, would repatriate a greater share of their profits as dividends; the likelihood that the corporation would be less efficient than its multinational competitors; the risk that the corporation would succumb to political pressure and, for example, build refineries in the wrong locations; the fear that national oil company executives, rather than government officials, would eventually dominate policy-making, and the possibility that Canadians might not prefer to "buy Canadian" at the gasoline pump.

It was a time when ideas were changing rapidly. In 1972, a plan to have a Crown corporation, Eldorado Nuclear, buy Home Oil, one of the largest Canadian-owned exploration and production companies, had fallen through when Bobby Brown Jr., Home's principal shareholder, decided that he did not want to sell to a government agency. This outcome was greeted with relief by some Cabinet veterans who had been worried about a negative reaction from the oil majors. But the OPEC explosion of 1973, sending world oil prices skyrocketing while its Arab members slashed production to support Egypt and Syria in a new Arab-Israeli war, suddenly made oil into something more than fuel. Oil – and with it, all forms of energy – became strategic commodities. No country could afford to rely on the weakened oil multinationals, whose allocations for scarce oil would be made in New York or other foreign corporate headquarters. Energy minister Donald Macdonald hurried to Venezuela to discuss continuity of supply for Canada. He returned to Ottawa with the announcement that "Venezuela would be quite prepared to enter into discussions with Canada on the long-range security of supply agreement . . . but they indicated to us that they would of course prefer to deal with a Canadian government entity in this regard, a national petroleum corporation, rather than the kind of private arrangements we have had heretofore."[11] A similar message was later received from Mexico. These external factors, however, were not the only ones at work. Canadians were discovering to their horror that the country did not have the readily available oil and gas supplies the oil majors had told them about. In 1973 the Trudeau government had assumed, based on earlier, rosy industry forecasts, that Canada could be self-sufficient in oil by 1980, but a later report by the National Energy Board showed that we would become increasingly dependent on imported oil as the country moved into the new decade. Not only did this increase the urgency of making secure arrangements for imports, but it also indicated a pressing need for Canadians to get better information on the oil and gas industry and Canada's true energy situation. The feeling was that a national oil company would give the government a clear "window on the industry," and thus help it to pursue better energy policies.

In the final month of 1973, the Trudeau cabinet was bent in analysis over the case for a national oil company and the role such a company might play. Interestingly, the use of a Petro-Canada to help Canadianize the oil and gas industry was not a high priority at the time. Macdonald, for example, was asked in a television interview whether he favoured takeovers of foreign-controlled oil companies by a national oil company:

Q. The oil industry is almost 100-per-cent owned abroad in this country. Are you in favour of going the whole way and nationalizing it and ensuring Canadian ownership of the companies that extract and refine the oil?

A. No, I think that would be a poor expenditure of our capital to in effect nationalize the whole industry and then have to pay for existing assets.

Q. That's what they did in Mexico.

A. They did it in Mexico 50 years ago. I don't think they would do that in Mexico now. I would see the using of the financial assets we have now in this country to develop other opportunities in the energy field rather than buying out existing assets.[12]

Finally, on 6 December 1973, Prime Minister Trudeau declared the government's intention of creating a national oil company, "principally to expedite exploration and development."[13] The government's goal was to speed up the drive for oil self-sufficiency – Trudeau said at the time that this could be achieved by the end of the 1970s – and it wanted its new oil company to accelerate exploration in the Canadian North and Atlantic offshore, where it felt that the oil majors were moving too slowly. Trudeau also wanted the national oil company to speed up the development of the Alberta tar sands, including a big push on tar sands research and development. Legislation to establish Petro-Canada was introduced in the Commons in May, 1974, but the minority Trudeau government was defeated a few days later. It was brought in again that fall, after Trudeau had won a majority in the July election, and finally passed in the following July over the bitter and drawn-out objections of a Conservative opposition that fought the measure adamantly as unwarranted government interference in the private sector, which for anything to do with oil and gas at this time was 90-per-cent foreign-controlled.

In the House debate, the three reasons energy minister Macdonald gave for Petro-Canada were to accelerate exploration and development, negotiate and possibly secure cheaper oil import arrangements, and give Canadians "a direct share in the wealth which development of our resources generates."[14] The most vital of these roles, however, was the first. "The government does not feel assured," Macdonald said, "that the private sector can be relied upon to mobilize all of the enormous amounts of capital which will be required to secure energy development consonant with Canadian needs over the longer term."[15] Petro-Canada was to spend the lion's share of the annual exploration budget it received from Ottawa in the frontier regions, working out joint ventures with the oil multinationals that held, and held idly, most of the exploration permits. The company would also own the federal government's 45-per-cent interest in Panarctic Oils and its 20-per-cent position in the Syncrude project. Like Trudeau, Macdonald saw Petro-Canada as an important tar sands catalyst: it could gain access to technology and share in tar sands profits.

The mandate as set out in the Petro-Canada Act, however, was much more sweeping. The national oil company had the authority to "explore for hydrocarbon deposits, to negotiate for and acquire petroleum and petroleum products from abroad to assure a continuity of supply for the needs of Canada, to develop and exploit deposits of hydrocarbons within and without Canada in the interests of Canada, to carry out research and development projects in relation to hydrocarbons and other fuels, and to engage in exploration for, and the production, distribution, refining and marketing of fuels."[16] In other words, with enough money and sufficient management resources, Petro-Canada could do everything that Exxon, Royal Dutch/Shell, Mobil Oil, British Petroleum, or Standard Oil of California could do, except that it would be owned and controlled by Canadians and, instead of automatically pursuing the most immediate profit opportunities, serve as an instrument of government policy to meet the country's long-term energy goals.

In addition to the opposition from the Conservatives in the House, the creation of Petro-Canada was greeted by strong criticism from the large oil companies. Jack Armstrong, then president of Imperial Oil, issued a statement shortly after the government's plans were announced: "The proposed national petroleum company will neither add skilled manpower to the country's pool of expertise, nor by edict will it increase the supply of energy. The federal government is already heavily committed to petroleum exploration and development through its participation in Panarctic, and indeed another tax-financed entity is redundant."[17] Armstrong passed in silence over the distinction between a stake in a company with noble but limited objectives and a state enterprise whose activity would encompass almost every aspect of the oil and gas business, thus coming up against the established position of the foreign-controlled majors. Jerry McAfee, president of Gulf Canada, took similar aim. "It seems to be fashionable these days for governments in Canada to have their own oil companies. Following the formation of provincial oil and/or energy companies in Quebec, Ontario, Saskatchewan, Alberta, and British Columbia, we now have Petro-Canada about to enter the scene," he told the Canadian Club of Toronto: "The stated purpose of these companies varies from case to case, as you know; to the extent they duplicate the efforts of the industry, and are given unfair competitive advantage, siphon off industry personnel, or channel tax dollars into the risky, highly technical business of exploration, I submit that these enterprises will prove counter-productive to Canada's overall effort to provide for future energy needs."[18] Texaco Canada was also among the majors denouncing the move. Its president complained that "the creation and force-feeding of a taxpayer-financed national oil company to compete with us in the manner of a referee who also fields his own team" was one more symptom of the oil industry's biggest problem – "too much government."[19]

This type of reaction, of course, was not without precedent. One need only recall the outcry that accompanied the public takeover of power companies in the Quebec of the 1960s, or, to go farther back but not very far away, the scare campaign whipped up against Ontario "radicalism" as the government of James Whitney prepared to launch Hydro in the early years of the century. The mood of Ontario then was summed up by *Saturday Night*, which said in 1906 that "if English capitalists are going to rise like a covey of scared partridges and quit the country whenever citizens stand up suddenly and object to being skinned, why, let them scare."[20] Petro-Canada in 1973, like Ontario Hydro seventy-five years earlier, had strong public support, but now as then, the industry whose ox had been gored was able to make life difficult in the early days. Maurice Strong, Petro-Canada's first chairman, reminded a Toronto audience of the "well-established Canadian tradition" of intervening in sectors of the economy considered vital to Canadian nationhood, as indicated by the presence of such Crown corporations as CN and the CBC, both created by the Conservatives, and Air Canada and others that had been launched by the Liberal governments. While some oil companies were accepting Petro-Canada as a fact of life by the time he spoke in 1977, "this does not mean that the initial hostility of the industry to Petro-Canada has fully abated. On the contrary, some elements in the industry, principally a few large foreign-controlled companies, are waging an unrelenting underground campaign against Petro-Canada, seizing every opportunity to restrict its role and undermine its credibility both with the public and with government. The influence of these interests should not be underestimated. It is greater than you think."[21]

The Canadian Petroleum Association, dominated, paradoxically, by foreign-controlled oil companies, refused to admit Petro-Canada as a member because of its government connection; yet the CPA included companies owned by the governments of

Britain and France. Nor did the oil industry let up in its campaign to restrict Petro-Canada's role. In a typical industry speech, Gulf Canada's president warned that the mere existence of Petro-Canada and the comparable provincial corporations might discourage private oil companies and undermine Canada's chance to increase energy supplies: "In deciding on Canada's energy policy options for the longer term, governments must balance very carefully the effect of increased direct involvement in the industry against the risk of discouraging the private sector which has the experience, the personnel, and the equipment to do the job most efficiently."[22] He argued, without explaining why, that "the measure of success of such Crown corporations as Petro-Canada will be whether they add to, or detract from, the total exploration effort. If given special advantage, they will discourage investment by the private sector." It was the common industry view that Petro-Canada's role should be restricted to areas too marginal or long-term to attract private capital – in other words, a sidelines presence in the industry.

While Ottawa's initial emphasis was on Petro-Canada's roles in frontiers and tar sands development and as a back-up source for oil imports, the new company's ambit expanded as policy-makers learned more about the industry and the world energy situation deteriorated. Foreign ownership also became a more perceptible issue as the importance and value of Canada's oil and gas reserves rose. The point had been reached when only the federal government had the resources to ensure that Canadians had a company which could soon emerge as one of the major actors in the industry. At the outset, Petro-Canada moved quickly to accelerate exploration in the Arctic islands, where it paid more than its 45-per-cent share of Panarctic to continue that company's exploration program, becoming part of the Arctic Islands Exploration Group with Imperial, Gulf, and Shell. It arranged a farm-in on Mobil Oil's Sable Island interests in order to revive exploration there after the parent company in New York had decided to postpone further activity. And it became a key player in exploration along the Labrador coast. In 1976, Petro-Canada was given a boost by the changes in the Canada Lands regulations, and soon made use of the 25-per-cent back-in provision to obtain a stake in what later turned out to be the rich Hibernia oil field. At the time, Petro-Canada had a back-in right when exploration permits expired and no significant discovery had been made; companies had the options of letting Petro-Canada back in, seeking other Canadian partners, or converting from an exploration permit to a lease with higher carrying costs. The national firm had also been given a seven-year right to select 25 per cent of Crown lands for exploration. Its arrival in the mid-1970s was timely, in fact, as Arctic and east-coast exploration were lagging badly.

With these policies and its own sense of adventure, Petro-Canada had become by the start of the 1980s the largest holder of frontier exploration lands, a participant in the Sable Island, Hibernia, Labrador, and Arctic island oil and gas discoveries, and the majority owner of Panarctic Oils. As Alberta political economist Larry Pratt has put it, "a state oil company can afford to view a disproportionate share of its capital budget as 'patient money' in high-risk projects, and on policy grounds it can afford to be more concerned with proving up national stocks of oil and gas reserves rather than with moving quickly into commercial production."[23] But since this requires the investment of hundreds of millions of dollars with little prospect of an early return, "to be an effective player, a state oil company must also be sufficiently large and competent to operate alongside the multinationals in some of the world's most hostile physical environments." There can be no doubt that Petro-Canada has invested an unusually large share of funds in these areas. In its first five years, it devoted roughly half its budget to frontier, tar sands, and heavy oil activities, and became an important catalyst in speeding up the pace of activity to meet future Canadian energy needs.

In fact it was the sheer cost of financing its exploration, plus the fact that as a taxable Crown corporation it needed a flow of revenue against which to write off exploration and other expenses, that propelled Petro-Canada into the takeover game. In 1976 it purchased Atlantic Richfield Canada, a subsidiary of the Atlantic Richfield Company of Los Angeles, for $342 million. The acquisition gave Petro-Canada ownership of oil and gas lands for exploration, a crucial asset for any oil and gas company, along with leases in tar sands country so that it could move into tar sands research and development, an established staff of experienced oil professionals, and producing properties that generated profits. These profits gave Petro-Canada access to tax incentives: it would have been ironic indeed had Canada's own oil company not been able to make use of the benefits provided by its own Canadian taxpayers. The Atlantic Richfield subsidiary was renamed Petro-Canada Exploration (PEX) and became the corporation's main operating arm. The process continued as, after an unsuccessful bid to acquire Husky Oil in 1978, Petro-Canada picked up Pacific Petroleums, another U.S.-controlled oil company, for $1.5 billion in 1978-79, and in 1981 bought the Belgian-owned Petrofina S.A. for $1.4 billion. Both added to Petro-Canada's proven reserves and strengthened its land position, as well as significantly boosting the company's cash flow. They also made Petro-Canada a national refining and marketing company, although its market share is probably still less than 6 per cent. While it is true, as Petro-Canada's critics pointed out, that such takeovers did not by themselves add one barrel of oil to the country's reserves, what is much more important is that they gave the company a chance to embark on an aggressive exploration program and reinvest all the cash flow of the acquisition. After all, it was part of the oil majors' credo that they could make better use of other companies' assets; they turned routinely to takeovers as means of achieving growth and market power.

While takeovers have been one way for Petro-Canada to build up its presence quickly, another important way has been buying into land permits held by other companies in so-called farm-ins, spending money on drilling to earn a share of whatever is found in the permit area. Petro-Canada's Sable Island drilling contribution not only led to important gas discoveries but earned the company, for $50 million in exploration spending, a 25-per-cent stake in all future oil and gas production from Mobil's land. It has gone on to make other farm-ins, an example being off the Labrador Shelf, where it picked up the principal interest in this promising area and in 1980 became the operator. Its 18-per-cent stake in the Arctic Islands Exploration Group was also earned in this way.

In addition to its frontier oil and gas activities, Petro-Canada has become an active participant in Alberta's tar sands and Saskatchewan's heavy oils. Beyond its 17 per cent of Syncrude and 17-per-cent stake in the proposed Alsands project, it will build the first all Canadian-owned and Canadian-engineered tar sands plant, Canstar, in partnership with Nova. Petro-Canada is also engaged in several pilot projects to improve tar sands and heavy oil technology, including PCEJ, a consortium of four companies (Petro-Canada, Canada-Cities Service, Esso Resources Canada, and Japan Canada Oil Sands) to test a new in situ technology, and MAISP, the Mine-Associated In Situ Process being studied by a five-company group. With Saskoil and Gulf Canada, Petro-Canada is participating in SHOP (the Saskatchewan Heavy Oil Project), is involved in several heavy oil projects in Alberta, and has become a partner with Husky Oil in a proposed heavy oil upgrader in Saskatchewan.

In other policy areas, Petro-Canada helped finance the feasibil-

270

ity study for the TQ and M (Trans Quebec and Maritimes) pipeline to bring natural gas into these markets and reduce the need for imported oil, and it holds an option to take a 10-per-cent interest in the project. It owns a controlling 35.2-per-cent interest in Westcoast Transmission in B.C., which in turn owns 50 per cent of the huge Foothills Pipe Line (Yukon) Ltd., the company building the conduit to deliver Alaskan gas to U.S. markets in California and the Middle West. And it is a 25-per-cent owner of Polar Gas, the consortium that wants to build a major gas pipeline from the far North to serve central Canadian and U.S. markets in the 1990s. In 1981 it purchased the bankrupt Come-by-Chance oil refinery in Newfoundland, which may be used again when Hibernia oil comes into production in the late 1980s. The company is investigating the potential for petrochemicals production in Atlantic Canada against the day when oil and gas are available there, and researching coal liquefaction to produce oil in Cape Breton. One Petro-Canada initiative with enormous ramifications is the Arctic Pilot Project, a plan to liquefy natural gas in the Arctic islands and move it by ice-breaking LNG tankers into an eastern Canada terminal where it would be reconverted. The national company has brought Nova, Dome Petroleum, and a group of Canadian shipping companies in as partners, and, subject to regulatory approval and financing, the project should be a reality by the late 1980s.

Petro-Canada has also taken important steps to stimulate research and development and capture industrial spin-offs from energy development for Canada. It is boosting Canada's drilling capacity in offshore waters and moving into refinery and heavy oil upgrading technology, as well as new tar sands technology. It opened a research and development facility in Calgary in 1980 and has quickly become one of the most important performers in the industry. In 1981, it expected to spend $60 million as compared with Imperial's $50 million, and in 1982 it has announced plans for a second Calgary laboratory. In a joint venture with Bawden Drilling, it will have a Canadian yard build one of the country's first semi-submersible drilling rigs at a cost of $100 million, and it may join with Canadian drilling companies to build up a large Canadian offshore drilling fleet that can also seek contracts in other countries to bring back export dollars. A good deal of Canadian technology should also come out of the Arctic Pilot Project.

Petro-Canada has moved into the oil import business as well, and has its own staff arranging foreign oil purchases and chartering tankers. When an oil import arrangement for 50,000 barrels a day was negotiated with Mexico in 1980, Petro-Canada handled the details. Mexico's president, Lopez Portillo, has announced more recently that his country plans to negotiate more of its oil sales with governments and national oil companies instead of the international oil majors which, he commented, were only "out for themselves."[24] In addition to the Mexican imports, Petro-Canada has been buying oil from Venezuela and Saudi Arabia. These state-to-state oil supply arrangements do not necessarily mean lower prices or even more secure relationships, as Petro-Canada chairman Bill Hopper has warned: "The most that can be claimed for such deals is that there is a presumption that with the range of powers and interests governments can employ, there may be greater durability to an agreement or, at least, greater reluctance on the part of suppliers to reduce or cease supply. I believe this is a reasonable presumption."[25] Morover, he added, "we will have to continue to offer – as do all other oil importers – food, technology, and capital goods and services in return for oil. It is this array of objects which only a government can marshal; it lies far beyond the capability of a private oil company to muster. These represent limited choices for any government. The fact is we have no options. We have to play in a new game."[26] But at the same time the new game, properly played, may also offer new export opportunities – for example, Canadian railway equipment, aircraft, and nuclear technology in exchange for oil – and the chance for countries like Canada and Mexico, Venezuela, and Saudi Arabia to develop closer ties as their national oil companies come together in joint ventures. For increasingly, exporting nations are preferring to negotiate oil supplies as part of broader trade and technology packages in state-to-state arrangements. Whereas the oil majors accounted for 92 per cent of oil moved in international trade in the early 1970s, by 1980 their share had dropped to about 35 per cent.[26] "The most important medium-run consequence of this change in the structure of international oil," according to one expert, "is simply that the world is going to get less oil in the 1980s, and possibly in the 1990s, than it would have done otherwise. The governments which now control the largest accumulation of OPEC reserves do not intend to develop production from them to the levels that the private companies which formerly controlled them probably would have."[27] Clearly, Petro-Canada's international role will be of critical importance until the early 1990s, when Canada's need for imported oil may have been nearly eliminated by new domestic supplies.

As this outline of Petro-Canada's activities to the start of the 1980s shows, through a program of aggressive public sup-

272

port – $520 million in federal common shares and $425 million in purchased preferred shares – Canadians now have a proven national oil company that has been able to establish itself in the space of five years as the country's fifth largest oil and gas enterprise. Though Hopper has pointed out with becoming realism that "we are still a small player in an industry that is dominated by a few major foreign-owned oil companies,"[28] the company's role so far almost guarantees an increasing influence in Canada's oil and gas world. It now has the backing, after all, of the National Energy Program and the Canada Lands reforms. In addition, Petro-Canada has a major part to play in the government's Canadianization goal, with the lion's share of financing to be provided by a special takeover tax – the Canadian ownership account – paid at the pump. This tax was applied for the first time to help finance the Petrofina deal in 1981.

Petro-Canada picked up some other new jobs under the National Energy Program. It is to consider construction of a central upgrading plant in the Montreal area to process 80,000 barrels of heavy fuel oil a day into gasoline, aviation fuel, and other products, helping reduce the need for imports. It is also expected to help build a $1-billion upgrading plant for Saskatchewan's heavy oil, using Canadian technology developed by the research laboratories of the federal energy department. Petro-Canada will be managing a new research and development subsidiary in Winnipeg, Canertech Inc., which has been given an initial $20 million to engage in joint ventures with, or provide equity capital for, Canadian companies working towards commercial production of renewable energy and conservation technology. As Canertech grows it will become a separate Crown corporation. Another Petro-Canada subsidiary, Petro-Canada International Assistance Corporation, is a child of the NEP, funded with $250 million. Its assignment will be to work with the national oil companies of such countries as Mexico and Venezuela as well as private Canadian firms, to assist the developing world in achieving its petroleum potential and reducing the burdensome cost of oil imports.

While Petro-Canada has made enormous progress, with a capital investment budget that has grown from under $200 million in 1977 to $1.5 billion in 1982, it is perhaps only recently that it has reached the point where its future is assured. Until 1980, the Progressive Conservatives seemed bent on destroying the Crown corporation. The key to their philosophy in this, one that they shared with the industry, can be caught in the flavour of a 1978 Commons debate in which the favourite new whipping boy came up.[29] One

273

Conservative spokesman, Harvie Andre, said that one reason his party would "dismantle Petro-Canada" was that in 1977, Petro-Canada's second year of operation, it had failed to be as profitable as the rest of the oil industry. Another Conservative, Marcel Lambert, argued that "public ownership has proved it cannot get itself out of a paper bag in the development of natural resources such as oil and gas," adding: "Petro-Canada will be the first expendable Crown corporation." And a third, Peter Bawden, contended that government was simply incapable of accomplishing anything positive. "There is no doubt," he said, "that Canadians have done much in the past of which they can be proud, but I think that it goes almost without question that the things which have been done by Canadians in the past have been done by the private sector. They have been done by free enterprise. It was the private sector which built this country. I do not think any of us can point with pride to anything which the government of Canada has been involved in, created, or is presently involved in." He concluded: "I do not give a damn, and I do not think Canadians should, about who owns the oil." The persistent view of the Conservatives was that Petro-Canada would inevitably, as a government enterprise, be less efficient than a private oil company, and that in any case the federal government had no need for an oil company of its own since the multinationals would respond to any guidelines laid down for them. These views defied history but they were strongly held, especially by Joe Clark. A task force set up by the Clark government in 1979 proposed that Petro-Canada be privatized, and in December 1979, Clark announced that the Conservatives would dispose of 70 per cent of Petro-Canada's shares, mainly in a public give-away. Such a move would have ended Petro-Canada's role as an agency of the country's energy policy and forced it to behave instead as another profit-maximizing oil company able to deliver immediate dividends to its new shareholders. The defeat of the Clark government early in 1980 prevented this emasculation from taking place.

Looking at the future scope of Petro-Canada's operations, one can easily see how it might become simply too big for any minister to keep in check. This is always one of the dangers in setting up a national oil company, or any aggressive national company. Once it reaches a certain size it can become a political force of its own, and defy political control. Since, however, Petro-Canada is to be an instrument of public policy and not just another oil firm, the government has special powers to reduce the risk of this happening. Cabinet must approve its capital spending budget every year, along with commitments for future years; Cabinet can issue policy directives, for example for the acquisition of other oil companies or the negotiation of an oil import arrangement with Mexico; Cabinet also has to approve any changes in corporate bylaws, appoints the corporate auditor, appoints the board of directors, and approves the choice of the president and chairman. If the government has a clear idea of its energy policy goals, there is little doubt it will impress them on Petro-Canada. But if the Cabinet is weak, there is the danger that Petro-Canada may set its own priorities; and if there is a negative Cabinet, as there was in the Joe Clark government, then Petro-Canada may lose its momentum and its best people out of demoralization.

The relationship between Cabinet and Petro-Canada, in fact, is a crucial one. Petro-Canada executive vice-president Joel Bell has called the mandate "a two-way street." In one direction, Petro-Canada "is to operate as an expression of the energy policy of the government, selecting its projects against the test of whether they contribute to the energy goal which the government sets from time to time for the country; and in the other direction, Petro-Canada is to add its input to the views heard by the government so that they might further understand the impact on their goals of various policies which are available to them, and that they might accept operating objectives for Petro-Canada which help to advance the energy goals they set for the country."[30] The relationship may be privileged, but it is not private. Petro-Canada is also subject to public scrutiny. It must publish details of its activities, just as any other company has to, in an annual report. It is also subject to parliamentary review through the Auditor-General, the right of opposition MPs to question the energy minister on its activities, and the appearance by Petro-Canada executives before the House of Commons Committee on National Resources and Public Works.

In pursuing its role as a special oil company with a mandate to carry out Canadian public goals, Petro-Canada could find itself facing several obvious difficulties. The first would be the failure by politicians, as in the days of the Clark government, to recognize that its role is actually unique. And Petro-Canada's position could be threatened as well if it is judged simply on its profit or bottom-line performance. As Petro-Canada vice-president Joel Bell has pointed out, the company has to select its investments by its public policy or mandate criteria, and even if exploration efforts are brilliantly successful, years of heavy spending may be required before these resources can be brought to market.[31] On the other hand, the presence of private partners in almost every project should help ensure that activities are conducted as efficiently as possible.

Another potential problem is associated with growth. In its drive to become a significant public presence, the company could outstrip its technical and operating expertise and stretch its top management too thin. This hasn't happened yet, but the development of management and technical expertise will be a major challenge for the company during the 1980s. It cannot afford to make costly blunders, or the kinds of strategic errors that can go unchallenged in the private sector. For example, the shift of exploration spending out of Alberta and into the Mackenzie Delta in the early 1970s by some major oil companies, and the costly buyback of land positions by the same companies later in the same decade, attracted little public attention. Were Petro-Canada to make this kind of mistake, however, the oil companies and opposition MPs would spring to the attack. Petro-Canada will also have to be careful to avoid the temptation to act like other oil companies in the pursuit of profits instead of living up to its mandate to guard the public interest. For example, as the Bertrand Report has argued,[32] the oil majors have made it difficult for independent service stations to provide competition in Canada, frequently buying out the independents when they become too successful. Petro-Canada raised apprehensions that it might fall into the same practice when it acquired the Merit independent chain in B.C. in 1980. Merit had in fact been offered to Petro-Canada by its owners, but the fears that were expressed at the time point up the need for committed top management and continuing political interest by Cabinet to ensure that Petro-Canada never becomes just another oil company. In a 1981 parliamentary hearing, energy minister Marc Lalonde was heard to say that the government expected Petro-Canada to help the consumer by being "a very aggressive competitor." This meant, he went on, "that all around I hope it will influence the margins, in the sense that if Petro-Canada is a strictly Canadian company, it does not depend on foreign subsidiaries for its supply, and this type of thing; we will avoid the possibility of unnecessary transfers of funds abroad through subsidiaries. Through aggressive competition I would expect that Petro-Canada will keep prices lower than they would have otherwise been. . . . We certainly would hope that Petro-Canada, being what it is, will indeed be in the sector an element that will keep competition very much alive indeed."[33]

Assuming that Petro-Canada maintains the calibre of management, combining entrepreneurial skill with a sense of the public interest, that it has had in its first six years, however, it should enjoy a highly promising future. It is likely to become a joint venture partner in a growing number of energy projects, a risk sharer for Canadians in projects where private industry wants public assistance but a risk sharer that will be able to collect a share of future profits as well. Petro-Canada will also be in a key position to provide opportunities for scores of smaller Canadian companies, including companies and co-operatives owned by Native peoples, to participate as junior partners in promising frontier and tar sands projects. And with its important role in helping Canadians gain engineering, technological, and manufacturing spin-offs from every project, it may play a significant role in expanding other important areas of the Canadian economy in the 1980s. Its foreign activities, especially its relations with other national oil companies, its developing third-world exploration assistance, and its participation in foreign oil exploration from Norway to China, are also likely to help spread Canada's reputation. Its joint venture research activities with such important countries as Mexico and Venezuela will make it a vehicle for better overall economic ties.

By the end of 1981, Petro-Canada had become an established and accepted fact of life in Canada. Royal Bank chairman Rowland Frazee told *The Financial Post*: "I'm a supporter of Petro-Can. I see a real role for a national oil company. Not in owning service stations, but in exploration and development, in tar sands, in the big frontier projects and Hibernia, in having a prominent position in the high-risk projects, and in bringing some federal clout to them. Where substantial financing is required, Petro-Can can play a very important role."[34] The fact was, Frazee said, that the creation of Petro-Canada was probably inevitable: "The sudden emergence of the international energy crisis together with the unusually high degree of foreign ownership of industry in Canada made it fairly clear that government would be required to take a much more direct role in energy development than it previously had. In that environment it was not surprising that Canada would choose an option that most other countries have chosen – a national oil company." And he told a U.S. audience in early 1982 that "Canada's Petro-Can is widely supported by the general public, not only as an instrument of government policy, but as a very capably managed enterprise."[35] Even the U.S. government's General Accounting Office found good things to say about Petro-Canada in a 1981 analysis. While Petro-Canada had not yet demonstrated that it could do a better job of finding oil than the private oil companies did, its "limited experience to date seems to indicate that a national oil company is not necessarily less efficient, as is often claimed."[36] In fact, "Petro-Canada operates as efficiently as the private sector." Moreover, the U.S. study said, "Petro-Canada's experience indicates that it is possible for a national oil company to accelerate the pace of exploration and development activities in high-risk/high-cost areas where private-company activity may be insufficient and currently uneconomic. Petro-Canada has demonstrated that a government-owned company can act as such a catalyst." The General Accounting Office also noted Petro-Canada's role in providing the government with useful information on the workings of the oil business, "a window on the industry."

Although Petro-Canada was born in political controversy and opposed by the oil multinationals, its establishment may turn out to have been one of the most important federal initiatives of the 1970s. To be sure, as it began to make its presence felt, its size was routinely exaggerated by its critics. While it had shown great growth, at the end of 1980 it still owned only about 4 per cent of Canada's oil reserves and 7 per cent of its gas reserves. But the process is well under way, and the effect has already been vital. By the 1990s, Petro-Canada is likely to be as important a part of our society as CN, the Wheat Board, Air Canada, or the CBC. It is one more example of the imaginative use of public enterprise to advance the basic interests of the Canadian people.

Notes

1. Herschel Hardin. *A Nation Unaware*. Vancouver, J. J. Douglas, 1974.
2. This is based on the unpublished study of Imperial Oil by John Ewing, cited chiefly in Chapter 2.
3. House of Commons, Debates, 20 May 1941.
4. Letter from Premier T. C. Douglas to an oil company executive, dated 21 March 1949; it is similar to letters Douglas sent to many oil company executives. Quoted in John Richards and Larry Pratt, *Prairie Capitalism*. Toronto, McClelland and Stewart, 1979.
5. Richards and Pratt, *Prairie Capitalism*.
6. Royal Commission on Energy. Report, vol. 2. Ottawa 1959.
7. Department of Energy, Mines and Resources. *An Energy Policy for Canada – Phase 1*. Ottawa 1973.
8. J. J. Greene to the American Association of Petroleum Geologists, Calgary, 20 June 1970.
9. Richards and Pratt, *Prairie Capitalism*.
10. *An Energy Policy for Canada*.
11. Donald Macdonald at the Royal Society of Canada Symposium on Energy Resources, Ottawa, 16 October 1973.

12. CTV Question Period, 9 September 1973.
13. House of Commons, Debates, 6 December 1972.
14. House of Commons, Debates, 12 March 1975.
15. House of Commons, Debates, 12 March 1975.
16. *The Petro-Canada Act*, 1975.
17. Imperial Oil press release, 17 December 1973.
18. Jerry McAfee, president, Gulf Canada, to the Canadian Club of Toronto, 25 November 1974.
19. R. W. Sparks, president, Texaco Canada, to the annual general meeting of shareholders, Toronto, 23 April 1976.
20. *Saturday Night*, 12 May 1906. Quoted in H. V. Nelles, *The Policies of Development*. Toronto, Macmillan, 1974.
21. Maurice Strong, Petro-Canada chairman, to the Canadian Club, Toronto, 18 August 1977.
22. J. L. Stoik, president, Gulf Canada, to the Northern Development Conference, Edmonton, 4 November 1976.
23. Larry Pratt, to the conference on "Managing Public Enterprises: Purposes and Performance" sponsored by the Institute for Research on Public Policy and the University of California, Vancouver, 13-14 August 1981.
24. "Mexico Now to Favor Government Oil Buyers." *New York Times*, 18 July 1981.
25. W. H. Hopper, Petro-Canada chairman, to the Empire Club, Toronto, 11 October 1979.
26. J. E. Hartshorn. "From Multinational to National Oil: The Structural Change." Middle East Economic Survey. Cyprus, 28 April 1980.
27. Hartshorn, "From Multinational to National Oil."
28. W. H. Hopper, Petro-Canada chairman, to a *Financial Post* Conference, Calgary, 27 October 1981.
29. House of Commons, Debates, 20 June 1978.
30. Joel Bell, Petro-Canada senior vice-president, finance and planning, to the Society of Management Accountants of Ontario, Toronto, 28 November 1980.
31. Joel Bell, Toronto speech of 28 November 1980.
32. Robert Bertrand, Director of Investigation and Research, Combines Investigation Act. *The State of Competition in the Canadian Petroleum Industry*. Ottawa 1981.
33. House of Commons Committee on National Resources and Public Works, 19 March 1981.
34. *The Financial Post*, 19 December 1981.
35. Rowland Frazee, Royal Bank of Canada chairman, to the Economic Club of Detroit, 22 February 1982.
36. U.S. General Accounting Office. "Petro-Canada: The National Oil Company as a Tool of Canadian Energy Policy." Washington, 15 October 1981.

Chapter 10

Big Oil Branches Out

In the lush headquarters of the world's big oil companies, top corporate brains are bent over strategies for recycling oil profits into a wide range of new activities, from coal, uranium, metals, and petrochemicals, to real estate, forest products, bio-technology, micro-electronics, food processing, and even department stores. The multinationals are preparing for the day when oil and gas will be less important and less profitable. Atlantic Richfield led the pack in 1977 with its $600-million takeover of the big Anaconda mining company. In 1978, Standard Oil of California unsuccessfully bid $1.8 billion for 80 per cent of Amax Inc., another huge U.S. mining multinational, and in 1981 its offer went up to $4.3 billion, which tells us, if nothing else, what kind of money the majors are willing to spend to lay hold of other resources. In 1981, Standard Oil of Ohio, controlled by British Petroleum, paid $1.8 billion to acquire Kennecott, the largest copper producer in the United States, while BP itself paid about $1 billion for the huge mining multinational Selection Trust and another $700 million to buy coal properties from U.S. Steel.

Few companies have spelled out their diversification strategies as clearly as British Petroleum has. According to company chairman Sir David Steel, BP's oil and gas activities are not an adequate basis for growth.[1] Accounting for 83 per cent of BP's assets in 1980, they will make up only 50 per cent by 1990, while chemicals will rise from 9 per cent to as much as 12 per cent, coal from 2.5 to 8 per cent, minerals from 3 to 8 per cent, and other interests such as food and detergents will expand from 2.5 per cent of the company's holdings to 22 or even 24 per cent. The range of diversification, in fact, is almost inexhaustible. Exxon has moved heavily into office equipment in competition with IBM, and in 1979 spent $1.2 billion to acquire Reliance, the largest electric-motor manufacturer in the United States. Mobil Oil paid $1.5 billion in

1975-76 for the Montgomery Ward department store chain and Container Corp., one of the biggest U.S. packaging companies. In mid-1981 Occidental Petroleum, which in 1978 bid $900 million for the giant Mead forest products company, picked up Iowa Beef Processors, the largest meat-processing company in the United States, for $795 million. As Occidental's president explained, "we think food will be in the 1990s what energy has been in the 1970s and 1980s."[2]

The oil companies are also active in the big consortia planning deep-water nickel and other mineral recoveries for later in this decade. Shell and Standard Oil of Indiana (Amoco) are both members of Ocean Minerals, while British Petroleum and Kennecott have the Kennecott consortium, and Sun Oil Co. is a member of a third consortium, Ocean Mining Associates. The oil majors are also looking for opportunities in the high-technology areas that will be increasingly important in the future, examples being Exxon, Shell, and BP involvements in bio-technology or genetic engineering, and some of them have set up venture capital subsidiaries to buy into new businesses at an early stage: Exxon has its Exxon Enterprises, Sohio its Vista Ventures Corp., and Texaco, whose venture arm is Harrison Capital, has even gone into the banking business with Ful-Tex Euro Services in partnership with a London foreign-exchange broker.

In Canada, under FIRA's careful eye, the oil majors have been able to expand aggressively into coal, uranium, and metals, as well as petrochemicals, real estate, and electronics – even though the agency has made it harder for them to take over big Canadian mining companies such as Noranda, and pulp and paper firms such as Abitibi-Price. Imperial Oil president Jack Armstrong told the company's 1977 annual meeting about plans for heavy expansion into coal and uranium, as well as other metals and petrochemicals: "We are no longer solely an energy company."[3] Imperial employees 30 years hence, Armstrong said, "will be busily engaged in the mining and production of frontier oil and gas, large-scale coal mining, the production of nuclear fuels, solar energy, and, most likely, the development of other forms of renewable energy. Our chemical enterprises will undoubtedly have expanded beyond all recognition and a growing amount of our revenue will be generated from the development and production of other minerals." And he continued this strategy shortly after the introduction of the National Energy Program: "The aggressive program of diversification we have pursued for a number of years means that we don't have all our eggs in one basket – in fact, we have identified far more opportunities than we have the resources to pursue."[4] Imperial, of course, is not alone in seeking out new profit opportunities in Canada. Shell Canada, Gulf Canada, Texaco Canada, and BP all have extensive non-oil activities here. Mobil Corp., in its 1980 annual report, noted that it was increasing its coal activities in Canada, while Standard Oil of California told its shareholders in its 1980 annual report that it had "accelerated its search for minerals in the United States, Canada and Australia."

From 1977 to mid-1981, the oil industry spent $469 million on ventures in coal, not including the cost of takeovers, of which over 80 per cent came from the major foreign-controlled integrated companies. In the same four and a half years, the oil industry spent $117 million to explore for and develop uranium, 80 per cent or $94 million of this coming from foreign-controlled companies. And of the $3.1 billion spent by the oil industry on refining-marketing and petrochemicals, $2.1 billion was spent by foreign-controlled firms, with the handful of major foreign-controlled integrated companines accounting for the bulk of these investments.[5] Though this represents just 2 per cent of total capital spending in the four years, the figures will rise significantly during the 1980s as mining projects are brought to the production stage. Investment in petrochemicals and metal mining is also expected to climb sharply.

Even with higher taxes and other restraints, the oil companies will have plenty of money in the 1980s for diversification. For all the much-hated National Energy Program, cash flow will grow fourfold; the 1981 agreement between Ottawa and the Alberta government provided the industry with an additional $10 billion up to the end of 1986. A leading Bay Street oil analyst, Robert Robinson, calculated after the NEP was introduced that after-tax profits from oil and gas production would still grow at an average annual rate of 22 per cent from 1982 to 1989, while cash flow for reinvestment, not counting Ottawa's new exploration grants, would be at least 3.5 times greater in 1990 than in 1982 and total $115 billion in the decade.[6] And the oil share of total profits in non-financial industries had already risen from 15 per cent in 1972 to 30 per cent in 1980, giving the industry a powerful base from which to expand and diversify.[7] As Imperial's president James Livingstone told the Canadian Association of Petroleum Investment analysts: "After record earnings last year, we started 1981 with a billion-dollar cash base and a prime credit rating. With expenditures approximating $8 billion for petroleum exploration and development and mineral projects, plus $5 billion for petroleum products and chemicals, Imperial expects to recover from this year's setbacks and have plenty of momentum in this decade."[8]

Coal is one of the chief areas in which the oil majors will invest in Canada, and forecasts of coal production show why. According to the Coal Association of Canada, westbound coal exports could climb from 14.1 million metric tons in 1980 to about 53.3 million metric tons by 1990.[9] A British investment house has estimated that Canada's export potential for steam coal alone will rise from one million metric tons in 1980 to 31 million in 1990.[10] Even within Canada, according to the National Energy Board, the demand for thermal coal to generate electricity will triple over the next 20 years, with coal's contribution to electricity supply rising from 9 per cent in 1979 to nearly 25 per cent in the year 2000.[11] While Canada probably has no more than 2 per cent of the world's coal supplies – most of the world's coal is in the United States, China, and the Soviet Union – its reserves in the West alone are accessible and certainly more than enough to meet future Canadian needs. And as the energy board has noted, "indications are that the resources of northern Canada will be shown to be very large when reliable information becomes available." But the most optimistic forecast has been issued from the Canada West Foundation, which announced in 1981 that "the resource base is huge and its potential for development is great. Twenty billion tonnes of recoverable coal reserves exist in the western provinces of Saskatchewan, Alberta, and British Columbia. This estimate is conservative and excludes inferred reserves or resources of future interest."[12] By the foundation's estimate, production will increase from 33.8 million metric tons in 1980 to 82.6 million in 1990 and 154 million in 2000. The export share was forecast to decline from 43 per cent in 1980 to 36 per cent in 2000, but the actual volume of exports would climb from 14.4 million metric tons in 1980 to 56 million in 2000, an almost fourfold increase. "The greatest potential development for coal may lie in its conversion to fuels and chemicals to supplement the products from conventional and heavy oils and from natural gas," according to Canada West: "Coal gasification and liquefaction are increasingly being considered as alternative sources of supply for oil and gas. In western Canada, given the abundance of natural gas reserves, coal gasification seems unlikely, at least in this century. Coal liquefaction, however, remains a distinct possibility. The conversion of coal to liquid fuels appears to be on the threshold of becoming an economic alternative source for oil." The foundation held that at least one conversion plant producing 75,000 barrels a day would be built during the 1990s.

It is because they believe that coal is "an energy bridge to the future," as one Imperial Oil executive has put it,[13] that the oil companies have invested so heavily. It is expected that Canadian subsidiaries of the oil majors will spend about $1 billion over the next five or six years developing massive coal projects in Canada. According to Imperial, "we possess the equivalent of 50 billion barrels of oil in our coal reserves, and in time, as energy prices rise and as new technology in the form of coal gasification and liquefaction is developed, we may be able to turn much of this coal into a more mobile and economic source of energy."[14] Gulf Corp. in the U.S. is developing a process for the solvent refining of coal, and, "assuming our coal mining projects go well," the company's Canadian president has declared, "we could perhaps see some future application in Canada for this new Gulf liquefaction process."[15] Moreover, as Shell Canada has pointed out, "gasification is just the starting point for the further synthesis of ammonia, methanol, liquid hydrocarbons, and a host of petrochemicals which can be transformed into anything from carpet fibres to packaging materials."[16]

Several oil majors are now operating mines or planning to open mines in the near future. At Byron Creek Collieries in British Columbia, acquired in 1980, Imperial has promised to quadruple production by 1985 to 3.6 million tonnes a year, provided sufficient reserves and markets can be found, and the company has made an undertaking with FIRA to increase Canadian ownership to 50 per cent. Esso is also considering a $350-million coal project near Judy Creek in Alberta for the late 1980s or early 1990s; in addition, at the end of 1980, it held or had applied for 390,000 net hectares of coal leases in Alberta and British Columbia. "Development costs could run as high as $35 billion" to meet rising demand for thermal and metallurgical coal, Imperial's chairman has predicted, and he has expressed concern that coal could come under Canadian ownership rules: "Coal mining is a high-risk industry, and one which is relatively dependent on external financing. Investor confidence would seem a prime prerequisite for expansion of the industry. Yet given the philosophical direction of current energy policy, this would seem a prime candidate for NEP-syle treatment."[17] However, Imperial continues generally optimistic, expecting that coal will be supplying 14 per cent of our overall energy needs in the year 2000 as compared with 10 per cent today, and predicting that by 2000, 2 million metric tons of coal a year will be used to produce gas for use in oil sands upgrading or in the production of ammonia and other saleable chemicals. "We project that after the turn of the century when oil and gas production plateau, coal use as a feedstock for coal synthetic plants will dramatically increase,'' one of Imperial's coal experts has announced.[18] While Canada's potentially abundant natural gas supplies could delay coal gasification for domestic use, synthetic plants could be built to supply export markets, according to this same expert, who also believes that within 20 years it could be economic to make oil from coal.

Shell Canada began buying coal properties in 1972, and in 1978 it acquired the B.C. Crows Nest Industries Company, now reorganized as its wholly-owned subsidiary, Crows Nest Resources. It is currently spending about $200 million on its Line Creek mine to fill long-term contracts for metallurgical coal with Japan and South Korea. In addition to Crows Nest's 300,000 hectares of land holdings, Shell has other coal prospects in Alberta and B.C., and is also negotiating coal leases on a Blackfoot reserve near Calgary as the first step towards a $700-million coal mine and electric-power project for the late 1980s. In 1978, Gulf Canada acquired a 40-per-cent interest in its first major coal project, a 116,000-acre metallurgical coal property in Belcourt, B.C., with Denison Mines holding the other 60 per cent. Gulf has also picked up 76,000 acres in the Chip Lake area west of Edmonton and an interest in another property in southwestern Alberta. Altogether, in late 1980, Gulf Canada had coal leases on about 700,000 net acres in British Columbia and 135,000 net acres in Alberta, with Alberta applications outstanding for another 267,000 net acres. The company has also taken out extensive exploration licences in the Canadian Arctic, and it is part of a consortium, Scotia Coal Synfuels Projects, looking at the possibility of liquefying Nova Scotia coal into oil. Other companies have been building up their holdings as well, with Suncor reporting what it calls promising results at its Chip Lake property west of Edmonton, where recoverable reserves are estimated at 260 million metric tons of thermal coal, and Texaco Canada announcing in its 1980 annual report that it had substantial holdings.

At the end of 1980, BP Canada held 15,178 net hectares of coal, 340,897 of minerals, and major minerals options on a further 114,670. In 1977, BP paid $30 million for extensive coal licences to two Canadian companies, Teck Corp. and Brameda Resources. Proven reserves of metallurgical coal at its main property, Sukunka-Bullmoose in B.C., are 182 million metric tons with, the company says, another 117 million indicated. The company has other interests in the B.C. northwest and Vancouver Island, where it hopes to find high-quality thermal coal, and it is looking for coal in Alberta. Union Oil Canada Ltd., a subsidiary of Union Oil of California, is proceeding with a $400-million mine at Obed Marsh in Alberta, and in 1980 nearly doubled its coal leases for a total of 549,078 net acres. Other international oil companies active in Canadian coal include Conoco, which is embarking on a $510-million expansion of its Consolidated Coal operation in Canada, and Superior Oil, whose controlling interest in McIntyre Mines gives it extensive coal operations in Alberta.

The probability is that the industry's burgeoning cash flow will put it in a strong position to build up its coal land holdings just as it built up land holdings in oil and gas years ago. And although the 1980 National Energy Program states that "the government is anxious to ensure that the coal industry does not become dominated by foreign-controlled firms,"[19] the Department of Energy, Mines and Resources has remarkably little data on foreign ownership in coal, nor does it have Canadian ownership targets as it does for oil, natural gas, and uranium; it has stated, however, that it will require all coal liquefaction plants to meet a Canadian ownership test. Moreover, with so much of the growth in demand for coal to come from foreign markets, some Canadians are asking whether an all-out export drive is in Canada's best interests. Jack Davis, a former federal and B.C. cabinet minister, has argued that it makes greater economic sense to process more of the coal in Canada: "The best bet is generating electricity from coal in the Kootenays . . . British Columbia Resources Investment Corp. and B.C. Hydro, co-operating on an East Kootenay power plant, would create hundreds of well-paid jobs. And we would be converting a low-grade resource into the biggest form of energy that money can buy, electricity. The overall yield to the provinces from this kind of manufacturing would be much greater, therefore, than mining is today."[20]

As if coal were not enough, the oil giants are also rushing headlong into uranium, even though federal regulations limit foreign ownership to 33 per cent. Three oil companies are now either operating uranium mines or moving towards production. In 1980, about one third of uranium exploration was carried out by oil companies.[21] It is not hard to see why. The federal energy department has estimated that exports, in spite of current weak world demand, will double from 9,200 tons of uranium oxide in 1979 to 18,700 tons in 1987, with current reserves at 780,000 tons. The price of a pound of uranium was $6.85 in 1970; in 1980 it was $38.55.[22] The new focus for uranium has been northern Saskatchewan, where important new finds give that province about half the Canadian total. Saskatchewan's NDP government has been stimulating this development, using its Mining and Development Corporation as a joint venture partner.

Gulf and Imperial are the oil companies expanding most vigorously into uranium. October 1975 saw the opening of the Rabbit Lake mine in Saskatchewan, the first new uranium mine in Canada in 25 years, with an annual production of 2,530 metric tons of U308 that made it the biggest producer in Saskatchewan. Rabbit Lake is owned 45.4 per cent by Gulf Minerals, a wholly-owned subsidiary of U.S. Gulf, 5.1 per cent by Gulf Canada, and 49 per cent by Uranerz of West Germany. Gulf Minerals and Uranerz are also planning a new uranium mine at Collins Bay with an annual production of 2,300 tonnes of U308, while Gulf Minerals, Noranda Mines, and the Saskatchewan Mining Development Corporation, each have a one-third interest in an important uranium prospect at Eagle Point, south of Rabbit Lake. Gulf has been able to operate outside Canada's foreign-ownership rules on uranium because Gulf Minerals was active in uranium exploration in the early 1970s, and therefore exempted.

Esso Resources Canada plans a $600-million mine at Midwest Lake to open in 1988. Imperial has 50 per cent of the project and two U.S. investors 12.5 per cent; the remaining 37.5 per cent is held by two Canadian companies, Bow Valley Industries and Numac Oil and Gas. The foreign ownership had to be reduced, but, through an escape clause in federal regulations by which the project was judged to be under Canadian management and of significant potential benefit to Canada, only reduced to 50 per cent. That was clearly preferable to Imperial, though according to the company, "at first we had hoped we would not have to divest at all."[23] And a number of other oil companies are also getting into the act. Shell Canada, for example, is busy exploring for uranium in Newfoundland, Nova Scotia, and Saskatchewan. Shell's 1976 exploration agreement with the federal Crown corporation Eldorado Nuclear allows it to earn a 40-per-cent stake in the western venture: in Nova Scotia, it is a 50-50 partner with Ontario Hydro. Canadian Occidental Petroleum is looking at a major new uranium mine in Saskatchewan at a cost of some $300 million, with Inco as half partner. And though no other oil companies are about to develop uranium mines, most are on the watch for reserves. Suncor is looking in Saskatchewan, Manitoba, New Brunswick, Nova Scotia, and the Northwest Territories, Texaco Canada says that it is continuing to negotiate for the acquisition of additional mineral rights in the Northwest Territories and Saskatchewan, and British Petroleum is looking for uranium in the Territories, where it has promising properties, as well as in northern Alberta. Mobil Energy Minerals is also active in uranium exploration.

The multinational subsidiaries are moving equally, like their parents, into the area of copper, lead, zinc, tin, iron, gold, and other minerals, with commitments that will probably exceed $1 billion in the 1980s. Exxon's Imperial plans to be one of the leading players, spending $1.2 billion on coal, uranium, and minerals development combined, or 15 per cent of its resource investments, in the decade.[24] Imperial's chairman has called Esso Minerals "the baby of the Imperial family," adding that "although relatively new-born, it's already a lusty infant and ranks among the top ten mineral exploration companies in Canada. Our plans call for bringing one new minerals project on stream every two years throughout the 1980s and have this segment making a notable contribution to earnings by 1990."[25] In 1979, Imperial opened a lead-zinc mine at Gays River near Halifax, and was given the green light by FIRA for its takeover of Granduc Mines, a B.C. copper producer. It is considering a $200-million molybdenum mine at Trout Lake and a $180-million copper-zinc mine at Kutcho Creek, both in British Columbia.

Superior Oil has a major mining stake in Canada through its controlling interest in McIntyre and Falconbridge. It also controls Madelaine Mines, a Quebec copper producer. The wholly-owned Canadian Superior branch is actively engaged in mineral exploration in Canada and elsewhere, frequently in joint ventures with its parent. Its activities in Canada include exploration for molybdenum in British Columbia, lithium in the Northwest Territories, uranium in Saskatchewan, British Columbia, and the Yukon, gold and copper in British Columbia, tin in Manitoba, and lead-zinc in the Arctic islands. In addition, it has sought out coal interests in various parts of British Columbia and Alberta, including 33.5 per cent of a 66,000-acre metallurgical coal property at Monkman Pass-Belcourt in British Columbia. Outside Canada, it has a 24-per-cent interest in DeLamar Silver Mines in Idaho and is searching for minerals in the United States, Spain, Ireland, and Chile. If Superior Oil goes ahead with a major copper mine at Quebrada Blanca in Chile, Canadian Superior will become a partner in the project, quite possibly diverting its profits from Canadian oil and gas to help its parent.

Shell Canada Resources had been looking busily as well, and announced in 1981 that its tin discovery in Nova Scotia "may be the biggest tin mine in Canada."[26] Since that time, however, the company has decided to sell off its metals interests and concentrate on such products as coal. Gulf Canada is less active in mineral exploration since that sector is covered by Gulf Minerals, but the oil branch has a 50-per-cent interest in some important Gulf Minerals projects. BP has a mining subsidiary, BP Minerals, set up in 1972 and currently active in B.C., Manitoba, and Ontario minerals exploration, with a 100-per-cent interest in a New Brunswick potash property. Standard Oil of California owns 20 per cent of Amax, a mining multinational with extensive Canadian interests, while a branch, Chevron Standard, owns Crest Exploration, with huge Yukon iron ore reserves. Other oil companies with metal mining interests in Canada include Mobil and Union Oil, as well as Aquitaine and Hudson's Bay Oil and Gas, two foreign-owned companies that came under Canadian control in 1981. Amoco Petroleum, the Canadian subsidiary of Standard Oil of Indiana, established a separate mining division in 1969. In the five years 1976-80, it spent $20 million looking for minerals. It has 50 per cent of the Detour Lake Gold Mine, a $200-million project in northern Ontario, and 70 per cent of a molybdenum property at Red Mountain in the Yukon. In 1979, Standard Indiana acquired Cyprus Mines, which became an operating subsidiary of Amoco Minerals in 1980. The move gave Amoco a 63-per-cent interest in Cyprus Anvil Mining, a major silver, zinc, and lead miner in the Yukon. In 1980, however, FIRA turned down the Cyprus Anvil deal and Amoco announced in 1981 that it would sell its 63 per cent to a qualified buyer, which in the event turned out to be Hudson's Bay Oil and gas.

Big Oil's investment in renewable energy forms has been modest so far, although the subsidiaries, like their multinational parents, have staked a position for the future. Shell was the first company to set up a biomass division through its wholly-owned subsidiary, BioShell Inc., which transforms wastes from forest industry operations into fuel pellets. It opened its first facility at an Abitibi-Price site in northern Ontario in 1981, has announced a second facility that will start up in eastern Ontario during 1982, and is planning to build additional plants at other forest product operations in Quebec and Ontario. Imperial Oil's main effort has been in the solar energy field, with results that are so far disappointing. Imperial's shareholders heard at their 1977 annual meeting that "solar is still a long way down the road as a large-scale commercial proposition but, again, when that day does arrive, we fully intend that Imperial will be involved and are closely following progress in this field. We also stand to benefit from our involvement in the considerable amount of research and development being conducted in this area by the Exxon Corporation."[27] Suncor Inc. has a 15-per-cent interest in Solartech, a Toronto-based company engaged in solar research and development, and Texaco Canada has established its own alternative energy division. While these commitments are minuscule when compared with the oil companies' overall activities, interest is likely to increase as they plan for the long term. Clifton Garvin Jr., chairman of Exxon Corp., has speculated: "If you want to look into the future – say, 50 to 75 years – I think it's obvious that the world's going to have to move increasingly toward an electrical-based society. And that electrical base is going to have to come increasingly from renewable sources of energy. The renewable sources, in my judgement, are primarily the sun and solar. I'd put nuclear fusion in renewable sources, and of course, the other things like fermentations of alcohol and biomass."[28] If the U.S. oil industry's research pays off, it is probable that companies will use their Canadian subsidiaries as marketing and distribution agencies.

The oil giants are looking at other business areas as well. Property development is one of these, and at least two oil companies, Shell and Gulf, have built housing projects. In its 1979 annual report, Shell noted expansion in its "portfolios of major tracts of land for subdivision and servicing. Acquisitions for both future residential and industrial subdivisions were centred in southern Ontario but included one parcel in the Vancouver area." The company reported the completion of a residential subdivision in St. Albert near Edmonton and announced its first joint venture with a major land developer, George Wimpey Canada Ltd., near Burlington, Ontario. In addition to its housing activities, Gulf has built the Gulf Canada Square office complex in downtown Calgary that opened in 1979, 40 per cent of it leased by non-company tenants.

The Canadian petrochemicals and chemical fertilizer industry has entered an unprecedented boom of investment and expansion after years of slow growth, and the oil multinationals are making sure that they are in on it. Five foreign-controlled oil companies – Imperial, Shell, Gulf, Canadian Occidental, and Union Oil – will participate in a multi-billion-dollar package of world-scale petrochemical projects during the 1980s, and they have other major investments on their drawing boards as well. Much of the production will go into export markets as the world seeks secure and critical supplies of chemicals and fertilizers. With Canadian natural gas in abundant supply and feedstock prices held below international levels as a result of government policy, would-be petrochemical producers in Canada enjoy obvious advantages.

One indicator of the expected growth in Canada's petrochemicals industry is the National Energy Board's estimate of future feedstock requirements for oil and gas. According to the board, these will soar from the equivalent of 389 petajoules in 1980 to 762 petajoules in 1990 and 985 in the year 2000.[29] And just as exporting electricity instead of coal or uranium means more and better jobs, upgrading oil and natural gas into manufactured products here generates far more employment than simply exporting the raw material does. According to one estimate, the value of the gas and oil increases by 20 to 40 times when they are transformed into petrochemicals and such products as plastics.[30] The industry obtains its basic raw materials – ammonia, methanol, ethylene, benzene, and their principal derivatives – by the conversion of gas and oil, along with ethane, propane, and butanes: ammonia and methanol come largely from natural gas, while ethylene can be made from either oil or gas, and benzene is produced from either oil or natural gas liquids. These basic building blocks are converted in turn into such products as polyvinyl chloride, polystyrene, vinyl acetate, synthetic rubber and latex, and cellulose acetate. As the process continues, these materials are manufactured into an almost endless list of industrial and consumer products that ranges from tires, anti-freeze, cosmetics, plastics, and synthetic fabrics such as polyesters for use in clothing, sheets, and carpets, to adhesives, drugs, and household detergents. The ethane that winds up as polyester fibre in a shirt would have increased in value by several hundred times along the way.[31]

One reason for the special oil industry interest in this country's chemicals potential has been spelled out in a paper on the world chemicals future by a senior Dow executive: "Looking at the ownership of the industry, one has to conclude that the pressures will be greatest on the non-integrated producers who do not have access to raw materials. By 2000, at least ten of the top 20 organizations will be daughters of major private oil companies or state oil enterprises."[32] Oil- and gas-rich countries will enter the petrochemicals big league, while there is going to be a major shake-out in the business: "Out of today's top 30, 20 or less will survive as we know them now. Among medium-size organizations the concentration will take place faster, and the number of companies in this bracket will be halved." Of the top 20 chemicals companies in 1980, seven were in the U.S. and 13 in western

Europe. In 2000, one of the top 20 will be in Canada, with Japan, the Middle East, Latin America, and eastern Europe also joining the front ranks. Reorganizations and takeovers here will give FIRA an opportunity to nurture a strong Canadian-controlled presence. The agency will need to be watchful, for, as a group of business and labour leaders reminded Ottawa in their 1981 report on major projects, "foreign firms have invested in the Canadian energy and other natural resource sectors mainly for the purpose of acquiring captive sources of raw materials for processing abroad. As a consequence, sufficient linkages have not been established between Canada's strengths in natural resources and manufacturing goods such resources can produce."[33] Nor have world trading rules helped Canadians in their efforts to upgrade resources, the group pointed out: "The General Agreement on Tariffs and Trade (GATT), in its application to Canada, continues to favour the export of raw materials over finished products. As a result, Canadian exports have tended to be concentrated in low-technology areas, whereas Canada's requirements for high-technology products are often procured from abroad."

The companies behind Canada's current chemicals boom, in fact, are not the oil majors but a Canadian-controlled group, led by Nova and the Alberta Energy Corp., launching a world-scale industry based on Alberta's natural gas resources and using the pioneer research work of Edmonton's Dr. Charles Allard. Until these Canadian companies got into the act, the chemicals industry in Canada was, with the exception of government-owned Polysar, almost entirely foreign-controlled. "Just a few years ago," Nova chairman Robert Blair has noted, "Canada was importing 90 per cent of its methyl alcohol and that was accepted as the normal and proper status quo."[34] This situation has been turned around, but as the majors move in, they will pose the now familiar danger to the survival of a Canadian-owned and -controlled petrochemicals sector. It is no accident that the membership of the Canadian Chemical Producers' Association includes the top oil companies.

Like so many ventures in the oil business, the petrochemical sector now coming to the fore is a product of long-term planning. R. G. Reid, then president of Imperial Oil, told the company's annual meeting in 1975 that it had invested more than $200 million since 1957, and in the previous years, for the first time, petrochemicals had made "a respectable contribution to company earnings." In 1976 Imperial was earning net profits of 10.8 per cent on capital employed in chemicals. By 1979 this had risen to 31.3 per cent and it went up further, to almost 35 per cent, in 1980. Production also rose, from 1.7 million metric tons in 1976 to 2.3 million in 1980. In 1976, 7 per cent of Imperial profits came from chemicals; by 1980 the figure was nearly double, at 13 per cent. Moreover, as a senior Imperial executive told financial analysts in 1981, "since we built our first petrochemicals plant at Sarnia 24 years ago, Esso Chemical Canada has grown to be the most profitable chemicals company in Canada, and is sixth largest in sales. At the rate of expansion we are planning, we should be among the top three before the end of the decade."[35] Imperial is planning to invest about $900 million in chemicals projects in 1981-85 and expects to earn a 20- to 30-per-cent after-tax discounted cash flow rate of return on these investments. It is not hard to see why the company is so optimistic, with projects that include a new $400-million fertilizer plant and a $45-million expansion program for another such plant in Alberta, a $150-million polyethylene plant in Ontario, and a $37-million investment to double the capacity of an Ontario polyvinyl chloride plant. In addition, Imperial had been a half partner with the Alberta Energy Corp. in a $300-million styrene plant and a $375-million benzene plant – the so-called Petalta Project – but withdrew early in 1982, giving as its reason a reduction in cash flow under the NEP. Imperial remains a one-third partner in a proposed $700-million ethylene plant in Alberta. This adds up to an $865-million commitment to projects all of which are expected to be in production by 1986, a striking expansion in which Imperial is drawing heavily on the petrochemicals expertise of its Exxon parent.

Shell Canada, which in 1980 was Canada's seventh largest chemicals producer, also has a long history in the sector, having been an early arrival in Sarnia's chemical valley. Today it is rushing to establish itself as a major Alberta presence with its Shell Canada Chemical Co. In 1976-78, it invested $222 million, but that figure will be dwarfed by its planned investments for the next few years. In addition to building a $285-million benzene plant in Alberta, Shell Canada in 1980 became a 40-per-cent partner in a new company, Enesco Chemicals Ltd., to manufacture and sell petrochemical products, with the other 60 per cent held by Nova. The new company plans a series of world-scale projects in Alberta during the 1980s that will almost certainly mean investment of well over $1 billion. Two projects already under construction are a $250-million polyethylene plant and a $250-million styrene plant, and a third, a $275-million olefins plant, is planned. Shell's share will amount to $310 million.

Gulf Canada, the third major oil actor in the chemicals sector,

Proposed Coal Projects by Oil Companies

Project	Location	Company	Cost (1980 $ millions)	Construction (start to finish)
Sukunka Coal Mine	Chetwynd, B.C.	B.P. Explorations Canada Ltd.	400	uncertain
Line Creek Coal Mine expansion	Fernie, B.C.	Shell Canada Resources Ltd.	350	1984-86
New Line Creek Coal Mine	Fernie, B.C.	Shell Canada Ltd.	260	1979-83
Rescon Thermal Coal Mine	Obed, Alberta	Union Oil of Canada (90 per cent); Rescon Coal Holdings (10 per cent)	400	1982-84
Gleichen Thermal Coal Mine	Gleichen, Alberta	Shell Canada Ltd.	200	1982-87
Judy Creek Coal Mine	Judy Creek, Alberta	Esso Resources Canada Ltd.	200	1985-94
Houilliere, Monkman Pass	Monkman Pass, B.C.	Petro-Canada and Canadian Superior Oil Ltd.	500	1985-89

Total: $2,310 million

Major Metals Mining Projects by Oil Companies

Project	Location	Company	Investment (1980 $ millions)	Construction (start to finish)
Kutcho Creek Copper-Zinc Mine	Kutcho Creek, B.C.	Esso Resources (50 per cent)	150	1987-90
Midwest Lake Ukrainian Mine	Midwest Lake, Sask.	Esso Resources (50 per cent); Numac Oil and Gas, Bow Valley Exploration, Saskatchewan Mining Development Corp.	370	1987
Detour Lake Gold Mine	Ninety miles north of Cochrane, Ont.	Amoco Canada Petroleum Ltd. (50 per cent), Dome Mines Ltd. (25 per cent), Campbell Red Lake Mines (25 per cent)	200	1981-87

Source: "Major Capital Projects Inventory, October 1981." Office of Industrial and Regional Benefits, Department of Industry, Trade and Commerce.

Multinational Oil Company Petrochemical Plants
under Construction, Planned, or under Serious Consideration

Company	Production	Location	Cost	On stream
Esso Chemical Co.	1,600 tonnes/day ammonia	Alberta	$400 million	1983
Esso Chemical Co.	Expansion of fertilizer plant by one third to 600,000 tonnes/year	Alberta	$ 45 million	1982
Esso Chemical Co.	Polyethylene plant 135 kilotonnes/year	Ontario	$180 million	1983
Esso Chemical Co.	Double capacity of polyvinyl chloride plant to 100 kilotonnes/year	Ontario	$ 37 million	1983
Esso Chemical Co. (one third) with Alberta Energy Corp. and Hudson's Bay Oil and Gas	700,000 tonnes/year ethylene plant	Alberta	$700 million	1986
Gulf Canada and partners	Ethylene plant expansion	Quebec	$300 million	1988
Gulf Canada and partners	Pehnols plant expansion	Quebec	$150 million	1984
Gulf Canada Products Co.	700 cubic metres/day benzene plant	Alberta	$250 million	1985
Gulf Canada	Aromatics extraction plant	Alberta	$150 million	1984
Gulf Canada and partners	1.5 billion pounds/year ethylene plant	Atlantic Provinces	$500 million	1990
Gulf Canada and partners	1.2 billion pounds/year ethylene plant	Alberta	$500 million	1985
Shell Canada Ltd. and Nova	270,000 tonnes/year polyethylene plant	Alberta	$250 million	1984
Shell Canada Ltd. and Nova	300,000 tonnes/year styrene plant	Alberta	$160 million	1984
Shell Canada Ltd. and Nova	200,000 tonnes/year olefins plant	Alberta	$275 million	1985
Shell Canada	250,000 tonnes/year benzene plant	Alberta	$285 million	1984
Union Oil of California with Westcoast Transmission, Chieftain Development, and B.C. Resources Investment Corp.	Nitrogen fertilizer plant with 1,600 tonnes/day ammonia, 1,600 tonnes/day urea, and 900 tonnes/day nitrogen solutions	B.C.	$675 million	not definite
Canadian Occidental Petroleum, with Dome Petroleum, Westcoast Transmission, and Mitsubishi	2.7-million tonnes/day ethylene plant plus other plants	B.C.	$2 billion	1985

Total $6,857 million

has announced plans for a $250-million benzene plant near Edmonton and holds one third of the Petromont consortium, its partners being Union Carbide and Ethylec, a subsidiary of the government-owned Société Générale de Financement du Québec: Petromont is expected to spend $600 million on a modernization and expansion program for its Montreal petrochemical complex that includes doubling some Gulf facilities sold to the consortium. Gulf is also in a joint venture with Petro-Canada to study the feasibility of a world-scale petrochemicals operation in eastern Canada using future production from the Arctic islands and Atlantic offshore. On Canada's west coast, Canadian Occidental Petroleum, 81-per-cent controlled by Occidental Petroleum of Los Angeles, is part of the consortium with Dome Petroleum, Westcoast Transmission, and the Japan Mitsubishi group that is planning a $2-billion petrochemicals and LNG project. Union Oil of Canada, a subsidiary of Union Oil of California, is a partner with Westcoast Transmission and Chieftain Development in a planned $670-million fertilizer facility in British Columbia. Other oil companies with petrochemical operations include BP Canada in Ontario and Quebec, and Cities Service, Suncor, Texaco, and Amoco, all active in Ontario.

The great challenge of the 1980s will be to ensure that the oil multinationals do not overrun the coal, uranium, metals, and petrochemicals industries. These companies have the cash to diversify and they have the long-range corporate planning structures to make investments today that will pay off a decade or more down the road. Canadians will have not only paid them and subsidized them in their hold on the oil and gas business, but also aided them in their new evolution into enormous energy-mining-chemicals conglomerates tying up an increasing share of Canada's natural resources in the pursuit of a global strategy in which Canada's interest may take a distinctly second place.

Notes

1. *Financial Times*, London, 3 April 1981.
2. *New York Times*, 2 June 1981.
3. J. A. Armstrong, president, Imperial Oil, to the annual meeting, Toronto, April 1977.
4. J. A. Armstrong to the Oil Analysts' Group of New York, 20 Nov. 1980.
5. Data up to 1979 collected under the Petroleum Corporation Monitoring Act; 1980 and 1981 data collected by the Petroleum Monitoring Agency, Ottawa. Various annual reports were also consulted for this section.
6. Robinson, Robert. "The Canadian Oil Industry." Toronto, Gardiner, Watson Ltd., 1980.

7. Petroleum Monitoring Agency. *Canadian Petroleum Industry: 1980 Monitoring Survey*. Ottawa 1981.
8. J. G. Livingstone, president, Imperial Oil Ltd., to the Canadian Association of Petroleum Investment Analysts, Toronto, 25 June 1981.
9. Coal Association of Canada, Calgary.
10. *The Petroleum Economist*, August 1981. The study, "World Steam Coal 1980-1990," is by Sheppards and Chase.
11. National Energy Board. *Canadian Energy Supply and Demand 1980-2000*. Ottawa 1981.
12. R. A. D. Beck and D. K. E. Elton. "Western Canada's Coal: the Sleeping Giant." *Canadian Business Review*, Ottawa, Autumn 1981.
13. J. A. White, Esso Minerals Canada. "Coal: Energy Bridge to the Future." Canadian Institute of Energy, 18 March 1981.
14. J. G. Livingstone, president, Imperial Oil Ltd., to the Conference Board Marketing Conference, Toronto, 6 March 1980.
15. J. L. Stoik, president, Gulf Canada, to the Canadian Chemical Engineers Conference, 23 October 1978.
16. Shell Canada. "The Coal Option." Toronto 1981.
17. J. A. Armstrong, chairman, Imperial Oil Ltd., to the *Financial Times of London* Conference, Toronto, 26 March 1981.
18. J. A. White, "Coal: Energy Bridge to the Future."
19. Department of Energy, Mines and Resources. *The National Energy Program*. Ottawa 1980.
20. *The Financial Post*, 25 April 1981.
21. Department of Energy, Mines and Resources. "Uranium in Canada: 1980 Assessment of Supply and Requirements." Ottawa 1981.
22. *Oilweek*, 2 March 1981.
23. *Oilweek*, 6 July 1981.
24. J. G. Livingstone, president, Imperial Oil Ltd., to the Canadian Association of Petroleum Investment Analysts, Toronto, 25 June 1981.
25. J. A. Armstrong, chairman, Imperial Oil Ltd., to the Oil Analysts Group of New York, 20 November 1980.
26. *Oilweek*, 1 June 1981.
27. J. A. Armstrong, chairman, Imperial Oil Ltd., to the Annual General Meeting of Shareholders, Toronto, April 1977.
28. *Leaders*, January-March 1981.
29. *Canadian Energy Supply and Demand 1980-2000*.
30. W. G. Magee. "Canadian Petrochemicals: An Opportunity for the 1980s." Nesbitt Thomson Bongard Inc., Toronto, 19 June 1981.
31. Patricia Clarke. "Made of Oil." *Imperial Oil Review*, 4 November 1981.
32. Frank P. Popoff, Dow Chemical Europe, to the Colloquium "Frontiers of the Chemicals Industries 1985-2000," Amsterdam, May 1981.
33. Consultative Task Force on Industrial and Regional Benefits from Major Canadian Projects. "Major Canadian Projects, Major Canadian Opportunities." Ottawa 1981.
34. Robert Blair, chairman, Nova, to the Winnipeg Chamber of Commerce, 21 February 1980.
35. J. G. Livingstone, president, Imperial Oil Ltd., to the Canadian Association of Petroleum Investment Analysts, Toronto, 25 June 1981.

Chapter 11

What Others Do

When Canadians took the first steps towards controlling owner-ship of their oil and gas industry with the creation of Petro-Canada and its preferences in the 1970s and the National Energy Program in 1980, far from pursuing a radical path that was con-trary to international behaviour, they were simply catching up with what many other countries had already done. Canada had been slow to protect its interests in this respect, and by the mid-1970s was only beginning to realize what the Norwegians, British, Australians, Venezuelans, Nigerians, French, Japanese, Indone-sians, Mexicans, and Middle East producers had been doing to diminish the role and influence of the multinationals and entrench a strong domestic presence in their own oil and gas. Most major importing and exporting countries had their own national oil com-panies, and most producing countries had adopted policies to cap-ture a much bigger share of oil and gas revenues, ensure the max-imum use of local goods and services, and benefit from attendant industrial spin-offs and resource processing. Canada was a late-comer mainly because it had followed the American way. The United States did not have a national oil company, although some Americans wanted one, but it did have most of the world's privately owned oil companies. And it did not have a formidable array of local content rules, although it had some, because most of the major engineering companies and equipment suppliers were U.S.-based. For much of the oil industry's postwar history, Cana-dian policy-makers appeared to believe that there was no alter-native to the American way.

The experience of most countries has been that they had to change their policies, sometimes radically, as they learned more about the oil business and as oil's role and strategic importance in-creased. The almost universal pattern was early reliance on the ma-jor international oil companies, followed by a growing government role that was catapulted into prominence by the early-'70s OPEC increases. In some cases, producing governments resorted to nationalization; in others, they created national oil companies to help them learn more about the industry and thus how to maximize royalty and tax revenue, but also, by participation in development, to capture more value from production. Importing nations have also changed their policies, for reasons that have included concern about security of supply, dislike of excessive dependence on the externally controlled multinationals, the feeling that the companies were overcharging them as well as evading taxes through transfer pricing, a desire for greater domestic marketing competition, and the decision to seek out their own sources of supply through direct exploration at home and elsewhere. The importers, then, have imposed domestic ownership requirements in refining and marketing, either by setting up national oil companies or by giving protection to existing companies. They have also resorted to direct imports, regulation of refinery expansion, competition laws, and state-to-state negotiations with producing countries. For both producing and consuming countries, in view of the growing importance of oil in the world, it was hard to see how things could be otherwise. Øystein Noreng of the Norwegian School of Management has commented in defending the North Sea policies of his own and the U.K. government: "The argument here is that the oil industry is different and more difficult to control from outside than most other industries, particularly when compared with the traditional industries of the U.K. and Norway. The reasons are the capital intensity of the oil industry, the historically high rates of profit, the difficulty of entering the industry and consequently the tendency towards joint ventures and reduction of competition, vertical integration, the traditionally low price elasticities of supply and demand for oil, as well as the large cash flow handled by the companies. These factors distinguish the oil industry from most other industries, making it more resistant to outside interference. This has traditionally been the strength of the international oil industry, and it correspondingly has been the weakness of governments. Historically, no single government of any oil importing country has been able to control the oil companies, not even the United States."[1]

Some of the earliest challenges to the oil majors came in our own hemisphere, from Mexico and Venezuela. Public ownership of the oil and gas industry is a matter of deep pride for Mexicans, who nationalized their industry on 18 March 1938, a date which has been commemorated ever since as a national holiday.

299

Petroleos Mexicanos (Pemex) came at the end of a long struggle with the oil majors, in particular Standard Oil of New Jersey, Royal Dutch/Shell, Standard Oil of California, Cities Service, and Sinclair Oil, which, beginning in the early part of the century, had operated as if the country were their private preserve. Mexico supplied the bulk of the fuel oil used by the Royal Navy in World War I, and it let the majors amass huge fortunes. "For nearly four decades after commercial development began, revenues from this vital resource flowed principally into the exchequers of American, British, and Dutch corporations," G. W. Grayson's history tells us: "The arrogance and contempt with which they treated Mexicans and Mexico revealed a sense of superiority toward the people and land yielding their fortune."[2] The companies funnelled money out of the country, ran their businesses as though they were exempt from Mexican law, and treated local workers in the most brutal fashion. Brushing aside government statements to the contrary, they insisted that they had permanent ownership of the oil rather than simply the right to exploit it under terms and conditions set by Mexico.

The Mexicans had considered nationalization in an earlier period, during the Revolution of 1910-20, partly out of resentment at the fact that British and U.S. oil interests had, at the turn of the century, secured an exemption from virtually all Mexican taxes. It was decided that Mexico lacked the capacity at that time to run the industry itself, but the Mexicans did try to increase their revenues. As Grayson relates, "whenever the oil taxes were raised, and this happened regularly after 1912, the foreign oil companies would complain of 'confiscation,' and the American and British ambassadors would then lodge formal protests." In their new 1917 constitution, the Mexicans attempted to assert public ownership of the subsoil oil, gas, and other mineral rights, the system that exists in Canada. The U.S. promptly threatened to withhold recognition of the new Mexican government, cut off the supply of arms needed to fight rebel groups, and block the granting of loans to Mexico by U.S. banks: "The most important threat, however, was armed intervention. There is evidence that a declaration of war on Mexico was actively considered by the Wilson cabinet in 1919, and that, in the same year, Republican senators in league with the oil companies unsuccessfully attempted to secure Wilson's support for an invasion of Mexico."[3] Throughout the 1920s, the U.S. government continued to put pressure on the Mexicans to prevent them from changing their land rules, and this backing so emboldened the oil companies that they even turned down Mexican requests for joint ventures; by the mid-1930s, the foreign oil companies accounted for 99 per cent of the country's oil production. And when this was finally met by nationalization, Britain broke off diplomatic relations, while the U.S. cut back sharply on both oil imports and American lending. As World War II progressed, however, the U.S. became more conciliatory, in line with Roosevelt's "Good Neighbour" policy. The American president declared after the compensation issue was resolved: "We know that the day of the exploitation of the resources and people of one country for the benefit of any group in another country is definitely over."[4] This was in the wake of a vicious, worldwide campaign by the multinationals to discredit the Mexican government and restrict its ability to borrow money in financial markets, boycott Mexican oil, prevent Mexico from getting tankers, and persuade foreign companies not to supply the equipment, services, and other needs of Pemex. The majors were confident that the Mexicans would be forced to call them back in.

Pemex's success in the face of this hostility is a matter of great satisfaction for the Mexican people. Today, it is one of the world's largest integrated oil companies, with proven reserves estimated at 60 billion barrels, and it has also developed its own engineering and research expertise. In 1950, Mexican engineers built their first refinery, something Canadian engineers had yet to do in 1980. In 1956, Mexico set up its own research and development facility, the Instituto Mexicano del Petroleo (IMP), to carry out research and train skilled technical people for the industry. IMP is now a leading international centre for oil and gas research that employs several thousand people. Pemex does not have a perfect record; it has had more than its share of corruption, as well as problems with bloated bureaucracy and political interference. Yet it has won great benefits for Mexicans, with an impressive record in exploration that, for a $600-million investment in the years up to 1966, has yielded 7 billion barrels of oil and natural gas: if this is valued at between $1 and $2 a barrel, Pemex's return, spread over the life of the reserves, has been between 28 and 35 per cent.[5] And the company has gone far beyond exploration and development to extend Mexican know-how and technology and stimulate the growth of Mexican industries to supply its needs and upgrade its raw materials.

In Venezuela's case, nationalization proceeded much more smoothly, in large part because companies recognized its inevitability and worked with government to ensure a relatively painless transition. Venezuela's oil industry dates back to 1914, when Shell found the highly productive Mene Grande field, and, with other companies quickly moving in, the country was the largest oil exporter in the world by 1929. While relations with the companies were generally good, however, Venezuela cannot have been all that comfortable with such cartel arrangements as the one worked out in 1937 among Exxon, Shell, and Gulf, representing 99 per cent of Venezuela's oil play, and convening at Imperial Oil's Toronto offices, to curb production and relieve competitive pressure on world oil markets.[6] In 1943, new concessions were negotiated which were to run to 1983; the companies were required to build large refining facilities in Venezuela and pay higher royalties. As Peter Odell has recorded, "the first potential threat to the international companies came in 1948, when Venezuela came under the control of Accion Democratica – a left-wing party long pledged, while in opposition, to the nationalization of the country's oil. The new government concentrated, however, on increasing the nation's share of the profits from the international companies' oil operations – this it succeeded in doing, but only at the cost of a virtual cessation of growth in production as the companies sought their increasing requirements from the growing resources of the Middle East."[7] In that year, the government passed a law requiring companies to hand over half their profits to the state, and Juan Perez Alfonzo, who was later to emerge as the father of the Organization of Petroleum Exporting Countries, was appointed to formulate a new policy. Accion Democratica was almost immediately overthrown, however, to be replaced by the dictatorship of Marcos Perez Jimenez, and there followed a decade of corruption and repression during which the oil companies prospered. According to Odell: "The concept of an equal sharing of total profits was accepted by government and companies, and so long as almost all the country's oil was transferred to overseas associates of the producing companies at Caribbean posted prices – thus generating high returns on investment in Venezuela – the formula remained acceptable."

Jimenez was overthrown in 1958, and in 1959 Romulo Betancourt came to power as the leader of a new Accion Democratica government. He had promised to bring the oil majors under national control, increase the country's benefits from its oil, and make the enclaves of the oil majors a part of Venezuelan society instead of the havens of privilege they were. There was no immediate confrontation, however. The oil majors had $4 billion invested in Venezuela, and with little new investment could produce large volumes of low-cost oil from their concessions before they reverted to the state in 1983. For its part, the Betancourt government was not anxious to create a major rift, while the U.S., in the wake of Fidel Castro's successful revolution in Cuba, was anxious to avoid difficulties with Venezuela. At the same time, Perez Alfonzo returned as mines and hydrocarbons minister, a state oil company, the Corporacion Venezolana del Petroleo (CVP), was set up in 1960, and in that year, Alfonzo persuaded a number of Middle East countries to join with Venezuela in setting up the OPEC cartel.

The decade that followed was not a boom time for Venezuela's oil industry, as companies shifted exploration spending to other parts of the world where they held longer-term concessions, and government concern grew that a sector accounting for 20 per cent of the country's GNP and 90 per cent of its export revenues was "in foreign hands, with no degree of Venezuelan control over decisions taken in New York or London which vitally affect the Venezuelan economy."[8] Though it tightened up on the industry in this period, and used its much-needed and rising take to help finance the country's industrial diversification, Venezuela feared that rapid depletion of its oil reserves would leave it high and dry. Then the OPEC strategy, as adopted in the 1972 General Agreement on Participation, of acquiring a position in the oil resources of member countries, added to the 1973 price increases, brought the country the solution it had been looking for. Venezuela "raised its tax reference price from $3.10 in January 1973 to $14.08 a barrel in December. The resulting oil bonanza increased government oil income from $2 billion in 1972 to $3 billion in 1973 to $9.7 billion in 1974. Most important, it gave the country both an additional incentive to take over the industry completely and a cushion to insulate it from drops in income."[9] In 1974, the new regime of Carlos Andres Perez began working on plans to bring the industry under public ownership. In August of 1975, the oil nationalization law was passed: compensation would be for the net book value of the companies – that is, the original value of the investments minus amortization and depreciation – and was calculated at about $1 billion, part of this paid in cash but most of it transferred in the form of five-year 6-per-cent bonds. Nationalization came into effect on 1 January, 1976, with Exxon, Shell and Gulf staying in Venezuela to help operate the production and refining facilities on a fee basis. The new state oil company, Petroleos de Venezuela (Petroven), took charge of operations, expanded the country's oil technology research and development centre, Intevep, and embarked on new trading and technology ties

303

with other countries, one of them Canada. With estimated recoverable reserves in excess of 100 billion barrels of tar sands oil in the Orinoco Tar Belt, Petroven has signed technology sharing agreements with the Alberta Oil Sands Technology Research Authority, the federal government, and Petro-Canada.

The British and Norwegian experience in North Sea development has been remarkably different from that of Mexico or Venezuela, but the goals of national industrial benefits, revenue maximization, and public control to achieve national aspirations, have been the same. When, at the start of the 1960s, the two European nations looked to see how other countries had managed their oil and gas development, they could find no satisfactory model: old-style concessions were clearly out of the question, and their ideology and lack of experience precluded direct state-run development. Over time, they developed their own approach to the oil industry, allocating just a small part of the oil and gas lands for exploration and production, using national oil companies as partners with private industry, giving preference to domestically owned companies in allocating land rights, using the exploitation of oil and gas to develop new industrial and technological opportunities, and capturing a large share of the value of oil and gas production through taxes and royalties, with a portion to be used to diversify their economies. Their North Sea system was drawn on when the Canada Lands regulations were overhauled in 1980.

Britain, with, in BP, the longer experience in the use of a national oil company, passed its Continental Shelf Act in 1964. Under the allocation system that allowed it to control the rate and location of development, the U.K. awarded the first round of licences in 1964, the second in 1965, and then waited until 1970 to award the third. By the end of 1981, there had been seven rounds of awards. The Norwegians proceeded at a slower pace, awarding the first round in 1965 and the fifth only in 1981. One important advantage of the system is that it has made it much easier for the governments to change the rules as they learned more about the oil and gas businesses, avoiding the problem of retroactivity that plagued our own Canada Lands policy. Another reason in favour of this approach is that it allows governments to discriminate between various applicants. For example, the government of Margaret Thatcher decided that it wanted to increase British participation in the North Sea: in the seventh round of awards of offshore oil and gas concessions in 1981, it was made clear that British-owned companies were to get a large share, and in fact the awards brought in a number of British-owned companies which had not previously participated in the North Sea, or indeed in the oil and gas business at all. *World Business Weekly* reported on 30 March that "the presence of some of the more surprising North Sea entrants could have much to do with their nationality: they are British and, as such, welcome partners for overseas companies seeking licences." Moreover, since the British and Norwegians wanted certain designated areas explored quickly, the system allowed them to "impose working programs, and it also gave those applicants with the most comprehensive working programs the best chances of getting a licence."[10] The governments could also bargain for enlarged use of British or Norwegian goods and services. Thus, the British and Norwegian systems have proven to be more flexible and give greater public control than the original Canadian one. They too require that 50 per cent of the land revert to the state, after seven years in Britain and six in Norway.

Britain's tax policies for the oil industry have also evolved over time. The taxation of oil and gas companies became a matter of real public concern in that country when, in 1973, the Commons Public Accounts Committee published a report showing that a number of the big oil companies operating in the North Sea would not have to pay taxes on their North Sea profits for many years, and perhaps not ever, given their ability to write off their British tax liabilities against taxes paid on oil in the Middle East.[11] Laws were so generous that a company could actually get tankers for nothing. In fact, because the companies could accumulate artificial tax losses in their international operations and carry these losses forward, the oil majors had paid only £500,000 in taxes from 1965 to 1973. The report also urged that British-owned companies have preferential access to North Sea licences, and that much more be done to ensure British engineering and manufacturing content.

In the following year, the British government proposed a new petroleum revenue tax on North Sea profits that would capture a share of these profits before write-offs from other corporate activities could be used. In some respects, this was the model for the Canadian PGRT tax of 1980. It came into effect in 1975 at a rate of 45 per cent of income, after the deduction of royalties and operating costs plus a sufficient level of income to allow recovery of 175 per cent of original costs. In August 1978, the tax bite was increased to 60 per cent of net income and the capital recovery allowance reduced to 136 per cent. In early 1980, the tax was raised to 70 per cent. The British government introduced yet another tax increase in March of 1981, a new Supplementary Petroleum Duty of 20 per cent on gross revenues for all fields after an allowance of 7.3 million barrels of crude oil a year. The tax was retroactive to January 1981 and would run to 30 June 1982, raising more than $2 billion in additional state revenue. The effect of the new tax was to raise the marginal rate of taxation on North Sea oil fields from 87.4 to 90.2 per cent. "In spite of the industry's protests, there is no evidence to suggest that the overall level of taxation has become unbearable," the London *Financial Times* concluded.[12] In addition to this tax and duty, companies pay a 12.5-per-cent royalty on production and a 50-per-cent corporate income tax on profits. Thus, according to Petro-Canada, the after-tax rate of return in the British North Sea is 21.9 per cent as compared with 20.01 per cent in Norway and between 27.3 and 31.3 per cent in Canada's offshore fields, depending on the level of Canadian ownership.[13] Using Hibernia as an example, with the same reservoir, cost and price parameters, the present worth of a barrel of oil, at a 20-per-cent discount rate, would be approximately 25 to 30 cents under the British tax system. "Operating in Canada, however," as a Petro-Canada executive has pointed out, "a foreign-owned company would have a positive present worth under similar circumstances in the order of 75 cents a barrel while a Canadian company could expect a return of about $1 a barrel at this discount rate."[14] What the numbers show is that in spite of the outcry by the oil majors, the Canadian tax system under the NEP is still extremely favourable when compared with other countries'.

In another move to increase British control, the British National Oil Company (BNOC) was set up as a publicly owned oil operation under the Petroleum and Submarine Pipelines Act of 1975. According to L. E. Grayson, "Lord Balogh, long-time adviser of Harold Wilson and the chief architect of the act, saw the BNOC as the guardian of the British people's rights and a foundation for Britain's economic revival."[15] In its first year, it acquired the National Coal Board's North Sea oil interest plus a major part of Burmah Oil's North Sea interests. BNOC was to negotiate participation on a "voluntary" basis with companies that had already been awarded licences. The result was that BNOC secured the right to buy up to 51 per cent of production, and it also obtained access to information and representation on operating committees in the oil fields under the retroactive participation agreements. Starting with the fifth round of awards in 1976-77, BNOC was awarded a 51-per-cent stake in all new licences; in the 1978-79 sixth round, competing companies were told that they should consider offering BNOC more than 50 per cent and bear all or part of BNOC's share of exploration costs. With the election of the Conservative government of Mrs. Thatcher, BNOC's preferential position in future licence awards was reduced: it would not be an automatic 51-percent partner in each licence negotiation, but would have to bargain for an interest. Nonetheless, "there was every evidence that the oil multinationals were eager to enter into possible partnership discussions with BNOC in the seventh round of licences in 1980."[16] The government also eliminated BNOC's exemption from the Petroleum Revenue Tax and its right to sit on operating committees in fields where it was not an equity partner. Like Joe Clark, who wanted to privatize Petro-Canada, Margaret Thatcher had come to office determined to sell BNOC off to private investors. Such a sale, even with restrictions on foreign participation, could be the largest new equity issue in British history. The plan has been strongly criticized by many Britons, and the Labour Party has promised to renationalize when it is returned to office.

Policies to increase the flow of industrial spin-offs and engineering contracts were strengthened after it was found in 1972 that British firms were getting less than 30 per cent of the spending on goods and services. A consulting group reported at that time to the Department of Trade and Industry: "In overcoming the severe technological and operational difficulties of the North Sea environment, non-British enterprise is becoming progressively more entrenched."[17] The biggest problem for British companies, the consultants said, "is that usually met in seeking to start in a new field of activity, i.e. the unwillingness of the oil companies to risk inadequate performance by a contractor engaging in work not previously undertaken. This problem is magnified by the size of the investment and by the extreme effect on oil companies' profits which can be caused by a comparatively slight delay in completion." They saw the first need as being a strong position in offshore engineering and construction: "The sources of supply of equipment and materials of all kinds to go on or in the major facilities rests essentially on who specifies and who buys. At present, these functions are mainly in the hands of U.S. and U.S.-experienced engineers who tend naturally to favour proven equipment from known and trusted suppliers." The British share could rise to 70 per cent of $5 to $6 billion a year in spending by the late 1970s, given vigorous government policies and industry follow-through.

The British followed through in 1973 by setting up the Offshore Supplies Office (OSO) in the Department of Trade and Industry. In awarding offshore licences, the OSO looks at the projected industrial benefits for Britain as well as whether the company subscribes to a 1975 understanding reached with the industry's Offshore Operations Association which stated "the declared intention of the government that the U.K. offshore industry should provide, on a competitive basis, a major and progressively increasing share of the goods and services required for the development of our continental shelf, and should establish a growing export market."[18] The memorandum set out a detailed code of practice, one of its prime requirements being that companies notify OSO of coming orders for materials and manufactured goods greater than $250,000, and any construction or other service contracts in excess of $1.25 million. The OSO plays a strategic role, trying to anticipate future requirements, providing advice on joint ventures and licensing, developing technology through research and development programs, helping fund new companies entering the offshore supply market, and promoting new ventures. It also maintains a staff of audit engineers who monitor performance under the 1975 agreement. The industry must notify the OSO of any decision to place an order outside Britain, giving the body a chance to review the decision. It must also file quarterly reports on all contracts awarded and, in these reports, explain why, in the case of non-British awards, overseas suppliers have been successful. In announcing plans for the seventh round of offshore licence awards in 1980, the British Secretary of Energy stipulated that factors affecting the decisions would include "the extent of the contribution which the applicant has made or is planning to make to the economy of the United Kingdom, including the strengthening of the U.K. balance of payments and the growth of industry and employment," and "whether the applicant subscribes to the Memorandum of Understanding to ensure that full and fair opportunity is provided to U.K. industry to compete for orders of goods and services. Where the applicant is or has been a licensee, his past performance in providing full and fair opportunity to U.K. industry will be taken into account."[19] And the Department of Energy's 1981 "Brown Book" on North Sea activities showed just how important to the economy British industrial and engineering content in North Sea oil and gas activities could be. From 1965 to 1980, the oil and gas industry had chalked up about $53 billion, in 1980 prices, in investment spending, along with another $10 billion in exploration spending. In 1980, offshore oil and gas investments accounted for about 18 per cent of British industrial investment spending and 6 per cent of total capital investment that year in the British economy. In addition to offshore industrial and engineering jobs, about 22,000 people were employed directly on production platforms, exploration, supplier ships, dredging, and similar activities. Altogether during 1980, the oil and gas industry reported orders amounting to $6 billion, with British companies getting 71 per cent of the business as compared with a peak of 79 per cent in 1979.[20]

While Britain lacks a formal foreign investment review agency, its Monopolies and Mergers Commission can and does play a similar role in screening takeovers. And in spite of its well-known enthusiasm for free-market economics, the government of Margaret Thatcher endorsed the Commission's 1981 findings on the Davy takeover bid, described in a previous chapter, accepting that with the loss of "national character of Davy as a British bidder," Britain would suffer a loss of jobs and exports.[21] From the British point of view, the decision made good sense. The merger had been tested for significant benefit – FIRA's role in Canada – and none had been found. Yet on the day after the British government announced its refusal of a foreign takeover of its leading engineering company, Britain's high commissioner in Canada, Lord Moran, chose the occasion of his first speech in his new job to criticize the National Energy Program and FIRA. "Some British investors have been put off by what they have heard and have gone to the United States or elsewhere," he insisted: "Others who had applied to FIRA say they have encountered uncertainties and long delays. Most British applications to FIRA have been approved but some important ones have been refused. This gives me some concern, and I have discussed these problems with the ministers concerned, [Marc] Lalonde and [Herb] Gray, and with the FIRA administration. I hope we can see them resolved quickly and fairly."[22]

Norway has also devised strong policies to protect its interests in oil and gas development. Unlike most countries in the 1960s and '70s, Norway started from scratch in the oil industry, declaring sovereignty over its continental shelf in 1963, discovering oil in 1969, commencing production in 1971, and becoming a net exporter in 1975. Norway has had a clear, strategic goal: "The petroleum resources on the Norwegian Continental Shelf are the property of the Norwegian State. The central objective of the government's oil policy is that the administration and exploitation of these resources should take place in a way which will give the best result for Norway from a national economic point of view, and that the whole Norwegian society should benefit."[23] While the Norwegians had a strong energy department, they concluded that "the best knowledge of the petroleum activity is gained through active participation at all levels of the activity. This may only be attained through direct state involvement." Norway's national oil company, Statoil, was created in 1972. It has much greater privileges in Norway's North Sea than Petro-Canada has in our frontiers. While 40 per cent of exploration activity off Norway since 1975 has been carried out by Norwegian companies, "the Norwegian participation level is much higher," as a Canadian Commons committee learned in 1981, "because at the outset the Statoil company is supposed to have an initial interest of 50 per cent, which can rise up to 80 per cent of the production phase, depending on the production. This is one of the basic elements on which we choose the foreign companies; namely their offer on how big an interest they are willing to give to Statoil or, the other side of it, how much they are willing to yield in case production comes on."[25] And while the oil majors in Canada complained about the NEP's plan for a 25-per-cent carried interest for the Crown or Petro-Canada, the Norwegians are much more demanding. Like Canada, they expect the other oil companies to bear the exploration cost, but the carried interest or back-in for Statoil ranged up to 36 per cent in the 1969 round of licensing and 50 to 75 per cent in the 1974 round. The Norwegian national oil company also participates with full voting rights in all decisions of the exploration group. Once a field is declared to be commercial, Statoil's share automatically goes up to 51 per cent, giving it majority control, and, depending on the agreement, can be increased to about 80 per cent. In addition, Norwegian tax rates on the private-sector oil companies' profits on their share run from 80 to 84 per cent.

Like the British, the Norwegians had to learn how to tax oil companies effectively. Prior to the sweeping changes in tax policy made in Norway after the 1973-74 OPEC price increases, the government take was estimated at about 45 per cent.[26] In 1974, a special or excess profits tax was levied at 25 per cent of operating profits, after deduction of income taxes of 50.8 per cent and royalties ranging from 8 to 16 per cent. In the aftermath of the large international price increases in 1979-80 following the Iranian revolution, this tax was raised to 35 per cent, putting the overall Norwegian oil-profits tax rate in the 80- to 84-per-cent range. The move was expected to reduce oil company revenues by about one third in the six-year period from 1980 to 1985. In 1980 alone, oil taxes and production levies were expected to increase to $4.5 billion U.S. from about $2.5 billion.[27] But in spite of the higher rates, Norwegians are far from satisfied: "In Norway, total government take has been estimated to vary between 57 and 66 per cent. This indicates that governments are less able to reach taxation goals than to define ambitions. It also indicates that private industry may be better than governments in discovering loopholes and special provisions in taxation systems."[28]

Norway is also pushing for greater domestic ownership. According to a 1980 report to the country's parliament: "Norwegian companies will be given equity interests in the resources on the Norwegian continental shelf to an increasing degree. International companies may continue to participate in the petroleum activity in co-operation with Norwegian companies to the extent indicated by national interests."[29] In fact, the Ministry of Petroleum and Energy talked of allocating equity rights to resources in parts of the North Sea only to Norwegian-owned companies. The allocation on block 34/10 – Statoil with 85 per cent, Norsk Hydro with 9, and a third Norwegian company, Saga Petroleum, with 6 per cent – could become a model; Statoil is the operator and Exxon the technical assistant, to be paid in oil or gas. In addition to favouring Norwegian companies for new licences, the government will also favour companies that are willing to set up industrial enterprises in Norway.

Norway makes strong demands on companies to use Norwegian goods and services as well as carry out up to half their North Sea research and development in the country. As a result, Norwegian content has doubled, from about 28 per cent in the mid-1970s to 60 per cent in 1980. Norwegian legislation on the North Sea requires oil and gas companies to use a Norwegian base for exploration and production, employ Norwegian goods and services wherever feasible, and include Norwegian companies in initiatives for tender. In awarding licences in the fourth round in 1979, the Norwegian government told applicants that they had to spell out how they would co-operate with Norwegian industry in its policy of using oil activities for industrial development. In addition, a 10-per-cent share in one major block was held back for the company suggesting "an interesting industrial project." Mobil was awarded the share for its plans to work with Norwegian oil companies in data processing, subsea oil completion, and oil field maintenance work. And when, in the 1980 fifth round of concessions, Conoco, Elf, and Exxon were granted new concessions, each company had to come up with ways to strengthen Norwegian technology and know-how: these ranged from tanker orders to research projects. In fact the importance of research and development is always stressed: "Only through a strong and active research effort will it be possible to develop independent Norwegian expertise, to take care of safety and environmental questions, and to benefit from the challenges which the operations on the continental shelf represent to Norwegian industry."[30] Much of this research is directly sponsored by the government, but research activities are also negotiated with companies as part of North Sea licensing agreements. As a Norwegian official informed Canadian MPs, "originally, R and D activities were considered part of the goods and services, but we felt that R and D activity was somewhat behind the use of traditional services and the manufactured goods. So what we implemented for the last two rounds was a specific agreement between the ministry and the operator for each joint venture, stating that the operator has the responsibility of seeing to it that at least 50 per cent of the research and development work necessary for the activities of the specific concession area should be performed in Norway in co-operation with Norwegian industry or Norwegian research institutions. So for this specific sector, namely R and D, we have a percentage requirement."[31] This goes far beyond any requirement under the National Energy Program in Canada.

Ian Townsend Galt of the Canadian Institute of Resources Law has summed up the background of these North Sea policies: "To Britain and Norway, the oil companies are essentially foreign bodies. The idea that Statoil and the BNOC are out there, in a sense, doing it, tends perhaps to make it hurt less when one has to pay the gasoline prices one has to in Britain and Norway, which are considerably higher than here. . . . Statoil will itself have a production capability and that capability, of course, would not have to be particularly high, in North American terms, to satisfy the domestic requirements of Norway. But it would mean there is no requirement for foreign capital and what they still see as foreign bodies in order to ensure supplies of petroleum."[32]

The North Sea model provides some useful current comparisons with Canadian oil and gas policies; the experience of other countries with national oil companies goes back much farther in history. And based on the experience of those countries, the hostility of the oil multinationals and the Progressive Conservatives to the creation of Petro-Canada is all the more surprising.

In France, for example, the government was given a monopoly on oil in 1928 which it pieced out among private and public companies. One of its first steps was to acquire 25 per cent of the leading French oil firm, Compagnie Française des Pétroles (CFP), and empower it to refine 25 per cent of the country's requirements. In 1945, the French government created the Bureau de Recherches

312

Pétrolières (BRP) to search for oil in France and its colonies and protectorates, which at that time included Algeria. A government-owned oil company, Société Nationale de Recherche de Pétrole en Algérie (SN Repal) was set up and, with CFP, went on to make major oil and gas discoveries in 1956-57. The French government's exploration companies in Algeria were later merged into what is now the ELF/ERAP group which has oil and gas interests in many parts of the world, including Canada. France also has strict policies on foreign ownership in oil tankers, refineries, and service stations. While Exxon, Shell, BP, and Mobil are allowed to participate in the French market, government policy dictates that 50 to 60 per cent of the gasoline and other oil products market belong to French-controlled firms. Refining expansion is controlled by the French government, and its own SNEA has been favoured. The French-owned tanker fleet gets preferred treatment. And France has even had a special sales tax on gasoline and other oil products, the Fond de Soutien des Hydrocarbures, to finance the growth and development of SNEA (Elf Aquitaine) and its predecessor companies, much like the special oil levy in Canada's National Energy Program to finance Petro-Canada's acquisitions.

The Italian government moved into the oil and gas business in 1926 with the creation of a national company, Azienda Generale Petroli (AGIP), to carry out exploration in the country. Nothing came of its efforts, however, until after the end of World War II, when a remarkable Italian nationalist, Enrico Mattei, took over AGIP and other state enterprises and, in the face of strong opposition from the majors, set up the Ente Nazionale Idrocarburi (ENI) in 1953. ENI held Italy's gas deposits in the Po Valley and operated refineries, service stations, gas pipelines, and other facilities. Mattei's controversial role in world oil emerged in the mid-1950s, when he took some important steps to reduce Italy's dependence on the multinationals. He offered more favourable purchasing terms to countries such as Iran, Egypt, Nigeria, Algeria, and Libya, and he took ENI into refining and service-station activities in Africa, Latin America, and Europe, offering third-world countries opportunities for government participation. In 1958, Mattei purchased lower-priced oil from the Soviet Union, a move that also infuriated the majors because it introduced price competition into Europe. There were efforts by the industry to persuade NATO to put pressure on ENI, through the Italian government, to end Soviet oil imports. After Mattei died in a 1962 plane accident, ENI became more conservative, and worked closely with the oil majors. Today the company accounts for about a quarter of Italy's oil market and owns refineries, service stations, petrochemicals plants, gas pipelines, oil tankers, and oil and gas exploration affiliates. In addition, it has developed expertise in the design and manufacture of oil refineries, petrochemical plants, and nuclear reactors, and operates an internationally competitive engineering company to design and build these facilities.

In 1927, Spain became yet another country with a government presence in oil. CAMPSA, 30-per-cent owned by the Spanish government, controls petroleum distribution in Spain, buying refinery output and selling it to the public. A high level of public ownership in the refining industry is assured as all new refining construction must be licensed by the government. Oil imports are arranged through another government entity, INI or the National Institute of Industry, while Hispanoil, a 51-per-cent INI-owned subsidiary, engages in overseas oil exploration. Spain has insisted that its refining industry be 60-per-cent Spanish-owned, and in the highly profitable pre-OPEC days, the oil majors' imports from their own international affiliates were limited to 40 per cent, a measure that restricted the potential for abuse under the transfer pricing system then in general use.

Even West Germany, by the late 1960s, felt the need for government intervention in oil. For most of its postwar history, the country has pursued a free-market policy and credited its "economic miracle" to adherence to such principles. In the meantime, though, the oil majors had moved in. In 1960, German companies controlled 55 per cent of the German oil market; by the end of 1966, German ownership had slipped to 25 per cent as a result of foreign takeovers, with Germany's largest domestically owned oil company, Deutsche Erdol AG (DEA), picked up by Texaco in that year, and a bid made by CFP to acquire Gelsenburg, by then the largest German-owned company. This mobilized the German government to ensure that the takeover did not take place and then move to create a new exploration company, Deminex, that was a consortium of the larger remaining German-owned firms. The government announced in 1969 that 25 per cent of the refining industry had to be German-owned and -controlled and that Deminex, with government assistance, would begin an international search for oil reserves. Today, Deminex is an active exploration and development company with interests in many parts of the world, including Canada's east-coast offshore and Arctic regions. The German government owns 44 per cent of Germany's leading oil and gas company, Veba A.C.C., which in turn owns 54 per cent of Deminex.

Japan is another country that has taken steps to ensure a presence for domestically owned oil companies and reduce its dependence on the oil majors. In 1950, the Japanese legislated a 50-per-cent foreign ownership ceiling for Japanese refining companies. In 1955, the Japan Petroleum Exploration Co. (JAPEX) was established to explore for oil in the country, and it had some success. The government's Japanese Petroleum Development Corp. was set up in 1967 to finance oil and gas exploration by Japanese companies around the world. At the same time, through the unique Japanese system of government indicative planning in the economy, the Ministry of International Trade and Industry (MITI) regulates refining construction, oil imports, and the expansion of terminals, storage facilities, and marketing operations. These policies have led in turn to the creation of a Japanese national oil company that could serve the public interest. One observer has noted: "The sudden inability in 1979 of the majors to guarantee third-party sales – to Japanese companies – reinforced their apprehensions, and contributed to an ever-larger role by government in diversifying sources of supply and watching over prices. With over 75 per cent of oil imports now obtained through Japanese interests, some with government capital or sponsorship, Japan has today possibly the most extensive means of affecting its supply of any large, industrial importer."[33] Through the Japan National Oil Co., the Asian power is involved in oil and gas exploration around the world, with Canadian activities that include financial support for Dome Petroleum in the Beaufort Sea and participation in a joint venture with Petro-Canada and other companies in a pilot project to develop tar sands oil.

Brazil created its own national oil company, Petroles Brasileiro or Petrobras, in 1953. It is controlled by the National Petroleum Council, a government body set up in 1938 to set policies for oil and natural gas, including the development of Brazil's own resources. Petrobras has always had a monopoly on domestic exploration and development and new refining construction, and since 1967 it has been active in the petrochemicals industry through a subsidiary, Petroquisa, though without a monopoly position. As already mentioned, Petrobras made waves in the early 1960s when it disclosed that it was able to buy imported oil at a price 11 per cent lower than the high transfer price oil majors were charging their affiliated Brazilian refineries, $2.21 a barrel as against $2.48. Petrobras became responsible for all oil imports, and by 1966 it was bringing oil in under contract at $1.95 a barrel. Brazil's public actions prompted a number of countries to review the multinationals' transfer pricing policies. Petrobras is owned about 80 per cent by the Brazilian government, 10 per cent by states and municipalities, and 10 per cent by private Brazilian citizens.

The establishment of national oil companies has obviously had more to do with pragmatic considerations than with ideologies or philosophies. OPEC members such as Venezuela, Algeria, and Iraq acted because they found that they were being exploited by the majors. Such countries as Brazil, India, and Japan had a different concern, excessive dependence, linked to considerations of military and geopolitical power. And after the OPEC crisis, many importing countries also began to worry about the ability of the majors to supply their oil at all, even at high prices. With OPEC members and nations like Mexico seeking more state-to-state deals, it became prudent for oil importers to make their own direct arrangements for at least some of their supply.

More recently, Australia has also begun to show growing concern about the degree of foreign ownership of its natural resource industries, including oil and gas. In August 1981, for example, Australian treasurer John Howard told Shell Australia that he wanted the company to offer Australian investors 25 per cent of its equity. The announcement coincided with approval by that country's Foreign Investment Review Board of two large Shell coal projects. Earlier that same year, Caltex, a company jointly owned by Standard Oil of California and Texaco, had offered a portion of its local shares for sale to Australians, and according to press reports, the government's move was expected to "heighten pressure on other internationals to speed 'Australianization.' "[34] The reason was simple: "The 'resources boom' has fostered a massive growth in foreign capital, which reached record levels during the past year. There is mounting concern that Australians are not receiving adequate scope to participate."

Even the United States has considered setting up a national oil company to meet national security needs. In fact, the idea goes back to 1919, when private U.S. oil companies were having difficulty getting into the Middle East and other oil-rich areas because of restrictions imposed by the British, French, and Dutch colonial powers. The empires backed down, however, and the plan was dropped. In the 1940s, the U.S. government again considered a direct move into the Middle East, this time for security reasons. The government Petroleum Reserves Corp. established in 1943 was instructed to acquire control of Aramco, the huge producing company in Saudi Arabia owned jointly by Standard of California and

Texaco, as interior secretary Harold Ickes said, "in the interest of national defence and the economic needs of the nation."[35] Ickes observed that whereas the U.S. oil industry had operated in private-venture form, "the other principal nations, or most of them, have conducted their business through corporations or agencies entirely or partly owned or in effect controlled by the government itself." Though it died with the war, the proposal for a U.S. government oil company resurfaced in the early 1970s as Americans faced a potential oil crisis. In 1972, for example, Lee White, a former chairman of the Federal Power Commission, advocated a National Energy Resources Corporation to invest in areas where the oil industry was reluctant to go, maintaining that the electric power industry had shown how private and publicly owned companies could compete for the public benefit. White held that "a government-owned corporation to explore for and develop petroleum resources on publicly owned lands could serve to supplement the privately owned segment of the petroleum industry and, although it should manage the nation's resources in an efficient manner and on a profit-making basis, it would also be expected to be strongly motivated by the need to meet national energy requirements."[36] A government corporation, he said, could spearhead exploration and development in offshore areas and take the lead in developing shale oil. The idea of such a company was revived by Senator Adlai Stevenson Jr. in 1974; in 1975, a U.S. federal energy department study suggested a national oil company to negotiate oil imports. And in 1979, President Jimmy Carter called for a new $88-billion Synthetic Fuels Corporation to invest in shale oil, synthetic fuels from coal, and the American tar sands. The Synfuels Corporation was set up to help finance big shale oil, coal gasification, and other synthetic fuel projects.

Americans are also showing more and more concern about the foreign share of their own oil industry, although foreign ownership stands at only 18 per cent, with Shell and British Petroleum the leading foreign-owned oil companies in the Untied States.[37] BP acquired Sohio or Standard Oil of Ohio in 1970, in one of the biggest oil takeovers in U.S. history, and in 1978, Shell, already a large operation in the U.S., bought Belridge Oil, an important independent producer with valuable land rights. In addition, the 1973-74 oil shock raised U.S. fears that OPEC countries would use their billions of petro-dollars to gain control of major U.S. corporations. In 1975, the American government set up its Committee on Foreign Investment, headed by the U.S. Treasury, to monitor foreign takeovers. In 1981, the committee attempted to delay the takeover of Texasgulf, a leading U.S.-based resources company, by Société Nationale Elf Aquitaine (SNEA), 70-per-cent owned by the French government. While the committee lacks the legal power to block takeovers, acting only as an adviser to government, assistant treasury secretary for international affairs and committee chairman Marc Leland called in the French ambassador and asked that the purchase, worth $2.8 billion U.S., be put off until the committee had completed a study of its implications for the U.S. national interest. Said the *New York Times*: "The move is a further sign of concern by the government over mounting foreign investment activity in this country." The paper went on to quote a treasury official as voicing "concern that a foreign government would be taking over a position in a sensitive industry."[38] The French ignored the request, however, and proceeded with the acquisition; once the sale had been completed, the Canada Development Corporation, which owned 37 per cent of the American company, gave its shares to SNEA in return for Texasgulf's Canadian assets.

The committee has also scrutinized Renault's takeover of American Motors, Shell's Belridge acquisition, and a number of proposed investments by Kuwait and other OPEC members, though always in an advisory role. A level of concern exists. In a private defensive move, Conoco amended its corporate bylaws in 1981 to limit share ownership to U.S. citizens, but it was too late to prevent Dome Petroleum from acquiring a major block which it later exchanged for Conoco's controlling interest in Hudson's Bay Oil and Gas. U.S. policies on foreign takeovers remain liberal, except in the banking industry, where foreign buys have been blocked, but more activity in oil and gas or other resource areas at this point seems likely to prompt sterner measures.

Moreover, although the U.S. moved more rapidly than Canada towards world oil prices, it also brought in a windfall profits tax to capture a large share of the OPEC-induced price increases. In April 1979, President Carter announced plans for the tax as part of the price decontrol program, declaring on national television that "as government controls end, prices will go up on oil already discovered, and unless we tax the oil companies, they will reap huge and undeserved windfall profits." The levy would "capture part of this money for the American people."[39] He appealed to Americans to deluge their congressmen and senators with mail in support of the tax: "As surely as the sun will rise, the oil companies can be expected to fight to keep the profits they have not earned. Unless you speak out, they will have more influence on

Congress than you do." Almost a year later, on 2 April 1980, Carter signed into law the Crude Oil Windfall Profits Tax Act. The tax was 70 per cent in the windfall game on oil properties in production before 1979, 60 per cent on oil from so-called "shipper" properties, and 30 per cent on oil properties that were not in production before 1979. It was to be phased out in a 33-month period after the end of 1987 or when cumulative tax revenues reached $227.3 billion U.S., whichever came later. No matter what happens, however, the phase-out must be under way by the beginning of 1991. Although many Republicans had opposed the tax, it has not been repealed by the Reagan administration that came to office in 1981.

Canada's 1980 energy policies have been severely criticized by the oil majors and foreign investments as unfair, punitive, confiscatory, retroactive, and counter-productive. Viewed in the light of the policies of other countries, however, the Canadian moves are neither unique nor radical, simply belated. Like other countries around the world, Canada has had to reshape its policies to protect its own interests. Like other countries, Canada has found that it needs greater control over the development of these resources, greater participation by its own citizens in the oil and gas industry, greater knowledge for itself through a national oil company that can also serve as an instrument for national energy policies, and greater industrial spin-offs from resource development for its own citizens.

Notes

1. Øystein Noreng. *The Oil Industry and Government Strategy in the North Sea*. London, Groom Helm, 1980.
2. George W. Grayson. *The Politics of Mexican Oil*. Pittsburgh, University of Pittsburgh Press, 1980.
3. Paul E. Sigmund. *Multinationals in Latin America: The Politics of Nationalization*. Madison, University of Wisconsin Press, 1980.
4. Quoted in Sigmund, *Multinationals in Latin America*.
5. Grayson, *The Politics of Mexican Oil*.
6. U.S. Federal Trade Commission. "The International Petroleum Cartel. Report to the subcommittee on Monopoly of the Select Committee on Small Business. United States Senate." Washington 1952. Imperial Oil was a party because it owned 60.09 per cent of International Petroleum, Exxon's integrated oil affiliate which operated in Colombia and Peru. Venezuela was the principal source of oil for Imperial Oil refineries in Quebec and Atlantic Canada.
7. Peter R. Odell, "The Oil Industry in Latin America." In *The Large International Firm in Developing Countries*, Edith T. Penrose ed. Westport, Conn., Greenwood Press, 1968.

8. Odell, "The Oil Industry in Latin America."
9. Odell, "The Oil Industry in Latin America."
10. Noreng, *The Oil Industry and Government Strategy in the North Sea.*
11. *The Economist*, February 1973.
12. "The North Sea Tax Wrangle." *The Financial Times*, London, 27 August 1981.
13. Petro-Canada to the House of Commons Committee on National Resources and Public Works, 25 March 1981.
14. Joel Bell, Petro-Canada, to the Fifth International Energy Forum, Mexico City, 12 November 1981.
15. L. E. Grayson. *National Oil Companies.* Toronto, Wiley, 1981.
16. Grayson, *National Oil Companies.*
17. International Management and Engineering Group of Britain Ltd. "Study of the Potential Benefits to British Industry from Offshore Oil and Gas Developments." London, HMSO, 1972.
18. Memorandum of Understanding Between the Department of Energy and United Kingdom Offshore Operations Association, 3 November 1975.
19. U.K. *Gazette*, 1 May 1980.
20. Department of Energy. "Development of the Oil and Gas Resources of the United Kingdom, 1981." London 1981.
21. Monopolies and Mergers Commission. "Enserch Corporation and Davy Corporation Limited: A Report on the Proposed Merger." London, HMSO, 1981.
22. Lord Moran, British High Commissioner, to the Men's Canadian Club, Ottawa, 11 September 1981.
23. Norwegian Ministry of Petroleum and Energy. "Starting Report. No. 53 (1979-80) Concerning the Activity on the Norwegian Continental Shelf." Oslo 1980.
24. Norwegian Ministry of Petroleum and Energy, "Starting Report."
25. Ole Lindseth, senior executive officer, Norwegian Ministry of Petroleum and Energy, to the House of Commons Committee on National Resources and Public Works, Ottawa, 26 March 1981.
26. Noreng, *The Oil Industry and Government Strategy in the North Sea.*
27. *Wall Street Journal*, 24 March 1980.
28. Noreng, *The Oil Industry and Government Strategy in the North Sea.*
29. Norwegian Ministry of Petroleum and Energy, "Starting Report."
30. Norwegian Ministry of Petroleum and Energy, "Starting Report."
31. Lindseth to the Commons resources committee, 1981.
32. Ian Townsend Galt, Canadian Institute of Resources Law, to the House of Commons Committee on National Resources and Public Works, Ottawa 5 February 1981.
33. Joel Bell to the International Bar Association Energy Seminar, Banff, 27 April 1981.
34. *The Financial Times*, London, 13 August 1981.
35. Neil H. Jacoby. *Multinational Oil.* New York, MacMillan, 1974.
36. Lee C. White to the Congress Joint Economic Committee, 7 June 1972.
37. U.S. Department of Commerce. "Supply of Current Business, January 1979."
38. *New York Times*, 21 July 1981.
39. President Jimmy Carter, from the White House, Washington, 5 April 1979.

320

Chapter 12

1990 is Tomorrow

"It must be accepted that there are some challenges and responsibilities we expect our governments to accept, not pass on. Energy is so clearly a matter in the general interest that the management and development of these publicly owned non-renewable resources are basic functions that can be performed only by governments acting for the people who elected them. There is no market for politicians who promote the life, love, and pursuit of happiness of their citizens in a cold climate." These are the words of economic doyen and former federal cabinet minister Eric Kierans, who may have opposed some of the policies called for in this book and in these times, but whose highly developed sense of public service correctly identified the principle underlying them. He went on to argue in 1975 that "leaving the supply of petroleum to the private sector may not have been too costly when sources, both domestic and international, seemed limitless and low-cost. Pursuing the same policy when domestic reserves are declining, foreign supplies are in monopoly hands, and markets are producer-controlled, will increase the dependence and vulnerability of the Canadian economy. Energy, or the lack of it, can literally dictate the nature and shape of political, social, and economic developments in this country. Energy policy, therefore, must be integrated with investment priorities, government expenditures, balance of payments, and commercial policy. It is far too important, under today's rapidly changing conditions, to be left to the private sector."[1] Especially, Kierans might have added, when the private sector was overwhelmingly controlled by citizens and corporations of other countries.

The situation, as these words are recalled in early 1982, can only be described as crucial. We are in the presence of an opportunity that this time, for the last time, we literally cannot afford to miss. We Canadians have created in the past few years the policies and institutions – Petro-Canada, the Canada Development Corporation, the Foreign Investment Review Agency, Alberta Energy, and Saskoil, to name a few – that can do the job. Private companies have emerged to back them up that are either Canadian-controlled or on the way to becoming so. We have surrounded them with laws, regulations, and incentives which, though far from perfect, make it possible for them to do the job. And as we look around the world, we can observe numerous examples of how the job could be done. What now remains is for Canadians, through their governments and public and private oil companies, to insist on a steady widening of their role in oil and gas, as indeed in all of the expanding resource sectors; and, perhaps most importantly at this point, to see that no more political roadblocks, either here at home or from abroad, are placed in their way.

There are some encouraging signs, in practice as well as in the principle of the 1980 reforms. Most of them have already been mentioned in this book, but it is worth turning back once more to scan the wide range of entrepreneurial and at times daring activity that has been achieved by Canadian-controlled companies over the past few years. The installation of a gas-based petrochemical industry in Alberta and British Columbia, the big gas discoveries of the Arctic islands, the introduction of gasohol in Canada, the development of compressed natural gas as a motor vehicle fuel, and new technology for the Canadian Arctic, are all examples of enterprising Canadians at work.

Another encouraging sign is, of course, the rapid growth of Canadian-controlled companies. In the public sector, Petro-Canada has taken the lead, but a number of provinces have launched similar companies, including Nova Scotia Resources Ltd., Quebec's Soquip, and the Ontario Energy Corporation. Dome Petroleum, which is Canadian-controlled and now committed to majority Canadian ownership, has become an industry giant with its takeover of Hudson's Bay Oil and Gas. The Canada Development Corporation, with its takeover of Aquitaine Oil from its French owners, has established another substantial Canadian energy company, Canterra Energy Ltd. And a significant number of medium-sized Canadian companies have great potential.

The co-operatives and credit unions make up another group representing large numbers of Canadians that has come into play. We have seen in 1981 the creation of the Co-operative Energy Corporation, or Co-Enerco, based in Calgary. It is owned by co-operatives and credit unions from across Canada that are putting

322

up $100 million in equity, and the federal government, contributing another $100 million to help launch the new venture. The new energy company's board will be dominated by the co-ops, and its first president, David Martin, the former exploration vice-president of Amoco Canada Petroleum, has announced that "Co-Enerco may well end up being one of Canada's ten largest oil companies by 1990."[2] It will have two subsidiaries, one, Co-operative Energy Development Co., an operating arm, and the other, Co-Operative Energy Investment Funds, an investment channel. The operating subsidiary will sell shares to investors, while the fund will sell investment units through co-operatives, credit unions, and caisses populaires, and will be managed by the Co-operative Trust Co. of Canada. Here is an initiative that can tap the savings of Canadians in a completely positive way, working for the good of Canada.

There are other sources of Canadian treasure that could play a big role in the future. Pension funds are one example. Various investment and trust companies are busy organizing investment vehicles for these funds. One has set up an oil and gas company, Pencrown Resources Ltd., which will be owned by 15 different pension funds; other trust companies are setting up "energy trusts" which will allow pension funds to buy working interests in producing properties and help finance future exploration plays.[3] Native peoples are another range of Canadians who could be much more active in future oil and gas development. For some time now, Native groups in Alberta have been benefiting from oil and gas development on their reserves. In the North, aboriginal peoples could become strong actors in frontier projects. In 1976, for example, the Inuit Tapirisat set up the Inuit Development Corporation to participate in resource and other initiatives. In 1981 the Inuit company was in on the financing of Cullaton Lake Gold Mines, listed on the Toronto Stock Exchange, which has just opened a mine in the Northwest Territories.

Also mentioned in this book have been creative, rather than draining, relationships with governments and private companies outside Canada. Here again, most of the opportunities and examples have been indicated, but let us pause to consider one or two. Mexico, for example, made it clear on the occasion of its president's 1981 visit to Ottawa that Canada has been selected as one of the five countries with which it wishes to develop a closer and stronger relationship – the others being, interestingly enough, Japan, Brazil, Spain, and Sweden. Oil and oil technology, along with the opportunity to develop ties with Canadian-controlled companies, are among the reasons for Mexico's interest. In the private sector, lest its positive side seem to have been forgotten in a work necessarily preoccupied with the development of public policy, the Norwegian offshore drilling giant, Aker, has now entered into partnership arrangements with Saint John Shipbuilding and Dry Dock in New Brunswick, and formed a company with SNC of Montreal, one of Canada's largest engineering firms – SNC/Aker Ltd. – to provide engineering, procurement, and construction services to the offshore oil and gas industry. It is an example of how Canadian companies can work with foreign firms to gain access to technology and skills that will be vital in the years ahead.

The urgency of the task before us is kept taut by such warnings as this one issued in 1980 by Gordon McNabb, president of the Natural Sciences and Engineering Research Council, on his return from international energy conferences in Britain and Europe. The major industrial countries, according to McNabb, "will be looking to Canada, and to other resource-exporting countries, for new and rapid development of raw materials, especially of coal and uranium, to replace depleting supplies of oil."[4] Not only do these countries assume that resource-rich countries like Canada will produce whatever level of tar sands or Arctic oil or other materials is demanded, but, McNabb said, "in some quarters we will find resentment of any thought we might have for possible further processing of our resources before export." He quoted a speech made by a spokesman for 20 European electrical utilities, who was attacking Canada's desire to upgrade uranium before exporting it: "We see no reason why such [upgrading] installations should be built abroad, where they often require European finance anyway, when European industry is well qualified to provide the services concerned in Europe." What this means, McNabb concluded, is that "the next decade will see major demands on our exportable energy resources and increasingly we will find ourselves cast in the role of the resource villain as we strive to achieve realistic prices and economic spin-offs from our depleting resources." A major diplomatic effort will be necessary in the United States, Europe, and Japan, if Canada is to not only to achieve, but also to maintain, the position to which it aspires in the energy world.

In these circumstances, it is going to be tough to keep up our momentum. And while Canada has made important progress towards a higher level of Canadian control in its own oil and gas industry, it still has a long way to go before the three goals of the National Energy Program – at least 50-per-cent Canadian ownership of oil and gas production by 1990, Canadian control of a significant number of the larger oil and gas companies, and an early increase in the share of the oil and gas sector owned by the government of Canada – are reached. As the Petroleum Monitoring Agency reported at mid-year in 1981, Canadian ownership of production revenue stood at 28 per cent and Canadian control at 17 per cent; each percentage point of additional ownership was costing $1 billion.[5] There was, certainly, a large jump in Canadian ownership and control shortly after the NEP was announced in 1980, but by mid-1981 the move had ground to a halt. One reason for this was concern about the impact of takeovers on the Canadian dollar. In July, finance minister Allan MacEachen asked Canadian banks to slow down their financing of takeovers of foreign corporations by Canadian ones, although Prime Minister Trudeau did stress subsequently that this would apply "except in the energy field. In the energy field we intend to reach our goal of 50-per-cent Canadianization by 1990."[6] An outflow of funds would obviously have some short-term effect on the exchange rate of the Canadian dollar, as the Bank of Montreal pointed out in a special study,[7] but this would have to be weighed against the long-term advantages of the takeovers, which would be significant. Moreover there was a danger of exaggerating the impact of these takeovers by Canadian-controlled companies. As the chairman of the Economic Council of Canada told the Toronto Association of Business Economists, "if there were rather large transfers of capital out of Canada, the result would not likely be a disaster. Undoubtedly there would be some problems posed for Canadian debt management. But they would not be insurmountable."[8] Failure to act would lead to a potentially much more enormous drain of capital, in fact, as the oil majors repatriate their fast-rising earnings in the 1980s and beyond; greater Canadian ownership will reduce this threat to Canada's balance of payments and keep more money in the country for reinvestment by Canadians.

In view of Wall Street's negative reaction to Canadianization, there has also been the not surprising fear that the U.S. financial community would retaliate by rejecting Canadian bond issues or imposing higher interest costs. As Wood Gundy, a leading investment house, has put it: "Questions have been asked as to whether U.S. investor attitudes towards Canadian debt securities have changed. In particular, has the 'Canadianization factor' impacted yield spread relationships of 'U.S. pay' Canadian bonds versus other sectors within the U.S. domestic market?" But as the firm concluded in late 1981, " 'Canadianization' did not greatly influence the U.S. market perception of Canadian credits . . . [and] there is no evidence at all that the U.S. bond market is showing any spread resistance to Canadians."[9] Critics of Canadianization were still able to raise public fears that the Canadian economy would be damaged by the ownership drive, even though the real danger came instead from the high-interest-rate policy originating south of the border. Added to this was anxiety in some circles in Canada that further buy-back attempts would precipitate a confrontation with the United States. In spite of their denunciations of Canadian pricing, tax, and land policies, none of the big U.S.-owned oil companies in Canada was willing to sell; any acquisition move would almost certainly be regarded as an unfriendly one, and inevitably whip up an orchestrated threat of retaliation from the United States. Under the Reagan administration, the U.S. government had once again become an agency for the protection and advancement of the multinational brigades.

For their part, many of the leading foreign-controlled companies had adopted a sitting-it-out strategy, confident that they could outlast a strong-minded energy minister such as Marc Lalonde and then convince his successor that the National Energy Program should be changed. In the meantime, these companies have gone on a form of strike, holding back investment activities in a strategy that will make Canada's short-term energy situation worse but, from their point of view, strengthen their own future bargaining power: an impending increase in required oil imports would worry the public and make it easier for the industry to push a future government into making significant changes in oil and gas policies. There is no sign that companies such as Imperial Oil, Shell Canada, Gulf Canada, Texaco Canada, Amoco Canada, Mobil Canada, or Chevron Standard have any intention of increasing the proportion of shares held by Canadians or, in some instances, allowing any Canadian shareholders in at all. This being the case, it is difficult to see how the Canadian ownership target can be reached by 1990 without further big takeovers.

While this may create some difficulties for Canada's foreign relations, the goal of 50-per-cent Canadian ownership remains reasonable by any international standard. In the past, Canadians have paid fair prices for the companies they have acquired, so that there are no grounds for foreign panic cries of forced takeovers and fire-sale prices. The essential thing in dealing with the United States and other countries is to make it clear that Canada has its own priorities, its own traditions, and its own preferred pace of development. As Canada's ambassador, Peter Towe, told one

U.S. audience, "we are still in the process of nation building. And that is so and will be so for many decades to come. We need space to work out our problems and to forge our destiny."[10] While Canadians could not expect Americans to protect and advance their interests, Towe said, "I do expect you to take the longer view and accord to us the respect that is due us – recognition of our differences and of the right, even the desirability, of following different paths when national interest dictates."

There are, in any country's history, important and decisive turning points that alter its direction and sense of being. In Canada's case, the decision to seek Canadian ownership and control of at least half of one of the country's most vital economic sectors will, years from now, come to be seen as one of those points. Provided that the momentum of Canadianization is reinforced and not allowed to fall off, Canadians will attain a new level of confidence and sense of achievement that will echo far beyond the oil and gas industry and have broad ramifications for decades to come. This is a golden opportunity for a young but proud community. To falter now would be to condemn the country to become little more than a footnote in the story of nations.

Notes

1. Eric Kierans. "Notes on the Energy Aspects of the 1974 Budget." *Canadian Public Policy*, Toronto, Summer 1975.
2. Toronto *Star*, 16 February 1982.
3. *The Financial Post*, 12 December 1981.
4. Gordon McNabb, Natural Sciences and Engineering Research Council, to the Energy and Electricity Conference, Toronto, 14 October 1980.
5. Petroleum Monitoring Agency. "Canadian Petroleum Industry Monitoring Survey 1981: First Six Months." Ottawa 1981.
6. Prime Minister Pierre Trudeau. Press conference, Ottawa, 25 September 1981.
7. Bank of Montreal. Department of Economics release, Montreal, 19 August 1981.
8. David Slater, Economic Council of Canada, to the Toronto Association of Business Economists, Toronto, 16 February 1981.
9. Wood Gundy. "Fixed Income." Toronto, 1 October 1981.
10. Peter Towe, to the Carnegie Endowment and the American Foreign Service Association, Washington, 28 October 1981.

Index

333